D0340067

Richard Nelson's American Cooking

Richard Nelson's American Cooking

WITH A FOREWORD BY
James Beard

NAL BOOKS
NEW AMERICAN LIBRARY
TIMES MIRROR
NEW YORK AND SCARBOROUGH, ONTARIO

Published simultaneously in Canada by The New American Library of Canada Limited.

NAL BOOKS TRADEMARK REG. U.S. PAT. OFF. AND FOREIGN COUNTRIES
REGISTERED TRADEMARK—MARCA REGISTRADA
HECHO EN HARRISONBURG, VA., U.S.A.

SIGNET, SIGNET CLASSIC, MENTOR, PLUME, MERIDIAN and NAL BOOKS are published *in the United States* by The New American Library, Inc., 1633 Broadway, New York, New York 10019, *in Canada* by The New American Library of Canada Limited, 81 Mack Avenue, Scarborough, Ontario, M1L 1M8

Designed by Julian Hamer

LIBRARY OF CONGRESS CATALOGING IN PUBLICATION DATA
Nelson, Richard.
Richard Nelson's American cooking

Includes index.
1. Cookery, American I. Title. II. Title: American cooking.
TX 715. N435 1983 641.5973 83-8123
ISBN: 0-453-00442-3

PRINTED IN THE UNITED STATES OF AMERICA

I dedicate this book to the three people who most influenced my writing it:

the late June Platt,
my mentor and friend,
who said I would do it;

James A. Beard,
my friend, mentor, and advisor,
who said I should do it;

and

Charles Kofler,
my friend and critic,
who said I could do it.

Acknowledgments

Full-time assistants, past and present: Dede DeJager, Susan Mahony, Joan Murray, Janie Malarkey, Rawl Hovey, and Mark Snapp

Part-time assistants, past and present: Joanne Stoney, Charles Gautreaux, Jill Van Cleave, Bonnie Belknap, Judie Geise, John Hurst, Sharon Lane, Tom Newman, Michael Tompkins, and Irene and Steve Angelo

Yvonne Rothert and Gail Kelly, who advised me from the beginning of the manuscript to its end, William C. Nelson, who transcribed every recipe, and Molly Allen, my editor, who held my hand and gave me encouragement all the way through.

Contents

FOREWORD BY JAMES BEARD xi

INTRODUCTION xv

Soups and Chowders 1

Meats 29

Poultry 83

Fish and Shellfish 127

Special Dishes 171

Vegetables 223

Salads and Salad Dressings 279

Sauces, Condiments, and Accompaniments 309

Breads, Pastries, and Batters 341

Desserts 365

INDEX 429

Foreword by James Beard

RICHARD Nelson was born in South Dakota, never considered to be a paradise for gastronomy. However, during his childhood and youth he experienced well-prepared food from his mother's kitchen, his grandmother's and his aunt's, and he was wise enough to remember to add these recollections to his taste memory. He was indeed fortunate to be eating homey food that was *truly* American cookery. His venturings to the West Coast—to California and later to Oregon—have provided variation on his early themes, enriched his cooking vocabulary, and given him added palate excitements.

In this period of much too much written about something called "New American cookery," it is a joy to have someone who recognizes the fact that true American cookery is something with which we grew up. Good eating and good cooking are nothing new in our lives. To be sure, there was mediocre cookery and, to be sure, every mother was not Cordon Bleu. Basically, year in and year out, most of us, whether we had a "hired girl" or a mother or a father who cooked, experienced good food. It was probably good regional food, albeit seasonal.

Simply to have lived in the far reaches of the Dakotas, Idaho, or Michigan, and to have grown up in the period when Richard Nelson did, was different. One learned to look forward to and appreciate foods from the countryside. Such luxuries as wild mushrooms, wild fruits, as well as fish and wild game were delights to anticipate and enjoy. What boy growing up with an interest in living ever missed a chance to go fishing, coming home laden with fish, or clams or crabs, proud of having provided them? Even those of us who tied a piece of liver on a string and pulled in crayfish from the streams had this joy of accomplishment as we marched home with a hat full of live crayfish.

Richard savored these things, and his many years in the Northwest, along the coast and inland, have given him a great deal more to appreciate. To this day, when he teaches in the Oregon Country, right at the mouth of the Columbia River, he revels in the salmon, the sturgeon, the Dungeness crab, the razor clams, and he tells you as you read through and use AMERICAN COOKING how much he treasures these various joys of the coast.

Richard's association in New York and California with the Platts, and especially with June Platt, was a definite high point. I consider June Platt to have been one of the great cooks of her time. She was a person for whom I had the greatest respect. Her food was meticulous, beautiful, and carefully prepared—a joy to the palate. Richard confessed to me that he stood in awe of her when they met and at first was almost afraid to participate in what she provided for her kitchen and her table. He found her stimulating, and her influence has helped him develop his own conception of our native cooking.

With this rich background it's not surprising that Richard Nelson finally broke away from other pursuits and joined those of us who have championed the cause of good cooking in these United States. I had eaten Richard's cooking long before he decided that he was going to teach and write about food. As a matter of fact, I think I may have had a pretty strong influence on that decision, because I believe that Richard's first ventures into demonstration were with me on the West Coast. I remember one pretty colossal project—a benefit for the local art museum in Portland. It entailed two enormous demonstrations in one day; in addition to that, we were obliged to train people to prepare the same menus in the kitchen, so that everyone who came to the demonstrations could have a substantial taste of every dish. I can assure you that by the end of the second demonstration we were pooped!

I remember at other times when he worked with me for the Oregon classes Richard's ability to sense where we would shop for certain things. He seemed to literally smell out the people who could supply wild berries, herbs, and good fish; he was tireless, driving from one outlet to another to get the best possible food for each day, and he always succeeded! I'm sure that during that year he bought more bunches of fine parsley than he's ever seen since or will see again.

Richard became concerned that there was very little camaraderie among the various cooking teachers all over the country. As a result, he became very active in an organization that is now quite successful—The International Association of Cooking Schools. He traveled extensively in the cause of this organization and was made its first international president. He worked even more tirelessly during that first year for the organization, and his work with it has given him a good sense of our national cooking.

Richard Nelson's inquisitive nature makes him endlessly curious about food. His AMERICAN COOKING is a reflection of his early years and a continuation of his later culinary experience. It is a book for the cook. It's a book of traditions and a book of good-tasting food. It's not just another treatise on American cooking or regional cooking. It's an interesting, personal journey through the kitchens of the Middle West, the West, the Far West, and the East. It is a record of enjoying good food, cooking good food, and living a happy, amusing, and zestful life!

Introduction

I have been called a "maverick in the kitchen" by food writers and students. I am not at all. I simply cook as I see fit and allow nothing to intimidate me. I grew up on a ranch in South Dakota, eating wonderful food cooked by my maternal grandmother. She could create amazing things from the little that was at hand, and the memories of her skillet breads and baked goodies will never leave me.

I am forever indebted to two wonderful mentors, June Platt and James Beard, who got me started on my cooking career by teaching me an awareness of what I was eating and how best to prepare it.

Today one hears a lot about "American cuisine" and I think it is high time we took proper pride in it. From the beginning, the keynote of good American cooking has been simplicity. At its best, it is an unpretentious and straightforward approach to food—good basic ingredients properly cooked without any unnecessary seasonings or sauces to mask the true flavors.

In no other country in the world have so many ethnic cooking traditions come together, and it is this diverse mix of all the dishes brought to this country by its immigrants, adapted to available produce and local tastes, that forms the basis of my kind of cooking.

Every recipe in this book has been tested. Most of them are geared to the working cook, which means they can be prepared ahead. I refuse to be in the kitchen when my guests are in the living room, and I plan all meals so that I can join in the pre-dinner conversation. One trip to the kitchen to check on everything and then a final trip just before calling guests to the table—that's it.

While I would suggest that the basic recipe be followed the first time the dish is made, no one should be afraid to experiment. There is nothing more personal than food, and the addition of a spice or herb or the deletion of a seasoning to suit the cook's palate is exactly what personalizes the dish.

This is not a basic cookbook and I do not address it as such. This is a book of the food I love to cook. I hope you will too.

—Richard Nelson

Richard Nelson's American Cooking

Soups and Chowders

LOTS of people get very nostalgic about the soups of their childhood. I was converted to soup at college—which is unusual since most people remember college food without much enthusiasm. It was a delicious bean soup that did it, and my early love of bean soup has extended to all kinds of soups, especially those with body and flavor, the kind that can serve as a meal coupled with bread, salad, and maybe a fruit dessert.

The classic vegetable soup (generally beef-based with an imbalance of warring vegetable flavors) doesn't thrill me. Other kinds of not so traditional vegetable soups do. You'll find soups here that celebrate some rather neglected vegetables, like the turnip, the eggplant, and the squash, which can create whole new flavors and textures.

Of course, a lot of the romance about homemade soups comes from the fact that we are inundated by packaged soups these days. Nothing beats a soup made from scratch, and scratch often starts with a basic beef or chicken stock. You can make it up by the potful and then decant it into plastic containers to freeze for use weeks later. Just remember, whatever kind of soup you are making, use the freshest in-season ingredients—not hard in a country like ours which offers a cornucopia of top-quality fresh produce.

The soup pot on the stove, used as a catch-all for a bit of this and an end of that, won't give you as good a soup as one that has a master plan. There are flavors that complement one another; flavors that drown out everything else; flavors that enhance a specific food.

Although I use a roux to thicken some soups, I try to go easy when I do. Natural thickeners, such as pureed vegetables, are always the best, and with the advent of the blender and the food processor, you can puree bulk into a soup in a second.

Americans are lucky to be able to draw from a vast stockpot of traditional ethnic soups—I've included a few here, as well as some cold soups for summer and some hearty chowders for winter.

A Note About Stock

Technically speaking, the terms *stock* and *broth* have different meanings. Stock is the resulting drained and reserved liquid after water, meat, poultry and/or vegetables and seasonings have been cooked together until all their flavors have combined. Broth is stock from which all the fat has been removed. Consommé, the next refinement, is stock from which all fat and impurities have been removed and to which gelatin is then added.

For purposes of simplification, I use the term stock in this book. The basic stock recipes given here all call for the removal of fat and also include directions for clarifying should you want an even clearer end product. For practical purposes, I have not gone into the making of consommé. It is an arduous process and one that no longer seems worth the time, since good canned consommés are available today.

In the "good old days," making beef stock was not the expensive proposition it is today—the beef and veal bones were there for the asking at the butcher's, not sold by the pound. Chicken stock is still cheap to make because you get the bones with the chicken you buy to roast. Even so, the number of good commercially canned stocks (or broths if you will) are so inexpensive that it usually doesn't pay to make your own. If you do, however, freezing is the best way to keep it unless you plan to use it shortly after making it. Freeze stock in small batches since it should not be refrozen once it is thawed.

Chicken Stock

This is an excellent recipe and I always use it when I want a good chicken stock. However, when I need only a small quantity of stock in cooking and don't have it on hand, I simply buy canned stock. I prefer Stidd's, Swanson's, and College Inn brands because they are not as salty as some of the others.

Makes about 2 quarts

2 pounds chicken gizzards
2 pounds chicken necks and backs
1 onion, peeled and stuck with 3 whole cloves
1 leek, well washed and trimmed
1 carrot, scraped
2 garlic cloves, peeled
1 bay leaf
1 sprig parsley
1 teaspoon dried thyme
6 peppercorns
3 quarts water
1 tablespoon salt

Put the chicken pieces, vegetables, garlic, herbs, peppercorns, and water in an 8-quart pot or a stockpot and bring to a boil. After 5 minutes, use a wire skimmer or large spoon to remove the scum that forms on the surface. Allow to boil rapidly for another 15 minutes, continuing to skim off the surface. Reduce the heat, cover the pot, and simmer for 2 to 2½ hours. Season with salt.

Strain the stock through a sieve lined with several thicknesses of cheesecloth into a large bowl. Save the gizzards and discard the other chicken parts and vegetables. Place the stock in the refrigerator to cool. When it is cold, remove the layer of congealed fat that has formed on the surface.

Put the stock back in a pan and keep at a slow boil until it has been reduced to half or a third of its original volume. Strain through a sieve lined with cheesecloth or a linen towel into a 2½-quart pan in order to remove any lingering traces of fat. The stock must be absolutely fat-free and clear.

To clarify the stock, add 1 egg white, beaten to a froth, and 1 crushed eggshell. Beat well over medium heat with a rotary beater or a wire whisk until the stock comes to a boil and the egg white rises to the surface. Remove the pan from the heat, and let it stand for 5 minutes until the eggshells, egg particles, and remaining residue settle. Then, without agitating the stock, strain through a sieve or a colander lined with several thicknesses of cheesecloth or a linen towel that has been wrung out in cold water. The liquid should just drain through into the bowl beneath; don't attempt to hurry the process or you won't get a perfectly clear stock. When it has all dripped through, pour into plastic containers, cool, and refrigerate or freeze.

Beef Stock

Although you do not have to use baked onions in this recipe, they improve the flavor of the finished stock since baking brings out the natural sugar of the onion.

Makes about 6 quarts

- *4 pounds beef with bones*
- *3 pounds marrowbones, cut in pieces*
- *2 veal knuckles*
- *4 leeks, sliced and rinsed*
- *2 garlic cloves or 2 teaspoons Garlic Puree (see page 332)*
- *2 medium onions, baked (see page 253)*
- *1 teaspoon thyme*
- *1 bay leaf*
- *2 ribs celery with leaves*
- *8 peppercorns*
- *2 carrots*
- *Several sprigs parsley*
- *8 quarts cold water*
- *Salt*

Put all the beef and bones in a roasting pan and bake at 450°F. for about 1 hour until very brown. Put the browned bones and accumulated juices in a large stockpot and add all the remaining ingredients. Bring to a boil; skim off any scum that accumulates on the surface and lower the heat. Cook at a simmer for 3 to 4 hours, skimming occasionally. Remove from the heat and allow to cool. When cold, remove any fat and the vegetables and bones, and strain.

The strained stock should be clarified as follows: Allow 1 egg white and 1 crushed eggshell for each quart of stock. Beat the egg whites slightly with a whisk; combine with the crushed shells. Return the stock to the heat and stir in the egg mixture. Bring to a boil, stirring all the time with a whisk, and boil for 2 to 3 minutes. Remove the pan to a cold burner. Bring the stock to a simmer and let it simmer over very low heat for 15 to 20 minutes. Skim off any scum that forms and then strain the stock through several thicknesses of cheesecloth.

Vegetable Stock

Makes about 3 quarts

4 small onions, chopped
3 medium carrots, finely chopped
2½ cups finely chopped celery
3 leeks, thoroughly rinsed and sliced
¾ pound mushroom stems, chopped
1 bay leaf
3 quarts water
Salt

Combine all the vegetables in a 4-quart pot with bay leaf and water. Bring to a boil, then lower the heat and simmer, covered, for 3 hours. Strain and discard the vegetables and bay leaf. Season with salt to taste.

White Bean Soup

In this soup and the ones that follow it, I call for dried beans since only the dried variety imparts the necessary flavor.

Serves 6 generously

2 cups dried navy beans
1 ham bone
2 large onions, chopped
1 carrot, chopped
1 bay leaf
Salt and freshly ground black pepper
1 cup tomato juice
2 tablespoons butter

Wash the beans carefully before soaking in water overnight. (You want to be able to use the water they soak in for the soup.) Measure the soaking liquid and add water to make 2 quarts in a 4-quart pot. Add the ham bone, onions, carrot, bay leaf, salt, and pepper, and simmer for 3 hours (45 minutes in a pressure cooker). Add more boiling water if the soup appears to be cooking down too much. Add the tomato juice during the last 15 minutes of cooking. When the soup is done, remove the bay leaf and ham bone; add the butter. Mash a third of the beans through a sieve to thicken the soup.

Black Bean Soup

A refined, smooth pureed soup, this is the aristocrat of bean soups and the specialty of many fine restaurants.

Serves 6

4 cups dried black beans
¼ pound butter
3 ribs celery, finely chopped
3 large onions, finely chopped
2½ tablespoons all-purpose flour
½ cup finely chopped parsley
Smoked ham rind and bone
3 leeks, thoroughly rinsed and finely sliced
4 bay leaves
1 tablespoon salt
½ teaspoon freshly ground black pepper
1 cup dry Madeira wine
2 hard-cooked eggs, finely chopped
Lemon slices for garnish

Pick over and wash the beans; cover with cold water and soak overnight. Drain the beans and place in a large kettle; add 5 quarts fresh cold water, bring to a boil, and simmer for 1½ hours.

Meanwhile, melt the butter in a second large kettle and sauté the celery and onions for about 8 minutes, or until tender. Blend in the flour for 1 minute. Then add the beans and all their cooking liquid and stir to mix. Add the parsley, ham rind, and bone, leeks, bay leaves, salt, and pepper. Simmer over very low heat for 6 hours.

Remove and discard the ham rind, bone, and bay leaves. Force the bean mixture and broth through a fine sieve. Stir in the Madeira and bring to a boil. Remove from the heat immediately and mix in the chopped eggs.

Serve in prewarmed soup plates and garnish each serving with a thin slice of fresh lemon.

Mexican Bean Soup

Serves 6 generously

2 cups dried pink beans or dried chick-peas
2 onions, minced
2 garlic cloves, minced
4 tablespoons olive oil
2 strips bacon, minced and browned
Salt and freshly ground black pepper
½ cup tomato sauce
½ teaspoon chili powder
1 teaspoon oregano

Soak the beans or peas overnight; drain and cover with 2 quarts of lukewarm water. Sauté the onions and garlic in the olive oil until just limp. Add to the soup kettle with the bacon and salt and pepper. Cover and cook for 2 hours very slowly. Fifteen minutes before the soup is done, combine the tomato sauce, chili powder, and oregano and add to the soup.

Note: This soup may be pureed, the beans can be left whole, or you can compromise by pureeing half the beans, giving the soup body, and leaving the remainder whole.

Minestrone, Genoa Style

This Italian version of "vegetable soup" is my concession to that basic soup, and it's a winner. Although the original recipe called for dried kidney beans cooked in red wine, I have found that this is one place where canned beans work just as well—probably because the beans are only one of a number of ingredients.

Serves 6

4 tablespoons olive oil
2 ounces lean salt pork, chopped
4 cups canned, undrained kidney beans cooked in 1 cup red wine for 30 minutes
4 cups shredded or coarsely chopped raw spinach, tightly packed
1 cup peeled diced potatoes
1 cup shredded cabbage
1 leek (white part only), thinly sliced
2 medium yellow onions, chopped
2 quarts water (use liquid in which the beans have been cooked, supplemented with fresh water)
2 teaspoons salt
½ teaspoon freshly ground black pepper
1½ cups uncooked linguini, broken into 1-inch pieces
½ cup Pesto, Genoa Style *(see page 329)*

Heat the olive oil in a large, heavy pot and sauté the salt pork for about 2 minutes. Add the kidney beans, spinach, potatoes, cabbage, leek, and onions, and sauté for 4 to 5 minutes, stirring constantly.

Add the water, salt, and black pepper. Bring to a boil, then reduce the heat to low and cook, uncovered, for 1 hour. If the liquid reduces too fast, add more boiling water.

Add the linguini and cook for 15 minutes longer, stirring occasionally. Remove from the heat and add the pesto. Let stand for 2 minutes, then stir well and serve.

MANY of the soups that follow offer new or unexpected taste experiences and take advantage of some vegetables that haven't received their culinary due.

Bread and Squash Soup

This takes me back to Sicily and the beautiful San Domenico hotel in Taormina where I first tasted this wonderful soup. The recipe calls for fresh basil, but dried basil can be used if fresh isn't available. Although this soup can be served hot or cold (it's truly a soup for all seasons), it tastes best hot.

Serves 6

2 pounds butternut, yellow, or hubbard squash, peeled, seeded, and cut into small pieces
8 to 10 garlic cloves, peeled
3½ cups salted boiling water
2 slices bread, crusts removed and torn into small pieces
Salt and freshly ground black pepper
¼ cup olive oil
Fresh or dried basil, or parsley

Add the squash and garlic to the boiling water and cook, covered, at a light boil, for 25 to 30 minutes, or until the squash is puree-soft. Add the bread and simmer for a few minutes longer. Put the contents of the pan through a sieve or vegetable mill. Add salt and pepper and reheat. Stir in the olive oil just before serving. The soup may be garnished with fresh basil leaves torn into tiny pieces, a healthy pinch of dried basil, or finely chopped parsley.

Eggplant Soup

This is like a minestrone and is well received even by those who say they won't eat eggplant.

Serves 6 to 8

¾ cup minced onion
4 tablespoons butter
2 garlic cloves, minced
1 large eggplant
2 zucchini, cut in 1-inch slices
15½-ounce can kidney beans
35-ounce can Italian plum tomatoes
1 cup shell macaroni
¼ teaspoon minced red chili peppers
1 teaspoon salt
2 cups stock (vegetable, chicken, or beef)
Chopped parsley
Shredded Swiss cheese

Sauté the onion in butter with garlic until golden brown. Cut the stem from the eggplant and peel off skin lengthwise in alternating ½-inch strips. Cut the eggplant into cubes. Add to the onion mixture and sauté until golden. Add the remaining ingredients except the parsley and cheese. Simmer, covered, until the eggplant is tender, about 30 minutes.

Serve in soup plates and sprinkle with parsley and cheese.

Turnip Soup

A soup for "turnip lovers" only, because it has a flavor all its own and makes that statement very definitely. To change it a bit, substitute beef stock for chicken stock, or use plain or low-fat milk instead of light cream.

Serves 8

2 pounds small white turnips
3 tablespoons butter
4 cups hot chicken stock
3 cups light cream, heated
Salt and freshly ground black pepper
Nutmeg
2 tablespoons chopped parsley

Skin the turnips and cut into thick slices. Melt the butter in a heavy pan and stew the turnips in it very gently for about 10 minutes. Add the chicken stock and bring to the boiling point. Lower the heat and simmer for about 25 minutes until the turnips are quite soft. Put the soup briefly in a blender or through a medium-fine vegetable mill. Return to the pot and stir in the cream. Reheat and season to taste with salt, pepper, and nutmeg. Sprinkle with chopped parsley and serve.

Cream of Rutabaga and Watercress Soup

The rutabaga, which is very close to the turnip in flavor, has been passed over for some reason, so that there are many people who have never eaten it. In combination with watercress it makes a good winter soup.

Serves 6

2 medium rutabagas, peeled and diced
½ cup watercress, packed
1½ cups chicken stock
2 cups heavy cream
2 tablespoons butter
Salt and freshly ground black pepper
Pinch nutmeg
Homemade Sour Cream (see page 333)
Chopped watercress

Combine the rutabaga and watercress in 4 cups of water in a 2-quart saucepan and cook until the rutabaga is tender, about 15 to 20 minutes. Drain and puree in a processor or food mill, adding the chicken stock, cream, butter, and seasonings. Return to the saucepan and heat until hot. Serve with a dollop of sour cream on each bowl, and garnish with chopped watercress.

Pumpkin Soup

If you make this soup from scratch, be sure what you are using is indeed a pumpkin and not a jack-o'-lantern. There's a difference, and I didn't know that when I first tried this recipe. Pumpkin is pumpkin, and jack-o'-lantern is not edible. One is grown to eat, and one is decorative and only produced for Hallowe'en—a pearl of wisdom I learned the hard way.

Serves 6 to 8

3 medium leeks (roots and green stalks removed), finely chopped
¼ pound plus 2 tablespoons butter, divided
1⅓ cups cooked fresh pumpkin pulp, or a 10-ounce can pumpkin pulp
3 large potatoes, peeled and thinly sliced
1 bouquet garni: ½ teaspoon dried thyme, 1 tablespoon fresh parsley, and 1 bay leaf
1 quart chicken stock, divided
1½ teaspoons salt
½ teaspoon freshly ground black pepper
⅛ teaspoon freshly grated or ground nutmeg
3 cups whole milk, heated
½ pound fresh spinach, chopped
¼ teaspoon sugar
½ cup freshly grated Parmesan cheese

In a large, heavy pan or casserole, sauté the leeks in 4 tablespoons of the butter until golden. Add the pumpkin pulp, sliced potatoes, bouquet garni, 3 cups of the chicken stock, salt, pepper, and nutmeg. Mix well. Bring to a boil, then cook over moderate heat for 30 minutes, stirring constantly.

Remove the bouquet garni and puree the leek-pumpkin-potato mixture in a blender. Return mixture to the pan, add hot milk, and bring to a boil. Reduce the heat to low and cook for 20 minutes, stirring frequently.

Meanwhile, cook and thoroughly drain the spinach. Melt 2 tablespoons of the butter in a skillet and sauté the spinach for 2 minutes over low heat.

When the pumpkin mixture is cooked, add the spinach, the remaining cup of chicken stock, and the sugar. Mix well. Remove from heat, add the remaining 4 tablespoons of butter and the Parmesan cheese, and mix well.

Cream of Pumpkin Soup

Serves 8

1 large onion, finely minced
3 tablespoons butter
3 cups cooked fresh pumpkin pulp or a 26-ounce can pumpkin pulp
Salt and freshly ground black pepper
⅛ teaspoon nutmeg or mace
⅛ teaspoon turmeric
6 cups hot chicken stock
1 cup heavy cream
Finely chopped cilantro (fresh coriander leaves) or chopped parsley
Crème Fraîche (see page 334), Homemade Sour Cream (page 333), or commercial sour cream

Sauté the minced onion in butter until tender and transparent but not browned. Place the onion and pumpkin puree in a soup pot, add the seasonings, and gradually add the chicken stock over low flame, stirring until the mixture is smooth. Add the cream and stir to blend. Taste to correct seasonings. Simmer soup for another 5 minutes, or until piping hot. Sprinkle with chopped cilantro or parsley and serve in heated bowls with a dollop of crème fraîche or sour cream.

Sorrel Soup

I am indebted to my friend Gail Kelly for this recipe.

Serves 4

6 ounces sorrel
1 large, sweet onion, finely chopped
6 tablespoons butter, divided
1 pound potatoes, quartered lengthwise and finely sliced
Salt
1 quart boiling water
½ cup heavy cream
Pepper to taste
Handful chervil leaves or chopped chives

Pick over the sorrel and remove the stringy veins from the leaves; wash, drain, and cut into coarse shreds. Tender newly formed leaves may be used as is; older leaves should be parboiled in water for a few seconds.

Stew the onion gently in 2 tablespoons of the butter in a large pot, stirring, for 15 minutes until melting-soft but uncolored. Add the sorrel and continue cooking until it is "melted," about 5 minutes. Add the potatoes; stir and cook together for a few minutes. Add the salt and boiling water and cook, covered, at a light boil for 30 minutes. Uncover and continue cooking for 10 minutes, crushing regularly with a wooden spoon or pestle, until the potatoes are reduced to a coarse semi-puree. Stir in the cream; return to a boil, remove from the heat, and stir in the remaining butter and the pepper. Serve sprinkled with chervil.

Cream of Sorrel Soup

The slightly bitter but wonderfully fresh taste of sorrel makes this a superb soup, and the addition of farina lends a nice texture and taste.

Serves 6

2 quarts clear chicken stock
¼ cup farina
1 cup whole milk
Salt and freshly ground black pepper
1 cup melted and pureed fresh sorrel (see page 13)
4 egg yolks, beaten
1 cup heavy cream

Bring the chicken stock to a boil in a double boiler. Add the farina slowly and cook for 15 minutes. Add the milk and salt and pepper, and cook, stirring, until well heated. Add the puree of sorrel and stir into the mixture.

When ready to serve, beat the egg yolks into the cream and add slowly to the hot soup, stirring continuously until the soup has thickened.

White Wine Onion Soup

This differs from most onion soup recipes because it is made with white wine and chicken stock instead of the traditional red wine and beef stock. Although the basic idea is the same, the taste is quite unusual.

Serves 4

8 onions, thinly sliced
1/4 pound butter
Salt to taste
Freshly ground black pepper
1 teaspoon Dijon mustard mixed with chopped shallots
Pinch thyme
1 tablespoon unbleached all-purpose flour worked into a little softened butter
1/4 cup dry white wine
4 cups hot chicken stock
4 teaspoons apple brandy or French Calvados
4 slices French bread, cut into 3/4-inch-thick rounds
Freshly grated Parmesan cheese

Poach the onions gently in butter until soft and clear (about 15 minutes), adding salt and pepper, shallot mustard, and a little thyme. Thicken with the flour-butter mixture. Add the wine and chicken stock and stir well. Put into individual onion soup pots. Flavor each pot with 1 teaspoon of apple brandy or French Calvados. On each pot float a round of French bread heaped with cheese. Brown briefly under the broiler.

Leek, Carrot, and Cheese Soup

This is one of the best soups I have ever eaten.

Serves 8

3 medium leeks
3 large carrots, peeled and thinly sliced
5 cups whole milk
3 cups heavy cream
6 ounces Fontina cheese, freshly grated
Salt and freshly ground black pepper
Freshly ground nutmeg
3 tablespoons butter (optional)

Remove the tough outer green leaves from the leeks and discard. Cut off the roots, halve lengthwise, and cut into thin slices. Wash well to get rid of sand and place in a soup pot with the carrots, milk, and cream. Bring to a simmer and cook for about 20 minutes until the vegetables are tender. Stir in the cheese, a bit at a time, being careful not to let the soup boil, or the cheese will curdle. Season with salt, pepper, and nutmeg. If desired, stir in the butter, a tablespoon at a time.

Leek and Potato Soup

You might call this the poor man's vichyssoise. It is basically the same and very easy to prepare. For the traditional cold version, see the Variation.

Serves 6 to 8

1 pound leeks (white part only), cleaned and finely sliced
3 tablespoons butter
2 quarts boiling water
Salt
1 pound potatoes, peeled and quartered
Pepper

Sauté the leeks in butter in a saucepan. When they become slightly golden, add the water, salt, and potatoes. Simmer for 1 hour. Mash the potatoes with a fork to get rid of lumps, and serve piping hot with a sprinkle of freshly ground pepper.

Variation: Vichyssoise—Prepare Leek and Potato Soup and allow to cool; add 1½ cups of heavy cream and blend well. Chill in the refrigerator. Serve in chilled cups with chopped chives as a garnish.

Chilled Cucumber Soup

Tomato, cucumber, and avocado are wonderful bases for cold soups. All three are also good served hot, but if heated should never be allowed to boil after the cream, sour cream, or yogurt has been added or they will curdle. Although the taste isn't dreadful, the visual effect is.

Serves 6

- *2 cups chicken stock*
- *2 medium cucumbers, peeled, seeded, and cut into strips*
- *1 tablespoon finely chopped onion*
- *Salt and freshly ground black pepper*
- *1 teaspoon fresh dill or dillweed, or ½ teaspoon dried dillseed*
- *2 cups plain yogurt*
- *Finely chopped cucumber or chopped fresh dill*

Combine the stock, cucumbers, and onion, and cook over low heat until the cucumbers are just tender. Puree in a processor or blender with the salt, pepper, and dill or dillweed. If you do not have a blender or processor, mash through a medium-fine sieve. Combine with the yogurt and correct the seasoning and chill. Serve in chilled cups, garnished with either cucumber or dill—but not both.

Spinach Soup

Since this recipe calls for unsalted butter and suggests adding salt to taste, you can just as easily use regular butter and skip the salt—that's true with any recipe. And if chervil is not to your liking, substitute nutmeg, turmeric, or simply some chopped parsley. Spinach makes a strong enough statement so that additional seasoning is not a must.

Serves 4 to 6

1 pound fresh spinach
6 tablespoons butter, divided
4 cups chicken stock
6 egg yolks
1 cup heavy cream
Salt
1 teaspoon finely chopped chervil

Wash the spinach under running cold water. Trim away any bruised or blemished spots and discard the stems. Stack the leaves together, a handful at a time, roll them lengthwise into a tight cylinder, and cut it crosswise as fine as possible.

In a heavy skillet over moderate heat, melt 2 tablespoons of the butter without browning. Add the spinach and cook, stirring constantly, until tender. Remove from the heat and set aside.

In a heavy 3- to 4-quart saucepan, bring the chicken stock to a simmer. Beat the egg yolks and cream together with a wire whisk. Whisking constantly but gently, pour the eggs and cream into the simmering stock in a slow, thin stream. Reduce the heat and simmer, stirring constantly, until the soup is thick enough to cling lightly to the wires of the whisk. Do not allow the soup to approach a boil. Strain the soup through a fine sieve into another saucepan, add the spinach, and salt to taste.

Immediately swirl in the remaining 4 tablespoons butter, taste for seasoning, and serve sprinkled with chervil.

Note: If the soup is to be served cold, omit the butter. Allow it to cool to room temperature, then chill before serving.

Tomato Soup

Tomato soup is exactly what this is: no fooling around, and truly the taste of the tomato. If you feel it is too acid, add a second pinch of baking soda.

Serves 4 to 6

5 to 6 medium-large tomatoes, peeled
¼ cup cold water
Pinch baking soda
1 quart hot boiled whole milk
½ teaspoon sugar
Salt and freshly ground black pepper
2 tablespoons butter
3 tablespoons crushed soda crackers
Homemade Sour Cream *(see page 333)*
Chopped parsley

In a 2½-quart saucepan, stew the peeled tomatoes in the cold water to which a pinch of baking soda has been added. When the tomatoes are soft, transfer them to a sieve and strain them over the saucepan to remove all seeds, letting the liquid and strained pulp fall into the pan. To this liquid add the milk, sugar, salt, pepper, butter, and soda crackers. Heat until hot and serve. To each serving, add a dollop of sour cream and a pinch of chopped parsley.

Note: You may use a good brand of canned tomatoes, but if you do, add some fresh ripe tomatoes as well, to give the soup a "fresh" taste.

Egg Soup

Serves 6

8 cups water (use veal or chicken stock for a richer soup)
6 tablespoons butter
4 egg yolks
1 teaspoon salt
Generous amount freshly ground black pepper
6 eggs, poached or 4-minute boiled (minus the shells)
Chopped parsley or chervil for garnish

Boil the water or stock and butter together for 5 minutes. Drop the egg yolks into a soup tureen and sprinkle with salt and pepper. Pour the hot liquid very slowly onto the eggs, stirring with a wire whisk until all the liquid has been incorporated.

Place a poached or 4-minute egg in each serving bowl, and cover with the soup. Garnish each bowl with parsley or chervil.

Variation: Replace the water with milk in which 2 tablespoons of minute tapioca has been cooked. Garnish with a dash of paprika instead of the parsley.

Lemon and Meatball Soup

Before I added the lemon juice, this was a traditional Armenian soup.

Serves 6

½ pound ground lamb
¼ cup finely chopped onion
½ cup raw rice
½ cup finely chopped parsley
Salt and freshly ground black pepper
2 quarts chicken stock
3 eggs, well-beaten
Juice of 2 lemons

In a small bowl, combine the lamb, onion, rice, parsley, salt, and pepper, and shape into meatballs. Bring the chicken stock to a boil. Add the meatballs and simmer for about 1 hour. Remove the meatballs with a slotted spoon to a warmed tureen. Combine the eggs with lemon juice. Slowly add the stock to the egg mixture, beating constantly with a wire whisk. Pour the thickened broth over the meatballs and serve.

Tex-Mex Soup with Meatballs

This nice, mildly spiced soup was given to me by a cook who lives on the border between Texas and Mexico, and is reproduced here exactly as it was sent to me. Although the minced garlic is acceptable, I prefer this soup with a teaspoon of Garlic Puree, which you will find on page 332.

Serves 8

1 onion, minced
1 garlic clove, minced
2 tablespoons vegetable oil
2 6-ounce cans tomato sauce
3 quarts beef stock
1 tablespoon whole cumin
1 tablespoon chopped parsley
1½ pounds ground beef
1 tablespoon instant coffee
1 egg
1 cup crushed crackers
2 teaspoons minced garlic
Salt and freshly ground black pepper

In a kettle, wilt the onion and garlic in oil. Add the tomato sauce, beef stock, cumin, and parsley; heat to a low boil.

Combine the meat with instant coffee, egg, crackers, minced garlic, and salt and pepper. Form into small balls and drop into the boiling stock. Cover and simmer for 30 to 45 minutes.

Optional: Add a 10-ounce package of frozen corn for the last 5 minutes of cooking time.

Rassolnik

I am particularly fond of kidneys and barley and this is a good combination of the two. The late Harriet Coe, my friend and cooking colleague, gave me the recipe, which comes from a Russian cookbook long out of print, and I am told that it was a traditional soup. I have not eaten it anywhere except in my own home.

Serves 6

8 lamb kidneys
2 quarts very cold salted water
2 tablespoons pearl barley
1 cup water
6 cups beef stock, divided
2 cups diced potatoes
1 large onion, minced
3 tablespoons butter, divided
1 tablespoon unbleached all-purpose flour
2 small dill pickles
½ cup sour cream
Freshly ground black pepper
2 tablespoons minced parsley

Soak the kidneys in the salted water for 30 minutes. Remove from the water and cut away the central cortex. Cut the remaining portion of the kidneys into thin slices and set aside.

Cook the barley until soft in the water; drain and set aside for later use. Parboil the potatoes in 5 cups of the stock; add the barley and set aside, keeping hot.

In a large, lidded skillet, sauté the onion in 2 tablespoons of butter; add the kidneys and remaining butter and sauté for 2 minutes; sprinkle with the flour and cook for 3 minutes. Cover and simmer for 10 minutes. Add the remaining broth, bring to a boil, and reduce again to simmer.

Peel the dill pickles and squeeze the liquid into the kidney-onion mixture. Add the kidney-onion mixture to the broth and diced potatoes, bring to a boil, then reduce the heat and simmer for 15 minutes.

When ready to serve, put the sour cream into a warm soup tureen and pour in the soup. Sprinkle with pepper and minced parsley.

Cream of Turtle Soup

This goes back to the days when I first moved to New York. I had never heard of turtle soup and wasn't sure I would like it at all when I did. Well, I not only liked it, I all but overdosed on it. It is delicious. One can hardly be criticized for using canned turtle soup in this recipe, since fresh turtles are pretty hard to come by.

Serves 6

- ***3 quarts shelled peas***
- ***1 large can or jar of turtle soup***
- ***2 cups heavy cream***
- ***2 tablespoons butter***
- ***2 tablespoons unbleached all-purpose flour***
- ***½ cup grated Parmesan cheese***
- ***Salt and freshly ground black pepper***
- ***½ cup sherry***

Cook the peas until tender and pass through a fine sieve, blender, or food processor. Heat the turtle soup in a double boiler; remove the turtle meat and cut it into small pieces. Place the meat in soup plates and keep warm.

Add the peas and cream to the turtle soup. In an enamel pan, melt the butter and add the flour; cook together for 1 to 2 minutes. Add 1 cup of the soup and stir until smooth. Add the remaining soup, the Parmesan cheese, and salt and pepper, stirring continuously; then add the sherry. Pour over the reserved turtle meat and serve very hot.

Salmon Soup

This should only be made with fresh fish, preferably salmon if it is available, although red snapper, cod, flounder, and haddock are good substitutes. When I say fresh, I don't rule out frozen fish, just canned.

Serves 8

2 pounds fish bones and heads
1½ quarts water
Salt and freshly ground black pepper
3 large ripe tomatoes, peeled, seeded, and chopped
7 tablespoons butter, divided
1½ pounds salmon fillets, cut in strips
1 tablespoon chopped black olives
1 tablespoon chopped green olives
4 dill pickles, finely chopped
2 teaspoons capers
2 onions, finely chopped
1 bay leaf
Chopped parsley, additional chopped olives, and lemon slices for garnish

Cook the fish bones and heads in water seasoned with salt and pepper for 1½ hours over medium-high heat. Drain off the broth and reserve.

Simmer the tomatoes in 3 tablespoons of butter for 10 minutes. Season to taste. Arrange the salmon strips in a deep pot with the tomatoes, olives, pickles, capers, and onions. Cover with the fish broth, add the bay leaf, and simmer for 15 minutes. Swirl in the remaining 4 tablespoons of butter.

Serve in bowls, garnished with chopped parsley, chopped olives, and lemon slices.

Greek Fish Soup

A really wonderful fish soup, this is hearty and can easily serve as a meal in itself. The addition of lemon juice is the Greek touch, which gives it its name.

Serves 4

1½ pounds halibut
1½ quarts salted water
12 small new potatoes
12 small whole white onions
1 green onion, minced
1 rib celery, sliced
⅓ cup olive oil
¼ cup lemon juice
Salt and freshly ground black pepper
2 tablespoons minced parsley

Simmer halibut in salted water for 20 to 30 minutes until tender. Drain, reserving the liquid; skin and bone the fish, and keep it warm.

Strain the cooking liquid; bring it to a boil and add the potatoes, white and green onions, and celery. Cover and simmer for 20 minutes, or until the vegetables are tender.

Mix together the oil, lemon juice, salt, and pepper. Pour half of this over the fish and stir the remainder into the soup. Sprinkle parsley on the fish and serve the fish as a side dish to the soup.

THERE seems to be some misconception that in order for a soup to qualify as a chowder it's got to be thick enough to hold the soup spoon upright, or maybe to keep the wallpaper on the walls. That's taking "stick to the ribs" too literally. Although the addition of a roux isn't absolutely necessary for chowder, it does lend a slight thickening and a nice smooth quality—but remember to use a light hand.

Corn Chowder

Corn chowder comes to mind in the fall and winter because it is hearty and bone-warming and very filling. I often prepare it for a Sunday supper with a light salad and fresh-baked bread.

Serves 8 to 10

16-ounce can whole-kernel corn, drained
2 16-ounce cans cream-style corn
2 cups light cream
1½ quarts whole milk
½ pound lean bacon, minced
1 medium onion, minced
2 medium potatoes, peeled and finely diced
½ cup warm water
6 tablespoons butter
Salt and freshly ground black pepper
Several drops hot pepper sauce

For the Roux

4 tablespoons butter
4 tablespoons unbleached all-purpose flour
2 cups whole milk

Place the corn, cream, and milk in a 6-quart kettle over medium heat.

Fry the bacon until it is almost crisp and drain on paper towel. Discard most of the fat from the skillet. Add the onion to the remaining fat in the skillet and cook over medium-high heat until limp and slightly browned. Add the cooked onions and drained bacon to the corn mixture in the kettle.

Using the same skillet, fry the diced potatoes. As they cook, add the warm water and butter. Raise the heat to high to reduce the liquid as the cooking continues. The potatoes will cook and brown at the same time. After they are almost cooked (about 10 minutes), add them to the kettle. Add the salt, pepper, and hot pepper sauce, and let the mixture simmer.

To make the roux, melt the butter in a 1-quart saucepan. Blend in the flour; cook and stir briefly to remove the raw taste of the flour. Add the milk and whisk to the thickness of a medium-thick gravy. Add this sauce to the soup kettle and continue to simmer for another 30 to 40 minutes.

Adjust the seasonings, if necessary, before serving.

Note: This recipe can also be used to make clam chowder or fish chowder. Use 4 cups of minced clams or 1½ pounds of mixed fish in place of the corn in the basic recipe.

Clam Chowder—New England Style

Everyone has a clam chowder recipe and everyone thinks theirs is the best. I'm no exception.

Serves 4

1 pint shelled clams with their liquid
or
2 10-ounce cans minced clams
¼ pound salt pork or bacon, diced
1 medium onion, chopped
3 medium potatoes, diced
½ teaspoon salt
Freshly ground black pepper
1 pint whole milk
Paprika
Butter

Drain the clams, measure the liquid, and add enough water to make 1 pint. In a large saucepan, brown the salt pork or bacon; then stir in the chopped onion and cook over very low heat for about 5 minutes. Add the potatoes, clam liquid, and seasoning, and simmer for about 15 minutes, or until the potatoes are tender.

Chop the clams, if whole, and add to the pan with the milk. Bring the chowder slowly back to the boiling point. Top each serving with a sprinkling of paprika and a pat of butter.

Brittany Chowder

The ideal combination for this recipe is flounder and halibut or snapper. If fresh cod is used, add two cups of milk to the boiling water to remove some of the strong taste of the cod.

Serves 4

1 pound sweet onions, peeled and quartered
3 tablespoons olive oil (or handful of chopped-up fat salt pork)
2 pounds potatoes, peeled and cut into large pieces
¼ teaspoon thyme, bay leaf, or oregano
Dash salt
2 quarts boiling water
2 pounds fish (2 or more varieties), cut into 1-inch slices
Dried bread slices

Accompaniment

Handful coarse salt
2 to 3 ladlefuls of fish broth
2 tablespoons peppercorns, coarsely crushed and mixed with 1 cup red wine vinegar

Over medium heat cook the onions in a large, heavy saucepan with the oil or salt pork for 2 minutes. Add the potatoes and herbs and continue cooking, stirring regularly, for 8 to 10 minutes, or until the onions begin to color lightly; add a little salt and pour on the boiling water.

After about 15 minutes, add the fish, holding back the soft-fleshed varieties (like sole) until the last minutes of cooking time. Continue to cook at a light boil for 10 to 15 minutes. Remove the fish and the vegetables to a hot serving platter. Reserve 2 or 3 ladlefuls of broth and set aside.

Place a slice of bread in each soup plate and cover with the remaining broth. When the bread has soaked, top with the fish and vegetables. Dissolve the coarse salt in the reserved fish broth and serve it in individual ramekins with the vinegar-crushed peppercorn mixture.

Note: You can substitute sea scallops for the snapper or halibut.

MEATS

FOR over two centuries, meat has been the mainstay of the American diet. At first, game meat played an important role because domestic animals like cattle, pigs, and sheep were raised to further the herd, not to be eaten. However, as the herds increased in size, domestic animals began to be used for food.

Beef was our most popular meat until very recently. Now lamb and even pork are close rivals for first place on the American table. Still, one cannot compare American beef with any other because the feed and care of the cattle are of extremely high quality, and proper aging lends the final touch. In beef and mutton, aging improves the tenderness and flavor. The government determines the grades of beef through inspection, but these grades change from time to time. It is best to know one's butcher and find out from him which cuts of meat are best for the intended use.

Veal and pork are never aged. Fine-quality lamb is sometimes aged. Meats with a thick outer coating of fat (that is, the highest quality meats) are aged from three to six weeks. Personally, I prefer meats aged three to four weeks. Anything under that is lacking in flavor and tenderness, and anything over seems soft and mushy in texture and strong in flavor.

All meats shrink during cooking. The temperature and length of cooking time determine the amount of shrinkage, which also affects the flavor and tenderness. Obviously, the less shrinkage the better, so the shorter the cooking time the better.

Cooking charts have changed considerably over the years. For far too long, Americans thought that all meats had to be thoroughly cooked to destroy bacteria, and the results were dull and tasteless, as well as difficult to chew and swallow.

Today there are two schools of thought on the cooking of most meats. One school prefers the long, low-heat method, claiming that there is less shrinkage. The other prefers a higher heat for a shorter period of time. I have tried both and find little difference in either shrinkage or flavor. Consequently, I prefer the fast method using very high heat. There are times when a combination works best, starting a roast on very high heat for a 20-minute period, then reducing the heat to medium and continuing the cooking. Whichever method is used, you should get into the habit of cooking with an instant-reading thermometer at hand so that you know precisely when the meat has reached the desired internal temperature.

The following chart will serve as a guide in cooking meat.

Type of Meat	*Internal Temperature*	
BEEF		
(rib, rolled rib, rib eye, tenderloin)	Rare:	110° to 115°F.
	Medium Rare:	115° to 120°F.
	Medium:	130° to 135°F.
(boneless rolled rump)	Well Done:	145° to 150°F.
VEAL		
(leg, loin, rack, boneless shoulder)	Well Done:	160°F.
LAMB		
(leg, shoulder, boneless cushion, rib)	Medium Rare:	125° to 130°F.
	Well Done:	145° to 150°F.
PORK		
(fresh loin, leg, fresh ham)	Well Done:	160° to 170°F.

You can suit yourself in using this chart; personally I follow it very closely. I remove the roast from the oven when it reaches the lower internal temperature given, because whatever is roasting will continue to cook for a while after it is moved to room temperature. If I want a beef roast rare, I always take it out the minute it reaches the desired temperature reading.

All meat should be at room temperature before you start cooking it, and once cooked, it is important for any roast to "rest" for at least 15 minutes to give the juices time to settle down. Always wait 15 minutes before carving, for with the juice goes a lot of the taste.

BEEF

In selecting prime beef, look for a liberal marbling of fat throughout the lean, and a heavy outside covering of fat. The tender cuts can be roasted, broiled, or pan-fried; the less tender cuts should be cooked more slowly in liquid. Where good beef is concerned, less is really more, which is why the recipes that follow are very simple and unadorned.

Rib Roast of Beef

This basic American dish is part of our English heritage, although we have perfected the raising of cattle and vastly improved the cooking techniques for beef. There is little brought to the table that is as impressive as a perfectly done standing rib roast.

Serves 6

4- or 5-rib beef roast*
½ teaspoon freshly ground black pepper
½ teaspoon thyme
3 tablespoons melted butter
Salt

Preheat the oven to 500°F.

Rub the meat thoroughly with pepper and thyme. Roast on a rack in a shallow roasting pan, bone side down, for 40 minutes, basting twice with melted butter.

Reduce the heat to 325°F. and roast for 30 minutes longer. Test the internal temperature with a meat thermometer thrust into the thickest part of the eye of the rib. It should register 115°F. for rare.

For a medium to well-done roast, remove the thermometer and continue roasting for 30 minutes, basting after 20 minutes with pan juices. Salt the roast after the second basting. Test the internal temperature after 30 minutes. When it reaches 130°F. (medium) or 150°F. (well done), remove to a hot platter and allow to rest in a warm place for 15 to 20 minutes before carving.

* Have the butcher remove the short ribs and chine bone from the beef, leaving the ribs intact.

Marinated Eye of Rib Roast

The secret of this recipe is fast cooking at high heat. Follow the cooking instructions exactly and you will have a beautifully rare success. Be sure the meat is at room temperature before it goes into the oven, or the 30 minutes roasting time will not be enough.

Serves 8

1 cup vegetable oil
4 cups soy sauce
¾ cup shredded fresh ginger
6 garlic cloves
¾ cup Madeira wine
5-pound eye of beef rib, at room temperature

Preheat the oven to 500°F.

Combine all the ingredients, except the meat, and mix well. Marinate the roast in the mixture for several hours or overnight.

Remove the meat from the marinade and place in a roasting pan. For rare, roast for 30 minutes, basting with the marinade (the internal temperature should be 110°F.). Let the cooked roast stand for 15 minutes before slicing.

This is particularly good with Potato Custard.

Note: Save any excess marinade and pour into a sealed container. It can be kept in the refrigerator for several weeks and reused.

New York Steak with Mushrooms

This is the world's simplest recipe—all it takes is a good cut of beef and the right cooking time. It's good all by itself, but somehow, to me, steak tastes even better with mushrooms. I prefer fresh chanterelles, which are reddish-yellow cup-shaped mushrooms that grow wild in this country; if they are not available, the commercially grown "button" mushroom is also flavorful. Just steer clear of the canned or frozen variety.

Serves 2

1½ pounds mushrooms, cleaned
3 tablespoons butter
2 tablespoons vegetable oil
Salt and freshly ground black pepper
½ teaspoon hot pepper sauce
3 tablespoons finely chopped beef suet
2 New York strip, shell, or club steaks, about 1 inch thick
⅓ cup chopped parsley

Separate the mushroom caps from the stems. Cut the caps into thin slices. Chop the stems very fine; put them in a dish towel and twist very hard to squeeze out all the moisture.

Heat the butter and oil in a heavy skillet. Add the sliced mushrooms and cook briskly over medium heat for 6 to 8 minutes, or until they have absorbed most of the fat. Shake the skillet well and continue to cook until the mushrooms are lightly browned. Add the chopped mushroom stems, salt, pepper, and hot pepper sauce; cook for 2 to 3 minutes, tossing. Keep warm while preparing the steaks.

Heat the suet in a heavy skillet until the fat is rendered. Discard the suet. Over high heat, sear the steaks quickly on both sides. Reduce the heat and add salt and pepper to taste. Continue cooking, turning from time to time, until the steaks are done to your liking (4 minutes per side for rare, 6 minutes per side for medium rare). Remove from the heat and spoon the mushrooms over the steak. Sprinkle with parsley and serve.

Brisket of Beef

Not to be confused with corned brisket of beef, this is one of the best "lesser" cuts that I know of. This recipe and the ones that follow make use of the longer-cooking cuts of beef that offer not only greater mileage for your money but extremely satisfying flavor.

Serves 8 to 10

5- to 6-pound beef brisket, at room temperature
Unbleached all-purpose flour for dredging
2 teaspoons salt
4 tablespoons butter or other fat
3 cups water
5 peppercorns
1 bay leaf
4 ounces fresh caraway-rye bread, crumbled

Coat the meat with a mixture of flour and salt. Heat the butter (or other shortening) to hot in a large Dutch oven or stewpot and brown the brisket on both sides. (Since brisket is large and will need to be folded over—not cut in half—to fit into the cooking container for the browning process, it will have to be turned four times in order to brown both sides.)

When well browned, add the water, peppercorns, and bay leaf. Cover the pot and lower the heat to a simmer. Cook for about 3 hours.

When the meat is tender, remove from the pot to a heated platter and keep hot while preparing the sauce.

Remove the bay leaf and the peppercorns from the cooking liquid. Turn the heat to high and add the bread to the pot. Stir continuously over high heat; when the liquid starts to thicken, lower the heat and continue to cook, stirring until the bread and liquid are completely cooked together.

Pour the sauce over the brisket; slice and serve. Lemon Sweet Parsnips go well with this roast.

Pot Roast of Beef

In cooking any pot roast, don't be afraid of over-browning the meat when you first start. It needs a good crust before the liquid is added to finish the cooking. That brown crust adds to the flavor of the finished dish. And for heaven's sake, don't taste the cooking liquid until it has cooked for about two hours, because it won't taste like anything until it has had time to draw flavor from the meat. Make any seasoning adjustment you want just before serving.

Serves 6 to 8

4-pound top round roast
2 to 3 tablespoons unbleached all-purpose flour
Salt and freshly ground black pepper
Beef suet
1 small bay leaf
⅓ cup seedless raisins
1 sprig parsley
1½ cups water
8 carrots, peeled and halved
8 medium-size new potatoes, peeled and halved
8 small white onions
6 tablespoons heavy cream
Additional flour for the sauce
1 tablespoon chopped parsley

Wipe the roast with a damp cloth to clean it. Mix the flour with salt and pepper and sprinkle over the roast until it is completely coated. Slowly render the beef suet in an iron pot or other heavy utensil, being careful not to burn it. Place the roast in the pot and brown on all sides, turning it carefully with tongs to avoid puncturing the meat. When nicely browned, add the bay leaf, raisins, parsley sprig, and water; cover and simmer gently for about 2½ hours.

During the last hour of cooking, add the carrots, potatoes, and onions, and a little more salt and pepper. When ready to serve, remove the roast and vegetables and keep warm. Drain off the pan juices into a bowl; as the fat rises to the surface, remove it by skimming off with a spoon and reserve.

For each cup of juice in the bowl, put 2 level tablespoons of the fat in a small saucepan, add an equal quantity of flour, and cook the fat and flour together for a few minutes. Add the cream and the hot juice from the bowl, and simmer this gravy for a few minutes to remove any taste of raw flour.

Place the roast on a heated serving platter and arrange vegetables around the edge; garnish with chopped parsley and serve with gravy on the side.

Pot Roast with Ginger

Beef chuck and rump roast are not tender cuts of meat. To tenderize them, I dredge them generously in flour seasoned with salt and pepper, then poke the flour mixture into the meat with the tines of a fork, forcing the flour a little way into the meat.

Serves 6 to 8

3-pound boneless beef chuck or rump roast
1 cup unbleached all-purpose flour
Salt and freshly ground black pepper
3 tablespoons lard
¾ cup chopped onion
1 garlic clove, minced
½ scant teaspoon thyme
16-ounce can whole tomatoes, undrained
1 teaspoon chopped fresh ginger root

Dredge the meat in flour seasoned with salt and pepper. In a Dutch oven heat the lard to hot, add the meat, and brown on all sides.

Pour off the fat and add the onion, garlic, and thyme. Stir until the onions are light brown; then add the tomatoes and ginger. Cover and simmer until tender, about 2 hours.

Remove the roast to a serving platter. Prepare the gravy by adding 1 tablespoon of flour mixed with ¼ cup of water to the pan juices. Serve with Sautéed Green Peppers.

Short Ribs of Beef

Who doesn't like short ribs? It's a very popular dish, and there is nothing better when it's well prepared. This recipe is one of my favorites. It takes a while, but it's worth it.

Serves 8

5 pounds short ribs of beef (about 12)
Salt and freshly ground black pepper
Unbleached all-purpose flour for dredging, plus an additional ¼ cup
4 tablespoons vegetable oil
2 cups finely chopped carrots
1 cup finely chopped celery
1 cup finely chopped onion
2 garlic cloves, finely minced
½ teaspoon dried thyme
1 bay leaf
3 cups peeled, chopped fresh or canned tomatoes
1 cup Port wine
1 cup fresh or canned beef stock

Preheat the oven to 375°F.

Sprinkle the meat with salt and pepper and dredge lightly in flour. Heat the oil in a heavy skillet or Dutch oven and brown the meat well on all sides. (This may take about 20 minutes.)

Remove the meat from the skillet and pour off all the accumulated fat. Return the meat and add the carrots, celery, onion, garlic, thyme, and bay leaf. Bake uncovered for 15 minutes. Turn the pieces of meat and bake for 15 minutes longer. Add the tomatoes and wine. Cover and continue to bake for 1½ hours. Add the beef stock and bake for 30 minutes to 1 hour longer, or until the meat is thoroughly tender.

Remove the meat and keep it warm. Skim as much fat as possible from the surface of the sauce in the skillet. Strain the sauce into a saucepan and simmer for 15 minutes. Skim off all the fat that has risen to the surface. Spoon the sauce over the short ribs and serve hot. Serve with buttered noodles seasoned with nutmeg.

Note: Madeira wine may be substituted for the Port.

Short Ribs of Beef with Cornmeal Dumplings

Cornmeal dumplings add another dimension to short ribs. To ensure light dumplings, do not let the batter stand very long.

Serves 6 to 8

4 pounds short ribs of beef, cut in serving-size pieces
Salt and freshly ground pepper
1 medium-size onion, cut in thin slices
1 garlic clove, minced
2 28-ounce cans tomatoes
12-ounce can beer
1 fresh or dried red chili pepper, seeded and chopped
2 tablespoons soy sauce
1 tablespoon sugar
¾ teaspoon salt
¼ teaspoon freshly ground black pepper
¼ teaspoon ground nutmeg

Cornmeal Dumplings (recipe follows)

Trim the excess fat from the short ribs and brown them on all sides in a Dutch oven; season with salt and pepper.

When well browned, remove the ribs and drain off all but about 2 tablespoons of the fat. Add the onion and garlic to the reserved fat; cook until the onion is transparent. Add the tomatoes, beer, chili pepper, soy sauce, sugar, salt, pepper, and nutmeg. Return the meat to the Dutch oven and bring to a boil. Reduce the heat and simmer, covered, until the meat is tender, about 1½ to 2 hours. Cool; skim off the fat, then return to the heat and bring to a boil. Meanwhile, prepare dumplings.

Cornmeal Dumplings

Makes 8 to 10 dumplings

1 cup water
½ cup yellow cornmeal
½ teaspoon salt
1 egg, beaten
½ cup unbleached all-purpose flour
1 teaspoon baking powder
Dash pepper
7-ounce can whole-kernel corn, drained

In a saucepan, combine the water, cornmeal, and salt. Bring to a boil, stirring constantly. Cook, stirring, until the mixture is the consistency of medium cream sauce. Remove from the heat and stir 2 tablespoons of the hot cornmeal mixture into the egg. Add to the rest of the cornmeal mixture. Mix the flour, baking powder, and pepper. Add to the cornmeal mixture and beat well. Stir in the corn.

Remove the short ribs from the cooking liquid. Drop the batter by rounded tablespoons into the boiling short-rib liquid. Cover and simmer until done, about 10 to 12 minutes. Be sure not to overcook.

Place the short ribs in the center of a platter and surround with the dumplings. Add some of the sauce in which the ribs and dumplings were cooked.

Beef and Onions in Beer

This is a tasty combination and one that is not exactly ordinary. A stew of sorts, it resembles the Flemish carbonnade. For maximum flavor, be sure to follow the directions for browning the meat. If the pieces of meat are touching, they don't brown—they steam. If they steam, you lose all the crusty bits left in the skillet during proper browning and have nothing to deglaze, thereby losing good flavor.

Serves 4 to 6

2 pounds lean beef shoulder, cut into ¼-inch-thick slices
1 pound sweet onions, halved and thinly sliced
⅓ cup lard, divided
Salt and freshly ground black pepper
2 teaspoons brown sugar
3 tablespoons unbleached all-purpose flour
2 cups beer
1 cup beef stock or consommé
2 bay leaves
2 teaspoons finely crumbled, mixed dried herbs (thyme, oregano, savory, and marjoram)

Preheat the oven to 325°F.

Slash the edges of the beef slices to prevent curling.

In a skillet over low heat, cook the onions in a little more than half the lard, stirring constantly, until softened and lightly caramelized. Empty them into a sieve over a mixing bowl. Pour the drained fat back into the skillet. Over fairly high heat, brown the slices of meat, a few at a time, adding a little more lard if necessary. Remove the pieces that are done to the strainer with the onions, and from time to time, remove the fat and juices that drain from the onions and seared meat to pour back into the skillet.

When all the meat slices have been browned, add salt and pepper and remove to a warm platter. Reduce the heat under the pan and add the sugar, stir, then add the flour and cook, stirring, for a few minutes. To deglaze the pan, add the beer slowly, stirring to scrape and loosen all the caramelized bits. Stir in the stock, bring to a boil, and remove from the heat.

Arrange the slices of meat in alternate layers with the onions (three layers of meat slices and two layers of onions), adding a bay leaf and a sprinkling of herbs to each layer of onions. Add the deglazing liquid; the contents should be well immersed, so add a little more beer, water, or stock, if necessary. Bring to a boil on the top of the stove. Then cover tightly and bake in a 325°F. oven for about 3 hours, testing for tenderness after 2½ hours.

Before serving, carefully remove all the fat from the surface, skimming it off first with a tablespoon, and then blotting up any remaining fat with absorbent paper. Adjust the seasoning just before serving. Accompany with steamed potatoes or fresh egg noodles.

Beef Stroganoff

It is my understanding that this dish is named for a Count Stroganoff and was invented by a peasant housewife to serve to him when he arrived unexpectedly. Although I doubt that she used beef tenderloin, the rest could be true. I hope this is close to what the man ate, because it is very good.

Serves 8

6 tablespoons butter, divided
2 tablespoons chopped onion
2 pounds beef tenderloin, cut in thin slices (see Note)
½ pound mushrooms, sliced
Salt and freshly ground black pepper
⅛ teaspoon nutmeg
1 cup sour cream at room temperature

Melt 3 tablespoons of the butter in a heavy skillet over medium heat. Add the onion and cook slowly until it is transparent. Remove the onion and set aside. Turn the heat to medium-high, add the beef to the skillet, and cook briefly, turning to brown on both sides. Remove the beef and set aside with the onion. Add the remaining 3 tablespoons of butter to the skillet. Stir in the mushrooms; cover and cook for 2 minutes. Season with salt, pepper, and nutmeg. Beat the sour cream lightly with a whisk and add to the pan. Do not allow to boil. Return the beef and onions to the pan and just heat through. Serve over noodles garnished with toasted sesame seeds.

Note: If you freeze the meat for an hour, it will be easier to slice.

Hunter's Stew

No ordinary stew, this can form the base of a sophisticated dinner as well as a casual meal. By shortening the cooking time to 30 minutes and increasing the heat to 350°F. the meat can be medium rare when the dish is finished. Since all the ingredients have been partially cooked before they are combined, the stew needs only time enough for everything to exchange and combine flavors. When I make this recipe for a dinner party, I use the tenderloin of either beef or venison, but on other occasions, I have used lesser cuts of either meats and longer cooking times with great results.

Serves 6

3 pounds beef tenderloin, cut in ¾-inch slices
Butter
6 whole carrots
1 green pepper, diced
1 zucchini, sliced
1 yellow squash, sliced
6 small onions, quartered
3 tomatoes, quartered
1 recipe Hunter's Sauce ***(see page 318)***

Preheat the oven to 325°F.

Sauté the beef slices in butter, allowing 2 to 3 minutes per side. Steam the carrots for 4 to 5 minutes. Steam the pepper and squash for 3 to 4 minutes. Sauté the onions with the tomatoes in butter.

Place the beef slices on the bottom of a casserole. Cover with the vegetables and top with Hunter's Sauce. Bake for 1 hour.

Note: The casserole may be prepared ahead of time if desired.

Casserole of Beef

One-dish meals are always good to know about, and this is one I fall back on frequently. Whether I use top sirloin or round steak, I always brown the pieces until they are very dark, cooking only a few pieces at a time to ensure a nice crusty coating, which adds to the flavor.

Serves 6

4 tablespoons butter, divided
1½ pounds boneless top sirloin or round steak, cut in 1-inch cubes
¼ cup brandy
12 small white onions
6 small whole carrots, peeled
6 small white turnips, peeled and halved
1 celery heart, quartered
4 large mushrooms, quartered
1 teaspoon commercial brown gravy sauce
3 tablespoons unbleached all-purpose flour
1½ cups beef stock
¼ cup dry red wine
Salt and freshly ground black pepper
1 bay leaf

In a heavy saucepan heat 2 tablespoons of the butter; add the meat and brown on all sides. Heat the brandy, flame it, and add to the meat. Remove the meat from the pan when well browned and set aside.

Heat the remaining 2 tablespoons of butter in the same pan, add the onions, carrots, turnips, and celery heart, and sauté until brown. Add the mushrooms and cook a few minutes longer.

Remove the pan from the heat and blend in the brown gravy sauce and flour; then add the stock and wine. Return to low heat and stir until the mixture boils. Season with salt and pepper. Return the meat and its juices to the pan and add the bay leaf.

Cover and simmer until the meat is tender, about 1½ hours. Discard the bay leaf before serving.

Note: If a tomato flavor is desired, add 1 teaspoon of tomato paste to the pan when blending in the brown gravy sauce and flour.

Meat Loaf

Serves 6 to 8

1 1/4 pounds top beef round, cubed
1 1/4 pounds veal cutlet, cubed
1 1/4 pounds fresh pork (minus all fat), cubed
1 cup finely rolled cracker crumbs
2 small onions, chopped fine
1 heaping tablespoon chopped parsley
1/2 teaspoon coarsely ground black pepper
1 scant teaspoon salt
3 eggs
2 tablespoons butter
3 strips bacon, cut in half
10 1/2-ounce can beef consommé
Parsley sprigs for garnish

Preheat the oven to 450°F.

Put the meats through the meat grinder twice (making sure all the pork fat is removed first). Place in a large bowl and add cracker crumbs, onions, parsley, pepper, salt, and eggs. Mix thoroughly with your hands.

Butter a 10 x 4 1/2 x 3-inch Pyrex dish and place 3 half-strips of bacon over the bottom. Fill the baking dish with the meat mixture, packing it in firmly and evenly. Place the remaining 3 half-strips of bacon over the top and bake in the oven. When lightly browned (after about 30 minutes), pour about 1/4 can of beef consommé over the meat loaf and reduce the heat to 375°F. Continue baking, basting with the remaining consommé every 15 minutes. Cook for 2 hours in all.

As soon as the meat loaf is done, run a knife around the edge and turn it out onto a hot platter. Garnish with sprigs of parsley and serve.

If you prefer to serve the meat loaf cold, turn out immediately, as above, and allow it to cool. When completely cold, wrap in waxed paper and refrigerate before using.

Puchero

(Mixed Boiled Meats, Argentine Style)

Every country has a boiled dinner, and they are not too unlike our New England boiled dinner. This one comes from Argentina. Chick-peas, or garbanzos, give it a bit of distinction. Traditionally, they should be started from scratch. However, using canned chick-peas is a permissible shortcut; just be sure you don't drain them. Include the liquid, or the taste of the final dish will be altered.

Serves 12

1 cup dried chick-peas (garbanzos)
2 pounds short ribs of beef, cut in serving-size pieces
1 pound lean salt pork, sliced thin
3-pound chicken, cut in serving pieces
2 chorizo sausages
6 carrots, peeled and halved
6 small turnips
6 medium onions
2 garlic cloves, crushed
6 large slices zucchini
6 tomatoes
1 cabbage, cut in 12 sections
1 tablespoon minced parsley
1 green pepper, chopped
6 leeks, white part only, thoroughly cleaned and sliced
6 white potatoes, peeled or unpeeled and halved
Salt and freshly ground black pepper

Soak the chick-peas overnight; drain and bring to a boil in 3 quarts of water. Add the beef, salt pork, and chicken. Cook for 2¾ to 3 hours. Add the sausages, carrots, and turnips and cook for another hour. Thirty minutes before serving, add all the remaining ingredients.

To serve, place the meats on a large platter surrounded by the vegetables. The cooking liquid is used as a soup that is usually served at the same time. Serve with a horseradish sauce.

Note: If canned chick-peas are used, they should be added halfway through the cooking time.

VEAL

Veal is very young beef; it has almost no fat and contains tissue that requires slower cooking to become tender. Veal cutlets are pounded flat in order to break down this tissue and shorten the cooking time. Top-quality veal must be very young; you can judge good veal by the amount of tissue in the cut and by the color, which should be the palest pink when raw. You can also judge good veal by the cost, alas. Veal has a very delicate taste that is enhanced by proper seasoning. It can be sautéed, roasted, or braised, and is delicious in stews.

Veal Scallops

There are numerous recipes for veal scallops—the scallopine of traditional Italian cuisine. It is an easy cut to work with and quickly absorbs the flavor of the butter, herbs, or wine in which it is cooked. This recipe and the ones that follow are some of my favorites.

Serves 4

8 veal scallops, about 4 inches square
Salt and freshly ground black pepper
1 egg, lightly beaten
Bread crumbs
4 tablespoons butter
1 tablespoon vegetable oil
½ pound mushrooms, thinly sliced
½ cup beef stock (or 2 tablespoons each stock and red or white wine)
½ cup grated imported Parmesan cheese

If the veal scallops have not been pounded, place them between sheets of waxed paper and pound them as thin as possible with a mallet. Cut each 4-inch-square piece into 2 equal rectangles. Season with salt and pepper. Dip each piece in beaten egg until lightly coated on both sides, allowing excess egg to drip off. Coat lightly on both sides with bread crumbs.

Preheat the oven to 375°F.

Heat the butter and oil in a large, heavy skillet and sauté the veal scallops on both sides until lightly browned (about 2 minutes per side). As each piece is browned, place it in an ovenproof casserole with a lid. When all the veal is in the casserole, sauté the mushrooms in the same skillet, adding more butter if necessary. Season with salt and pepper and add to the casserole. Pour in the stock, or stock and wine mixture, and sprinkle with grated cheese.

Bake, covered, for 5 to 7 minutes. Serve with buttered noodles and Puree of Broccoli.

Note: Filleted turkey breast can be substituted for veal if good veal is not available or if it is too much of a strain on the budget.

Veal Scallops with Lemon

This is my version of the classic Italian veal piccata.

Serves 6

- ***2/3 cup unbleached all-purpose flour***
- ***2 teaspoons salt***
- ***1/2 teaspoon freshly ground black pepper***
- ***6 veal scallops, pounded 1/16 inch thick***
- ***1/4 pound butter, divided***
- ***1/4 cup lemon juice***
- ***1/4 cup finely chopped fresh parsley***

Mix together the flour, salt, and pepper. Dredge the veal scallops in the seasoned flour.

In a skillet heat 6 tablespoons of the butter. When the butter foams, add the veal scallops and cook over very low heat, turning frequently, until brown and tender, about 5 minutes. Remove the scallops and keep hot.

Add the lemon juice, parsley, and the remaining 2 tablespoons of butter to the pan juices. Stir well and pour over the hot veal scallops.

Veal Scallops in Cream Sauce

This is a good entrée for luncheon or dinner. It has the advantage of being easy to put together and serve. You can assemble it in the morning and do the final cooking right before serving. Just be sure that it is at room temperature before it goes into the oven.

Serves 4

4 veal scallops
Unbleached all-purpose flour
4 tablespoons butter
Salt
Freshly ground black pepper
2 small onions, chopped
2 shallots, minced
½ pound mushrooms, chopped
3 ounces ham, cut in julienne strips
2 tablespoons unbleached all-purpose flour
1 cup whole milk
3 ounces grated Gruyère or other Swiss cheese
2 tablespoons heavy cream

Preheat the oven to 425°F.

Pound the veal scallops and dust them with flour. Heat the butter in a skillet and lightly brown the scallops on both sides over moderately high heat. Transfer to an ovenproof baking dish, season to taste, and set aside.

Add the onions and shallots to the skillet. Sauté briefly, then add the mushrooms. Cook until the onions are nearly tender.

Add the ham to the skillet, stir in the flour, and then slowly pour in the milk. Bring the sauce to a boil, stirring constantly, then lower the heat and cook until thickened. Season with salt and pepper to taste.

Cover the veal scallops with half the grated cheese, add the sauce, and top with the remaining cheese. Bake until nicely browned, about 15 minutes. Just before serving, sprinkle with heavy cream.

Veal Orloff

This is a very elegant if somewhat complex recipe, calling for more work than I usually like to do . . . but the end result really justifies the means.

Serves 14

28 veal scallops
Unbleached all-purpose flour
6 tablespoons butter, divided
½ cup rice
4 cups chopped onion
⅔ cup chicken stock
¼ cup heavy cream
1 tablespoon lemon juice
1 teaspoon salt
½ teaspoon freshly ground black pepper
2 egg yolks, lightly beaten
1 cup Duxelles (see page 338)
Mornay Sauce (see page 312)
Bread crumbs (optional)
Butter

Preheat the oven to 400°F.

Put the veal between sheets of waxed paper and pound lightly with a mallet. Flour the scallops lightly and sauté briefly in 2 tablespoons of the butter. Set aside.

To prepare the filling, boil the rice in 5 cups of salted water for 5 minutes; drain. Combine the cooked rice with the onion, chicken stock, cream, lemon juice, salt, pepper, and egg yolks. Cook this mixture in the remaining 4 tablespoons of butter until the onions are transparent. Add the duxelles and continue cooking over medium heat for 2 to 3 minutes. Remove from the heat and puree in a food processor or blender.

Spread each slice of sautéed veal with the filling and arrange, overlapping, in a baking dish. Spread any remaining filling mixture over the top of the meat. Cover with Mornay Sauce, sprinkle with bread crumbs if desired, and dot with softened butter.

Bake until the sauce bubbles, about 20 minutes. Serve with Glazed Carrots or Carrots and Leeks Vichy.

Note: If good veal is not available, use fresh turkey breast. Just fillet the breast meat and pound it as instructed above for veal.

Veal Chops with Fresh Herbs

Veal can stand a lot of seasoning and lends itself to many kinds. Ordinarily, I would be against a combination of herbs because too many can confuse the taste completely. In this case, however, the chives and parsley do not make a loud statement, and the tarragon and chervil are most compatible.

Serves 4

4 veal chops
4 tablespoons butter
2 tablespoons oil
Salt and freshly ground black pepper
4 shallots, finely chopped
4 strips bacon
8 tablespoons finely chopped mixed fresh herbs (tarragon, chives, parsley, chervil) or ½ the quantity if dried

In a large, heavy skillet, brown the chops on both sides in butter and oil until golden brown, about 10 minutes. Remove the chops to a platter and let cool; season with salt and pepper.

In the same skillet, cook the shallots for a minute or two, stirring constantly. Reserve the shallot–oil–butter mixture.

Put the bacon in a pot with 1 quart of cold water. Bring to a boil and simmer for 10 minutes. Drain, rinse in cold water, dry on paper towels, and cut each strip in half.

Cut 4 pieces of aluminum foil, each large enough to wrap a chop easily. Put a half-strip of bacon in the center of each piece of foil, then a chop that has been sprinkled on both sides with 2 tablespoons of the herb mixture. Put some of the shallot–butter–oil mixture on each chop, cover with another half-strip of bacon, and fold the foil so that the chop is tightly sealed.

Put the foil-wrapped chops on an outdoor grill or in a preheated 400° F. oven. Cook for 15 minutes. Serve immediately in the foil packets.

Note: A quarter of a chicken may be substituted for each veal chop.

Veal with Herbed Vegetables

First, be sure to have some wonderful breads to eat with this dish. My grandfather taught me early on that to eat any stew properly, bread for sopping is a must.

Serves 4 to 6

2 pounds veal, cut into 1½-inch cubes
Salt and freshly ground black pepper
2 tablespoons butter
2 tablespoons vegetable oil
1½ cups thinly sliced mushrooms
1 cup finely chopped onion
½ cup chopped celery
½ cup finely minced garlic
½ cup dry white wine
¼ cup unbleached all-purpose flour
1½ cups chicken stock, homemade or canned
1 cup crushed canned Italian plum tomatoes
3 sprigs fresh rosemary (1 teaspoon dried)
2 parsley sprigs
1 bay leaf
12 small white onions or 3 medium onions cut into quarters
2 tablespoons finely chopped parsley

Sprinkle the meat with salt and pepper. Heat the butter and oil in a skillet and cook the meat, a few pieces at a time, until browned on all sides. Set the browned meat aside.

Add the mushrooms, onion, celery, and garlic to the skillet and cook, stirring, until the onion is wilted. Add the wine and cook, stirring, until it evaporates. Return the meat to the skillet and sprinkle evenly with the flour. Gradually add the stock, stirring to blend.

Add the tomatoes, rosemary, parsley, and bay leaf. Cover and cook over low heat for about 1 hour. Add the onions; cover and cook for 45 minutes longer. Garnish with chopped parsley.

Veal Stew

I like this best when I make it in the morning and reheat it in the evening. The combination of flavors needs time to come together, and although stews are good when first made, they are always better later, or even the next day. When reheating stew, always start it on a very low heat and keep an eye out so it doesn't burn on the bottom. Burned stew is awful.

Serves 8 to 10

¼ pound butter, divided
4½ pounds leg or breast of veal, boned and cut into 1½-inch cubes
Salt and freshly ground black pepper
1 cup finely chopped onion
2 garlic cloves, mashed
4 tablespoons chopped fresh dill, divided
½ cup unbleached all-purpose flour
1 teaspoon freshly ground nutmeg
1½ cups chicken stock
1½ cups water
3 carrots
2 leeks
1 cup heavy cream

Preheat the oven to 375°F.

Melt 4 tablespoons of the butter in a large, deep casserole. Add the veal and sprinkle with salt and pepper. Add the onion, garlic, and 2 tablespoons of the dill. Cook, stirring, without browning for 5 minutes. Sprinkle with the flour and nutmeg, add the chicken stock and water. Bring to a boil; cover and bake for 1 hour.

Meanwhile, peel the carrots and cut into matchstick-size strips. Cut off and discard the roots and all but 2 or 3 inches of the green tops of the leeks. Cut in half lengthwise; wash thoroughly under running water. Cut into strips the same size as the carrots. Cook the carrots and leeks in the remaining 4 tablespoons of butter over medium-low heat until wilted but not browned.

When the veal is done, stir half the carrot–leek mixture into the stew. Stir in the cream and bring to a boil. Serve garnished with the remaining carrots, leeks, and dill, accompanied by buttered noodles.

Veal Stew with Olives

Unless you have a meat cleaver and really know how to use it, have the butcher cut the veal breast. From there on, this is a simple and uncomplicated entrée. Feel free to alter the seasonings to suit your palate, but try it my way the first time.

Serves 8 to 10

1 breast of veal with bones (about 4½ pounds), cut into 2- or 3-inch cubes
1 boneless shoulder of veal (about 3 pounds), cut into 2- or 3-inch cubes
Salt and freshly ground black pepper
½ cup unbleached all-purpose flour
1 cup vegetable oil
3 cups coarsely chopped onion (about ¾ pound)
6 whole cloves
3 garlic cloves
4 cups dry white wine
2 cups water
28-ounce can plum tomatoes
1 bay leaf
3 parsley sprigs
6 sprigs fresh thyme or 1 teaspoon dried thyme
24 stuffed green olives
24 good-quality pitted black olives

Preheat the oven to 375°F.

Sprinkle the veal breast and shoulder cubes with salt and pepper and dredge in the flour. Heat the oil in one or two skillets and add the meat, a few pieces at a time. Brown on all sides. As the meat is browned, transfer it to a large, ovenproof casserole. Sprinkle the meat with the onion and add the cloves, garlic, wine, and water. Drain the tomatoes, reserving the juice; set the tomatoes aside. Add the juice to the meat and stir. Add the bay leaf, parsley, and thyme (tie in a bundle if fresh sprigs are used). Add salt and pepper to taste and bring to a boil. Bake, uncovered, for 1½ hours, stirring occasionally. Chop the reserved tomatoes and add them to the stew with the olives. Bake for 30 minutes longer, skimming off any excess fat that rises to the surface. Serve with rice.

Veal Casserole

This is a dish that can be doubled or cut in half without any problem. Be sure to consider the oregano, though. In doubling the recipe, it's advisable to leave the quantity of oregano as is—one teaspoon (but if you halve the recipe use only a pinch). You need not be limited to this one herb. Try tarragon.

Serves 8

3 pounds veal shoulder, cut into 1-inch cubes
¼ pound butter (approx.), divided
2 large onions, peeled and chopped
1 garlic clove, chopped
6 carrots, scraped and sliced into large ovals
2 cups chicken stock
1 bay leaf
1½ teaspoons salt
1 tablespoon finely chopped parsley
1 teaspoon oregano
⅛ teaspoon freshly ground black pepper
3 tablespoons unbleached all-purpose flour
½ cup heavy cream
30 button mushrooms, wiped clean

Preheat the oven to 350°F.

Heat 2 tablespoons of the butter in a large skillet and sear the veal, a little at a time, until it is brown on all sides. Add more butter as needed. Drain the veal on paper towels and transfer to a 3-quart casserole.

In the same skillet, sauté the onions and garlic in about 2 tablespoons of butter until golden, adding the carrots for the last few minutes of the cooking time. Add to the skillet the chicken stock, bay leaf, salt, parsley, oregano, and pepper. In a separate dish, mix the flour to a smooth paste with a little soft butter. Add the paste to the skillet and stir over low heat until smooth and thickened. Pour this mixture over the veal in the casserole.

Cover the casserole. Bake for about 1¼ hours, or until meat is fork-tender, uncovering for the last half hour. When done, add the cream and stir gently. Keep warm.

Sauté the mushrooms in the remaining butter for 2 or 3 minutes and add to the casserole just before serving. Asparagus with Wine Sauce is a good accompaniment.

LAMB

There was a time when it was unusual to find lamb on any menu, and even today there are still some holdouts who refuse to eat it because it is too "strong." I grew up on a cattle ranch where sheep was a dirty word. No one in my family would mention the name, let alone eat it, so I never expected to like lamb when I first tried it. Surprisingly, I found that I not only liked it, I wanted it often.

Good-quality lamb is covered with white, brittle fat, and the texture of the meat should be fine-grained and velvety. Young lamb is pink-red, older lamb a darker red. The fell, or paperlike covering of the carcass, should be left on roasts because it shortens the cooking time and makes the meat juicier. However, it should be removed from chops before cooking. Most cuts of high-quality lamb are suitable for pan-frying, broiling, or roasting. Lamb necks, breasts, and shanks are usually stewed or braised. Lamb is best served pink because it is juicier and there is less shrinkage when cooked to this stage.

Rack of Lamb

This makes a very festive meal served with Spoonbread Soufflé and minted green peas or any other green vegetable you like.

Serves 4

1 rack of lamb (8 chops)
1½ teaspoons coarse salt
1 garlic clove, slivered
½ teaspoon medium-grind black pepper

Preheat the oven to 425°F.

The rack should be trimmed so that 1½ inches of bone are exposed on each chop, and the chine bone (back bone) should be removed so that it will be easier to carve the rack into chops. Rub the lamb with salt and pepper. Insert the garlic slivers with a sharp knife-point. Place the lamb, fatty-side up, on a rack in a baking pan and roast for 45 minutes. Remove to a serving board; let stand 10 minutes before carving.

Broiled Leg of Lamb with Orange Butter

This recipe and the one that follows call for a butterflied leg of lamb. There is really nothing to butterflying a leg of lamb. I have found that I do a better job of it than most butchers, with the exception of my butcher, who does it right. Even so, I do the job myself. Here's how. Lay the leg on its flat side and, with a sharp knife, cut in toward the bone through the fleshy side of the meat. Then cut around the bone, and the job is done. You will find the meat is pretty much the same thickness throughout and thus will broil evenly.

Serves 8

6- to 7-pound leg of lamb, butterflied
Salt and freshly ground black pepper
½ teaspoon rosemary
Vegetable oil
¼ pound butter
Zest and juice of 1 orange

Rub the meat with rosemary and oil. Season with salt and pepper.

Place the lamb on a broiler pan, skin-side up, and broil 6 inches from the heat for 20 minutes. Turn the lamb and broil for 15 minutes. The meat will be nicely pink.

Melt the butter with the orange zest and juice and let simmer for a few minutes. Pour over the lamb just before serving.

Variation: For a sharper sauce, add 3 tablespoons of Dijon mustard to the orange butter and whisk until it forms an emulsion.

Broiled Marinated Leg of Lamb

Whether broiling or grilling a butterflied leg of lamb, I never remove any of the fat, nor do I remove the fell. It needs the fat for flavor and moisture, and the fell helps to keep the juices in the meat. In broiling, I start with the fat-side up because that side should be closest to the heat source during the initial cooking. The juices work down during this cooking process. When the meat is turned, the juices are trapped and sealed in the middle. Because in grilling, the heat source is reversed, start with the fat-side down.

Serves 8

7-pound leg of lamb, butterflied*

Marinade

1 cup vinegar
1 garlic clove, grated
1½ tablespoons Worcestershire sauce
2 tablespoons sugar
⅓ cup catsup
1 teaspoon dry mustard
1 teaspoon salt
2 tablespoons lemon juice
¼ teaspoon freshly ground black pepper
Thin slices lemon

Combine all the marinade ingredients and simmer for 15 minutes. Pour over the butterflied leg of lamb and let it marinate overnight.

Preheat the broiler.

Drain the meat, reserving the marinade. Broil on both sides (start with the fat-side down) for a total of 5 to 10 minutes.†

Preheat the oven to 350°F.

Remove the rack from the broiling pan and place the lamb in the pan. Cover with lemon slices and pour the reserved marinade over the top.

Bake, basting occasionally, for about 40 minutes (if using a meat thermometer, to 130°F. for medium rare, 150°F. for well done).

Note: The same method may also be used for a thick sirloin of beef.

Variation: For an alternate cooking method, broil for 10 minutes on each side, starting with the fat-side up first; then lower the temperature to 425°F. and roast in the oven for 15 minutes, for medium rare; 25 minutes for well done.

* See page 55 for instructions on how to butterfly a leg of lamb.

† This may be done in the morning.

Braised Lamb Shanks

Lamb shanks should be baked until the meat is almost ready to fall from the bone—one time that lamb should be well done.

Serves 6

6 lamb shanks, outside fat removed
1 garlic clove, halved
½ cup unbleached all-purpose flour
2 teaspoons salt
1 teaspoon paprika
2 tablespoons vegetable oil
½ cup lemon juice
½ cup dry white wine
½ cup chicken stock
2 tablespoons grated lemon rind
1 small bay leaf
4 peppercorns

Preheat the oven to 350°F.

Trim the fat from the shanks and rub thoroughly with the halved garlic clove. Mix the flour, salt, and paprika on a piece of waxed paper and roll the shanks in the mixture. Brown in sizzling oil in a heavy skillet, and arrange in a large casserole. Stir the lemon juice into the skillet and loosen all the browned particles. Add the wine and chicken stock and pour over the lamb shanks. Sprinkle with the grated lemon rind; tuck in the bay leaf and peppercorns. Cover; bake for 1½ hours.

Lamb Shanks with Garlic

A much more pungent version of lamb shanks.

Serves 4

4 lamb shanks, outside fat removed
Salt
3 tablespoons olive oil
15 to 20 garlic cloves, unpeeled
Few tablespoons water
½ teaspoon finely crumbled, mixed dried herbs (rosemary, thyme, oregano)
½ cup dry white wine
Freshly ground black pepper

Season the shanks with salt. In a heavy pan, brown the shanks in the oil. Add the garlic and cover. Cook the shanks over very low heat, turning occasionally, for about 1½ hours, until tender. Sprinkle with the herbs after an hour's cooking time.

When the liquid disappears and the shanks begin to sizzle in the fat, add water, a spoonful at a time, so that a film of liquid always remains in the bottom of the pan. As the meat approaches the desired tenderness, stop moistening with water and allow all the liquid to evaporate. When the meat begins to sizzle in pure fat, remove it to a plate.

Pour off the fat and deglaze the pan with the white wine, scraping and stirring with a wooden spoon to dissolve all the caramelized bits. Put the juice from deglazing through a sieve to rid it of the garlic hulls. Return the liquid to the pan and reduce it.

Return the meat to the pan—there should be only enough sauce just to coat the pieces. Add pepper to taste.

Lamb Chops with Shallots

This recipe gives broiled lamb chops a slightly different touch without a lot of work. You can substitute scallions or green onions for the shallots, or use dried shallots, but don't expect them to taste the same.

Serves 8

8 loin lamb chops, 1½ inches thick
Pinch each salt, freshly ground black pepper, and cayenne
3 tablespoons lemon juice, divided
¼ pound plus 4 tablespoons butter, melted, divided
3 shallots, finely chopped
2 tablespoons minced parsley

Preheat the broiler.

Sprinkle the chops on both sides with salt, pepper, cayenne, and 2 tablespoons of the lemon juice. Set aside for 15 minutes.

Brush the chops on both sides with about ¼ cup melted butter. Broil until done (18 minutes in all), turning once while cooking.

After the chops are turned, pour the remaining melted butter (about ½ cup) into a saucepan. Add the shallots and cook for 5 to 6 minutes. Stir in the remaining lemon juice and the parsley. Season with salt, pepper, and cayenne. When the chops are done, transfer them to a heated platter, pour the lemon–shallot butter over them, and serve.

Lamb with Sour Cream and Dill

Use either the butt end of the leg or the meat from loin chops. Less tender cuts of lamb will also do, but the cooking time should be increased by 30 minutes. For a luncheon dish, cut the lamb into smaller cubes, and serve over hot biscuits or toast rounds.

Serves 8

3½ pounds lamb (butt end of the leg), cut into 1½-inch cubes
Salt and freshly ground black pepper
1 tablespoon butter
1 cup finely chopped onion
1 garlic clove, finely minced
1 cup dry white wine
2 cups chicken stock
1 bunch fresh dill or 1 tablespoon crumbled dried dillweed
1 cup heavy cream
¼ cup sour cream
½ pound fresh mushrooms (if small, leave whole; otherwise, slice)
Juice of ½ lemon
1½ cups freshly shelled peas (or a 10-ounce package frozen peas)

Hot cooked rice

Sprinkle the lamb with salt and pepper. Heat the butter in a large kettle and add the lamb, stirring and cooking until it loses its red color. It will release a good bit of liquid. Add the onion and garlic and cook briefly. Add the wine and stock. Cut the feathery tops off the dill and reserve. Tie the dill stems in a small bundle and add to the lamb. Cover and cook about 1¼ hours, or until the lamb is tender.

Stir in the heavy cream, sour cream, and dill leaves. Remove the lamb with a slotted spoon. Cook the sauce down for about 5 to 10 minutes; strain it through a fine sieve. Meanwhile, put the mushrooms in a saucepan with the lemon juice; add salt and pepper to taste, cover and cook for about 5 minutes. Cook the peas in boiling salted water until tender. Return the lamb to the sauce and add the mushrooms and peas. Reheat and serve with rice.

Lamb Stew

The shoulder cut of lamb and most other meats costs less than the choice cuts, but requires longer, slower cooking. Don't try to dress it up to be something it isn't. If you treat it simply but carefully, the results will be tasty and very interesting.

Serves 4

2 pounds lamb shoulder, cut into large cubes
6 tablespoons butter, divided
3 tablespoons unbleached all-purpose flour
6 cups water
Salt and freshly ground black pepper
3 tomatoes, peeled and chopped
4 large carrots, scraped and cut in half
2 medium turnips, peeled and quartered
12 small white onions, peeled
4 small potatoes, peeled and quartered
10-ounce package frozen peas, thawed
2 tablespoons chopped parsley

In a skillet, brown the lamb cubes on all sides in 3 tablespoons of the butter. When nicely browned, transfer to a Dutch oven. Sprinkle with the flour and add the water, salt, pepper, and tomatoes. Bring to a boil, cover, and reduce the heat to a simmer; cook for 1½ hours.

Heat the remaining 3 tablespoons of butter in the same skillet used to brown the lamb cubes. Add the carrots, turnips, and onions, and sauté until the onions are lightly browned.

Add the browned vegetables and the potatoes to the stew and cook, uncovered, until the potatoes are done. Stir in the peas and cook for 2 to 5 minutes.

Garnish with chopped parsley and serve.

Irish Stew

This stew can be made with either raw or leftover cooked lamb. I prefer to use raw lamb because I think it lends more flavor to the beans.

Serves 6

2 cups dried white beans
½ pound salt pork, cubed
5 tablespoons butter, divided
1 large onion, very thinly sliced
8 small white onions
2 pounds lamb shoulder, cut in small pieces
1½ cups canned beef consommé
¼ cup unbleached all-purpose flour
¼ cup dry white wine or dry sherry
3 sprigs parsley
1 garlic clove
Pinch marjoram
Pinch thyme
¼ cup chopped celery
1 leek (white part only), chopped
Salt and freshly ground black pepper

Wash the beans; soak overnight in warm water to cover. When ready to make the stew, pour off the water from the soaking beans, cover them with fresh cold water, and bring them slowly to a boil. Reduce the heat and simmer until the skins roll off the beans when blown upon (about 1½ to 2 hours). Drain the beans, saving the water in which they cooked.

Cover the salt pork with boiling water. Let stand briefly, then drain. Heat the butter and sauté the scalded salt pork with the sliced onion and the small onions. When the salt pork and onions are golden brown, transfer to a hot casserole with a small lump of butter. Brown the lamb cubes in salt pork fat. As the pieces brown, add them to the pork and onions. Discard the fat from the frying pan and replace it with the consommé and stir until hot.

Sprinkle the meat in the casserole with the flour, stirring until the flour is well mixed. Stir in the wine and blend well. Add the parsley, garlic, marjoram, thyme, celery, and leek.

Cover the meat with the reserved beans, and add just enough of the bean water to barely cover. Season with salt and pepper. Cover tightly; reduce the heat to very low and cook for about 2 hours. Set aside for 5 minutes; then skim off as much fat as possible. Reheat to the boiling point and serve.

Lamb, Pork, and Beans

This is a simplified American version of the formidable French cassoulet, with nothing lost in that simplification.

Serves 8 to 10

- *1 garlic clove plus 1 extra sliver*
- *1 shoulder lamb roast (about 2½ pounds), boned and rolled—reserve the bone*
- *Butter or chicken fat*
- *2 to 3 small white onions, chopped*
- *2 to 3 shallots, chopped*
- *Salt and freshly ground black pepper*
- *15-ounce can tomato puree*
- *½ cup catsup*
- *1½ cups canned beef consommé, divided*
- *12 ounces cooked ham, cubed*
- *1 bay leaf*
- *8-ounce can or jar cocktail sausages*
- *4 15½-ounce cans oven-baked pork and beans*
- *2 cups tomato juice*
- *Few strips bacon*

Preheat oven to 350°F.

Insert garlic sliver into the lamb and brown the meat in butter or chicken fat. Add the chopped onions, garlic clove, shallots, salt, and pepper, and add the bone from the roast. Cover and bake for about 1½ hours. Add the tomato puree, catsup, and ½ cup of the consommé. Cover and return to the oven for 30 minutes longer.

In an enamel pan simmer the ham with the remaining cup of consommé and the bay leaf.

Remove the lamb and pass the gravy through a fine sieve. Remove the strings from the lamb and slice the meat. Pour the liquid from the ham into the strained gravy. Slice the ham into strips or cubes. Brown the sausages lightly in a little butter.

Cover the bottom of an earthenware casserole with 1 can of baked beans. Add a layer of sliced lamb, cover with another layer of beans (1 can), top with a layer of ham, another layer of beans (1 can), and then a layer of sausages, and a final layer of beans. Pour the tomato juice over all. Top with strips of bacon and bake, covered, for 30 minutes. Remove the cover and bake slowly for 30 minutes longer, or until brown on top.

Serve directly from the baking casserole with a green salad.

Lamb Casserole

This is a good way to use up leftover leg of lamb.

Serves 6

2 tablespoons butter, margarine, or vegetable oil
2 tablespoons unbleached all-purpose flour
½ teaspoon dry mustard
10½-ounce can beef consommé
½ cup dry red wine
½ cup heavy cream
1 tablespoon Worcestershire sauce
2 hard-cooked eggs, chopped
½ cup sliced mushrooms, lightly sautéed
2½ cups cooked lamb, cut in small slices or diced
½ cup buttered crumbs
1 teaspoon minced parsley

Preheat the oven to 350°F.

Melt the butter in a medium casserole on top of the stove. Stir in the flour and mustard; then blend in the consommé gradually, stirring constantly. Add the red wine. Cook a few minutes and then stir in the cream, Worcestershire sauce, eggs, mushrooms, and meat. Top with the buttered crumbs mixed with parsley. Bake uncovered for 20 to 25 minutes until the top is bubbly and golden. Serve with Rice Casserole.

PORK

While smoked ham is a national favorite, pork hasn't always been a best-seller. It has, however, gained in popularity in recent years.

The best-quality pork is fine-textured, firm, and delicately pink. It loses its pinkness when cooked and, when roasted, should be removed from the oven once the internal temperature reaches 155°, and allowed to stand so that the juices can settle. It will continue to cook for a bit while standing and should reach an internal temperature of 160° by the time it is sliced for serving. Cooked past an internal temperature of 160°, pork is usually dried out instead of nice and moist—which is how it should be when served.

Most cuts of pork are tender and therefore may be roasted. Pork chops are usually pan-fried or baked rather than broiled. And if you think pot roast has to be beef, try a braised pork shoulder and broaden your horizons.

Roast Loin of Pork with Pepper and Thyme

Serves 8

4-pound loin of pork, boned but not rolled
1 garlic clove
2 tablespoons coarse salt
½ teaspoon freshly ground black pepper
½ teaspoon thyme

Preheat the oven to 450°F.

In a mortar, crush the garlic with the salt, pepper, and thyme.

Rub the surface of the loin of pork with the garlic mixture; let stand at least 2 hours. Wipe off the garlic mixture, roll the roast, and tie at 2-inch intervals. Put the roast in a pan and roast for 30 minutes. Reduce the heat to 325°F. and roast for 2 hours more, or until meat thermometer registers 155°F.

Note: If you have an already rolled roast, simply work the herb mixture into the center, using your fingers or a wooden spoon handle.

Pork Loin in Egg-Lemon Sauce

This roast requires some watching. There should always be liquid in the cooking container, so if the stock cooks away, add more. The final sauce should be the consistency of thin gravy.

Serves 4

1½-pound loin of pork, boned, rolled, and tied
1 teaspoon salt
4 tablespoons butter
½ cup chopped celery
½ teaspoon finely minced garlic
Freshly ground black pepper
¼ teaspoon freshly grated or ground nutmeg

Egg-Lemon Sauce

4 cups hot beef stock, divided
3 egg yolks, beaten
¼ cup lemon juice

Rub the loin of pork with salt. Melt the butter in a Dutch oven, a large, heavy casserole, or a large electric frying pan with a domed lid. Add the pork loin, celery, and garlic and brown the meat on all sides over low heat. Season with pepper and nutmeg. Add 2 cups of the stock; stir. Cover, bring to a boil, then cook over moderate heat for 1½ hours, or until the internal temperature reaches 155°F. Remove the meat from the pan and keep hot.

To make the Egg-Lemon Sauce, strain the pan juices and put in the top of a double boiler. Slowly add about ½ cup of the beef stock to the egg yolks, stirring. Mix in the lemon juice. Add egg–lemon–stock mixture to the pan juices, beating constantly. Add remaining stock, mix, and let the sauce thicken.

Slice the roast and pour the Egg-Lemon Sauce on top; serve with Puree of Peas and Watercress.

Braised Loin of Pork

Here's an easy way to prepare pork loin; the marinade has the advantage of keeping the roast nice and moist while it adds flavor.

Serves 8

5-pound loin of pork, boned
1 garlic clove, peeled
½ teaspoon paprika
2 cups coarsely chopped onion
1 cup coarsely chopped leeks (optional)
¾ cup sliced carrots
1 bay leaf, crushed
½ tablespoon rosemary
1 teaspoon coriander
Salt and freshly ground black pepper
2 sprigs fresh thyme or 1 teaspoon dried
1 bottle Burgundy or other dry red wine
3 sprigs fresh parsley
¼ cup unbleached all-purpose flour
½ cup beef stock
¼ teaspoon nutmeg
2 tablespoons butter

Rub the pork all over with the garlic clove. Sprinkle with paprika and place in a deep casserole. Add the onion, leeks, carrots, bay leaf, rosemary, coriander, salt, pepper, thyme, wine, and parsley. Cover and let stand in the refrigerator for 24 hours, turning the meat occasionally.

Preheat the oven to 400°F.

Remove the meat from the marinade. Strain the liquid, reserving both the liquid and the vegetables. Heat a clean Dutch oven and place the pork loin fat-side down in it. Cook for about 5 minutes until it is well browned. Place the pork in the oven, uncovered, and bake for 30 minutes.

Remove the pork and pour off the fat. Place the pork fat-side up in the Dutch oven and scatter the vegetables from the marinade around it. Return to the oven and bake for 10 minutes, uncovered. Sprinkle the vegetables with flour and bake for 5 minutes longer. Stir in the wine marinade and beef stock. Bake uncovered for 1 hour.

Remove the meat and strain the sauce, pressing to remove as much liquid from the solids as possible. Skim off the fat. Pour the sauce into a saucepan and reduce it over moderate heat for about 20 minutes. Add the nutmeg and swirl in the butter. Slice the meat and serve it with the sauce accompanied by Polenta with Pine Nuts and Raisins.

Crown Roast of Pork with Sausage–Apple Stuffing

There is no more impressive roast than a crown roast of pork. For me, 22 ribs is a must, so I never serve this unless I have 8 or 10 guests. There is, however, no reason to avoid having roast pork left over. Nothing makes a better sandwich.

Serves 14

1 crown roast of pork*

Stuffing

3 tablespoons butter
¾ cup finely chopped onion
¼ cup finely chopped celery
½ cup peeled, cored, and coarsely diced tart apple
½ cup fresh bread crumbs
1 pound ground pork
½ pound well-seasoned sausage meat
½ cup finely chopped parsley
½ teaspoon dried sage leaves, crumbled
1½ teaspoons salt
Freshly ground black pepper

Preheat the oven to 350°F.

To make the stuffing, melt the butter over moderate heat in an 8- to 10-inch skillet. Add the onion and cook, stirring frequently, for about 5 minutes. Add the celery and apple. Cook without browning about 5 minutes longer. Scrape the contents of the pan into a large bowl.

Add the bread crumbs, ground pork, sausage meat, parsley, sage, salt, and pepper, and mix thoroughly.

Fill the center of the crown with the stuffing, mounding it slightly. Cover with aluminum foil and wrap the ends of the chop bones in foil to prevent them from burning.

Roast in the center of the oven for 3 hours, or until a meat thermometer reads 160°F.; 1½ hours before the roast is done, remove the central foil and allow the stuffing to brown. Transfer roast to a platter and remove the foil from the chop bones to serve. For decorative effect, the foil can be replaced with paper frills. Brussels Sprouts Gratinée is a good accompaniment.

* A proper crown roast of pork consists of 22 ribs and weighs about 8 or 9 pounds.

Pork Pot Roast

Pork shoulder is usually an inexpensive cut of meat, and one that has an excellent taste. Cook it with the bone left in, or you will lose a good part of the natural flavor. For additional flavor, substitute beef stock for the water. The brown gravy sauce called for in this recipe can be any concentrated, commercially prepared gravy sauce—it is used to add color to the pot roast. Partially pureeing the vegetables adds additional thickness to the sauce, but is only a suggestion and not necessary.

Serves 8

2 tablespoons lard
4- to 5-pound pork shoulder roast
3 cups water or beef stock
1 cup chopped onion
2 teaspoons salt
½ teaspoon pepper
2½ cups diced carrots
1 cup diced turnips
½ cup cold water
2 tablespoons unbleached all-purpose flour
1 teaspoon brown gravy sauce
Salt to taste
Freshly ground black pepper
2 tablespoons chopped parsley

Heat the lard to very hot in a Dutch oven and brown the pork on all sides. Add 3 cups of water or stock, onion, salt, and pepper, and bring to a boil. Reduce the heat to a simmer and cook, covered, for 1½ hours, or until the meat is nearly tender (140°F. on a meat thermometer). Add carrots and turnips and continue cooking until the meat is fork-tender and the vegetables are done, about 25 minutes.

Transfer the meat to a heated serving platter and keep warm.

Drain the vegetables, reserving the stock. Keep the vegetables warm. Remove all fat from the stock.

In a saucepan, blend the ½ cup cold water slowly into the flour; over heat add 1 cup of the reserved stock and the brown gravy sauce. Cook and stir until thickened. Season to taste with salt and pepper.

Partially puree the warm vegetables in either a blender or food processor, leaving some texture, and add to the gravy. Add the parsley and serve the sauce over slices of the meat. Crusty Potatoes with Parmesan Cheese go well with this dish.

Fresh Ham (Leg of Pork)

This recipe is straight from one of James Beard's cooking classes at Seaside, on the Oregon coast, and it is wonderful. There is a tricky part, however, and that's the sauce. It takes a while for it to start tasting like anything. The alcohol must be cooked off the marinade, and the flavor of the raisins and pine nuts allowed to come through as the sauce is reduced. As Jim said, Don't give up, it does work—and that's exactly right.

Serves 14

1 whole fresh ham (about 14 pounds)
Madeira wine
2 teaspoons nutmeg
2 teaspoons cinnamon
2 teaspoons mace
2 teaspoons ground ginger
Kosher salt
Sage
Freshly ground black pepper

Sauce

1 cup raisins
½ cup pine nuts
3 cups reserved marinade

Preheat the oven to 450°F.

Place the fresh ham in a deep dish and add the Madeira until it is halfway up on the ham. Add the nutmeg, cinnamon, mace, and ginger to the wine. Marinate overnight, turning occasionally.

Remove the roast from the marinade and score the skin. (Reserve the marinade.) Rub the ham with kosher salt, sage, and pepper. Roast, uncovered, for 30 minutes; reduce the heat to 400°F. and continue roasting for 1½ hours. Reduce the heat to 350°F. and roast until the internal temperature is 155°F. (about 1½ hours longer). Baste with some of the marinade frequently during the entire roasting period.

To make the sauce, add the raisins and pine nuts to the reserved marinade and heat until the alcohol has burned off and the sauce is reduced to approximately 1½ cups. Serve with the roast.

Baked Ham in a Crust

Not many people refuse ham. It has become a traditional dish at Easter, and it is served at almost every party during the Christmas holidays. Since ham goes a long way and is easy to prepare, it is naturally a favorite for the host or hostess. The following method of baking a whole ham was popular in the 1940s and 50s, and has remained popular with me. It has the advantage of keeping the ham nice and moist, and it really concentrates the added flavors because there is no way for them to escape. Of course the crust is useless once the ham is done, and it really does take a mallet to break it, but the ham inside is beautiful. You might think that foil will do the same thing, but unfortunately the foil creates too much steam, whereas the dough crust absorbs that moisture and doesn't "sweat" the ham.

Serves 16

Ham

12-pound precooked ham
24 whole cloves
4 tablespoons cider vinegar
6 tablespoons light brown sugar
1 teaspoon dry mustard

Dough

4½ cups unbleached all-purpose flour, divided
1 tablespoon dry mustard
⅔ cup cider vinegar
1⅓ cups cold water

Bottom of Pan

⅓ cup cider vinegar
⅔ cup water

Preheat the oven to 450°F.

To prepare the ham, trim off only the brown rind from the ham. Score the remaining fat in a diamond pattern. Place the ham fat-side up in a large roasting pan and stud it with cloves. Pour vinegar over it. Mix the sugar and mustard and pat over the ham.

To make the dough, mix the mustard into 4 cups of the flour. Combine the vinegar and water and add enough of the mixture to the flour to make a stiff dough. Roll out on a pastry cloth sprinkled with ½ cup of flour to prevent sticking. Make a "blanket" large enough to cover the top and sides of the ham. Pick up the dough by rolling it onto a rolling pin and drop it over the ham, repairing any tears with dough and tucking the edges under.

To cook the ham, pour ⅓ cup of vinegar and ⅔ cup of water into the bottom of the pan. Bake for 4 hours, or 20 minutes to the pound. When done, crack the crust with a mallet and discard before serving.

Pork Chops and Apples in Mustard Sauce

This is a great dish to serve at any dinner party and a natural combination. Just don't use "hot dog" mustard; it will ruin it.

Serves 4

2 pounds crisp, tart apples (Newtown or Granny Smith)
1 tablespoon butter
4 loin pork chops, about ¾ inch thick
Salt and freshly ground black pepper
¼ cup dry white wine
1 cup heavy cream
⅓ cup Dijon mustard (approx.)

Preheat the oven to 400°F.

Quarter, core, and peel the apples; slice thin. Spread them in a lightly buttered baking dish and bake for 15 minutes.

Trim the excess fat from the pork chops; salt them lightly. Cook them in a bit of butter in a frying pan over medium heat, allowing about 7 to 8 minutes per side, until nicely colored on both sides. Arrange the chops over the apples. Deglaze the frying pan with the white wine; reduce the sauce by half and dribble it over the chops.

Mix the cream and mustard, adding the mustard gradually to taste. Season with salt and pepper. Pour the mixture over the chops and apples. Bake for 15 minutes longer.

Pork Chops with Beer Sauce

I specify thick pork chops only because that is the kind that I like. Use thin ones if that's your choice; just don't cook them as long.

Serves 4

¼ cup pork fat or drippings
2 to 3 onions, thinly sliced
2 to 3 large tart apples, peeled and sliced
1 to 2 garlic cloves, chopped
4 thick pork chops
Salt and freshly ground black pepper
Beer Sauce (recipe follows)

Heat the fat in a skillet. Layer with half the onions, all the apples, the remaining onion, and garlic. Cook gently on top of the stove until the onions are soft and the apples are cooked.

In the meantime, prepare the chops. With a small knife, score them in two or three places around the edges to prevent curling. Cook them quickly in a dry pan, or under the broiler, until brown on both sides. When the chops are brown, place them on top of the simmering onions and apples. Sprinkle with salt and pepper, cover, and cook over low heat until the chops are tender (about 30 minutes). Meanwhile, prepare the sauce.

Beer Sauce

Makes about 1 cup

2 tablespoons butter
2 tablespoons unbleached all-purpose flour
1 cup beer
Salt
Cayenne pepper
Finely chopped parsley or chives
1 tablespoon brown sugar

Melt the butter; add the flour, stirring well to make a roux. Gradually add the beer to make a thickish sauce. Add the salt, pepper, parsley or chives, and sugar. Stir well. Serve either separately or poured over the chops.

Terrine of Pork and Veal

Excellent as a first course or hors d'oeuvre, this makes a very nice presentation on a buffet table and is well worth the time it takes to prepare. One might call it a fancy meat loaf, served cold. A word of caution: Be sure to taste for seasoning *before* the mixture goes into the terrine. This is best done by making a patty from a tablespoon of the mixture and sautéing it in butter. It is the only effective way to test for seasoning. Whatever you do, do not taste any pork mixture raw.

Serves 20

¼ pound boneless lean ham
1¼ pounds boneless lean veal, divided
¼ cup cognac
¼ teaspoon salt
⅓ teaspoon freshly ground black pepper
¼ teaspoon dried thyme
¼ teaspoon ground nutmeg
1 tablespoon finely chopped shallot or onion
2 truffles, finely chopped (optional), divided
¾ pound lean fresh pork
½ pound fat salt pork
2 large eggs, beaten
¼ teaspoon ground ginger
½ teaspoon poultry seasoning
1 garlic clove, crushed
Thin strips fat salt pork
1 bay leaf
Parsley for garnish

Preheat the oven to 350°F.

Slice the ham and ½ pound of the veal ¼ inch thick and cut into strips 4 inches long. Marinate for 2 to 3 hours in the cognac with the salt, pepper, thyme, nutmeg, shallot or onion, and 1 chopped truffle (if used). Put the fresh pork, salt pork, and the remaining ¾ pound of veal through a food chopper twice, using the finest blade. Add the eggs, ginger, poultry seasoning, and garlic. Drain the marinade from the veal and ham strips. Add the marinade to the ground meat mixture and mix well.

Line the bottom and sides of a 2-quart terrine mold or casserole with thin strips of salt pork. Put a third of the meat mixture on the bottom. Cover with half the veal and ham strips. Sprinkle with chopped truffle (if used). Repeat with the second third of the meat mixture and the remaining veal and ham strips and truffle. Cover with the rest of the meat mixture. Cover with two thicknesses of foil, tied down; bake for 1½ hours, or until the pâté shrinks from the sides of the mold and the juices are clear yellow with no trace of pink. Remove foil, cool, refrigerate to chill thoroughly, and unmold.

Return the pâté to the terrine. Serve it from the mold, or pour aspic flavored with sherry or Madeira over it and chill it again, then turn it out on a tray and slice. Garnish the tray with parsley.

Cotechino Sausage

This spicy sausage is available in many markets but it is easy to make your own. Order sausage casings from the butcher before you plan to make sausage. Although the first time around this might seem a bit of a job, when you have done it once, the next time will be easy. Be sure to *poach* the sausage—if the poaching liquid boils, the casings will explode and there is no recovery, unless you want sausage soup.

Makes 3 pounds

1 pound fresh pork rind
2 pounds lean pork shoulder
1 pound pork fatback
2 teaspoons salt
½ teaspoon freshly ground black pepper
¼ teaspoon powdered marjoram
¼ teaspoon powdered bay leaf
¼ teaspoon powdered thyme
¼ teaspoon powdered sage
¼ teaspoon vanilla
Sausage casing

Simmer the pork rind in water to cover for 2 hours; drain. Put the pork, pork rind, and fatback through a meat grinder twice, using the finest blade. Season with salt, pepper, marjoram, bay leaf, thyme, sage, and vanilla. Place the mixture in a pastry bag fitted with a large round tip and fill the sausage casing, tying it at 3-inch intervals.

Poach in water for 1 hour.

VARIETY MEATS

Under this heading I've grouped all the "other parts" of the animal, a category that suffers from too little public relations and poor preparation. Generations of children have grown up hating liver because it was overcooked—and it *is* dreadful that way. To many people the idea of eating kidneys, brains, tongue, or sweetbreads is unattractive, so they deny themselves a number of culinary treats. Many of these meats are economical as well as being delicacies when properly prepared. In this section, I've brought together a few of my favorite recipes.

Lamb Kidneys and Mushrooms

Serves 4

12 lamb kidneys
6 to 8 shallots, finely chopped
4 tablespoons butter, melted
1 pound mushrooms, sliced
½ cup dry white wine
¼ cup dry Madeira wine
¼ cup cognac
½ tablespoon unbleached all-purpose flour
½ tablespoon butter, melted
Salt and freshly ground black pepper
1 teaspoon tarragon vinegar

Remove the fat and membrane from the kidneys. Wash them and cut into thin slices. Place the shallots in an earthenware casserole with the melted butter and gently cook until a delicate brown. Add the prepared kidneys and mushrooms, the white wine, Madeira, and cognac. Simmer, covered, for 1½ hours, stirring occasionally.

Just before serving, combine the flour and butter and add to the liquid to thicken it slightly. Cook 3 to 4 minutes longer, season to taste, and add the vinegar. Serve over toast or rice.

Beef Tongue with Ham Mousse and Mayonnaise Collée

Beef or ox tongue is available fresh, salted, or smoked. Fresh tongue should be soaked in cold water for several hours after the cut end has been trimmed. It can then be braised or poached, and skinned. A salted or smoked tongue should also be soaked for several hours before being braised, poached, or baked, to get rid of excess salt or a smoky taste (poaching will take about 3½ hours and braising about 2½ hours) and then skinned.

If you want a really elegant presentation on a party buffet table try this recipe.

Serves 12 to 14

4-pound smoked beef tongue
1 recipe Ham Mousse (recipe below)
1 recipe Mayonnaise Collée (recipe follows)
Stuffed ripe olives, sliced
Watercress and cherry tomatoes

Soak the tongue for several hours to remove excess salt. Place the tongue in water to cover and simmer until tender (about 3½ hours). Let it cool in the cooking liquid. Remove the skin and tough root portions and chill for 1 hour. Cut the tongue into thin diagonal slices. Spread Ham Mousse between the slices and reshape the tongue. Coat with Mayonnaise Collée and decorate with olive slices. Transfer the tongue to a chilled platter. Garnish with watercress and cherry tomatoes.

Ham Mousse

2 cups cooked ham, finely chopped
2½ tablespoons golden raisins
1 tablespoon tomato paste
1 tablespoon dry Madeira wine
1 teaspoon horseradish
1 teaspoon prepared mustard
1 envelope (1 tablespoon) unflavored gelatin
½ cup boiling hot chicken stock
1 cup heavy cream, whipped

Put the ham and white raisins through the finest blade of a food grinder 5 or 6 times or combine in the food processor, using the metal blade; add the tomato paste. Stir in the Madeira, horseradish, and mustard.

Soften the gelatin in 1 tablespoon of cold water for 5 minutes. Add the chicken stock to the gelatin and stir until the gelatin is dissolved. Add the gelatin to the ground ham. Mix well. Cool. Fold in the whipped cream.

Mayonnaise Collée

1 envelope (1 tablespoon) unflavored gelatin
¼ cup cold water
1 cup Homemade Mayonnaise (see page 307)

Soften gelatin in cold water for 5 minutes in the top of a double boiler. Stir over hot water until the gelatin is dissolved. Add to the mayonnaise and blend well.

Baked Ox Tongue

Since tongue is usually poached before being baked, it is basically cooked, so the baking time should be about 45 minutes in a 350° F. oven.

Serves 8

2 10½-ounce cans clear beef stock
Few drops vinegar
6 shallots, finely chopped, divided
Parsley sprigs, finely chopped, divided
2 tablespoons finely chopped sweet pickles, divided
1½ cups fine bread crumbs, divided
1 cooked ox tongue, sliced ¼ inch thick (beef tongue may be substituted)
Salt and freshly ground black pepper
2 tablespoons butter

Preheat the oven to 350° F.

Pour 1 can of the stock into a shallow, oblong, ovenproof glass baking dish. Add the vinegar and half the shallots, parsley, pickles, and bread crumbs. Lay the tongue slices on this bed and sprinkle the remaining ingredients on top, ending with the bread crumbs. Season with salt and pepper. Dot with butter and bake for 45 minutes until brown.

Simmer the second can of beef stock until it is reduced to almost a glaze. When ready to serve the tongue, pour the glaze on top and serve very hot with fluffy mashed potatoes.

Oxtail Stew

Oxtails are not always available, so take advantage of them when they are and make this hearty stew.

Serves 6 generously

4 pounds oxtail, disjointed
2 cups unbleached all-purpose flour, for dredging
Salt and freshly ground black pepper
4 tablespoons fat
4 cups beef stock
2 tablespoons cider vinegar
1 large onion, coarsely chopped
3 medium to large carrots, coarsely chopped
2 cups finely diced celery
1 green or red pepper, coarsely chopped
2 tablespoons butter, for the roux
2 tablespoons unbleached all-purpose flour, for the roux

Dredge the sections of oxtail in the flour seasoned with salt and pepper. Heat the fat in a large skillet; add the oxtail pieces and brown on all sides. When nicely browned, transfer to a large Dutch oven or a lidded kettle and add the stock and vinegar. Cover the kettle and simmer the meat until almost tender, about 2 hours. Add the onion, carrots, celery, and pepper, and continue to simmer for about 30 minutes longer, or until the vegetables are tender.

Remove the meat and vegetables to a warmed serving platter. Pour off 2 cups of the cooking broth and set aside; reserve remaining broth.

Make a roux of the butter and flour in a 1-quart saucepan over medium heat, stirring constantly until the mixture is well blended and the flour is cooked. Stir in the reserved 2 cups of cooking broth; mix well and add to the broth remaining in the cooking pot. Bring to a boil, stirring for a minute or two; taste for seasoning, and make sure there is no taste of raw flour, and pour over the vegetables and meat.

Pan-Fried Liver

Beef liver, the liver I like best, is about the least expensive item at the meat counter—I suppose because no one seems to want it. Contrary to what many people think, it needs no soaking in milk or scalding in boiling water—just a simple dusting with flour and a 30-minute rest before it is fried in butter over high heat. Allow only a few minutes per side, until it is just pink. Although I call for calf's liver in some of the recipes that follow, you can substitute beef liver just as easily.

Serves 2

4 slices of beef liver, cut ½ inch thick
1 cup unbleached all-purpose flour
4 tablespoons butter
Salt and freshly ground black pepper

Dust the slices of liver generously with the flour; allow to rest for 30 minutes. This helps seal the liver (the flour will stick to the liver, not to the bottom of the pan).

Melt the butter in a 12-inch skillet over high heat. When really hot, add the slices of floured liver and season with salt and pepper. Leave the meat in the skillet until it has a chance to seal completely. After 1½ minutes, turn the meat to the other side and cook for another 1½ minutes.

Remove the liver from the skillet and allow to rest for 5 minutes before serving. Serve with Sautéed Onion Rings.

Calf's Liver in Red Wine Vinegar

I often substitute beef liver for the calf's liver called for in this recipe. To me it is more flavorful and seems to have more texture.

Serves 4

½ cup unbleached all-purpose flour
Salt and freshly ground black pepper
1 pound calf's liver, thinly sliced and deveined
¼ pound butter, divided
¼ cup finely chopped parsley
¼ cup red wine vinegar

Blend the flour with the salt and pepper to taste and dredge the liver slices on all sides with the mixture. Heat half the butter in a heavy skillet. Add the liver and cook on one side for 2 to 3 minutes. Turn and cook the other side for 2 minutes. Do not overcook. Transfer the liver to a heated platter and sprinkle with parsley.

Add the remaining butter to the skillet and allow it to brown. Pour over the liver. Add the vinegar to the skillet and bring to a boil. Swirl it around in the skillet and pour over the liver. Serve with boiled potatoes or rice.

Calf's Liver with Cream

Serves 4

8 small slices calf's liver, cut ½ inch thick
Unbleached all-purpose flour
Salt and freshly ground black pepper
¼ pound butter
1 cup heavy cream
Chopped parsley for garnish

Dust the liver with seasoned flour and allow to rest for 15 minutes. Melt the butter in a frying pan and, when hot, add the liver, cooking the slices 2 minutes on each side. Place the meat on a hot platter. Pour the cream in the frying pan, stir well until heated through, season with salt and pepper, and pour over the liver. Sprinkle with chopped parsley.

Sautéed Sweetbreads

Sweetbreads are about as controversial as liver—in this case probably because of their texture. Served in a sauce, they tend to be mushy, which puts a lot of people off, but when they are sautéed until crisp, it's a different story. You should purchase sweetbreads from a butcher; usually you don't have any choice because they seldom come prepackaged at the supermarket. Veal or calf sweetbreads are generally bought in pairs; 1 pair serves 2 persons.

Because sweetbreads are small, they don't need a lot of cooking; in fact, they shouldn't have a lot of cooking. For this recipe, and the variations that follow, they should be slightly crusty.

Serves 4

2 pairs sweetbreads
4 tablespoons butter
Salt and freshly ground black pepper
1 lemon, quartered

Soak the sweetbreads in cold water for ½ hour, then simmer in salted water for 20 minutes. Refresh in cold water and remove the membrane, tubes, and excess fat.

Cut in serving-size pieces. Melt the butter in a skillet. Season the sweetbreads with salt and pepper and sauté until nicely browned and slightly crusty on both sides, about 5 or 6 minutes. Serve with lemon quarters.

Variations:

With Madeira—Dredge the sweetbreads in unbleached all-purpose flour and season with salt and pepper. Sauté in 6 tablespoons of butter until lightly browned. Add ¼ cup of Madeira wine to the pan and cook for 1 to 2 minutes. Serve at once.

With White Wine and Ham—Sauté the sweetbreads as above. Add 1 tablespoon chopped parsley and ¼ cup of dry white wine to the pan and cook for 1 to 2 minutes. Serve on a slice of grilled ham.

With Bacon—Sauté the bacon until crisp, allowing 2 to 3 slices per person. Drain the bacon on absorbent paper. Sauté the sweetbreads in 2 tablespoons of bacon fat and 2 tablespoons of butter for 1 to 2 minutes. Season with salt and pepper to taste and serve with bacon.

POULTRY

"CHICKEN every Sunday" has become chicken every day and sometimes twice a day. Poultry is versatile, lending itself to many seasonings and cooking methods; it is plentiful, always available, and still the number one favorite on the American table. Along with fish, it is the dieter's special. Both have low calorie counts and are quick and easy to prepare. The only real difference is that fish, unlike chicken, still has its natural taste.

There was a time when poultry had a very special flavor all its own, but that day is gone forever. We will never again experience that home-grown taste unless we go back to the old methods of raising chickens and turkeys. Mass-production, hormones and chemical treatment got in the way of what poultry is all about. The taste of the cooked product got left behind, too, when quality was sacrificed to quantity. Since we no longer select a Rhode Island Red, or White Leghorn, or Buff Orpington, but buy chickens in packages, and since we now have turkeys that are pumped up with butter and whatever else, and sealed in plastic packages, we must work with what is available.

Chicken purchased in plastic wrap should not be stored in the refrigerator that way for very long. It needs to breathe or it will spoil. Remove it from the plastic and rewrap it loosely. If it is wrapped for freezing, it should be stored for only a short time before being used; freezer-burn is almost as bad as ordinary spoilage.

Allow frozen turkey or chicken to thaw slowly. Transfer the frozen bird from the freezer to the refrigerator section and let it stay there until it is completely thawed. That can take a couple of days (allow about 4 hours per pound) in the case of turkeys, only a few hours for a two- or three-pound chicken.

Poultry should not be overcooked. Slow heat and prolonged cooking used to be the rule. That's still all right for those who prefer it and I include some recipes that conform to this method, but I find that a shorter cooking time at fairly high heat gives far better results. The end product should be moist and tasty, and that doesn't happen if the bird cooks past an internal temperature of 160° F.

Broiling, grilling, frying, poaching, and stewing, as well as roasting and baking, are fine for turkey and chicken alike, although it isn't easy to come by a turkey small enough to broil, grill, or fry. However, a six- or seven-pound turkey can be treated just like a chicken—same seasonings, same marinades, same everything.

When broiling, grilling, or frying, remember that the meat continues to cook after being removed from the heat. The best way to learn is trial and error. If fowl comes out overcooked, shorten the cooking time the next time around. Everyone seems to think that it takes far longer than it really does. A total of 10 to 12 minutes is enough to fry a chicken breast with the bone in. If the breast is boned, 4 minutes on each side is sufficient. In broiling, I allow about 15 minutes per side, with the chicken pieces about 6 inches from the broiling element.

Since dark meat takes longer to cook than white meat, I simply start the dark meat first and add 7 or 8 minutes to the cooking time when frying; for broiling or grilling, the 15-minute per side rule takes care of both white and dark meat.

Stewing is generally used for a tougher, older bird, and for a tender and edible result, a long time is required. If the bird is young and is to be fricasseed or stewed, cut the cooking time considerably or the meat will be off the bone and stringy by the time the dish is finished.

Chicken Liver Terrine

This is the world's easiest terrine to make. It is great as a first course served over chopped lettuce and garnished with a little chopped egg. If it is to be used on a buffet table, unmold it and coat it with either a chicken or veal jelly made from clear stock with gelatin added. It should always be served well chilled.

Serves 8 to 10

1 cup rich beef stock
3 ounces day-old bread, crusts removed, crumbled
1 small garlic clove, pounded to a paste in a mortar
1 pound chicken livers
5 ounces raw beef marrow (from one leg bone)
Salt, freshly ground black pepper, and cayenne pepper
Large pinch mixed powdered herbs (thyme, savory, oregano, and marjoram)
3 eggs
½ cup heavy cream
2 tablespoons cognac
Butter

Preheat the oven to 350°F.

Combine the stock and bread crumbs in a small saucepan and reduce, stirring with a wooden spoon, to the consistency of a firm paste. Stir in the pounded garlic.

Pass the livers, marrow, and bread mixture through a grinder. Season with salt, pepper, and cayenne and pass through a fine sieve, a ladleful at a time. Discard any fiber that remains in the sieve.

Whisk in the eggs, cream, and cognac. Pour into a buttered 1-quart mold and place in a pan of hot but not boiling water in the oven for about 1 hour, or until the center is firm to the touch.

Unmold the loaf when it has cooled to tepid, pressing a sheet of plastic wrap around it to protect it from contact with the air. Serve well chilled. It should have a beige crust and be a uniform pink inside.

Note: Once chilled, the terrine may be decorated with a chicken or veal jelly, made by adding 2 tablespoons of gelatin powder to 2 cups of clear chicken or veal stock. Cook the mixture for 5 minutes, then cool it and spoon over the chilled terrine. Refrigerate and then add a second layer of jelly. The terrine may need a third layer of jelly. Be sure to refrigerate the terrine between layer additions.

Chicken Liver–Walnut Pâté

The ingredients of this elegant and rich pâté make a very strong statement. This is perfect party food and can be served with crackers or toast as an appetizer, as a salad accompanied by cherry tomatoes, olives, and assorted greens, or as a cold dish at a buffet, garnished with sliced radishes, strips of carrot, and lots of parsley or watercress.

Serves 8 to 10 generously

- *¼ pound butter*
- *½ cup chopped onion*
- *½ cup chopped celery*
- *1 garlic clove, quartered*
- *1 pound chicken livers, cut up*
- *½ cup brandy or cognac*
- *2 hard-cooked eggs, quartered*
- *1½ cups chicken stock, divided*
- *1 envelope (1 tablespoon) unflavored gelatin*
- *¾ teaspoon salt*
- *¼ teaspoon freshly ground black pepper*
- *½ cup walnuts, filberts, or almonds, finely ground*

In a heavy pan, heat the butter until it foams. Sauté the onion, celery, and garlic for approximately 10 minutes, or until all are tender. Remove to the container of a blender or food processor.

In the same pan sauté the chicken livers until they are a pale pink-beige color (less than 4 minutes). Add the brandy and cook for 1 minute. Add to the blender container with the eggs and ½ cup of the chicken stock.

Blend for about 1 minute at moderate speed. The mixture should be smooth and homogenous.

Meanwhile, soften the gelatin in ¼ cup cold chicken stock, then heat to the boiling point in the remaining stock. When the gelatin crystals have disappeared, stir in the salt, pepper, nuts, and the pureed liver mixture. Pour into a rinsed 1½-quart mold and chill for 4 hours or longer. Unmold and serve.

Chicken Liver Custard

This custard is excellent served as a first course with toast triangles or on a buffet table for cocktails. It will keep for up to a week in the refrigerator; after that it deteriorates and should be discarded.

Serves 4

6 to 8 ounces chicken livers
2 ounces raw beef marrow (pried out of the bone)
1 garlic clove, crushed
1¾ cups whole milk
2 eggs
3 egg yolks
Salt and freshly ground black pepper
Butter for the mold

Preheat the oven to 325°F.

Puree the liver, marrow, and garlic in a blender or food processor (or use a mortar and pestle). Add the milk, eggs, and seasoning to the puree and stir until blended; pass the mixture through a fine sieve and whisk until smooth. Pour into a generously buttered 3-pint charlotte mold, into the bottom of which a round of buttered parchment paper has been pressed.

Place the charlotte mold on a folded towel in a larger container of hot water. Bake for about 1¼ hours, or until the center is firm to the touch and the edges have just begun to shrink from the sides. Let cool for 5 minutes before unmolding. When unmolded, carefully peel off the round of paper. Serve with toast triangles.

Plain Fried Chicken

Fried chicken is just about the most American dish there is, and there are as many ways of frying chicken as there are Americans frying it. Some use batter prepared with egg, flour, and milk; some soak the chicken pieces in milk for a time before frying; some use crumbled cereals as a coating, and some simply sauté their chicken in butter with no preparation at all. I have never found a method of frying chicken that I did not like, but I do have some favorites. I grew up thinking that my Grandmother Cooper's old-fashioned recipe was the only way to fry chicken, and I still feel that this method gives the nicest crust with the least amount of preparation—and being an "unmasked" preparation, it lets the taste of the chicken prevail.

Serves 6

2 1½- to 2-pound fryers, each cut into 8 pieces
3 tablespoons vegetable oil
2 cups unbleached all-purpose flour
Salt and freshly ground black pepper
¼ pound butter
¼ pound lard
¼ cup water

Gravy

3 tablespoons unbleached all-purpose flour
2 cups light cream
4 cups whole milk

The chicken should be at room temperature. Roll the pieces in oil, then dust with flour mixed with salt and pepper. Lay the chicken pieces on waxed paper. Allow to rest for 30 minutes before frying.

Combine the butter, lard, and water in two skillets and heat until hot. (The chicken will absorb the water.) Fry the chicken, starting with the dark meat, as it takes longer to cook. To assure better browning and crispness, do not crowd the chicken pieces in the skillet. When the pieces start to brown, lower the heat to medium and continue to cook until done, about 20 minutes. Drain on paper towels and keep warm in a 150°F. oven.

To make the gravy, drain all but 4 tablespoons of fat from one of the skillets. Discard the fat from the other skillet (or treat it in the same way if extra gravy is desired). Add the flour to the remaining fat.

Combine the fat and flour thoroughly over medium heat. When the mixture is smooth and begins to bubble, add the cream and milk. Cook, stirring, until the gravy is the consistency of heavy cream. Season with salt and pepper. If a thicker gravy is desired, reduce the amount of milk.

Serve with Corn Batter Cakes.

Cinnamon Fried Chicken

The touch of cinnamon mixed with flour gives an elusive taste to the finished dish as well as a wonderfully golden color to the chicken pieces as they fry. The amount of cinnamon used must be small, however, or it becomes a case of more is less.

Serves 4

1 cup unbleached all-purpose flour
½ cup whole wheat flour
Salt and freshly ground black pepper
¼ teaspoon cinnamon
3- to 3½-pound fryer, cut into 8 pieces
¼ pound butter
3 tablespoons vegetable oil

Preheat the oven to 325°F.

Combine the flours, salt, pepper, and cinnamon in a paper bag and shake to mix thoroughly.

Shake the chicken pieces in the flour mixture to coat liberally and place on waxed paper. Let stand for at least 30 minutes. (If you do this, you will find that the flour sticks to the chicken instead of to the skillet.)

Heat a large skillet; add the butter and oil. Fry the chicken, a few pieces at a time, until golden brown (about 8 minutes per side).

Transfer the browned pieces to a baking dish and bake until all the pieces are cooked (about 30 minutes).

Note: Since dark meat takes a few minutes longer, I usually cook the dark meat first. The cinnamon taste should be subtle, not overpowering.

Chicken with Calvados

If you cannot find French Calvados, apple brandy works just as well.

Serves 4

3-pound fryer, cut into 8 pieces
2 tablespoons butter
1 tablespoon vegetable oil
⅓ cup Calvados or apple brandy
4 shallots, minced
½ teaspoon salt
¼ teaspoon white pepper
2 tablespoons chopped parsley
Pinch thyme
½ cup apple cider
½ cup heavy cream

Sauté the chicken in butter and oil over medium-high heat for 10 minutes until golden, turning occasionally. Lower the heat and continue cooking, turning the chicken, for 10 minutes more. Add the Calvados or apple brandy, ignite, and shake the pan until the flame dies. Add the shallots and cook for 2 minutes. Sprinkle the chicken with salt, pepper, parsley, and thyme. Add the cider and cover; simmer gently for 15 minutes, or until the chicken is done. Remove the chicken to a warm platter. Stir the cream into the pan, bring to a boil, pour over the chicken, and serve.

Chicken and Mushrooms with Sour Cream

Serves 4

3- to 4-pound fryer, disjointed
1 rib celery, minced
1 carrot, minced
1 yellow onion, minced
1 cup water
1 pound mushrooms, cleaned and sliced
3 tablespoons butter
6 small white onions, sliced
1 cup Homemade Sour Cream *(see page 333)*
Salt and freshly ground black pepper
1 teaspoon dry mustard
½ cup dry sherry

Rinse the chicken pieces in warm water, pat dry, and set aside. Arrange the celery, carrot, and onion in the bottom of a heavy skillet and add the water. Lay the chicken pieces on top. Cover and steam over medium heat until tender (at least 30 minutes). When the chicken is done, debone and cut the meat into good-size pieces and set aside. Discard the steamed vegetables.

Sauté the mushrooms in butter for 10 minutes and remove with a slotted spoon. Set aside with the chicken. Sauté the onion in the same skillet as the mushrooms. When tender, add the mushrooms and the chicken pieces. When the chicken, mushroom, and onion combination is heated through, add the sour cream, salt, pepper, mustard, and sherry, and mix well. Serve immediately over pasta or rice.

Chicken in Mushroom and Truffle Sauce

The truffle is nice but not essential.

Serves 4

1 large broiler or roasting chicken, cut into 8 pieces
2 cups water
Bouquet garni: parsley, chervil, tarragon, thyme, and bay leaf
Salt and freshly ground black pepper
4 tablespoons olive oil
7 tablespoons butter, divided
¾ cup sherry
¼ cup cognac or brandy
3 shallots, finely chopped
½ pound fresh mushrooms, washed, dried, and finely chopped
1 white or black truffle
½ cup dry white wine
½ cup heavy cream
1 teaspoon each parsley and chervil, minced
2 egg yolks

Place the chicken back, gizzard, heart, liver, and neck into a 1-quart pan with the water and bouquet garni and bring to a boil; lower the heat to medium and cook for 15 minutes. Set this stock aside.

Season the legs, second joints, and split breast of the chicken with salt and pepper. Fry to a golden brown in hot olive oil. Remove from the skillet and pour off any oil that remains. Replace the oil with 3 tablespoons of the butter and return the chicken pieces to the skillet. Add the sherry and cognac and simmer over medium-low heat for about 30 minutes. (The chicken should be tender and thoroughly cooked but not so done that the meat falls from the bones.) Pour off the juice into a saucepan; add 2 tablespoons of butter to the chicken pieces and keep hot in the oven.

Melt the remaining 2 tablespoons of butter in a sauté pan and brown the shallots lightly. Strain the reserved chicken stock and add 1 cup to the mushrooms; simmer for 15 minutes. Boil the truffle in the white wine for 5 minutes; then drain and chop fine. Combine the remaining stock with the mushrooms, shallots, and truffle; add the heavy cream. Let this combination simmer for a few minutes. Season to taste and add the parsley and chervil. Beat the egg yolks, thinning them slightly with a little cream, and slowly add to the hot sauce. Stir constantly while the sauce thickens. Arrange the chicken on a platter and blanket with the sauce.

Chicken Breasts with Grapes and Wine

This version of Chicken Véronique uses only the breasts. A whole chicken can also be used, and I often do, but for a party the breasts look a little nicer. Actually I prefer the dark meat because it is moister and more flavorful, but in this dish, the sauce provides both flavor and moistness.

Serves 6

3 whole chicken breasts, halved
6 tablespoons butter
2 teaspoons fresh tarragon or 1 teaspoon dried tarragon
Salt and freshly ground black pepper
⅓ cup dry white wine
2 cups seedless grapes
1 cup heavy cream
3 egg yolks, beaten

Preheat the oven to 350°F.

In a large, heavy casserole brown the chicken breasts in butter and add the tarragon, salt, and pepper. Remove from the heat and add the wine and grapes.

Cover the casserole and bake until the chicken is tender, about 45 minutes.

Heat the cream to a boil and add to the egg yolks, a little at a time, so that the yolks do not cook too quickly. Pour this mixture over the chicken-and-grape combination and serve immediately over toast or rice.

Chicken Breasts with Tomato Sauce

In this dish, the chicken breasts and tomato sauce are cooked and served separately; only at the table do the two come together. Prepared this way, it is a great combination because the flavor and texture of each are preserved. Cooked together, the tomato flavor would tend to take over.

Serves 6

3 whole chicken breasts, cut in half
6 cups olive oil, divided
6 tablespoons lemon juice
1 tablespoon chopped fresh parsley
1 teaspoon finely minced garlic
1 teaspoon ground rosemary
1 bay leaf, crushed
3 teaspoons salt
½ teaspoon freshly ground white pepper
1 cup unbleached all-purpose flour
2 cups unflavored bread crumbs
12 whole parsley sprigs for garnish
2 lemons, cut in wedges for garnish
2 cups Easy Tomato Sauce *(see page 326)**, heated*
2 tablespoons chopped fresh basil leaves (optional)

Marinate the chicken breasts in a mixture of 1 cup olive oil, the lemon juice, parsley, garlic, rosemary, bay leaf, salt, and pepper for 2 hours. Turn the chicken occasionally. Remove the breasts from the marinade and drain well.

Dredge in the flour, then dip into the bread crumbs. Heat the remaining 5 cups of olive oil until almost smoking and fry the chicken until each piece is golden brown on all sides. Cover, reduce the heat, and cook for about 20 minutes, or until tender.

Remove the chicken breasts from the oil and drain on paper towels. Arrange on a heated platter and garnish with parsley sprigs and lemon wedges. Serve the tomato sauce in a separate bowl, sprinkled with fresh basil.

Chicken Breasts with Cornmeal Mush

This is a wonderful combination of flavors and a real "one-dish meal," perfect for a Sunday supper. All one needs to add is a green salad and dessert.

Serves 6

2 tablespoons butter
2 tablespoons lard
3 whole chicken breasts, halved and boned
½ pound ham, chopped into medium dice
1 small onion, finely diced
2 small carrots, finely diced
2 stalks celery, finely diced
Salt and freshly ground black pepper
⅓ cup red or white wine
1 tablespoon tomato paste dissolved in 1 cup hot water, or 1 cup thin tomato sauce
1 cup yellow cornmeal
1 quart whole milk

In a large skillet, melt the butter and lard over medium-high heat. Add the chicken breasts, ham, onion, carrots, celery, salt, and pepper. Cover and cook until the chicken is tender, about 30 minutes, basting from time to time with the fat. Turn the chicken to brown it on all sides.

When the chicken is browned, add the wine. When the wine is absorbed, add the tomato sauce. Cook a few minutes longer until the chicken is thoroughly cooked. Remove from the heat and keep warm.

Combine the cornmeal and milk over medium-high heat, stirring constantly. Cook until very thick; season with salt and pepper. Add 2 or 3 tablespoons of butter if desired. The mixture should be stiff.

Spoon the cornmeal mush onto a large, deep platter. Place the chicken breasts on the mush and pour on the remaining sauce from the skillet.

Chicken and Broccoli

There are other names for this dish, such as chicken divan, but to me it is just plain chicken with broccoli baked in a casserole.

Serves 8

4 whole chicken breasts, halved, skinned and boned (reserve skin and bones)
1 onion
2 tablespoons butter
2 tablespoons unbleached all-purpose flour
1 cup chicken stock
¾ cup mayonnaise
1 teaspoon lemon juice
2 10-ounce packages frozen whole broccoli
Grated Cheddar cheese
Homemade Bread Crumbs *(see page 335)*

Poach the chicken breasts in salted water with the onion and reserved skin and bones for about 12 minutes.

Make a roux of the butter and flour; cook long enough to remove the raw taste of the flour. Add the chicken stock and cook until the sauce is a medium-thick cream gravy. Combine the sauce with the mayonnaise and lemon juice.

Preheat the oven to 350°F.

Cook the broccoli until just tender. In an oblong baking dish, layer the chicken breasts and broccoli. Pour the sauce over all, cover with the cheese, and top with a thick layer of bread crumbs. Bake for 30 to 40 minutes.

Note: After the dish is baked, it may be cut into squares for easy serving for a buffet. This dish freezes very well. When you are ready to use it, defrost and complete the final baking step.

Chicken with Fresh Noodles

Although this recipe calls for chicken breast, thighs or legs can also be used. Dark meat is actually moister and more flavorful; it just doesn't look as attractive as the breast.

Serves 4

1 whole breast from 2½-pound fryer
Salt
3 tablespoons vegetable oil
2 teaspoons finely chopped parsley
1 teaspoon finely chopped fresh marjoram or a pinch of finely crumbled dried marjoram
2 to 3 garlic cloves, peeled and finely chopped
1 recipe for Fresh Egg Noodles (see page 199) or 1 pound commercial noodles, cooked and drained
Freshly ground black pepper
½ cup freshly grated Parmesan or Gruyère cheese (or a mixture of the two)
4 tablespoons softened butter or olive oil
Chopped parsley for garnish

Skin and bone the chicken breast. Cut, across the grain, into strips ¼ to ⅓ inch thick. Salt lightly.

In a large, heavy skillet, sauté the chicken strips in oil over high heat for 1 or 2 minutes until they are firm and springy and all the surfaces are opaque. Add the herbs and garlic and cook for a minute longer on high heat, stirring and tossing constantly. Add the noodles; toss thoroughly, using wooden forks. Remove from the heat. Grind pepper over the top; add the cheese and butter or oil and toss, mixing well. Serve immediately with a sprinkle of chopped parsley as a garnish.

Chicken Paprika with Sour Cream

The secret of this dish lies in using homemade sour cream. The difference between commercial and homemade is considerable: the homemade is far superior in texture and quality, and it will not curdle when placed over or under heat. This dish is meant to be on the delicate side, but I notice that some people prefer it spicier. Add more hot red pepper if you wish, and more of everything else for that matter if a stronger taste is what you are after.

Serves 6

1 medium onion, thinly sliced
1 tablespoon butter
1 teaspoon paprika
Salt and freshly ground black pepper
1 small, dried, hot red pepper, minced
3 whole chicken breasts, halved, skinned and boned
1 cup Homemade Sour Cream (see page 333)

In a covered skillet large enough to hold the chicken breasts, cook the onion slices in butter until transparent. Remove the pan from the heat; add the paprika, salt, pepper, and red pepper and mix well.

Add the chicken to this bed with ½ cup hot water and return to the stove; bring slowly to a simmer. Cook, covered, for about 30 minutes, adding a few drops of hot water from time to time if necessary.

Preheat the oven to 375°F.

When the chicken is cooked, remove and reserve; bring the liquid in the skillet to a boil. Cook on high heat until it is reduced about a third. Add the sour cream, and continue to cook for 5 to 10 minutes. Place the chicken pieces in an ovenproof baking dish, pour the sour cream mixture on top, and bake, uncovered, for 20 minutes. Adjust the seasonings and serve very hot with buttered noodles.

Note: If you are using unboned chicken pieces, follow the same instructions but cook them somewhat longer. If you use dark meat rather than white, add 15 minutes to the cooking time.

Roast Chicken

This is roasted at high heat, and I challenge anyone to have a moister or more perfectly done roast chicken. With the bacon slices it bastes itself and requires nothing more than occasional turning, replacing the bacon with each turn. Just don't cook it any longer than an hour. Nothing is less appealing than overcooked chicken.

Serves 4

2½- to 3-pound fryer, whole
Juice of ½ lemon
Salt and freshly ground black pepper
4 slices bacon

Preheat the oven to 400°F.

Rinse the chicken with warm water and dry thoroughly. Rub with lemon juice and sprinkle inside and out with salt and pepper.

Roast for 1 hour, starting the chicken breast-side down for 15 minutes, with the bacon slices distributed across the back. Then turn on one side, moving the bacon slices to the top side, and bake for 15 minutes. Turn on the opposite side, with bacon on the top side for 15 minutes.

To finish, turn the chicken on its back, place the bacon on the breast, and finish baking for a final 15 minutes.

Remove the bacon and serve. (The bacon will be overcooked, but will have served its purpose, so you can discard it—or eat it in the kitchen as the cook's reward.)

Roast Chicken with Cognac Cream Sauce

Cognac, white Port, and whipping cream combine to make a very special sauce for this roast chicken. The sauce actually makes itself as the chicken cooks and is basted.

Serves 4

5-pound roasting chicken
Salt and freshly ground black pepper
¼ pound butter
½ cup cognac, heated
½ cup Port, preferably white
3 to 4 tablespoons whipping cream

Preheat the oven to 425°F.

Salt and pepper the inside of the chicken thoroughly, place the butter in the cavity, and sew it up.

Spread a little butter on the bottom of a small roasting pan and place the chicken in it. Bake for about 10 minutes in the oven to brown lightly. Place the pan on top of the stove, pour the heated cognac over the chicken, ignite it, and let it burn a little. Extinguish the flames by pouring the Port over the bird. Baste and season well with salt and pepper. Reduce the oven heat to 325°F. and continue roasting, allowing 15 to 20 minutes per pound.

As the chicken continues to roast, baste with the pan juices, and each time you baste, add a tablespoon of whipping cream.

When the chicken is done, let stand for 15 minutes. Carve and serve immediately, accompanied by the sauce in a gravy boat.

Chicken Baked in Madeira

This classy and colorful dish tastes like a lot more work than it actually is.

Serves 4

2½- to 3-pound young chicken
9 small white onions, divided
¼ pound butter, divided
Salt and freshly ground black pepper
¼ pound salt pork, cut in ¼-inch squares
12 small carrots, peeled
1 tablespoon beef extract
1 cup dry Madeira wine
½ cup dry white wine
8 large potatoes, peeled
Olive oil for frying

Preheat the oven to 350°F.

Clean and truss the chicken. Chop 1 of the onions very fine and place with a generous tablespoon of the butter inside the chicken. Season with salt and pepper and brown the chicken carefully in a large, heavy saucepan.

Put 4 tablespoons of the butter in an earthenware casserole and add the salt pork and the chicken. Cover with a large piece of buttered paper, fit the lid of the casserole tightly on top, and place in the oven to cook for 30 minutes.

In a separate pan, lightly brown the remaining onions and the carrots in the remaining 3 tablespoons of butter.

Take the chicken out of the casserole and remove the string. Pour the cooking juices from the casserole and strain through a fine sieve. Dissolve the beef extract in the Madeira. Return the chicken and the strained juice to the casserole, add the carrots, onions, white wine, and the Madeira–beef extract mixture. Season to taste and place back in the oven for another 30 minutes.

Scoop out about 30 small potato balls from the raw potatoes. Wash and dry them thoroughly, then fry in hot olive oil until nicely browned, about 15 minutes.

Remove the chicken and vegetables from the casserole to a heated serving platter and keep hot. Pour the cooking juices into a small saucepan and reduce over high heat by a third. Pour over the chicken and surround with the vegetables and potato balls.

Baked Chicken with Cabbage

This is a most unusual dish and should be served with boiled carrots and turnips garnished with chopped chervil. I don't cook the vegetables with the chickens because I like them to retain their individual flavors.

Serves 8

2 2½- to 3-pound young chickens
1½-pound ham slice with a rim of fat
1 garlic clove
6 scallions, finely chopped
1 large white cabbage
2 cups chicken or beef stock
Salt and freshly ground black pepper
½ teaspoon crushed fennel seed
1 cup dry white wine
¼ cup brandy

Preheat the oven to 325°F.

Truss the chickens for baking. Cube the ham and brown it in a skillet with the garlic and scallions. When some of the fat has fried out, put the chickens in the pan and brown them lightly.

Quarter the cabbage and place it in a large, heavy casserole; pour the stock over it and add the chickens, ham, and seasonings. Cover and bake for 1½ hours, until tender. As soon as the casserole is removed from the oven, add the wine and brandy and allow to steep for 20 minutes before serving.

Cold Boiled Chicken

This is not a spur-of-the-moment dish, but, made a day ahead, it is a superb summer luncheon or supper entrée and great for a fancy picnic. It should be served with a good bottle of chilled champagne.

Serves 6

5- to 6-pound roasting chicken
8 carrots, peeled
2 stalks celery
Salt and freshly ground black pepper
3 white onions
½ pint heavy cream
1 large piece lemon peel
4 tablespoons butter
4 tablespoons unbleached all-purpose flour
Juice of ½ lemon
½ teaspoon mace
¼ teaspoon salt
⅛ teaspoon freshly ground black pepper
1 envelope (1 tablespoon) unflavored gelatin, dissolved in ¼ cup cold water
Chopped parsley
8 slices lean-bacon
Paprika
Boston lettuce
Cold vegetables (carrot sticks, cauliflower buds, turnip rounds, cucumbers, celery), marinated briefly in French dressing

Clean the chicken inside and out and truss as for roasting. Place it in a deep kettle and cover with boiling water. Add the carrots, celery, salt, pepper, and onions, and boil gently until tender, about 1 hour. Remove from the heat and let stand for 3 or 4 hours until it reaches room temperature.

About 2 hours before serving, place the chicken on a platter, making sure all the juice has drained out. Remove as much of the skin as possible without spoiling the shape of the chicken. Strain the cooking liquid through a fine sieve and reserve. Discard the vegetables.

Heat the cream and add the lemon peel to season the cream. In the top of a double boiler, melt the butter. Stir in the flour until smooth, and add the hot cream with the lemon peel. Cook over medium heat until the raw taste of the flour is gone, about 5 minutes, and until it is the consistency of a medium-thick sauce. If it becomes too thick, add a little of the reserved cooking liquid. Remove from the heat and discard the lemon peel. Add the lemon juice, mace, salt, pepper, and dissolved gelatin.

When the sauce has cooled, pour it carefully over the cold chicken until the chicken is completely coated. Decorate the platter with parsley. Place in the refrigerator to chill. Just before serving, fry the bacon until crisp and serve it around the chicken; sprinkle the breast of the chicken with a little paprika. Serve on a bed of Boston lettuce accompanied by various marinated cold vegetables.

Chicken in Consommé

This variation on chicken soup is like a pot-au-feu with the bird left whole and not cooked completely to pieces. It's a great Sunday supper dish in the winter and is very filling.

Serves 6

3- to 4-pound chicken, trussed
1½ quarts boiling water
1½ quarts chicken consommé
6 whole carrots, peeled and cut in ½-inch circles
2 small turnips, sliced
2 leeks, white only, sliced and rinsed
4 white onions, quartered
1 rib celery, coarsely chopped
Salt and freshly ground black pepper
½ head cabbage
Sea salt
Parsley for garnish

Place the chicken in a large pot and add the boiling water, consommé, and all the other ingredients except the sea salt and parsley. Cover and simmer gently until the meat is almost ready to fall from the bones, about 1½ hours.

Remove the chicken from the cooking liquid, take off the skin, and set the chicken on a hot platter. Sprinkle it with sea salt and decorate with parsley.

Remove all the grease from the cooking liquid and serve it and the vegetables piping hot in individual cups with the chicken.

Sautéed Chicken

Technically, sautéeing is done in a shallow pan or skillet, and frying in a deep pan or skillet. The real difference lies in the amount of fat used in the cooking process. Frying is really "deep frying" or cooking in an amount of fat that almost completely immerses the food being cooked. Actually most American chicken dishes are sautéed rather than fried.

Serves 6

½ pound butter
2 carrots, peeled and finely sliced
4 white onions, finely sliced
3- to 4-pound chicken, cut up into 8 pieces
Salt and freshly ground black pepper
2 teaspoons unbleached all-purpose flour
2 cups hot chicken stock
2 small tomatoes, peeled and chopped
¾ pound small mushrooms, cleaned and quartered
1 teaspoon chopped parsley
1 cup red wine

Melt the butter in a large frying pan and add the carrots and onions. Cook for 10 minutes, stirring occasionally. Add the chicken and a little salt and pepper. Cook for another 10 minutes, turning the chicken to brown on all sides. Sprinkle with the flour and add the stock and tomatoes. Stir until the mixture boils and then let it simmer for 20 to 30 minutes. Add the mushrooms and parsley. When the chicken is almost tender, add the red wine and let simmer for 10 minutes longer. Correct the seasoning and serve.

Chicken Curry I

Curry is not a spice but a mixture of spices that combine to become a seasoning. There are many curry powders on the market and most of them are quite acceptable, but any cook can make up a curry powder with a spiciness and strength to suit his or her taste.

Serves 6

1⅓ cups chopped onion
2 garlic cloves, crushed
4 tablespoons clarified butter (see Note)
2 teaspoons turmeric
2 medium-size apples, peeled, cored, and chopped
2 teaspoons ground cumin
2 teaspoons ground ginger
½ teaspoon freshly ground black pepper
1 teaspoon ground mustard seed
6 teaspoons ground coriander seed
½ teaspoon ground red pepper
1 teaspoon cinnamon
3 pounds chicken legs and breasts
3 teaspoons salt, divided
2 cups hot water
1 teaspoon fresh lemon juice
1 cup canned coconut milk

Cook the onion and garlic in hot clarified butter for 2 to 3 minutes. Add the turmeric and cook over moderately low heat for about 10 minutes until the onions are very soft. Stir constantly so the turmeric does not scorch. Add the apples and the remaining spices; cook for 2 to 3 minutes.

Rub the chicken with 2 teaspoons of the salt; add to the onion mixture and cook over moderate heat for 10 to 15 minutes, turning until the chicken is lightly browned. Add the remaining salt and the hot water. Cover and cook for 50 minutes, or until the chicken is tender. Remove the chicken. Strain the sauce through a sieve (if the sauce is too thin, reheat it, stirring, until it thickens). Return the chicken and sauce to the skillet and heat through. Add the lemon juice and coconut milk. Heat just before serving. Serve with a selection of condiments (see page 337).

Note: To clarify butter place it in an ovenproof dish in a 350°F. oven until the butter is completely melted. Remove from the heat and allow to approach room temperature. Then refrigerate until the butter hardens. Remove, wipe off any impurities that have come to the top, and transfer the hardened butter to another dish, leaving the liquid that has formed under the butter in the ovenproof dish. Wipe the hardened mass of butter with a damp cloth, and discard any liquid. The butter is now clarified. It can be stored in the refrigerator or freezer, depending on how soon it will be used. It makes sense to clarify a pound or two at a time, rather than by the tablespoonfuls that most recipes call for. It is a good item to keep on hand, and very nice to cook with. Clarified butter does not burn as easily and gives more uniform browning.

Chicken Curry II

You can use a commercially blended curry powder to make this. I suggest trying the homemade curry powder that appears in this book if you decide you'd like to try your hand at making your own.

Serves 8

2 1½- to 2-pound fryers, cut into 8 pieces each
2 carrots, whole or halved
2 ribs celery, cut in large pieces
¼ pound butter
3 to 4 small yellow onions, finely chopped
3 to 4 tablespoons Homemade Curry Powder (see page 336)
4 egg yolks
½ pint heavy cream
Parsley sprigs for garnish
Suggested condiments: chutney, pine nuts, shredded coconut, raisins or currants, pickled onions, quince preserves, chopped hard-cooked egg

Place the chicken in a large saucepan with the carrots and celery in just enough water to cover (about 1½ cups). Simmer, covered, until the meat is tender, about 1 hour. Remove the chicken pieces, pour the broth into a bowl, and discard the vegetables.

Over medium-high heat, melt the butter in a skillet, add the onions, and lightly brown them. Remove the onions with slotted spoon and reserve. Put the chicken pieces in the skillet and cook for 5 minutes over medium heat. Sprinkle with the curry powder and pour the reserved broth over the chicken. Stew for 5 or 10 minutes.

Beat the egg yolks and add the cream. Cook in a pan over medium heat until the sauce thickens. Whisk constantly, being sure not to cook too quickly or the eggs will curdle.

Arrange the chicken on a warm platter. Pour the curried broth over the chicken and then pour the egg and cream sauce on top.

Garnish with sprigs of parsley and serve with a bowl of hot rice and as many different condiments as you wish.

Chicken Casserole

This is not a casserole in the usual sense. It is just chicken in a quickly baked custard. And here's a word of warning, just so you don't think something has gone wrong: the combination of wine and lemon with the cheese gives a curdled quality to the custard when the dish is baked.

Serves 4

1 frying chicken, cut into 8 pieces
Salt
2 tablespoons butter
Large handful finely crumbled fresh bread crumbs
⅓ cup white wine

Cheese Custard

¾ cup heavy cream
3 egg yolks
Salt and freshly ground black pepper
3 ounces freshly grated Gruyère cheese
Juice of ½ lemon and the deglazing liquid

Salt the chicken pieces and cook them in the butter in a skillet over medium heat until nearly done and lightly colored on all sides, about 20 minutes, adding the white meat only after the dark meat has cooked for 10 minutes. Transfer the browned pieces to shallow baking dish just large enough to hold them, arranged side by side in one layer. Cook the crumbs in the butter remaining in the skillet, stirring, until they are slightly crisp and only slightly colored. Remove and set aside; deglaze the pan with the white wine, reducing it by about half.

Preheat the oven to 400°F.

To make the custard, whisk together the cream, egg yolks, salt, pepper, and cheese, then incorporate the lemon juice and the deglazed pan liquid. Spoon or pour the mixture evenly over the chicken pieces, sprinkle the surface with the bread crumbs, and bake for 20 to 25 minutes, or until the surface is nicely colored and the custard is firm.

Chicken Crepes

A good crepe needs a lot of consideration. The batter must be light, the cooking brief, and the filling right. A wide range of foods have had a whirl at being in a crepe, but not many have survived the first try. This chicken crepe recipe is one that really works; it should be served as a first course, rather than a main course.

Serves 6 as a first course

6 tablespoons butter, divided
4 tablespoons unbleached all-purpose flour
1 cup whole milk, heated
1 cup chicken stock, heated
½ teaspoon salt
½ teaspoon freshly ground black pepper
2 tablespoons minced shallots
1 garlic clove, minced
1 cup diced cooked chicken
½ cup dry white wine
½ teaspoon dried tarragon
2 egg yolks, divided
½ cup heavy cream, divided
1 teaspoon lemon juice
Grated Gruyère cheese
6 crepes (see page 366)*

Melt 4 tablespoons of the butter and remove from the heat. Blend in the flour and return to the heat; let the flour and butter cook slowly for 2 minutes. Add the milk and chicken stock. Beat the sauce vigorously with a wire whisk and cook over moderate heat for 2 to 3 minutes until the sauce has thickened. Remove from the heat and beat in the salt and pepper; set aside.

Cook the shallots and garlic in the remaining 2 tablespoons of butter over low heat for 2 minutes. Stir in the chicken and cook slowly for 2 more minutes. Add the wine. Cover and simmer for 1 minute. Uncover, raise the heat, and cook rapidly until the liquid has almost evaporated. Stir in the tarragon.

Take 1 cup of the sauce and add to it 1 egg yolk, ¼ cup of the cream, the lemon juice, and a dash of pepper. Boil for 1 minute and add to the chicken mixture. Fill the crepes with this mixture and roll them up, tucking in the ends. Arrange the rolled crepes in a buttered ovenproof dish.

To the remaining sauce add the other egg yolk and the remaining ¼ cup of cream, and boil for 1 minute. Pour over the crepes. Sprinkle the crepes with cheese and brown under the broiler.

* Omit the sugar from the crepe recipe; these should not be sweet.

Chicken Pot Pie

I never cared for chicken pie until I discovered that part of the secret lay in really starting from scratch. So don't try to make this with leftover chicken—you'll ruin the dish. The wonderful taste depends on fresh chicken cooked with fresh vegetables and proper seasoning.

Serves 8

Pastry

2 cups unbleached all-purpose flour
8 tablespoons butter
4 tablespoons lard
Salt to taste
2 to 3 tablespoons cold water

Filling

5 tablespoons butter, divided
2 2½-pound chickens, cut into serving pieces
Salt and freshly ground black pepper
½ cup coarsely chopped carrots
½ cup coarsely chopped celery
1 cup small white onions, peeled
½ pound mushrooms, thinly sliced
3 fresh parsley sprigs
2 whole cloves
3 fresh thyme sprigs or ½ teaspoon dried thyme
4 tablespoons unbleached all-purpose flour
1 cup dry white wine
4 cups chicken stock
Few drops hot pepper sauce
5 strips bacon
3 hard-cooked eggs, peeled and cut into sixths
1 cup heavy cream
1 teaspoon Worcestershire sauce
1 egg, beaten

For the pastry, put the flour in a mixing bowl and add the butter, lard, and salt. Using a pastry blender, work the mixture until it resembles coarse cornmeal. Add the water a little at a time, working the mixture lightly with the fingers. Add just enough water to hold the dough together. Shape the dough into a ball, wrap in waxed paper, and refrigerate for at least 30 minutes.

To make the filling, melt 3 tablespoons of the butter in a skillet and add the chicken pieces, skin-side down, sprinkling with salt and pepper.

Cook over low heat, without browning, for about 5 minutes, turning once. Scatter the carrots, celery, and onions over the chicken. Heat the remaining 2 tablespoons of butter in another skillet and add the mushrooms. Cook, stirring, until they give up their liquid. Continue cooking until most of the liquid evaporates. Add the mushrooms to the chicken.

In a cheesecloth square, tie together the parsley, cloves, and thyme; add to the chicken mixture. Cook, stirring frequently, for about 10 minutes, being careful not to let the chicken burn. Sprinkle with the flour, stirring to distribute it evenly. Add the wine and stock. Add the hot pepper sauce, cover, and simmer for 30 minutes.

Preheat the oven to 400°F.

Cut the bacon into 2-inch lengths and cook until crisp and brown; drain. Remove the chicken and vegetables and transfer the cooking liquid to a saucepan. Discard the cheesecloth bag of spices. Arrange the chicken and vegetables in a baking dish. Arrange the hard-cooked eggs over the chicken. Scatter the bacon bits on top.

Skim the fat from the cooking liquid. Bring to a boil and add the cream. Bring the sauce to a boil and simmer for 20 minutes. Add the Worcestershire sauce with salt and pepper to taste. Pour this sauce over the chicken mixture.

Roll out the pastry and cut a round or oval just large enough to cover the baking dish. Arrange it over the chicken mixture and cut a small vent in the center. Brush with beaten egg and bake for 30 minutes.

Chicken-Beef Pie

Serves 10 to 12

3 eggs
8 ounces fresh or sour cream
¼ pound butter, melted
Salt and freshly ground black pepper
½ teaspoon baking soda
Unbleached all-purpose flour
5-pound roasting chicken
3 carrots, peeled
3 onions, chopped, divided
3 ribs celery, chopped
3 pounds round steak, chopped
Butter
3 hard-cooked eggs, chopped
1 cup crushed soda crackers
1 egg yolk, lightly beaten

Make a paste by combining the eggs, fresh or sour cream, butter, salt, pepper, soda, and enough flour to obtain a not-too-thick paste; reserve.

Put the chicken in 4 cups of water with the carrots, two thirds of the onions, and the celery. Simmer for 1 hour until the chicken is done. Remove the skin and bones and dice the meat. Reserve the stock and vegetables.

Sauté the remaining onion and the chopped steak in butter, being careful not to brown the onion. Add the hard-cooked eggs to the mixture.

Preheat the oven to 325°F.

Grease a deep baking dish with butter, powder it with the cracker meal, spreading it over the sides and the bottom of the baking dish. Place a layer of chopped meat, then a layer of chicken, repeating alternately until the dish is full. Cover the pie with the reserved paste and brush the top with the egg yolk. Bake for 30 minutes and serve with the heated chicken soup and vegetables.

Brunswick Stew

There can be no more American dish. I don't know that anyone has been able to pinpoint its origin; both North and South claim it, and there are many variations. The main differences are in the seasonings, which can be adjusted to suit individual tastes. A very thick Brunswick stew usually indicates a Southern influence, but thick or thin, it is a great one-dish meal. You can use either fresh or canned vegetables where canned are called for in the recipe. My grandmother's recipe called for home-canned tomatoes, beans, and corn, but commercially canned will do.

Serves 8

2 4-pound chickens
4 carrots, peeled
3 ribs celery
5 or 6 small white onions
Salt
15-ounce can peeled tomatoes, drained
16-ounce can lima beans, drained and rinsed
16-ounce can white corn with juice
1 cup celery cut in 1-inch pieces
Salt and freshly ground black pepper
Dash cayenne pepper
1 teaspoon sugar
2 cups heavy cream

Cut up and bone the chickens. Put the chicken bones in 6 cups of water. Cover and bring to a slow boil; skim carefully. Add the carrots, celery, and onions. Simmer for 2 hours, adding 1 teaspoon of salt 15 minutes before the soup is ready. Strain and cool.

Wipe the boned chicken pieces and place in a deep cooking pot. Pour the strained broth over them and bring slowly to a simmer. Skim, reduce the heat, and cook until just tender. Add the tomatoes, lima beans, corn with its juice, and the celery pieces. Simmer for 20 minutes longer, stirring frequently. Season to taste with salt, black pepper, cayenne, and sugar. When ready to serve, add the cream; heat through.

Pour into a large soup tureen. This should be eaten from soup plates.

Mexican Chicken Stew

Not all Mexican dishes are spicy hot; in fact, most of them are not. I have not specified what kind of green pepper to use in this recipe—it can be either a green bell pepper or a green jalapeño, and therein lies the spiciness. Either way, the dish is good. I would serve this with Spoon Bread Soufflé, or some other cornmeal dish, and a green vegetable.

Serves 6

5-pound roasting chicken, cut into 8 pieces
Lard
2 large whole onions
2 garlic cloves, finely minced
1 tablespoon unbleached all-purpose flour
2 tablespoons tomato paste or sauce
1 cup water
3 to 4 cloves
1 tablespoon cider vinegar
1 cup sherry
1 large green pepper, sliced in half
Salt and freshly ground black pepper
12 pitted black olives
Handful seedless raisins

In a skillet, fry the chicken pieces in hot lard. Remove from the pan and place in a deep flameproof casserole.

In the same skillet sauté the onions and garlic, and add the flour. Add the tomato paste or sauce and water as soon as the flour is browned. Mix thoroughly; bring to a boil and pour over the chicken. Add the cloves, vinegar, sherry, and green pepper. Add salt and pepper to taste.

Cover the casserole and simmer until the chicken is tender, about 1½ hours. About 15 minutes before serving, add the olives and raisins.

Chicken Stew with Vinegar

Granted, it sounds terrible, but the big surprise is that the combination works so well. It just has to be tried to be appreciated.

Serves 4

12 large anchovy fillets
Whole milk
1 teaspoon finely minced garlic
¾ cup white wine vinegar
2½-pound fryer, cut into 8 pieces
2 teaspoons salt
¼ cup unbleached all-purpose flour
¾ cup olive oil
1 teaspoon ground rosemary
¼ teaspoon freshly ground black pepper

In a bowl soak the anchovies in milk to cover for 10 minutes; drain and discard the milk. Mash the anchovies with the garlic into a smooth paste; stir in the vinegar and set aside.

Wash and dry the chicken pieces. Season with salt and dust lightly with flour.

Heat the olive oil in a heavy frying pan. Add the rosemary, pepper, and chicken. Brown the chicken on all sides. Reduce the heat to moderate; cover and cook, turning the chicken pieces occasionally, for 20 minutes, or until tender. (Check the white meat, as it cooks faster than the dark, and remove it about 2 to 3 minutes earlier.) Remove the chicken and keep hot.

Pour out a little more than half the oil from the pan. Add the garlic-anchovy-vinegar mixture to the remaining pan juices. Stir, scraping the pan bottom for browned particles, and cook over moderate heat for 10 minutes, or until the liquid is reduced by half. Add the chicken pieces to the sauce and cook over very low heat for 2 minutes, stirring. Remove the chicken and arrange on a hot platter with a cover. Pour the sauce over the chicken and serve in a covered casserole.

I LIKE turkey twice a year, once at Thanksgiving, and again at Christmas. It's always been a mystery to me why people prefer the white meat; compared with dark, I think it lacks moisture, flavor, and texture.

In buying a turkey, look for one that is young and plump-breasted and that has not been frozen or pumped full of "self-basting" fluids. That is a large order in itself. I try to avoid those packaged turkeys with the pop-up thermometer inserted in the breast because they tend to be overcooked.

The ideal size is a 14- to 16-pound bird, but obviously the number of guests determines the size of the turkey you buy. Allow ¾ of a pound to 1 pound per person; no one is going to eat that much, but the bones make up part of the weight.

Today the plastic wrapping on most turkeys gives instructions for roasting; they are certainly all right, although it is my experience that most of them err on the side of overcooking.

Boiled Turkey with Butter Sauce

Better than boiled chicken because it's more flavorful and there's more to it. This is one way to guarantee having a nice, moist turkey.

1 hen turkey (not more than 10 pounds)
4 carrots, peeled and chopped
3 small white onions
2 white leeks, trimmed, split, and carefully rinsed
6 ribs celery
6 sprigs parsley
Pinch thyme
½ bay leaf
1 small slice salt pork
Parsley bunches for garnish

For the Butter Sauce

½ pound butter
Grated rind of 2 lemons
Salt and freshly ground black pepper
Dash nutmeg
Pinch unbleached all-purpose flour
2 tablespoons chopped chives

Clean the turkey and tie securely. In a large pot, place the carrots, onions, leeks, celery, parsley, thyme, bay leaf, and salt pork. Cover with warm water and let come slowly to a boil. Skim carefully and let simmer for 2½ hours, or until quite tender. Remove the turkey to a large platter.

Strain the juice and remove all the grease. Replace the turkey in a large pot and cover with the strained juice.

To make the sauce, clarify the butter by heating and skimming off any foam that rises to the surface. Let stand a minute, then pour off the clear part, being careful not to take any of the milky sediment. Pour into a saucepan, add the lemon rind, salt, pepper, nutmeg, and flour. Heat and, when ready to serve, add the chives.

Before serving, reheat the turkey in its broth to the boiling point; remove to a large platter, discard as much of the skin as possible, and decorate with large bunches of parsley. Pour a spoonful of broth over it and serve the remaining broth in individual bowls; serve the sauce separately.

Basic Roast Turkey

I cook my turkeys via the fast or high-heat method. The standard technique calls for a 325°F. oven and allows 20 minutes to the pound to determine cooking time. I prefer starting high and not going below 350°F., and generally allow only 15 minutes to the pound because there's less risk of having a dried-out, overcooked bird.

14- to 16-pound turkey
Salt and freshly ground black pepper
Lemon juice
Stuffing of choice (see pages 119–121)
½ pound butter, divided

Preheat the oven to 475°F.

Wash and dry the turkey thoroughly inside and out. Rub the inside of the bird with salt and pepper and a little lemon juice before stuffing. Fill the breast cavity of the turkey, fold the neck skin over the opening, and sew or skewer it down carefully. Stuff the body, but not too full, as most stuffings swell during the roasting. Truss and sew, or use aluminum pins, lacing them with white string and tying securely.

Place the bird breast-side up in a roasting pan containing at least ¼ pound of melted butter. Rub the turkey all over with the remaining ¼ pound of butter (melted or soft).

Bake in a very hot oven for about 30 minutes, or until the breast is light golden brown, basting occasionally with melted butter in the pan.

Turn the bird over carefully, breast-side down, and continue roasting until the back is lightly browned. Then salt and pepper the back, turn the bird breast-side up again, and salt and pepper the breast. Add more butter if necessary for basting.

Reduce the heat to 350°F. and continue roasting, basting occasionally.

To determine the cooking time, allow 15 to 20 minutes to the pound. The turkey is done when the internal temperature reaches 160°.

During the roasting process, it is a good idea to make a tent covering of aluminum foil to prevent the breast from browning too rapidly. This covering should not be applied until after the first 30 minutes of cooking, and should be removed during the last 30 minutes to give that wonderful golden color that everyone wants to see.

Let the finished bird rest for at least 20 minutes to let the juices settle before carving.

Boned, Rolled Turkey with Sausage Paste Stuffing

When I first decided to do this, I simply did it. No one had showed me how to bone a turkey, and I could find no directions in any book that I owned. I found that it is not in the least difficult and needn't take very long. Follow the directions in the recipe and I guarantee you will be successful. There is one giant advantage to boning the turkey and that shows up in carving—no bones to deal with means infinitely easier slicing.

The paste stuffing should be made first before the turkey is boned, because it is a cooked stuffing and must cool before it is spread over the turkey and rolled up.

Sausage Paste Stuffing

2 tablespoons butter
1 medium onion, minced
3 ribs celery, minced
½ pound mushrooms, cleaned and chopped
2 pounds unseasoned pork sausage
16-ounce can whole-berry cranberry sauce
Salt and freshly ground black pepper

Melt the butter in a medium skillet and sauté the onion and celery until limp and translucent. Add the chopped mushrooms (after putting them in a cloth and wringing out the moisture) and sauté until they have lost their raw taste (3 or 4 minutes). Remove from the skillet and reserve.

Cook the sausage in the same skillet until all the pink changes to gray. Add salt and pepper to taste. Add the sautéed vegetables, mushrooms, and the cranberry sauce. Continue cooking, stirring occasionally, until the liquid from the cranberry sauce has reduced by half. Remove from the heat; taste for seasoning and allow to cool.

To Bone and Roll a Turkey

Lay the bird on its breast. Using strong poultry shears, cut up the back from the tail to the neck cavity. Do not try to cut up the exact center because you cannot cut through the backbone, but start the shears on either side and cut as close as possible all the way up the backbone.

Once the cut is complete, force the rib cage open wide enough so that it remains open when you release the sides. Now work to the left or right, using a sharp boning knife, and remove the skin and meat from the bones. Be careful not to cut through the skin as you work; you don't want the stuffing to leak out during cooking.

Leave the wings, thighs, and legs until last. When the rib cage and back have been completely removed and the body is flat, remove the two end sections from the tip ends of the wings and reserve them to cook during the roasting. The section of the wing remaining should be slit on the up-side of the bone from the tip of the joint to the body. Now slit the up-sides of the legs and thighs the same way. Remove the bones, and the turkey is ready to be spread with the stuffing paste, rolled, and roasted.

Pile the sausage stuffing mixture about 1 inch thick over the inside of the bird, slathering it to within 2 inches of the outside edge. Fold the bird from left to right about two thirds of the way across the stuffing mixture. Now fold from the right, pulling as tight as possible without squeezing the stuffing out. Pin across the fold with skewers, about 1 inch apart, from the bottom to the top; lace with string to hold in place. (Pinning and lacing will help tighten the rolling process.)

Now bring the skin flap from the neck of the bird back to cover the top opening; skewer in place. Turn the turkey over on its back and skewer the remaining opening (where the innards were removed in cleaning).

Preheat the oven to 400°F. Place the turkey breast-side up on a broiling pan. *Do not use a roasting pan;* the sides make it difficult to remove the bird after cooking.

A 20-pound boned, rolled turkey takes about 2 hours and 45 minutes. If the bird is browning too fast, make a tent of aluminum foil and lay it over the turkey. Don't cook the turkey with a thermometer inserted in it; that simply allows the juices to flow out. Use an instant-reading thermometer, and only insert it in the dark-meat area, close to the end of the cooking time, just long enough to check the temperature. The turkey is done when the reading is 160°.

When the turkey is cooked, carefully remove all the skewers and lacing string. Allow to rest for 15 to 20 minutes before carving and serving. The turkey will continue to cook for some minutes after it is removed from the oven; the standing time allows the juices to settle.

Note: The sausage stuffing can be transformed into a super stuffing for chicken, capon, or wild or domestic duck by adding about 10 ounces of fresh crumbled white or whole wheat bread. It is also very nice with pork chops; when I use it, I bake the chops, prepare the stuffing on the stove top, and then combine the two for the last 10 minutes in the oven.

NOW we get to the good part. If turkey is a bit too predictable, stuffings are another story. I like all sorts of stuffings, although admittedly some are better than others. Unfortunately, there was a time when sage was the principal seasoning in all stuffings and many cooks tended to be heavy-handed. Stuffings take imagination and a great deal more care in preparation than many realize. They should always be moist, buttery, and never overseasoned.

Wild Rice Stuffing

Since roasting a turkey is usually an indication of a special occasion, spring for some wild rice and try this stuffing. It is a delicious combination of flavors and textures.

Enough for a 14-pound turkey

3 cups wild rice
4 quarts cold water
2 tablespoons salt
¼ pound plus 4 tablespoons butter
3 tablespoons finely chopped onion
¾ cup finely chopped celery
3 tablespoons finely chopped parsley
Salt and freshly ground black pepper

Wash the wild rice thoroughly in several waters. Bring to a boil in cold water and salt. Do not stir, but shake the pan occasionally to avoid sticking. Cook for 15 minutes, counting from the boiling point. Drain well in a colander and return the rice to the pan, shaking it over low heat to dry it a little.

Melt the butter in a small frying pan and cook the onion slowly for 5 minutes, stirring constantly to avoid browning. Add the celery and cook a minute longer. Then add all the wild rice, stirring constantly with a fork. Add the parsley, and season with salt and pepper. Mix well and stuff the cavity of the turkey.

Potato Stuffing

If you like mashed potatoes and plan to serve them with a turkey, this recipe is ideal. It takes care of everything in one swoop.

Enough for a 14-pound turkey

16 medium potatoes, peeled and quartered
18 slices bacon
1 medium onion, chopped
¼ pound butter
1 cup heavy cream
1 tablespoon chopped parsley
Salt and freshly ground black pepper

Cook the potatoes in boiling salted water until tender; drain. Fry the bacon until crisp; drain on paper towels and break into small pieces. Brown the onion lightly in the bacon fat. Mash the potatoes, adding the butter and cream. When light and fluffy, add the bacon, parsley, and onions. Season to taste with salt and pepper; blend thoroughly.

Stuff the cavity of the turkey.

Orange–Sweet Potato Stuffing

I do not recommend this stuffing if the menu is going to include sweet potatoes as a side dish, but if the turkey is stuffed with this combination, then the cook is free to have another traditional side dish, such as corn bread dressing baked in a casserole or Spoon Bread Soufflé.

Enough for a 14-pound turkey

6 to 8 sweet potatoes
Grated rind of 1 lemon
Grated rind of 1 orange
Pulp of 3 navel oranges (cut in half crosswise and scooped out)
Salt and freshly ground black pepper
¼ pound butter
2 tablespoons cognac

Peel and quarter the potatoes; cook in boiling salted water until tender; drain. Put the cooked sweet potatoes through the potato ricer into a large bowl. Add to them the lemon and orange rind and the orange pulp, seasoning to taste with salt and pepper. Add the butter cut in pieces and sprinkle with cognac. Toss with a large fork. Do not mash the potatoes.

Stuff the cavity of the turkey.

Note: Make a clear gravy for the turkey in the usual manner, substituting 1 cup of strained orange juice for part of the water or stock.

Whole Wheat–Pecan Stuffing

Fancy, and maybe a bit outrageous if you use the chopped truffles called for in the recipe. Even without the truffles, this is a very good stuffing. However, under no circumstances substitute black olives for truffles. They do not do the trick.

Enough for a 14-pound turkey

4 medium slices firm whole wheat bread
1/3 cup whole milk (approx.)
1/2 pound sliced boiled ham, finely chopped
2 hard-cooked eggs, finely chopped
4 small white onions or 6 scallions, finely chopped
4 to 6 tablespoons butter
2 tablespoons finely chopped parsley
Salt and freshly ground black pepper
1/4 pound salted pecans, coarsely chopped
3 chopped truffles (optional)
1/2 cup brandy

Barely moisten the bread in milk and squeeze dry. Place in a bowl and add the ham. Mix well and add the eggs. Cook the onions slowly in butter without browning. Add the parsley and blend thoroughly. Add the mixture to the bowl of bread and season to taste with salt and pepper. Add the pecans and truffles, if used. Add the brandy last. The stuffing should be moist and fall apart easily.

Turkey Fillets in Lemon Sauce

Buy the breasts already filleted at the market, or buy the whole breast and fillet it yourself. It is easier if the breast is partially frozen, but with a good sharp knife it isn't too difficult to cut completely thawed. In taste and texture turkey fillets are similar to young veal and are far less expensive.

Serves 4

- ***6 thin fillets turkey breast***
- ***Salt and freshly ground black pepper***
- ***1/4 cup unbleached all-purpose flour***
- ***4 tablespoons butter, divided***
- ***2 tablespoons olive oil***
- ***2 tablespoons lemon juice***
- ***4 tablespoons finely chopped parsley***
- ***18 thinly cut lemon slices***
- ***4 anchovies, chopped***

Cut the turkey fillets into 2½-inch squares; season with salt and pepper. Coat the pieces very lightly on both sides with flour. Heat 2 tablespoons of the butter with the oil in a large, heavy skillet until bubbling hot. Sauté the fillets until golden brown (2 to 4 minutes). Remove to a warm serving platter.

Pour the fat out of the pan. Add the remaining butter, lemon juice, and parsley and heat through. Arrange the turkey squares and lemon slices in an alternating pattern, and pour the pan juices over them. Garnish with anchovies.

Turkey with Tuna Sauce

This is an inexpensive version of Vitello Tonnato, a classic Italian dish. It is made the same way and tastes almost identical to the veal traditionally used in this dish. It is not the "poor man's version," simply another dish with the same theme.

Serves 6

6 thin fillets turkey breast
Salt and freshly ground black pepper
4 tablespoons butter
2 tablespoons vegetable oil

Tuna Sauce

2 egg yolks at room temperature
3 tablespoons lemon juice, divided
½ teaspoon dry mustard
½ teaspoon salt
¼ teaspoon freshly ground black pepper
1 cup olive oil
3½ ounces drained, canned tuna, mashed
2 to 3 anchovies, mashed, or 1½ teaspoons anchovy paste
1 tablespoon capers

Season the turkey lightly with salt and pepper. Sauté in very hot butter and oil until golden on both sides (2 to 5 minutes). Arrange in one layer on a very large serving platter and let cool to room temperature.

To make the sauce, prepare a very thick mayonnaise by beating the egg yolks until thick and lemony in color. Add half the lemon juice and the seasonings and beat well. Add the oil drop by drop, stirring continuously. Add the tuna to the finished mayonnaise with the remaining lemon juice. Stir in the anchovies or anchovy paste. Cover the turkey fillets completely with the sauce and sprinkle with capers. Keep in the refrigerator at least 3 to 4 hours and remove 20 minutes before serving.

Goose with Onion and Sage Stuffing

This recipe applies to wild or domestic geese, but the wild are never predictable because one never knows the age of the bird. It has been my experience that most wild geese tend to be pretty tough, and although the sage and onion stuffing can eliminate any unpleasant gamy taste, nothing seems to really tenderize the birds if they are on the tough side. Because all geese, wild or domestic, have a heavy fat coating, it is wise to puncture the bird all over as the cooking starts. I know of no other way to extract the fat that must come out before the finished dish is served.

Serves 6

10- to 12-pound goose
6 large onions, boiled until tender, drained, and finely chopped
6 fresh sage leaves or ½ teaspoon dried sage
1 teaspoon salt
1 teaspoon sugar
1 teaspoon prepared mustard
Freshly ground black pepper
1 large apple, pared and finely chopped
Dash nutmeg
2 cups fine bread crumbs
2 tablespoons melted butter
1 small lemon, peeled (retain as much of the thick white part as possible)
1 large strip salt pork
Unbleached all-purpose flour
1 cup hot water
1 teaspoon dry mustard
Pinch cayenne pepper
3 tablespoons Port

Preheat the oven to 500°F.

Singe, wash, and dry the goose inside and out. Lightly mix together the onion, sage, salt, sugar, mustard, pepper, apple, nutmeg, bread crumbs, and melted butter. Stuff the cavity of the goose with this mixture, placing the lemon in the center of the dressing.

Sew up the bird, truss well, cover the breast with the salt pork, and bake for 45 minutes.

Remove from the oven, pour out all the fat that has accumulated and discard the fat and the strip of salt pork. Sprinkle the goose with salt and pepper, dredge with flour, and return to the oven. Reduce the heat to 350°F. When the flour has browned, add the hot water and baste the goose often. Continue cooking for 3 hours.

When ready to serve, mix the dry mustard with a little water until smooth. Add the cayenne and Port and heat gently. Make a slit in the apron of the goose, remove the lemon, and pour the hot Port mixture into the body of the bird.

Garnish and serve hot with the following gravy.

Gravy for Goose with Onion and Sage Stuffing

1 large onion, sliced
1 teaspoon butter
1 pound beef, cubed
1 pint boiling water
Parsley
Pinch thyme
1 whole clove
3 peppercorns
1 tablespoon butter
1 tablespoon unbleached all-purpose flour

Lightly brown the onion in butter with the beef. Add the boiling water and skim off the fat; add the parsley, thyme, clove, and peppercorns. Simmer for 1 hour, or until reduced to about 1 cup. Strain and add the drippings from the goose, skimmed of all the fat. Reserve this liquid. Make a roux of the butter and flour. Cook together for several minutes and add the reserved liquid to make a gravy. Simmer for a few minutes and serve with the goose.

FISH AND SHELLFISH

NO food has been so maligned or badly treated as fish, and yet the guidelines for preparing it couldn't be more streamlined: a real case of "less is more." The fact that so many kinds of fish may be eaten raw lets us know. that fish requires minimal cooking, but more often than not, it is overcooked until it is dried out and tasteless, or is over-breaded and deep-fried to a fare-thee-well. Recently I had a meal where the fish tasted exactly like gun oil. That's pretty hard to do, and more's the pity, since the cook could have used that energy to produce a natural, fresh taste.

Cooking fish well is an art easily achieved by any cook simply by following a few basic rules. First of all, start with fresh fish. Contrary to what many people think, you can't always go by smell, because some fish have a strong "fishy" odor that can be removed simply by a light rinsing in water with a squeeze of lemon juice. To determine freshness, check the eyes; they should be clear. If the eyes are milky, it is a pretty good indication that the fish is not fresh. For this reason, never buy a whole fish that has already had the head removed.

I grew up eating fish poached in milk. Whatever the fish was, I remember that it was seasoned only with butter, salt, and pepper, and it was very tasty. The method was simple enough so that the flavor of the fish predominated, and that is what is essential to well-cooked fish.

The best rule for cooking was developed in Canada and is therefore known as the "Canadian rule": *allow 10 minutes of cooking time to the measured inch of thickness.* To do this, lay the fish on its side and measure at the thickest part by holding a ruler at the back side and, using a knife laid horizontally on the fish, point directly to the measurement on the ruler. If it is 3 inches, that means 30 minutes of cooking time; if it is 3½ inches, cook for 35 minutes.

To a certain extent, the kind of fish determines the cooking method. Fish with a high fat content, such as sea bass, salmon, or sturgeon, can be baked or broiled, although it is preferable to cover such fish with bacon strips if it is being baked, and baste it from time to time. For leaner fish, baking in a wine stock is a good way to ensure a moist final dish. If a lean fish is being broiled, it is a good idea to coat it with flour and dip it in oil first.

Sautéeing is recommended for small whole fish, fillets, steaks, and for shellfish. They should be coated in seasoned flour or crumbs and cooked at a low temperature in a small amount of butter mixed with oil. These fish can also be oven-fried—in this case, melted butter or fat is poured over the fish and it is cooked in a 450°F. oven until it flakes easily with a fork.

Like fish, shellfish requires a very short cooking time and should not be overcooked. It should be at room temperature before it is cooked. There are all kinds of formulas for preparing cooking liquids for crab, and for the most part I find them too strong. The delicate, sweet natural taste of crab meat should not be overpowered by either the cooking medium or any accompanying sauce. The exception is the spicy mixture traditionally used to cook the Atlantic and Gulf Blue crab. The Dungeness crab, however, is best cooked in water with only a little salt and lemon. The Florida Stone crab and the Alaskan King crab need only salted water, ideally sea water. A cooking time of 12 to 15 minutes in boiling water is enough; crabs continue to cook a bit after being removed from the boil and will become rubbery if cooked too long. All varieties can be frozen and may be used interchangeably in almost any recipe calling for crab meat.

Lobster, considered the ultimate delicacy, also needs only a short cooking time, about 12 minutes, in plain boiling water. Shrimp are done in about 1 minute. Clams and mussels are done the minute the shells open in the steamer. Razor clams should be sautéed for no more than a minute on each side. Scallops are done when they turn from translucent to opaque; allow 1 minute for bay scallops and about 3 minutes for sea scallops.

Seviche

As is, this is a good first course. It is to be found everywhere in the Caribbean and on the west coast of Mexico. An interesting South Seas variation calls for the addition of coconut milk and chopped scallion, carrot, and green pepper. This is very popular in the Pacific Islands, where it serves as a first course or an entire meal.

Serves 4 to 6

- *1½ pounds fillets of sole*
- *1 cup fresh lime juice*
- *½ cup olive oil*
- *¼ cup finely chopped green onion*
- *¼ cup finely chopped parsley*
- *2 tablespoons finely chopped, canned, peeled green chilis*
- *1 garlic clove, finely chopped*
- *1½ teaspoons salt*
- *1 teaspoon freshly ground black pepper*
- *Dash hot pepper sauce*
- *1 tablespoon chopped fresh coriander (or cilantro or Chinese parsley)*

Cut the sole into thin strips about ½ inch wide. Arrange the strips in a baking dish and pour the lime juice over them. Refrigerate for 4 hours, by which time the juice will have turned the fish opaque and made it firm. Drain off the lime juice. Combine the remaining ingredients except the fresh coriander, and pour over the fish, tossing the pieces lightly in the mixture. Chill for 30 minutes, then sprinkle with chopped coriander and serve.

Marinated Salmon

Here is another excellent first course or buffet luncheon dish. It needs some advance planning and should be made only with very fresh salmon. Other very fresh fish such as sturgeon or halibut may be substituted.

Serves 10 to 12 as a first course

3 tablespoons salt
1 teaspoon coarsely ground white pepper
1½ tablespoons plus ½ teaspoon sugar, divided
1 tablespoon plus ½ teaspoon powdered anise, divided
2½ pounds fillet of salmon (one long flat piece with skin and bones removed)
1 teaspoon Dijon mustard
½ cup French Dressing (see page 304)
Chopped parsley for garnish

Two days before serving, mix together the salt, pepper, 1½ tablespoons of the sugar, and 1 tablespoon of the anise. Pat this mixture into both sides of the fillet. Refrigerate for 2 days, turning from time to time.

Remove from the refrigerator, drain off the accumulated liquid, scrape off the seasonings, and dry with paper towels.

Add the remaining ½ teaspoon of sugar, the ½ teaspoon of powdered anise, and the mustard to the French dressing. Combine thoroughly. Arrange the salmon on a platter, pour the seasoned dressing over it, and garnish with chopped parsley.

Cioppino

This California fish stew is very versatile and can take just about anything you want to add to it. I know because I have had it served to me with every possible combination, depending on what was in the market that day. It's up to the cook to vary the ingredients to his or her taste. Try this recipe as I have written it and then decide what you might like to change. You can leave out what you don't like and add what you do.

Serves 12

½ cup olive oil
1 tablespoon chopped garlic
¼ cup chopped parsley
1 tablespoon chopped celery
1 tablespoon chopped green pepper
2 cups solid-packed canned tomatoes
1 cup tomato puree
Salt and freshly ground black pepper
Paprika
1 cup dry red wine
3 sweet basil leaves or 1 teaspoon dried basil
2 dozen clams
1 quart mussels
6 fillets of bass or other whitefish
1 pound cooked crab meat
1 pound raw shrimp, shelled and cleaned
1 pound scallops

Heat the olive oil in a Dutch oven. Sauté the garlic, parsley, celery, and green pepper until lightly browned. Add the tomatoes and tomato puree. Season with salt, pepper, and paprika. Add the red wine and basil. Simmer for 1 hour.

While the sauce is cooking, prepare the seafood. Wash the clams and steam them in a little water until the shells open. Add liquid from the clams to the sauce. Clean and steam the mussels. Cut the fish into pieces.

After the sauce is cooked, add the fish, crab meat, and shrimp and cook until the shrimp change color, about 8 to 10 minutes. Add the clams, mussels, and scallops at the last minute—they should cook for only about 3 minutes. Serve the stew in bowls accompanied by a green salad with Mustard Vinaigrette.

Sautéed Tuna with Tarragon

I was twenty years old before I found out that tuna came any way other than canned. This tuna dish is excellent with tiny new potatoes smothered in butter and glazed small onions. Use the Canadian rule (page 127) to determine the cooking time.

Serves 4

2-pound tuna steak
4 tablespoons butter
⅔ cup dry white wine
1 teaspoon dried tarragon, or 1 tablespoon fresh

Select a tuna steak at least 1 inch thick. Melt the butter in a skillet, add the fish, and brown lightly on both sides over high heat. Meanwhile, soak the tarragon in the wine. When the steak is browned, add the wine mixture and let it cook down rapidly; spoon it over the fish as it cooks. Remove the fish to a hot platter and pour the wine sauce over it.

Baked Tuna

This recipe tastes best with light tuna. If only the dark is available, cut the oil to a couple of tablespoons, since the dark meat contains considerably more natural oil than the light.

Serves 9 to 12

1 medium onion, chopped
3 tablespoons chopped green pepper
3 celery ribs, chopped
½ cup chopped parsley
1 garlic clove, chopped
½ cup olive or vegetable oil
1 teaspoon salt
1 teaspoon freshly ground black pepper
1 teaspoon oregano
1 cup dry red wine
28-ounce can tomatoes
3 to 4 pounds tuna steaks or fillets

Preheat the oven to 350°F.

Sauté the onion, pepper, celery, parsley, and garlic in the oil. Season with salt, pepper, and oregano, and stir in the wine and tomatoes.

Place the fish in a well-oiled baking dish and pour the sauce over it. Bake until the internal temperature of the fish registers 140°, or until the fish flakes easily when tested with a fork, about 45 minutes. Baste frequently during cooking.

It can be served in the dish in which it was baked. Sourdough bread with garlic butter or garlic bread is a good accompaniment.

Fillet of Sole in Herbed Butter

Petrale sole, a large Pacific flounder, is shipped all over the United States. It is desirable because of its delicate flavor and firm texture, which make it easier to handle than other varieties of sole. However, if it's not available, any sole will do. In any case, a nonstick pan makes turning the fish and removing it to a platter easy. You can select from the various herbed butters below the one that appeals to you.

Serves 6

2 pounds fillets of Petrale or lemon sole
Herbed butter (see below)
Salt and freshly ground white pepper

Melt the desired amount of herbed butter in a hot skillet. Quickly sauté the fillets, allowing 1 or 2 minutes per side—*do not overcook.*

Fennel Butter: Combine 4 tablespoons of soft butter with ¼ teaspoon of ground fennel and let stand a few minutes.

Tarragon Butter: Combine 4 tablespoons of soft butter with ¼ teaspoon of dried tarragon and let stand for a few minutes.

Lemon Butter: Combine 4 tablespoons of soft butter with 1 teaspoon of grated lemon peel and let stand for a few minutes.

Baked Halibut

This can be prepared ahead and baked later. It can be either a first course or main course for luncheon or dinner, and is simplicity itself. If it is prepared in advance and refrigerated, let it come to room temperature before it is baked, or the 10-minute cooking time will not be enough.

Serves 4

1 cup sauterne
1 tablespoon salt
1 pound halibut fillets
1 cup mayonnaise
½ cup sour cream
¼ cup chopped onion
Fine bread crumbs
Paprika
Lemon wedges

Mix the wine and salt and marinate the fish for 1 to 2 hours in the mixture.

Preheat the oven to 500° F.

Drain the fish thoroughly on paper towels. Dip both sides in bread crumbs and arrange the fillets side by side in a greased, shallow baking dish. Mix the mayonnaise, sour cream, and onion and spread evenly over the fish. Cover with a thin layer of crumbs. Dust with paprika and bake for 10 minutes, or until the fish flakes when fork-tested. Serve with lemon wedges.

Broiled Scrod

Scrod started out as another name for the catch of the day—what came in on the top of the pile in the fishing boats.

Serves 6

2 young cod, flounder, haddock, or any other white fish, split, with backbones removed
Soft butter
Salt and freshly ground black pepper
1 lemon, quartered, for garnish
Parsley for garnish
Clarified butter (see page 105)

Wipe the prepared fish with a damp cloth and rub well with butter. Season lightly and place skin-side down on a buttered grill.

Place the grill under the broiler and cook until the fish loses transparency; turn over and cook until the skin is brown and slightly crisp. The total cooking time is only a few minutes.

Garnish with quartered lemon and parsley. Serve with clarified butter.

Salmon Fillets with Sorrel or Spinach Sauce

This is an elegant presentation, but should be served only to those who like sorrel and spinach. The salmon makes its own statement and can handle the sauce nicely. Serve the sauce either over, under, or as an accompaniment.

Serves 4

4 thin salmon fillets
Butter

Pound the fillets and sauté in butter for 2 to 3 minutes on each side. Serve accompanied by Sorrel Sauce (recipe follows).

Sorrel Sauce

½ pound fresh sorrel or spinach
4 egg yolks
2 tablespoons lemon juice
½ teaspoon salt
Dash hot pepper sauce
¼ pound butter, melted and hot
½ cup heavy cream, whipped

Thoroughly wash the sorrel or spinach; discard stems and ribs and cook in a dry skillet for 3 to 4 minutes, or until limp. Set aside for later use.

Place the egg yolks, lemon juice, salt, and hot pepper sauce in the food processor.

Process for 3 seconds and, while still processing, pour in the bubbling melted butter. Fold the whipped cream into the finished sauce and add the sorrel or spinach.

TO poach a whole fish it is best to use either water or wine seasoned with vegetables and herbs and brought to a boil. This liquid is called a court bouillon. After the court bouillon has cooked for 15 to 30 minutes, add the fish and immediately reduce the heat to simmer. Never cook fish in boiling liquid, as it toughens the flesh.

When the fish is added, the cooking liquid is again brought to a boil, and the fish is then simmered, allowing 10 minutes to the measured inch (the Canadian rule). Be sure to remove the fish immediately because it will continue to cook even though it is no longer in the liquid.

A final word: there's a mystique about the necessity of court bouillon that I'd like to dispel. The fact is, you can poach fresh fish in plain water, a combination of milk, water, and butter, or in tomato juice for that matter. Don't be stopped from poaching fish because you have no court bouillon on hand. Just remember that the fish itself, plus liquid, is the base of court bouillon.

Court Bouillon for Poached Fish and Shellfish

Makes about 2 quarts

6 cups water
Salt
3 garlic cloves, crushed
1 carrot, peeled and thinly sliced
1 onion, peeled and thinly sliced
10 parsley sprigs
1 bay leaf
1 teaspoon thyme
1 tablespoon fennel seed
½ teaspoon oregano
1 teaspoon freshly ground white pepper
1 leek, trimmed, split, and carefully rinsed
1 rib celery
2 cups white wine

Bring the water to a boil. Add all the ingredients except the wine, and simmer, covered, for about 15 minutes. Add the wine, return to a boil, and continue to cook, covered, for another 20 minutes.

Note: This recipe may easily be doubled or tripled. The amount of bouillon needed depends on the size or quantity of the fish to be cooked.

Cooking Times

For Fish: Follow the Canadian rule of 10 minutes cooking time per measured inch of thickness for all fish.

Bring the court bouillon to a boil, immerse the fish in the hot liquid, and immediately reduce the heat to a simmer. Cover with a tight-fitting lid and continue to simmer until the time is up. Remove from the court bouillon immediately.

Note: The bouillon in which fish has been poached forms an excellent base for soups or sauces.

For Crayfish: First dislodge the central tail flap and pull out the attached thread of intestine. Plunge alive into boiling court bouillon, and cook, covered, for no longer than 5 minutes. Turn off the heat and leave to steep, covered, for another 15 minutes before serving.

For Frozen Lobster weighing 1½ pounds: Thaw, then plunge into boiling court bouillon, reduce heat, and simmer for about 10 minutes. Turn off the heat and leave in the cooking liquid for an additional 20 minutes. Both crayfish and lobster are better served warm with a combination of melted butter and court bouillon mixed in equal portions.

Court Bouillon with White Wine

I sometimes use this stock recipe when I poach frozen fish and am unsure how long it has been in the freezer. A fish that has been frozen for a long time loses much of its natural moisture and this stock helps correct that. However, if the fish is absolutely fresh, plain water is all that is needed.

Makes about 4½ quarts

2 cups dry vermouth or dry white wine
½ cup chopped onion
½ cup chopped carrot
½ cup chopped celery
2 teaspoons salt
8 peppercorns
1 bay leaf
3 parsley sprigs
1 whole clove
½ teaspoon dried thyme
4 quarts cold water

Put all the ingredients into a large kettle and bring to a boil. Boil rapidly for 30 minutes. Cool and strain.

Court Bouillon with Red Wine

Makes about 4 quarts

- *2 pounds fish bones and heads*
- *3 quarts water, divided*
- *1 quart red wine*
- *Bouquet garni (thyme, parsley, leek)*
- *2 ribs celery*
- *1 onion stuck with cloves*
- *3 carrots, cut in quarters*
- *1 tablespoon salt*

Over medium-high heat, cook the bones and heads of the fish in 2 quarts of water for 30 minutes. Add the remaining water and all the other ingredients and continue cooking for 20 minutes. Cool, strain, and reserve the stock.

Cold Poached Salmon

Serves 12

- *1 whole 8- to 10-pound salmon with the head*
- *4 quarts Court Bouillon with Red Wine (see above)*
- *3 envelopes (3 tablespoons) unflavored gelatin*
- *Salt and freshly ground black pepper*
- *1 cup small peas, cooked*
- *1 cup finely cut snap beans, cooked*
- *1 cup finely diced potatoes, cooked*
- *Mayonnaise*
- *12 small tomatoes*
- *4-ounce can whole ripe olives, divided*
- *15 hard-cooked eggs (reserve two yolks for garnish)*
- *4-ounce can ripe olives, chopped*
- *1 cucumber, sliced for garnish*
- *1 to 2 lemons, sliced for garnish*

Wrap the fish in cheesecloth and place it on a rack; poach it in the court bouillon according to the fish poaching technique (page 136). Remove the fish carefully to a large board or platter and allow it to cool. Remove skin, cutting sharply at the tail, and stripping up to the head.

Reduce the court bouillon to about 2 quarts. Clarify it with the crushed shell and white of an egg and strain it through a linen napkin. Dissolve the gelatin in ¾ cup of cold water. Stir 6 cups of the hot court bouillon into it to make an aspic. Season with salt and pepper to taste.

While the aspic is cooling, prepare the garnishes. Mix the peas, beans, and potatoes with enough mayonnaise to bind them stiffly. Peel and scoop out the tomatoes and stuff them with the vegetable salad. Brush the tops with a thin layer of aspic and top each one with a ripe olive. Cut the eggs in half horizontally and remove the yolks (putting 2 aside). Mash the yolks and mix them with salt, pepper, the chopped olives, and mayonnaise. Heap this mixture into the whites or pipe it through a pastry tube. Glaze the tops with aspic.

Brush the salmon with aspic, giving it a thick coating. It is sometimes better to give it a first coating, allow it to set, and then apply a second. Decorate the fish with thin cucumber slices, lemon slices, the remaining ripe olives, quartered, and the reserved hard-cooked egg yolks, sieved.

Shrimp-Stuffed Petrale Sole

Petrale sole lends itself perfectly to stuffing, whereas other types of sole are not always so easy to work with, although they can be used. This recipe, served as a first course, could be followed by lamb, beef, or pork as an entrée.

Serves 6 as a first course

6 medium petrale sole fillets
1 pound cooked baby shrimp
3 cups (approx.) water or fish stock
Salt and freshly ground black pepper
1 recipe Velouté Sauce (see page 311)

Prepare the fillets by folding them around lengthwise and securing them with toothpicks. Leave a center opening about 1 inch across. Place the fillets upright on a square of cheesecloth large enough to encase them. Using the fingers, fill the centers with the cooked shrimp. Do not pack tightly, just fill. Tie the cheesecloth around the fillets, leaving a piece of string so that they can be removed from the poaching liquid.

Place the cheesecloth-covered sole in simmering poaching liquid in a 10-inch skillet with a lid, and poach for about 3 or 4 minutes.

Take the shrimp-stuffed sole from the liquid and remove the cheesecloth. Keep warm until ready to serve. Serve with Velouté Sauce.

Fish Rolls Florentine

I always make this recipe when local spinach first comes on the market. There are many ways to dress up this dish, and I've included several. A word of caution though: don't overcook the fish—no sauce on earth can repair the damage.

Serves 6

6 whole fillets of sole or other whitefish
½ pound sole fillets, chopped
1 pound spinach, parboiled, squeezed dry, and chopped
3 tablespoons softened butter
3 egg yolks
Salt and freshly ground black pepper

Flatten the fillets gently with the blade of a large knife and slit the skin-side membrane at 1-inch intervals. Fit each fillet along the side of a buttered, individual round ramekin, with the skin-side facing in, forming a circular wall, leaving the bottom of the ramekin uncovered.

Preheat the oven to 375°F.

Combine the chopped sole, spinach, butter, egg yolks, salt, and pepper. Pack into the center of the fish-lined ramekins. Cover the ramekins with foil, place them in a large pan of hot water, and poach them in the oven for 10 to 12 minutes, or until the centers are firm to the touch. Unmold onto a flat wire rack or slotted spoon to drain.

Serve with Velouté or White Butter Sauce.

Codfish Stew

Whether fresh or salted, cod is high on my list of fish, and I am always on the lookout for new ways to prepare it. Fresh cod is good just poached, its delicate flavor enhanced with butter, salt, and pepper. Salt cod, like that called for in this recipe, must be soaked for several hours in many changes of fresh cold water to eliminate the excess saltiness.

Serves 8

2 pounds dried salt cod
2 boiled potatoes
1 garlic clove, halved
1¼ cups lukewarm olive oil, divided
Grated rind of 1 lemon
1¼ cups whole milk or light cream
Salt and freshly ground black pepper
¼ cup chopped, pitted green olives
Whole pitted green olives for garnish

Soak the cod in cold water for 12 hours, changing the water frequently. Drain, cover again with cold water, and bring to a gentle simmer. Reduce the heat, cover, and continue to simmer for 1 hour. When done, drain well and pick the fish over carefully, removing bones and any discolored pieces.

Rub the inside surface of a large, heavy enamel pan with the garlic. Pass the potatoes through a ricer or crush thoroughly with a fork into the pan and add the fish, broken into pieces.

With a masher, work the two together vigorously until well mixed. Add 1 cup of the oil, drop by drop, beating continuously. Place the pan on very low heat and beat constantly as it heats. Work in the remaining oil. Add the lemon rind to the milk or cream and heat to the scalding point. Work into the fish mixture. Season to taste with salt and pepper.

When hot and very light and fluffy, pile the "stew" in a mound on a hot platter. Heat the chopped olives in a little oil and sprinkle over the mound. Garnish the edge of the platter with whole olives.

Cod, Potatoes, and Eggs

Try this recipe before you pass judgment. It is a wonderful combination for a Sunday night supper or a lunch any day. All it needs is a green salad with a tangy vinaigrette dressing and a sweet dessert.

Serves 4

1½ pounds dried salt cod
1 bay leaf
Pinch thyme
2 to 3 garlic cloves, peeled and pounded to a puree in a mortar
Large handful chopped parsley
4 hard-cooked eggs, cut into pieces
⅔ cup olive oil, divided
2 pounds potatoes, boiled in their skins, cut in thick slices, and kept hot
Freshly ground black pepper

Soak the cod in water for several hours; then drain and poach it in water with the bay leaf and thyme until the fish flakes easily. Drain, skin, and flake the cod, and keep it warm in a warm oven or over hot water. Mix the garlic puree and parsley together. Add the eggs and stir gently with half the olive oil. In a large skillet, heat the remaining oil over medium heat and add the potatoes. Add the flaked cod and toss to mix. Gently stir in the egg-garlic-parsley mixture. Add pepper generously and turn out onto a heated serving platter.

Note: Salt will probably not be needed since the cod is generally salty.

Codfish Balls

Serves 6

¾ pound dried salt cod
4 medium potatoes, peeled and quartered
1 egg
¼ cup whole milk
Oil for deep-frying

Soak the cod in cold water for 2 hours. Drain off the soaking water and remove any skin and bones from the cod. Combine the fish with the potatoes. Cover with cold water, bring to a boil, and cook until the potatoes are tender. Drain well and mash at once with a wire masher. Beat the egg with the milk and add to the fish. Beat together until light and smooth.

Heat the oil to 375°F. in a large pot or deep-fat fryer. Using a spoon and fork, form small balls of the cod mixture and drop them into the heated oil. No more than 6 balls should be in the pot at the same time. Cook until golden brown. Lift the fish balls out and drain on paper towels in a pan in a warm oven while the remainder are fried.

Turban of Salmon and Sole

Use a pastry brush to completely cover the inside of the mold with oil, and don't be afraid of using too much. If you have to remove or adjust one of the fillets, be sure to add more oil. It is most important that the turban not stick to the sides of the mold.

Serves 8

10 sole fillets
Juice of 1 lemon
Vegetable oil
1½ pounds skinned, boned fresh salmon
2 egg whites
1 cup light cream
2 teaspoons salt
1 teaspoon freshly ground black pepper
1 teaspoon dry tarragon
2 tablespoons chopped fresh parsley
½ pound cooked baby shrimp
½ pound mushrooms, sliced and sautéed

Preheat the oven to 350°F.

Wash the sole fillets in lemon juice and water. Dry and set aside. Brush a 10-inch ring mold with oil. Line the mold with the fillets, placed skin-side up and overlapping, the narrow ends in the center. Set aside.

Grind the salmon. Place in a mixer bowl and beat in the egg whites. Slowly beat in the cream, salt, pepper, tarragon, and parsley. Beat hard to mix well. Spoon into the fish-lined mold and fold the fillet ends over to cover the top. Cover with buttered foil and set in a deep baking pan half filled with boiling water. Bake for about 25 to 30 minutes. When done, let stand for 5 minutes before unmolding. Carefully run a knife around the edges and unmold on a platter. Garnish with shrimp and mushrooms.

Note: To avoid having juices run onto the platter, the mold may be inverted on a wire rack with a pan underneath to catch any liquid.

Smoked Salmon Soufflé

This soufflé is simplicity itself, but its success depends in part on the quality of the salmon used. Select one that is not too oily and does not have an overpowering flavor of the wood used in smoking. If smoked salmon is not available, you can substitute canned salmon, but *not* lox.

Serves 6

½ cup chopped shallots
4 tablespoons butter, divided
1 cup flaked smoked salmon, all bones removed
4 eggs, separated
2 tablespoons unbleached all-purpose flour
1 cup whole milk

Preheat the oven to 350°F.

Sauté the chopped shallots in 2 tablespoons of the butter until they are dark and transparent. Combine the shallots, smoked salmon, and well-beaten egg yolks.

Make a Béchamel sauce (see page 310) using the remaining 2 tablespoons of butter, the flour and milk. Combine the Béchamel and salmon-shallot mixture. Beat the egg whites to stiff peaks. Combine a third of the egg whites with the salmon mixture to bind. Carefully fold in the remaining two thirds.

Bake in a buttered 8-inch soufflé dish for 35 to 40 minutes. Serve immediately.

Codfish Soufflé

Serves 6

2 cups (about ¾ pound) flaked fresh cod
4 tablespoons butter
4 tablespoons unbleached all-purpose flour
1 cup whole milk
Nutmeg
Freshly ground black pepper
4 egg yolks, beaten
6 egg whites
Medium Béchamel Sauce (see page 310)

Preheat the oven to 375°F.

Soak the cod in milk for 30 minutes; drain and poach in water to cover for about 15 minutes. Drain and shred; there should be 2 cups.

Combine the butter and flour in a saucepan over medium heat. When they are well blended, gradually add the milk, stirring until thickened. Season with a little nutmeg and black pepper. Add a little of the hot mixture to the egg yolks. Blend the egg yolk mixture into the sauce. Add the cod. Beat the egg whites until stiff and fold into the mixture. Pour into a buttered 1½-quart soufflé dish and bake for 35 to 40 minutes, or until puffy and brown.

Serve with Béchamel sauce.

Smoked Cod Casserole

This winter dish is one of my favorites. Add boiled potatoes and a green vegetable and finish the meal with something sweet.

Serves 6

2 pounds smoked cod, cut in serving pieces
¼ pound plus 4 tablespoons butter
½ cup plus 1 tablespoon unbleached all-purpose flour
1½ cups white wine
3 cups light cream
Freshly ground white pepper
Grated Parmesan cheese
Homemade Bread Crumbs (see page 335)

Preheat the broiler.

Prepare a modified Béchamel sauce by combining the butter and flour in a 1½ or 2-quart saucepan over medium heat. When the butter is melted and the flour combined, allow to cook for a couple of minutes to get rid of the flour taste. Add the wine, cream, and pepper and cook until the sauce is medium thick.

When the sauce is hot, arrange the pieces of cod in a shallow casserole. Pour the sauce over all and sprinkle with the cheese and bread crumbs. Allow to stand for a few minutes, to heat the cod through, then broil until the cheese is melted and the top becomes a golden brown.

Seafood Casserole

This recipe can be prepared as it is written, or with any substitutions the cook wants to make, depending on what is available. Just make sure there is some contrast in the types of seafood selected.

Serves 8

- *1 teaspoon chopped shallots or green onions*
- *3 tablespoons butter or margarine, divided*
- *10 mushroom caps, sliced thin*
- *1 tablespoon unbleached all-purpose flour*
- *½ cup dry white wine*
- *1 cup water*
- *20 small shrimp, cooked, shelled, and deveined*
- *½ pound fresh, frozen, or canned crab meat*
- *½ pound cooked scallops, sliced thin crosswise*
- *½ pound cooked lobster meat (if available)*
- *12 anchovy fillets, rinsed, dried, and cut up*
- *Juice of 1 lemon*
- *1 teaspoon chopped chives*
- *1 teaspoon Worcestershire sauce*
- *1 tablespoon chili sauce (optional)*
- *¼ cup heavy cream*
- *Salt and freshly ground black pepper*
- *2 tablespoons buttered bread crumbs*
- *2 tablespoons freshly grated Parmesan cheese*

Sauté the shallots in 1 tablespoon of the butter until golden in a heavy skillet. Add the mushrooms and cook for 3 or 4 minutes. Sprinkle with the flour and stir until the flour is absorbed. Blend in the wine and cook until very thick. Add the water and simmer gently about 5 minutes, stirring occasionally, until the sauce is smooth and thick.

Stir in the seafood carefully and simmer over very low heat for a few minutes. Add the anchovies, the remaining 2 tablespoons of butter bit by bit, the lemon juice, chives, Worcestershire, chili sauce, and cream. Season to taste. Pour into a 2-quart casserole, top with the crumbs, sprinkle with the cheese, and brown under the broiler.

Note: If prepared early in the day and refrigerated, bring the casserole to room temperature (allow about 1 hour) and bake it for 20 minutes in a 375°F. oven before broiling it.

Mousseline of Scallops and Sole

This is an excellent first course. It can be baked in small, individual ramekins or in a shallow 1½-quart ovenproof dish. I bake this uncovered because I prefer a brown, slightly crusty top. If you don't, use buttered waxed paper or foil as a cover, but be sure to leave it loose to prevent steaming. No matter how the dish is cooked, a sauce forms in the bottom of the baking container. It is good poured over the top when served.

Serves 6 to 8

1 pound sole fillets
1 pound scallops
1 teaspoon lemon juice
Pinch tarragon
Salt and freshly ground black pepper
2 eggs
1 cup heavy cream

Preheat the oven to 350°F.

Clean the sole and scallops in water to which lemon juice has been added. Pat dry with a paper towel and grind in a food processor. Add tarragon and salt and pepper to taste. Mix thoroughly. Add the eggs and continue to mix until it is the texture of a puree. Whip the heavy cream until stiff and fold into the puree.

Spoon into well-buttered ramekins. Place in a pan filled with hot water halfway up the side of the ramekins and bake for 25 minutes, or until done.

Salmon-Crab Loaf

Here's a recipe where canned salmon is every bit as good as fresh. I have used both and it is impossible to tell the difference. This loaf puffs up like a soufflé, but unlike a soufflé, once spooned into, it does not fall.

Serves 8

1 medium-size onion, chopped
2 to 3 ribs celery, chopped
3 tablespoons butter
16-ounce can salmon
½ pound fresh crab meat
2 cups crushed soda crackers
½ cup whole milk
4 tablespoons chili sauce
4 eggs
Salt and freshly ground black pepper

Preheat the oven to 325°F.

Sauté the onion and celery in the butter until limp.

Drain the salmon (do not run water over it) and combine with the crab, onion, celery, soda crackers, milk, and chili sauce. Mix well. Add the unbeaten eggs and stir until thoroughly mixed. Add salt and pepper to taste. Pour the mixture into a well-greased 2-quart soufflé dish and bake for 1 hour. Serve with Egg Sauce, Cucumber Sauce, or Shrimp Sauce (see pages 322 and 324).

Salmon Mousse

Serves 8 to 12

2 pounds boned, skinned fresh salmon
Salt and freshly ground black pepper
3 cups heavy cream
⅛ teaspoon nutmeg
⅛ teaspoon cayenne pepper
2 eggs
½ tablespoon butter
White Butter Sauce (see page 324)

Preheat the oven to 400°F.

Cut the salmon into 1-inch cubes and add to a food processor or blender. (If you are using a processor, you may process the salmon, cream, seasonings and eggs at one time. If you are using a blender, divide all the ingredients into four parts and blend one quarter at a time.)

Add the salt, pepper, and cream and gradually begin processing or blending. Add the nutmeg and cayenne, and the eggs, one at a time. Process or blend thoroughly.

Grease a 2-quart ring mold with the butter. Spoon in the mousse and smooth the top with a spatula. Clean around the rim of the mold and cut a ring of waxed paper to fit. Butter one side of the paper and place the buttered side directly against the mousse.

Place the mousse in a large round baking dish; add water to a depth of about 2 inches. Bring to a boil on top of the stove, then place the mousse in the water bath in the oven.

Reduce the heat to 350°F. and bake for 45 minutes to 1 hour. Test the center for doneness with a long needle. The needle should come out clean when the mousse is done.

Unmold the mousse into a round dish and spoon about ½ cup of White Butter Sauce over it. Serve the remaining sauce in a sauceboat.

Baltimore Lobster Stew

This is ideal if one has only one lobster and two people. Perfect on a cold winter evening with a light salad and Robert Pamplin Biscuits.

Serves 2

1 small lobster, steamed or boiled
Salt and freshly ground black pepper
Pinch dry mustard
1 cup light cream
1 cup whole milk
Hot buttered biscuits
Sherry

Remove the meat from the lobster shell and cut it into small slices. Put in an enamel pan and sprinkle with salt, pepper, and mustard. Pour the cream and milk over it. Simmer gently for 7 minutes.

Serve in hot soup plates accompanied by hot buttered biscuits. Serve with a small bottle of sherry and let each person flavor his or her stew.

Note: You can substitute ½ pound fresh or frozen crab meat for the lobster.

Scalloped Clams

Serves 6

¼ pound plus 4 tablespoons butter
½ cup toasted bread crumbs
1 cup cracker crumbs
Salt and freshly ground black pepper
Dash paprika
*2 cups minced clams**
2 tablespoons minced onion
2 tablespoons minced parsley
⅓ cup heavy cream

Preheat the oven to 375°F.

Melt the butter and mix it with the bread and cracker crumbs. Add salt, pepper, and paprika. Set aside ⅓ cup of this mixture for the top of the casserole. Mix the remainder with the clams, onion, and parsley. Pour into a well-buttered baking dish and top with the reserved crumb mixture. Dot with butter and pour cream over the top.

Bake for 20 to 25 minutes.

* You can also use canned clams.

Fried Razor Clams

The Pacific Northwest razor clam is best just battered, fried over high heat for a minute on each side, and served at once. Unlike its eastern cousin, it is not good steamed.

Serves 6

1 egg
½ cup whole milk
1 teaspoon salt
Freshly ground black pepper
12 razor clams
2 cups finely crushed saltine crackers
4 tablespoons vegetable oil
2 tablespoons butter

Mix the egg, milk, salt, and pepper. Dip the clams into the egg mixture and then into the cracker crumbs.

Allow the clams to rest for an hour on waxed paper, unrefrigerated. (This will make them crisp when fried.)

Fry the clams in the oil to which the butter has been added. (The mixture should cover the bottom of the pan and be hot, but not smoking.) Fry the clams a few at a time, browning them on both sides. Allow about 1 minute per side.

Clam Fritters

You can use any kind of clam to make fritters, but it seems a shame to use fresh ones when the canned will do just as well. These are good as an appetizer or as an entrée with french fried potatoes, a green vegetable, and coleslaw.

Serves 6

2 eggs, separated
2 cups minced canned or fresh clams
1 cup cracker crumbs
Salt and freshly ground black pepper
Pinch cayenne pepper
Clam juice
¼ pound butter
2 tablespoons vegetable oil

Beat the egg yolks until very light and slowly add the clams, cracker crumbs, and seasonings. Add enough clam juice to make a thick batter. Beat the egg whites until stiff and fold into the batter.

In a skillet heat the butter and oil until hot. Drop the batter by spoonfuls into the skillet and sauté for 4 or 5 minutes, turning once.

Hot Clam Pie

Serves 10 to 12

3 garlic cloves, minced
1 large onion, minced
2 ribs celery, minced
1 large carrot, minced
4 tablespoons butter
2 cups parsley
2 pints clams, minced
3 cups toasted bread crumbs
½ pound bacon, minced
Juice of 1 lemon
3 to 4 bay leaves, chopped
Salt and freshly ground black pepper
1 recipe Plain Pie Crust *(see page 414)*

Preheat the oven to 375°F.

Sauté the garlic, onion, celery, and carrot briefly in butter, without browning. Combine with the other ingredients (except the pastry) and blend lightly. Place in a shallow 1½-quart casserole and top with pie crust. Bake for about 45 minutes, until crust is lightly browned.

Clam Loaf

This recipe is a favorite at festivals, church functions, and potlucks along the northern Pacific coast when razor clams are plentiful.

Serves 8

24 razor clams or 5 pints of steamers, shucked
½ pound pork sausage
½ pound lean ground beef
1 egg
12 rolled soda crackers
Worcestershire sauce
½ teaspoon salt
Freshly ground black pepper
1 onion, minced
½ cup whole milk

Preheat the oven to 350°F.

Chop the clams and combine with the sausage, ground beef, egg, crackers, seasonings, onion, and milk. Mix thoroughly and put in a greased loaf pan. Bake for 1 hour.

French-Fried Butterfly Shrimp

There are two schools of thought when it comes to rinsing shrimp clean. I don't buy the school that says not to clean them. I always run them under cold water, sometimes add a bit of lemon juice to the water to get rid of the accumulations of "fishiness," and always remove the black veins. I don't know that it is all that important, but I don't like to see veins when I am eating shrimp. When frying butterflied shrimp, be careful not to crowd them. It only takes a couple of minutes cooking time, and those that finish first can be kept hot in the oven while the others are cooking.

Serves 4

1 pound fresh or frozen raw shrimp
Salt
1 egg, beaten
1/3 cup fine, fresh bread crumbs
1/4 cup unbleached all-purpose flour
2 tablespoons paprika
Fat for deep-frying

Remove the shells from the shrimp, taking care not to break off the tail meat. With a sharp knife, slit along the back of the shrimp, cutting almost through. Wash away the black veins. Salt the shrimp lightly on both sides.

Beat 1 tablespoon of water into the egg. In another dish, combine the bread crumbs, flour, and paprika and mix well. Dip each shrimp in the egg mixture; then roll in the crumb mixture. Heat fat or oil to 350°F. and fry the shrimp for about 2 minutes, or until golden. Drain on paper towels and keep warm while you finish frying the remaining shrimp.

Gingered Shrimp

This makes an excellent first course. If you use jumbo shrimp, consider using the recipe as a main course and add a minute or two to the cooking time. Large or small, shrimp should be cooked only until they change color, and that's a very short time.

Serves 8 as a first course; 4 as a main course

- *6 tablespoons butter*
- *3 tablespoons finely chopped fresh ginger*
- *2 pounds raw, peeled and deveined shrimp*
- *Salt and freshly ground black pepper*
- *3 tablespoons finely chopped parsley*
- *Toast triangles*

Heat the butter until it sizzles. Sauté ginger briefly. Add the shrimp and continue to sauté just to heat through, about 3 minutes. Season to taste with salt and pepper. Sprinkle with parsley and serve with toast triangles.

Broiled Shrimp

Serves 4

- *1 pound large raw shrimp, washed in cold water*
- *¼ pound butter, melted*
- *½ cup olive or vegetable oil*
- *1 tablespoon chopped shallots*
- *3 garlic cloves, minced*
- *Juice of 1 lemon*
- *Salt and coarsely ground black pepper*
- *1 cup dry white wine, heated*
- *Finely chopped parsley*

With scissors, snip open the shells of the shrimp from head to tail along the center of the back and remove the black vein with the point of a knife, discarding the shells. Rinse the shrimp in cold water and dry.

Pour the butter mixed with oil over the bottom of a flat ovenproof dish. Sprinkle the dish with the shallots and garlic. Roll the shrimp in butter and oil until they are well coated, to prevent their sticking together. Squeeze the lemon juice over them.

Place the dish under a hot broiler for 4 minutes. Remove. Sprinkle lightly with salt and pepper. Turn the shrimp over and grill them for 3 minutes on the other side, or until they are a light brown. Remove from the broiler, sprinkle lightly again with salt and pepper, and pour the hot wine over them. Place under the broiler again for just a few seconds. Remove, sprinkle with chopped parsley, and serve.

Shrimp Steamed in Vermouth

This is a particularly good way to prepare shrimp. Following the cooking directions will yield a "just right" shrimp that can be served hot or cold, with additional seasonings or "as is." The cooked shrimp can be added at the last minute to a fish soup or broth, or to a cream sauce served over toasted bread or muffins.

Serves 4 to 6

1 cup dry vermouth
1 cup water
1/3 cup thinly sliced yellow onion
1/3 cup thinly sliced celery
1/3 cup thinly sliced carrots
3 parsley sprigs
1 bay leaf
1/4 teaspoon thyme
3 peppercorns
2 pounds fresh shrimp

Simmer dry vermouth, water, onion, celery, carrots, parsley, bay leaf, thyme, and peppercorns in a tightly covered enamel casserole for 15 minutes. Add the shrimp in their shells and simmer, covered, for 4 to 5 minutes, shaking the casserole frequently.

Let shrimp cool in the cooking liquid. Peel and devein the shrimp and serve hot or cold.

Note: It is important to use enamel cookware for this dish.

Curried Shrimp Soufflé

I first had this dish at a dinner in Honolulu, and the hostess cautioned that it was only really good if the curry powder was fresh and of good quality. You know, she was dead right. I tried it and purposely used an ordinary commercial brand, and it was a near disaster. It is a wonderful dish when the ingredients are right.

Serves 4 to 6

1½ cups yogurt, beaten
2 teaspoons dark brown sugar
¼ cup freshly grated coconut
¼ cup grated toasted coconut
2 tablespoons olive oil, divided
2 tablespoons butter
2 medium onions, chopped
1 garlic clove, chopped
2 teaspoons curry powder (see Note)
2 tablespoons finely chopped fresh ginger
3 tablespoons unbleached all-purpose flour
2 tablespoons whole milk
4 egg yolks
¾ cup cooked, pureed peas
1 cup shelled, cooked, chopped shrimp
6 egg whites
Salt
Cayenne pepper
Chopped parsley

Put the yogurt, brown sugar, and both kinds of coconut into a bowl. Stir well and set aside for at least an hour. Brush an 8-inch soufflé dish with a little of the olive oil and set aside in a warm place.

Preheat the oven to 375°F.

Melt the butter and the rest of the oil in a heavy pan. Add the onion and garlic and cook slowly for 2 to 3 minutes. Stir in the curry powder and cook slowly for another 2 to 3 minutes. Add the ginger, carefully stir in the yogurt mixture, and cook over low heat for about 10 minutes. Mix the flour and milk to a smooth paste and slowly add this to the yogurt mixture. Continue cooking for another 5 minutes, stirring. Add the pea puree and shrimp; mix well.

Beat the egg whites to stiff peaks with the salt and cayenne. Fold into the shrimp mixture and pour into the soufflé dish. Bake for 40 to 45 minutes. Remove and sprinkle with chopped parsley. Serve at once.

Note: The curry powder is extremely important and should be your own favorite blend or the recipe on page 336.

Skewered Shrimp and Ham

For a nice treat, skip the skewers and stir-fry this combination. It works beautifully and takes only a short time—an even shorter time if the shrimp are cooked in fish stock before being shelled and deveined. The seasoning can be adjusted to suit your taste.

Serves 4

20 uncooked shrimp, shelled and deveined
20 1-inch squares of ham (1/4 inch thick)
6 tablespoons butter
Salt and freshly ground black pepper
Dash Worcestershire sauce
2 lemons, halved

Preheat the oven to 350°F.

Thread the shrimp onto skewers, alternating with pieces of ham. Melt the butter and stir in salt, pepper, and Worcestershire. Pour the seasoned butter into a flat baking dish and lay the skewers on the dish.

Bake for 10 to 15 minutes, turning the skewers occasionally and basting the shrimp often with the seasoned butter. Serve with lemon halves.

Whole Shrimp à la Nage

Anything "à la nage" means it's "swimming" in something. In this case, the shrimp is cooked in a liquid that forms the court bouillon, in which the shrimp is served.

Serves 6

2 to 3 carrots, scraped
2 medium onions, very thinly sliced
½ cup parsley sprigs
1 teaspoon thyme
1 bay leaf
1 tablespoon salt
4 peppercorns
4 cups dry white wine
1 to 2 cups water
4 dozen large shrimp in the shell
Butter
Lemon wedges

With the tines of a fork, score the outside of the carrots and slice them very thin. Put the carrots, onions, parsley, thyme, bay leaf, salt, peppercorns, wine, and water in a deep pot over high heat and bring to a rolling boil. Drop in the cleaned shrimp and cook for 3 minutes at the boiling point. Remove at once and arrange in deep serving bowls or soup plates. Ladle over the shrimp some of the cooking liquid with carrots, onions and a dollop of butter. Serve with lemon wedges.

Crab Pâté

Makes about 2 cups

8 ounces Dungeness crab meat
3 hard-cooked eggs
¼ pound butter
½ cup Homemade Mayonnaise (see page 307)
2 tablespoons lemon juice
¼ cup minced parsley
¼ cup minced onion
Salt
Dash white pepper

Rinse the crab meat in cold water and drain. Separate the hard-cooked egg yolks from the whites. Place the yolks, butter, and mayonnaise in the bowl of a mixer or food processor and combine until completely blended. Add the lemon juice, parsley, and onion, mixing until just combined. Chop the egg whites coarsely. Fold the chopped whites and the crab meat into the yolk mixture. Season with salt and pepper.

Place the pâté in a crock and refrigerate overnight to allow the flavors to mellow. After it is removed from the refrigerator, the pâté should stand at room temperature for at least 30 minutes so that the flavor can develop. It will not be as pronounced if the pâté is eaten cold. Serve with sesame melba rounds or other crisp crackers.

Crab Puffs

Makes 36

1 medium onion, minced
1 rib celery, minced
1 tablespoon vegetable oil
½ pound fresh or canned crab meat
½ cup Béchamel Sauce (see page 310)
2 eggs, well beaten
½ teaspoon freshly ground black pepper
½ teaspoon sesame salt
½ cup cracker crumbs
Fat for frying

Sauté the onion and celery in oil until transparent. Drain on absorbent paper. Combine with the crab meat, Béchamel sauce, eggs, seasonings, and cracker crumbs. Shape into bite-size balls and fry in 1 inch of oil in a skillet until golden brown. Drain and serve.

Crab and Mushroom Sandwich

Ideally, this sandwich should be made with fresh crab meat, but since it is not always available, go ahead and use a reliable brand of canned or frozen crab. Once it is mixed with the rest of the ingredients, the fact that the crab is not fresh doesn't make that much difference. Just make sure the cheese is the real thing—not a processed fake.

Serves 6

3 bacon strips, cut in small pieces
4 ounces mushrooms, sliced
¼ cup chopped onions
1 cup crab meat
1 cup (4 ounces) grated Swiss cheese
⅓ cup grated Parmesan cheese
½ cup mayonnaise
6 English muffins or 12 thick slices French bread
Dash cayenne pepper
Dash paprika

Cook the bacon pieces over medium heat until crisp; drain on a paper towel. Sauté the mushrooms and onions in bacon drippings until the mushrooms begin to turn brown. Cool.

Preheat the oven to 400°F.

Mix the crab meat with the cheeses and mayonnaise; combine with the bacon, mushrooms, and onions. Spread the mixture on sliced, buttered muffins or bread. Sprinkle with cayenne and paprika.

Place the sandwiches, open face, on a cookie sheet and bake for 15 minutes.

Note: Shrimp may be substituted for crab meat.

Deviled Crab

This has to be my most favorite dish. James Beard first introduced me to deviled crab, and since that time I have eaten miles of it. It is really a hot salad, and can be made with any kind of fresh crab—Dungeness, King, Blue, or Stone—but try not to use canned crab, the difference is noticeable.

Serves 8

2 pounds Dungeness crab meat
2 cups cracker crumbs
1 cup finely diced celery
¾ cup chopped onion
¼ pound plus 4 tablespoons butter, melted
¾ cup light cream or whole milk
1½ teaspoons dry mustard
½ teaspoon salt
Dash cayenne pepper
2 tablespoons chopped parsley
1 tablespoon chopped green pepper
Dash hot pepper sauce

Preheat the oven to 350°F.

Rinse the crab meat in cold water; drain and combine with the crumbs, celery, and onion. Add the melted butter and cream. Season with the mustard, salt, cayenne, parsley, green pepper, and hot pepper sauce. Mix thoroughly and bake, covered, in a casserole for 30 minutes.

Variations: Combine scallops, shrimp, and crab, or substitute shrimp or scallops for crab meat, making sure the amount totals 2 pounds.

Note: This is best cooked in a shallow casserole. For a crustier top, bake uncovered.

Crustless Crab Quiche

My friend and colleague Marlene Sorosky gave me this prize-winning recipe and it is so good that I include it here.

Serves 6 to 8

8 ounces fresh mushrooms, sliced
2 tablespoons butter
4 eggs
1 cup sour cream
1 cup small-curd cottage cheese
½ cup grated Parmesan cheese
¼ cup unbleached all-purpose flour
1 teaspoon onion powder
¼ teaspoon salt
4 drops hot pepper sauce
2 cups (8 ounces) shredded Monterey Jack cheese
8 ounces fresh or frozen crab meat

Preheat the oven to 350°F.

In a medium skillet, sauté the mushrooms in butter until tender. Remove with a slotted spoon and drain on paper towels.

In a blender or food processor fitted with a steel blade, blend the eggs, sour cream, cottage cheese, Parmesan cheese, flour, onion powder, salt, and hot pepper sauce. Fold in the mushrooms, Jack cheese, and crab meat. Pour into a 10-inch porcelain quiche dish or a 9½-inch deep-dish pie plate.

Bake for 45 minutes, or until a knife inserted near the center comes out clean. The quiche should be puffed and golden brown. Let stand for 5 minutes before cutting into wedges.

Gingered Scallops

This is one of my favorites; it works equally well as a first course or a luncheon main course. You can use either bay scallops or sea scallops, the only difference being that bay scallops cook faster. To refresh scallops before cooking, rinse in water to which 1 teaspoon of lemon juice has been added and pat dry. Bear in mind that scallops take only a few minutes to cook—any longer and you end up with golf balls.

Serves 8 as a first course; 4 as a main course

6 tablespoons butter
3 tablespoons finely chopped fresh ginger
2 pounds bay scallops
Salt and freshly ground black pepper
2 tablespoons finely chopped parsley

Heat the butter until sizzling. Sauté the ginger briefly. Add the scallops and continue to sauté just to heat through. Season with salt and pepper. Sprinkle with parsley and serve with toast triangles.

Note: If you use sea scallops, simply cut them into smaller pieces.

Scallops in Heavy Cream

When I say 2 minutes to simmer the scallops after the liquid comes to a boil, that's just what I mean. Longer and the gems are bounceable, and that's not what you want.

Serves 8 as a first course; 4 as a main course

1½ pounds sea scallops
1 tablespoon chopped shallots
¼ teaspoon salt
Dash white pepper
½ cup dry vermouth
1 cup heavy cream
1 tablespoon unbleached all-purpose flour
4 tablespoons softened butter
Minced parsley

Preheat the oven to 475°F.

Wash the scallops and put in a saucepan with the shallots, salt, pepper, and vermouth. Bring the liquid to a boil, cover the saucepan, and simmer over low heat for only 2 minutes. Remove the scallops with a slotted spoon and set aside.

Cook the liquid remaining in the saucepan over high heat until it is reduced by half. Add the cream to the reduced liquid. Boil rapidly until the cream is reduced and the sauce is the consistency of syrup. Combine the flour and butter. Reduce the heat and gradually stir this mixture, bit by bit, into the cream sauce.

Return the scallops to the sauce; transfer to an ovenproof dish or individual dishes, sprinkle with parsley, heat in the oven for 5 minutes, and serve immediately.

Oysters Rockefeller

I gave up shucking oysters almost before I got started. It's a terrible job and borders on being dangerous, particularly if you lack the proper equipment, namely a thick rubber or double-leather mitt to protect the hand holding the oyster. Only a purist is going to shuck the oysters for this recipe anyway. I buy them either in bulk, when available, or in a jar. By jar, I do not mean canned; I use only fresh oysters.

Serves 6

3 dozen oysters on the half shell
½ 10-ounce package frozen chopped spinach, thawed
½ cup chopped parsley
½ cup chopped scallions
½ cup chopped Boston lettuce
1 garlic clove
Clam juice (optional)
¼ pound butter
1 cup bread crumbs, divided
1 tablespoon Worcestershire sauce
1 teaspoon anchovy paste (optional)
4 drops hot pepper sauce
1 tablespoon Pernod
½ teaspoon salt
¼ cup freshly grated Parmesan cheese
Melted butter
Rock salt

Open the oysters or have them opened for you—but never more than 2 hours before serving. Reserve the oyster juice.

Combine the spinach, parsley, scallions, lettuce, and garlic in a blender or processor with about 2 tablespoons of the reserved juice (use clam juice if there is not enough oyster juice), and blend thoroughly.

Cream the butter in a bowl, blend in ¾ cup of the bread crumbs, and combine with the spinach puree. Add Worcestershire, anchovy paste (if desired), hot pepper sauce, Pernod, and salt. Mix thoroughly. Drain from the oysters any excess liquid that remains; add it to the sauce, and cover each oyster with a spoonful of the sauce. Sprinkle with Parmesan cheese and the remaining ¼ cup of bread crumbs; drizzle with melted butter. (The recipe may be prepared ahead to this point and refrigerated. Bring to room temperature before baking.)

Twenty minutes before you are ready to bake the oysters, spread an ovenproof serving dish with a layer of rock salt and place it in a preheated 450°F. oven to heat the salt. Place the oysters on their half shells on the hot rock salt and return the pan to the oven to bake for about 20 minutes, or until the oysters are lightly browned. Do not overcook.

Baked Oysters

This is generally best made with medium to large oysters; however, if one is using Olympias, the tiny, succulent oysters from Washington State, shorten the baking time to 20 minutes. Be careful not to overcook the oysters or they will become rubbery. If this is to be a first course, bake the oysters in individual shallow dishes.

Serves 6

1 quart oysters, drained
¼ cup chopped fresh parsley, divided
¼ cup finely chopped shallots, divided
Salt and freshly ground black pepper
1½ teaspoons Worcestershire sauce, divided
Dash hot pepper sauce
1 tablespoon lemon juice, divided
4 tablespoons melted butter, divided
1 cup cracker crumbs, divided
Paprika
½ cup light cream

Preheat the oven to 375°F.

Spread half the oysters in the bottom of a greased, shallow 1-quart baking dish; sprinkle with half the parsley, shallots, seasonings, lemon juice, butter, and crumbs. Make second layers of the same ingredients. Sprinkle with paprika. Just before baking, pour the cream into evenly spaced holes so as not to totally moisten the crumb topping. Bake for 30 minutes, or until firm.

Oysters Casino

I use catsup rather than cocktail sauce because I prefer it. I like to taste the oysters, not just feel them, but if you think the dish needs jazzing up, add some cayenne pepper or hot pepper sauce.

Serves 8 as a first course; 4 as a luncheon course

24 oysters on the half shell
Catsup
½ pound butter
½ cup chopped parsley
½ cup chopped green onion
½ cup lemon juice
Salt and freshly ground black pepper
8 to 10 partially broiled bacon strips

Place a spoonful of catsup under each oyster in the shell. Blend the butter with the parsley, onion, lemon juice, salt, and pepper to make a paste. Top each oyster with a spoonful of the paste and cover with a piece of the partially broiled bacon.

Place under the broiler and broil just long enough to heat the oysters and finish cooking the bacon.

Oyster Stew

If only I had a dollar for every oyster stew recipe and method of preparation I've come across. Here is the one I like best, plus a variation. There is no secret to the preparation—it couldn't be more basic. The variation is simply for those who want to think or believe that their oysters are done a bit more.

Serves 4

4 tablespoons butter
1½ pints oysters and liquor
1 cup whole milk
2 cups light cream
Salt and freshly ground black pepper
Cayenne pepper
Chopped parsley or paprika

Heat 4 soup bowls; add a pat of butter to each and keep hot. Drain the oysters, reserving the liquor. Heat the milk, cream, and oyster liquor to the boiling point. Season to taste with salt, pepper, and cayenne. Reduce the heat to low; add the oysters and poach for 2 minutes. Ladle into the heated bowls and add a sprinkling of chopped parsley or paprika. Serve with crisp biscuits or buttered toast.

Variation: Sautéed Oyster Stew—Drain the oysters and reserve the liquor. Combine the drained oysters and butter in a skillet and cook until the edges curl. Combine the reserved liquor with the cream and milk and bring to the boiling point. Season, add the sautéed oysters, and ladle into hot bowls.

Fried Oysters

Oysters, like scallops, become golf balls when overcooked. It only takes 2 to 3 minutes to cook them properly. Use a light hand in cooking these—they should not be deep-fried.

Serves 4

4 dozen oysters, shucked
Unbleached all-purpose flour for dusting
2 whole eggs, beaten
2 cups finely crushed cracker crumbs
6 tablespoons butter
Freshly ground black pepper
8 lemon wedges

Dip the oysters in the flour, then the egg, and then the cracker crumbs. Sauté quickly in butter until golden on both sides. They should be just heated through, not blackened. Season with pepper and serve at once with lemon wedges.

Oyster Pie

Both the East Coast and the West Coast claim this recipe. It doesn't really make any difference where it started, and there are so many variations that I am sure the original couldn't be spotted. I prefer to use small to medium oysters because they are easier to work with and look nicer. Once you try this, you can adjust the seasonings and the amount of flour to suit yourself.

Serves 6 to 8

1½ pints oysters with their liquor
1 teaspoon onion juice
Salt and freshly ground black pepper
1 teaspoon grated lemon rind
Dash mace
Scant ½ cup unbleached all-purpose flour
Butter
1 egg, beaten

Pastry

2½ cups unbleached all-purpose flour
1 teaspoon salt
½ teaspoon baking powder
½ cup lard
¼ pound butter
½ cup ice water

Arrange the oysters and their liquor in a deep 9-inch dish; sprinkle with onion juice, salt, pepper, lemon rind, mace, and flour; dot with butter and paint the edges of the dish with beaten egg.

Preheat the oven to 425°F.

To make the pastry, sift together the flour, salt, and baking powder and work into this the lard and butter with the fingertips. Moisten with ice water until the paste holds together. Roll out the dough on a lightly floured board. Cut 2 inch-wide strips and place around the edge of the dish. Paint the strips with beaten egg. Cover the dish with the remaining dough, secure the edges by pressing them together, and crimp. Cut a few slits on the top, brush the surface with egg, and bake for 10 minutes. Reduce the heat to 325°F. and bake for 30 minutes longer.

Oyster Soufflé

I serve this only as a first course because it is very delicate in both texture and flavor, and does not hold up for a long period of time. Moreover, served in larger amounts it somehow seems to lose its eye appeal, and that should not happen to anything one eats.

Serves 8 as first course

4 tablespoons butter
4 tablespoons unbleached all-purpose flour
Salt and cayenne pepper
1½ dozen oysters, with ½ cup liquor
¾ cup whole milk
½ teaspoon finely chopped sautéed garlic
1 teaspoon chopped fresh thyme, or ¼ teaspoon dried thyme
1 tablespoon chopped fresh parsley
½ cup chopped, sautéed shallots
4 egg yolks
2 tablespoons sour cream
6 egg whites, stiffly beaten
Grated Parmesan cheese
Bread crumbs

Heat the oven to 375°F.

Melt the butter in a pan; remove from heat and stir in the flour. Season with salt and cayenne pepper. Mix in the oyster liquor and milk. Heat to a boil, stirring, and add the garlic, herbs, and shallots.

Beat in the egg yolks. Mix in the sour cream and add the oysters. Fold in the egg whites. Place an oiled collar on an 8-inch soufflé dish and pour in the mixture. Sprinkle with cheese and bread crumbs.

Bake for 45 minutes, or until just firm to the touch. Serve at once.

Oysters in Cream

This is an elegant dish that can serve as a first course, luncheon, or Sunday supper. Don't pass it up simply for want of a patty shell. There is absolutely nothing wrong with using commercially prepared patty shells for this. Very good ones exist for cooks who don't want to attempt puff pastry.

Serves 6 as a first course

1½ dozen oysters with their liquor
4 tablespoons butter
¼ cup unbleached all-purpose flour
½ cup dry white wine
1 teaspoon salt
¼ teaspoon freshly grated nutmeg
2 cups light cream, divided
2 eggs, beaten
6 puff patty shells or toast rounds
Minced parsley

Heat the oysters in their liquor just until the edges curl. Melt the butter in a saucepan, stir in the flour until smooth, and cook until the butter foams. Add the wine, salt, and nutmeg. Stir over low heat. Stir in 1 cup of the cream and cook, stirring constantly, until the sauce has thickened.

Add the oysters with their liquor. Next add enough of the remaining cream to bring the sauce to a smooth consistency. Stir a couple of tablespoons of the sauce into the eggs, then combine with the oysters in sauce. Heat through but do not boil, or the sauce will curdle. Spoon into hot patty shells and sprinkle with minced parsley.

Note: The patty shells can be baked ahead of time and reheated just before serving.

Variation: Use 2 cups flaked cooked crab meat or lobster cut in serving pieces in place of the oysters.

SPECIAL DISHES

ALTHOUGH this may be a bit of a catch-all title, the recipes herein include some of my favorites. You'll find egg and cheese dishes, pastas, rice and bean dishes, cornmeal dishes, and a few others that don't quite fit into the meat, fish, or vegetable categories. Most of these dishes can form the centerpiece of a lunch, supper, or even a dinner, complemented by a salad and a dessert.

Potato Gnocchi

This recipe and its variations make good use of the potato without the usual look or taste. Gnocchi are great with roast chicken and all meat dishes, particularly if the entrée is an Italian specialty.

Serves 6

5 medium potatoes, peeled and quartered
3 quarts boiling water
2 tablespoons plus 1 teaspoon salt, divided
2 egg yolks
1½ cups unbleached all-purpose flour (more, if needed)
6 tablespoons butter, melted (more, if desired)
1½ cups freshly grated Parmesan cheese, divided

Cook the potatoes in boiling water to which 1 tablespoon of salt has been added for about 30 minutes, or until tender. Drain and place in a saucepan. Mash the potatoes over very low heat to get rid of excess water.

Mix together the mashed potatoes, egg yolks, 1 teaspoon of salt, and flour. Knead the mixture well in a bowl and roll by hand on a floured board into long sausage-like rolls about the size of a thick cigar. Cut into pieces about 1 inch long. Press the pieces over the tines of a fork, rolling gently to flute and curve them slightly.

Plunge the gnocchi in an additional 3 quarts of boiling water to which the remaining tablespoon of salt has been added. As soon as they rise to the surface, remove with a slotted spoon; place in a heated serving dish and repeat the process until all the gnocchi are cooked. Add the butter and ½ cup of the Parmesan cheese. Toss and serve accompanied by the remaining Parmesan cheese.

Variations: Gnocchi Bolognese—Serve with 2 cups of Bolognese Sauce (see page 327).

Gnocchi Salvia—Use the same amount of butter but brown it with 1 tablespoon of fresh sage and then toss with the gnocchi.

Gnocchi Piedmontese—Use the same amount of butter but brown it and toss with the gnocchi. Thinly slice ¼ pound of Fontina cheese; place on hot gnocchi. Serve with 2 cups of tomato sauce in a separate bowl.

Gnocchi Buongustaio—After tossing the gnocchi with butter, slice 1 medium white truffle paper-thin and sprinkle on top just before serving. Accompany with 2 cups of consommé in a separate bowl.

Sausages with Vegetable Puree

Serves 4 to 6

¾ pound carrots, cut in 1-inch pieces
¾ pound turnips or rutabagas, quartered
¾ pound potatoes, quartered
4 to 6 tablespoons butter, cut into small pieces
Grilled pork sausages, 3 per serving
Salt and freshly ground black pepper
2 tablespoons chopped parsley

Cook each vegetable separately in boiling salted water for 25 minutes; drain and dry well. Use a processor, or sieve through the medium mesh of a vegetable mill into a saucepan. Stir constantly over low heat until the combination is smooth and well mixed. Add the butter, salt, and pepper. Put into a serving dish, accompanied by grilled sausages and sprinkled with parsley.

Carla's Tamale Pie

This party dish can be made ahead and frozen. However, wait to add the grated cheese topping until the pie is ready to go into the oven. Since it is already cooked, let it defrost for 1 hour, and allow an hour to reheat it in a 300°F. oven.

Serves 8

Meat Sauce

2 tablespoons vegetable oil
2½ tablespoons chopped onion
1½ pounds lean ground beef
1½ tablespoons salt
⅛ teaspoon freshly ground black pepper
2 garlic cloves, minced
2 dashes cayenne pepper
½ teaspoon oregano
2 tablespoons chili powder
28-ounce can whole, peeled tomatoes
8-ounce can tomato sauce
12-ounce can whole-kernel corn
24 whole ripe, pitted olives

Cornmeal Mixture

1 cup yellow cornmeal
½ cup cold water
1 teaspoon salt
1½ cups boiling water

Topping

1½ cups grated mild Cheddar or Jack cheese

To make the meat sauce, combine all the ingredients except the corn and olives and simmer for 1 hour. Add the corn and olives to the finished meat sauce and remove from the heat while preparing the cornmeal mixture.

In a saucepan, mix the cornmeal and cold water; stir in the boiling water and cook over low heat for 10 minutes. Add ½ cup of the liquid from the meat sauce.

Preheat the oven to 325°F.

Combine the cornmeal mixture with the simmered meat sauce. Put in a 3-quart casserole and top with the grated cheese. Bake for 2 hours.

Pizza with Eggplant Crust

Unlike ordinary pizza, this one has a vegetable crust. It makes a nice first-course serving for any Italian dinner, but be sure to serve it hot from the oven. Once it gets cold, it might as well be tossed out.

Serves 8

Crust

8 slices unpeeled eggplant, ½ inch thick
Salt
3 tablespoons unbleached all-purpose flour
3 to 4 tablespoons olive oil
Freshly ground black pepper

Topping

8 tomato slices, ½ inch thick
16 flat anchovy fillets
16 ripe olives, pitted and halved
1 tablespoon chopped fresh oregano or basil or 1 teaspoon dried
1 teaspoon freshly ground black pepper
2 tablespoons freshly grated Parmesan cheese
8 thin slices mozzarella cheese

Sprinkle the eggplant slices generously with salt. Cover with a dish and a heavy weight and leave for 30 minutes. Press out the bitter juice and drain. Wipe the slices dry and dredge in flour. Fry in oil until golden brown. Season generously with pepper and very sparingly with salt.

Preheat the oven to 325°F.

Arrange the eggplant slices in a single layer in an oiled baking dish. Cover each slice with a tomato slice. Decorate with two crisscrossed anchovy fillets and place 4 olive halves between the anchovies. Sprinkle with herbs, pepper, and Parmesan cheese. Cover each "pizza" with a slice of mozzarella cheese. Bake for 10 to 15 minutes, or until the mozzarella has melted.

EGG DISHES

We use eggs daily in countless ways in breads, pastries, soups, desserts, in soufflés, as garnishes, and as thickening agents—as well as the main entrée of a meal. Only in America are eggs associated almost exclusively with breakfast. In other countries, egg dishes are more likely to appear as the main course of a lunch or dinner, which is how I often enjoy them. I've included recipes here for first-course dishes, for main-dish meals for lunch or dinner, and for brunches and breakfast. As with almost everything else, the secret of eggs is proper cooking, and since hard-cooked eggs are the most abused eggs of all, I give a recipe for preparing them (see page 183).

Eggs Surprise

This is as fancy as I ever get in the kitchen, and the occasion has to be special before I go to this much trouble, but the results are spectacular.

Serves 12 as a first course

12 extra-large or jumbo eggs
1 cup plus 2 tablespoons heavy cream
1 cup plus 3 tablespoons consommé
3 tablespoons butter, melted
¼ cup dry Marsala wine
½ teaspoon freshly ground white pepper
¼ teaspoon freshly grated or ground nutmeg
1½ cups unbleached all-purpose flour
½ cup water
6 slices white bread, crusts removed, each slice buttered, quartered, and toasted

Puncture a small hole on the large end of each egg with a small needle or pin. Make a larger hole at the other end, using a fine knitting needle, nut pick, or a similar sharp-pointed instrument. This must be done very carefully. The best procedure to follow is to first make a very small opening and then remove tiny bits of the shell until you have an opening approximately ¼ inch in diameter. Try to avoid making small lateral cracks.

Blow hard through the smaller holes of 9 of the eggs, so that the egg yolks and whites come out through the larger hole into a bowl. Set them aside to use for omelets or for other purposes. Repeat the process with the 3 remaining eggs, reserving the yolks and whites; these will be used in the fillings. Beat these 3 eggs very lightly.

Lightly mix the beaten eggs, cream, consommé, butter, Marsala, pepper, and nutmeg. Put this mixture in a pastry syringe and refill the egg shells through the larger holes. Stir the filling lightly but frequently during this operation, as the ingredients tend to separate. Avoid making the mixture frothy. As each egg is filled, replace it in the egg carton, pin-hole down.

Mix together the flour and water and knead into a dough. Roll scant tablespoons of dough into 12 small balls. Pinch part of each ball into a small, pointed cone. Insert the point of the dough ball into the large opening of each egg. Gently flatten the dough around the top of the egg until it is not quite halfway down the egg. Wet your fingers in water and press the edges of the dough firmly to each egg so that it will adhere. It is very important that the dough sticks tightly at the edges. Replace the eggs in the carton, dough-side up, and let the dough dry completely. Do not place the eggs in the refrigerator.

Place the eggs, dough-side up, into a small 12-cup muffin tin. Since the eggs do not fit perfectly into the muffin-tin cups, line the sides of each cup with folded aluminum foil, so that the eggs will not bounce around when cooking.

Place the muffin tin on the bottom of a large, deep pot or a roasting pan that has a cover. Add cold water to the pan, being careful not to pour it on top of the eggs, until the water comes just below the dough caps of the eggs. Bring the water slowly to a simmer. Turn off the heat, cover the pan tightly, and let stand for 5 minutes.

Carefully remove the eggs from the muffin tin and place each, dough-side down, in an egg cup or demitasse cup with a saucer underneath. Accompany the eggs with buttered toast squares.

Note: Thin Italian bread sticks (*grissini*) wrapped in very thin slices of lean prosciutto may be substituted for the buttered toast squares.

Eggs Scrambled with Tomato and Basil

Use only tomatoes that are ripe yet firm to the touch, or canned tomatoes. If canned tomatoes are used, add one fresh tomato to give a fresher taste. The olive oil can be mixed half and half with vegetable oil to cut the flavor if it seems too strong, and if fresh basil is not available, use 1 teaspoon of dried instead of the fresh called for in the recipe.

Serves 4

3 to 4 medium tomatoes, peeled, seeded, and chopped coarsely
Salt and freshly ground black pepper
3 to 4 garlic cloves, crushed
Bouquet garni (bay leaf, thyme, and celery rib tied in cheesecloth) or a pinch of mixed, crumbled bay leaf, thyme, and chervil
½ teaspoon sugar
¼ cup olive oil
4 tablespoons butter
8 to 10 eggs
2 tablespoons fresh basil leaves and flowers

Cook the tomatoes, seasonings, garlic, bouquet garni, and sugar in the olive oil over a low flame, tossing from time to time, until the liquid has evaporated and the tomatoes seem coated with oil. Discard the garlic and the bouquet garni.

Add the butter, cut into small pieces, to the eggs, season to taste, and beat lightly with a fork. With a wooden spoon, stir this mixture into the tomatoes over a low flame, beating constantly. When the eggs begin to thicken, add the basil. This should be done at the very last moment to avoid blackening the basil.

Remove from the heat when the desired consistency is achieved and continue stirring. Serve immediately.

Spanish Eggs

Serves 6

2 onions, finely chopped
1 small garlic clove, finely chopped
3 tablespoons olive oil
3 tomatoes, seeded and cubed
2 small squash, cubed (zucchini or yellow squash)
3 large green peppers, finely chopped
Salt and freshly ground black pepper
8 eggs
1 tablespoon melted butter

Brown the onion and garlic in olive oil. Add the tomatoes, squash, and peppers, season to taste; cook slowly for 45 minutes. Cool slightly.

Break the eggs into a bowl, beat well; add the vegetables and transfer the mixture to a heavy-bottomed saucepan containing the melted butter. Cook over medium heat, stirring constantly with a table fork. When the mixture reaches the desired degree of doneness, remove from the heat and serve immediately.

Eggs Scrambled with Cheese and White Wine

Any number of combinations are nice with eggs, but this is one of the best. Serve with heated bran muffins or toast and plenty of butter.

Serves 4

3 garlic cloves, finely chopped
1 cup dry white wine
4 tablespoons butter, divided
10 eggs
5 ounces Swiss cheese, freshly grated
Salt and freshly ground black pepper

In a small, covered saucepan simmer the garlic in the wine for about 30 minutes, or until the wine has reduced to about ⅓ cup. Strain, discarding the pieces of garlic. Set aside to cool.

Butter the interior of a 2-quart earthenware casserole liberally and cut the remaining butter into small pieces. Add all the ingredients, grinding in a generous amount of pepper. Beat with a small whisk. Place the casserole on an asbestos pad or other heat diffuser over fairly high heat. Keep beating the mixture, slowly at first, increasing the speed as the pieces of butter begin to melt, and scraping the sides and the bottom of the casserole constantly.

When the mixture begins to thicken noticeably, remove the casserole from the heat and continue stirring for a minute or so. The consistency should be that of a thick, pourable cream.

Serve directly from the cooking casserole onto well-warmed plates.

Cheese-Scrambled Brunch Eggs

To keep scrambled eggs from drying out and lumping is a problem. The only solution I have found is to add a light Béchamel sauce to the scrambled eggs the minute they reach the desired doneness. Of course, the amount of sauce depends on the number of eggs being cooked; I suggest ½ cup for every 8 eggs scrambled. If the eggs are for breakfast, there is usually no need to add the sauce because the eggs will generally be served directly from the skillet and eaten immediately. But for a brunch or a buffet, when the eggs are going to be served from a chafing dish or casserole, the addition of the sauce will keep them moist.

Serves 8

4 tablespoons butter
12 eggs, lightly beaten
1 cup heavy cream
8 ounces (2 cups) grated Port Salut, Gruyère, or Cheddar cheese
Salt and freshly ground black pepper
8 slices toast, brioche, or English muffins, buttered
8 slices cooked ham or Canadian bacon
Avocado slices for garnish

Heat the butter in a small, heavy-bottomed saucepan. Add the eggs and whisk over very low heat for about 5 minutes, until soft curds form. Stir in the cream and cheese and continue to cook just until the cheese melts. Season with salt and pepper and spoon over buttered toast slices that have been topped with ham or bacon. Garnish with avocado slices.

Making an Omelet

Heat a heavy, seasoned omelet pan over medium-low heat and add butter to coat. When the butter begins to sizzle, pour the beaten egg mixture into the pan. Increase the heat to medium-high and immediately begin to stir with the flat side of a fork. At the same time, shake the omelet pan over the heat. Do this for about 15 seconds. Smooth the eggs, which will look scrambled, and as they start to set up, put any filling you are using across the eggs, perpendicular to the skillet handle, and closer to the handle than to the center of the skillet. If right-handed, turn the skillet slightly to the right, and change your hand-hold from over the top of the handle to under the handle. This will enable you to lift the skillet up easily and turn it over to fold the omelet onto the plate. To fold the omelet onto the plate, place the plate or other serving dish against the front edge of the skillet and tilt the skillet at the same time.

Chili Relleno Omelet

Commercially canned jalapeño peppers are available in most markets. They have been roasted and packed in light oil with the seeds only partially removed. If you want the chilis hot, retain the seeds; discard them to remove some of the "hot." Ideally, an omelet is best made using 3 eggs. Don't be bashful about using a nonstick omelet pan; nothing is more devastating than having the omelet stick to the pan, since it is the bottom of the omelet that is going to show when it is turned out on the plate.

Makes 1 omelet

2 tablespoons butter
1 jalapeño pepper
¼-inch slice Jack cheese the length of the pepper
1 tablespoon cold water
3 eggs
Salt and freshly ground black pepper

Melt the butter in an omelet pan. (Use a nonstick pan, if desired, but be sure to use an omelet-size pan.)

Pat the jalapeño pepper dry with a paper towel. Stuff the pepper with the slice of Jack cheese. Set aside until ready to place in the omelet.

Add the cold water to the eggs and beat lightly with a fork.

When omelet pan is hot, add the egg and water mixture and stir with a fork as for any omelet (see page 180). When the omelet is ready to turn, lay the stuffed pepper in the omelet and turn out. The pepper will heat and the cheese will melt from the heat of the omelet. Serve salt and pepper on the side.

Eggs in Tomatoes

This is a colorful as well as different and delicious dish for brunch or luncheon.

Serves 6

3 large tomatoes, cut in half, centers scooped out
4 tablespoons olive oil, divided
Salt and freshly ground black pepper
3 shallots, finely chopped
¼ cup chopped parsley
6 eggs
2 tablespoons buttered bread crumbs
2 tablespoons freshly grated Parmesan cheese

Preheat the oven to 375°F.

Fry the tomatoes carefully in 2 tablespoons of the oil without letting them lose their shape. Place them side by side in a buttered baking dish. Sprinkle with salt, pepper, shallots, and parsley. Break an egg into each tomato half. Combine the buttered crumbs and Parmesan cheese, mix together, and sprinkle on top of each tomato half. Drizzle the remaining 2 tablespoons of oil over the tomato-egg combinations and bake for 10 minutes or until the egg whites are set.

Baked Eggs in Cream and Bacon

This is Sunday breakfast about once a month at my house, especially during the winter.

Serves 4

4 strips bacon, cooked until crisp, crumbled
8 eggs
Salt and freshly ground black pepper
4 tablespoons heavy cream

Preheat the oven to 300°F.

Heat individual ramekins and butter them. Sprinkle them well with crumbled bacon. Break 2 eggs carefully into each dish, add salt and pepper, and pour a tablespoon of cream over each. Bake for about 10 minutes, or until the whites are set.

Tabasco Eggs

Serves 4

½ pint heavy cream
½ cup whole milk
½ teaspoon salt
Pinch cayenne pepper
Freshly ground black pepper
Hot pepper sauce
8 eggs
½ cup Homemade Bread Crumbs (see page 335)
½ cup grated mild Cheddar cheese
8 slices hot buttered toast

In a chafing dish heat the cream, milk, salt, cayenne, black pepper, and hot pepper sauce to the boiling point. When the mixture is about to boil, add the eggs, one at a time, as quickly as possible. With a small ladle, dip the liquid over the eggs. When the eggs begin to set, sprinkle with the bread crumbs mixed with cheese. Keep dipping the sauce over the eggs until they are firmly set and the cheese and the crumbs are well mixed.

Put each egg on a square of hot buttered toast and top with some of the sauce. Serve with sliced tomatoes and extra buttered toast.

Hard-Cooked Eggs

Use medium to large eggs at room temperature. Place in an uncovered saucepan with enough cold water to cover by 1 inch. Bring to a boil over high heat. Immediately reduce the heat to just below the boil and begin timing the eggs. Medium-size eggs take 10 minutes to reach the hard-cooked stage; large, approximately 12 minutes. Remove from the heat, crack lightly, and plunge into cold water. Peel and use, or refrigerate.

Eggs Stuffed with Sorrel

These are good as a first course, as canapés with cocktails, or as picnic fare. If sorrel is not available, use watercress or fresh or frozen spinach. Just be sure, if you are using frozen spinach, to wring out all the moisture before combining it with the yolks.

Serves 4

6 ounces sorrel
¼ cup olive oil, divided
Salt and freshly ground black pepper
6 hard-cooked eggs, peeled and halved
1 cup freshly grated Parmesan cheese, divided

Remove the stems from the sorrel. Wash the leaves, sponge dry, and chop fine.

Preheat the oven to 400°F.

Oil the bottom of a baking dish with 1 tablespoon of olive oil; line with a third of the chopped sorrel and sprinkle with salt. Remove the egg yolks and mash them with a fork; add the remaining sorrel, ¾ cup of the cheese, and salt and pepper. Work in 2 to 3 tablespoons of olive oil, enough to bind the mixture. Stuff the halved egg whites with this mixture, packing gently and mounding the stuffing with a spoon.

Arrange the stuffed eggs on the bed of sorrel, sprinkle with the remaining cheese, dribble with olive oil, and bake for about 15 minutes.

Curried Eggs in Brown Rice

This main dish should be served with thick slices of fried fresh ham. A green salad and a citrus dessert go well with it.

Serves 6

3 white onions, sliced
2 tablespoons butter
1 teaspoon unbleached all-purpose flour
1 tablespoon curry powder
2 cups chicken stock
Salt and freshly ground black pepper
1 cup heavy cream, heated
8 hard-cooked eggs, peeled and quartered
2 cups cooked brown rice

Cook the onions without browning in the butter; sprinkle with the flour mixed with curry powder. Add the chicken stock, season to taste, and cook until the onions are well done. Pour in the hot cream and the quartered eggs. Heat well but do not boil. Make a nest of the rice and pour the curried eggs in the center. Serve with a good chutney.

Baked Eggs with Onions

This can be served as a breakfast, brunch, luncheon, or supper dish. If it is breakfast, accompany it with fresh fruit and toasted muffins. Otherwise, add a green salad or a fruit salad with sweet rolls or a pastry.

Serves 6

7 tablespoons butter, divided
4 medium onions, thinly sliced
12 hard-cooked eggs, thinly sliced
Salt and freshly ground black pepper
3 tablespoons unbleached all-purpose flour
2 cups light cream, heated
3 tablespoons grated Swiss or Parmesan cheese
Additional butter for topping

Preheat the oven to 400°F.

Melt 4 tablespoons of the butter in a large, heavy pan; add the onions and cook over low heat until soft but not brown, about 10 minutes.

Butter a medium-size baking dish and layer the eggs and onions alternately, starting with the eggs. Sprinkle a little salt and pepper between the layers.

Melt the remaining butter in a saucepan, stir in the flour, and cook for a minute or two, stirring constantly. Do not allow to brown. Add the hot cream and stir the sauce constantly with a whisk over moderate heat until thickened. Pour over the eggs and onions. Sprinkle the top with the grated cheese and dot with butter. Bake for about 10 to 12 minutes until the cheese has melted and the top of the casserole is lightly browned.

Casserole of Hard-Cooked Eggs in Creamed Sorrel

A good luncheon entrée with a green salad and a nice white wine. If sorrel is not available, use spinach instead.

Serves 4 to 6

10 ounces sorrel
¼ pound butter, divided
1 cup heavy cream
Salt and freshly ground black pepper
1 cup crumbled bread crumbs
6 hard-cooked eggs, peeled and halved

Pick over the sorrel. If it is young and tender, shred it fine; if older, plunge the leaves into boiling water, remove them when the water returns to a boil, drain, and then shred.

Melt 3 tablespoons of the butter in a pan; add the sorrel and salt and cook gently, stirring, for about 10 minutes, or until the liquid has evaporated and the sorrel has melted into a puree. Stir in the cream, a little at a time, allowing the sauce to thicken before adding more. Grind in some pepper and add salt to taste. Brown the bread crumbs lightly in 4 tablespoons of butter.

Preheat the oven to 400°F.

Using the remaining tablespoon of butter, grease a 1-quart ovenproof baking dish. Arrange the halved eggs, cut surface up, side by side in the buttered baking dish. Spoon the sauce over the entire surface. Sprinkle with bread crumbs and bake for about 15 minutes, or until the dish is well heated and has a light brown crust.

Eggs in Spinach

This side dish is a dressy way to treat spinach, which is often served with just chopped egg. This version is party fare and not a vegetable-egg treatment you are likely to find often. It is especially good with rare roast beef and oven-browned potatoes.

Serves 6

3 pounds spinach, washed, with stems removed
4 tablespoons butter
1 tablespoon unbleached all-purpose flour
1 cup whole milk, heated
Pinch sugar
Salt and freshly ground black pepper
Pinch nutmeg
1 cup heavy cream
4 egg yolks
6 hard-cooked eggs, peeled and cut in half

Cook the spinach in boiling salted water. Drain well and press dry. Puree in a food processor.

In a 2-quart saucepan, melt the butter, add the flour, and cook together without browning. Add the spinach puree, hot milk, and sugar, and cook well, stirring constantly. Season to taste with salt, pepper, and nutmeg. Remove from the heat and stir in the cream into which 4 egg yolks have been beaten. Return to very low heat and when ready to serve, pour the spinach mixture into a deep dish and decorate with a circle of hard-cooked eggs.

Hard-Cooked Eggs with Potatoes

This hot egg-and-potato salad should be reseasoned at the table to suit individual tastes. Potatoes tend to absorb a lot of salt, and since some people want less salt than others, leave the final seasoning up to your guests. Scallions may be substituted if shallots are not available.

Serves 4

2 tablespoons finely chopped shallots
1/4 pound butter
2 pounds potatoes, boiled in their skins
6 hard-cooked eggs
Salt and freshly ground black pepper
1/3 cup chopped parsley
2 to 3 tablespoons wine vinegar

Cook the shallots in the butter over a very low flame until they soften and turn yellow.

Peel the potatoes while very hot, holding each one in a towel; slice them onto a heated serving platter, then cut the eggs in thick slices over the potatoes. Mix them together gently, breaking the eggs no more than necessary.

Sprinkle the shallots with salt and pepper, raise the heat a little, add the parsley and, a couple of seconds later, the vinegar. Pour the contents of the pan over the potatoes and eggs.

CHEESE DISHES

Green Pepper and Tortilla Cheese Dip

This should be served directly from the broiler; as it cools, reheat it so that the cheese stays melted while it is being passed or served. This is best as an appetizer with cocktails before dinner. If it is to be served on a buffet table, make the dish in smaller serving sizes so there is always a fresh replacement.

Serves 4

4 green peppers
4 tablespoons butter
½ pound fresh tomatillos (Mexican green tomatoes), husked, or an 8-ounce can, drained
1 or 2 fresh or canned jalapeño peppers
1 large green onion, chopped
2 garlic cloves, minced
1 tablespoon coriander leaves (optional)
½ cup (4 ounces) tightly packed crumbled cream cheese
Salt and freshly ground black pepper
1 cup (4 ounces) lightly packed, freshly grated Danish Fontina or Port Salut cheese

Roast the green peppers under the broiler for about 10 minutes, turning frequently until they are completely blistered on all sides. Place in a plastic bag to steam for at least 10 minutes. Peel the peppers, discarding the stems and seeds, and cut into ¼-inch-wide strips.

Melt the butter in a heavy-bottomed skillet. Add the pepper strips; cover and cook gently over low heat for 30 minutes, stirring occasionally.

Meanwhile, place the tomatillos, jalapeños, onion, garlic, and coriander in a blender or food processor and puree until smooth. Sieve this tomatillo sauce over the cooked peppers. Add the cream cheese and stir over low heat until the cheese melts. Season with salt and pepper. Transfer to a flat baking dish, sprinkle with Fontina, and set aside until ready to serve. Heat under the broiler until the cheese melts and browns.

Serve at once with tortilla chips.

Hot Olive-Cheese Appetizers

Makes 36 canapés

4½-ounce can chopped ripe olives
1 tablespoon minced onion
¾ cup grated Cheddar cheese
¼ cup mayonnaise
¼ teaspoon salt
¼ teaspoon chili powder
6 English muffins, halved

Preheat the oven to 425°F.

Blend all the ingredients except the muffins. Spread the mixture to the very edge of each muffin half.

Bake for 10 minutes, then broil to brown the tops. Cut in sixths to use as appetizers, or serve whole as open-faced sandwiches.

Soufflé of Cheese and Chicken

A good use for leftover cooked chicken, whether white meat or dark. If you use Parmesan cheese in place of Swiss, cut back a bit on the amount of salt you use.

Serves 6

1 carrot, chopped
1 onion, chopped
1 rib celery, chopped
2 tablespoons butter
2 tablespoons unbleached all-purpose flour
3 cups whole milk, heated
1¼ cups minced chicken
1 teaspoon onion juice
Salt and freshly ground black pepper
1 cup grated Swiss or Parmesan cheese
5 egg yolks, beaten
6 egg whites, stiffly beaten

Preheat the oven to 350°F.

Brown the carrot, onion, and celery in the butter. Add the flour and cook for 5 minutes. Gradually pour in the hot milk. Continue to cook, stirring, for several minutes.

Remove from the heat and pass through a fine sieve. Add the chicken and the onion juice. Season with salt and pepper to taste. Return to the heat until hot and remove again to add the cheese and egg yolks. When cold, fold in the egg whites, transfer to a buttered dish, and bake for 35 minutes.

Cheese Soufflé

You will find this a most successful soufflé. The Camembert should be forced through a coarse sieve so it will be distributed through the mixture; mashing it with a fork first will make it easier. If it is well chilled, it is even possible to grate it.

Serves 4

1 cup whole milk
1 small bay leaf
1 shallot, sliced
1 small garlic clove
1 small piece celery
1 teaspoon salt
6 peppercorns
3 tablespoons butter
3 tablespoons unbleached all-purpose flour
1/8 teaspoon white pepper
1/8 teaspoon English dry mustard
1/2 teaspoon Dijon-style mustard
1/4 cup Camembert cheese, forced through a coarse sieve
1/4 cup freshly grated Gruyère cheese
1/4 cup freshly grated Parmesan cheese, divided
5 egg yolks
Bread crumbs
7 egg whites
Paprika

Put the milk, bay leaf, shallot, garlic, celery, salt, and peppercorns in a pan; stir over low heat and bring to a boil. Cover, remove from heat, and allow to steep for 5 minutes.

Melt the butter in a small, heavy pan; remove from the heat and stir in the flour. Add the pepper and mustards, and strain the prepared milk into the butter mixture. Stir over heat until it boils. Add the Camembert and Gruyère cheeses and half the Parmesan; mix well. Beat the egg yolks until light and fluffy and mix into the sauce.

Preheat the oven to 375°F.

Butter a 2-quart soufflé dish, dust with the bread crumbs and a little Parmesan cheese. Beat the egg whites to stiff peaks and add the egg-yolk-cheese mixture. Fold gently but not too thoroughly, so that a little of the egg white still shows. Fill the soufflé dish, leaving a ¼-inch rim at the top. Sprinkle the top with the rest of the Parmesan cheese and bread crumbs. Place in a shallow pan of hot water and bake for 45 to 50 minutes, or until just firm to the touch. Do not open the oven door during the first half of the baking. Remove, sprinkle with a little paprika, and serve at once.

Quiche Lorraine

The quiche has come to be the most popular egg-and-cheese combination around. Of all the quiches currently in favor, Quiche Lorraine, which is probably the original quiche, is the best in my opinion, and this recipe is the creamiest and tastiest I have found to date.

Serves 6

Crust

1½ cups unbleached all-purpose flour
½ teaspoon salt
¼ pound butter
4 tablespoons ice water

Filling

18 strips bacon
4 eggs
2 cups heavy cream
Pinch nutmeg
Pinch sugar
¾ teaspoon salt
Pinch cayenne pepper
Freshly ground black pepper
Soft butter
1 cup (4 ounces) grated Swiss cheese

Preheat the oven to 450°F.

To make the crust, sift together the flour and salt. Work the butter into it, using your fingers. Moisten the pastry with the ice water. Make into a smooth ball, wrap in waxed paper, and place in the refrigerator for about 30 minutes before rolling out thin on a lightly floured board. Line a large tart or pie pan with the pastry; trim the edges and crimp them. Prick the surface with a fork and refrigerate until ready to use.

To make the filling, grill the bacon until crisp and break it into small pieces. Break the eggs into a bowl and add the cream, nutmeg, sugar, salt, cayenne, and black pepper. Beat with a rotary beater just long enough to mix thoroughly. Rub soft butter over the surface of the pie shell and sprinkle the bacon over the bottom. Sprinkle with the grated cheese and pour the egg mixture on top. Bake for 15 minutes. Reduce the temperature to 325°F. and continue cooking for 25 to 35 minutes, until the quiche is a light golden brown.

Cheddar Cheese Pudding with Mushroom Sauce

You can use either a mild or sharp Cheddar to make this dish for brunch, lunch, or supper. Although the combination of ingredients may be changed to suit the cook, try the recipe exactly as it is written the first time around so you know what you might want to change, if a change is necessary.

Serves 4

½ pound (approx.) sourdough, French, or other white bread
¼ pound butter, melted
3 cups light cream
5 eggs
¼ cup Port or sherry
1 teaspoon Worcestershire sauce
1 teaspoon prepared Dijon mustard
½ pound Cheddar cheese, freshly grated
1 teaspoon salt
¼ teaspoon freshly ground black pepper
¼ teaspoon paprika
Mushroom Sauce (recipe follows)

Generously butter a 2-quart soufflé dish, charlotte pan, or other mold. Cut the bread in ½-inch-thick slices and remove the crusts. Dip the bread in melted butter, a slice at a time, and arrange in the soufflé dish, cutting or overlapping slices, if necessary, so that the bottom and sides of the mold are completely covered.

Preheat the oven to 325°F.

Thoroughly mix the cream, eggs, wine, Worcestershire, mustard, cheese, salt, pepper, and paprika. Pour into the bread-lined mold and place in a pot of water that comes three-quarters up the sides of the mold. Bring to a simmer on top of the stove and then transfer to the oven to bake for about 1 hour, until the pudding is puffed and browned and a knife inserted into the center comes out clean.

Remove from the water bath and let sit for 5 minutes. Cut off the edges of the bread that extend above the cheese mixture; run a knife around the edge and invert. Pour Mushroom Sauce over the mold and serve with a green salad or vegetable.

Mushroom Sauce

Makes 1½ cups

2 tablespoons butter
1 pound mushrooms, thinly sliced
1 tablespoon minced scallions
¼ cup Port or sherry
¼ cup heavy cream
1 teaspoon salt
½ teaspoon freshly ground black pepper

Melt the butter in a skillet. Add the mushrooms and scallions, and sauté over medium-high heat until the liquid has evaporated and the mushrooms have browned. Pour in the wine and cook until the liquid is reduced by half. Add the cream and continue cooking until most of liquid is absorbed. Season with salt and pepper.

Easter Cheese

This traditional Ukrainian custard entrée or dessert can be made ahead of time and reheated when you are ready to use it, or it can be served cold.

Serves 8 to 10

1½ pounds dry cottage cheese
¼ pound butter
4 tablespoons sugar
Pinch salt
6 eggs

Preheat the oven to 350°F.

Over a large bowl, work the cottage cheese through a strainer with a wooden spoon. Beat in the butter until completely blended and airy. Add the sugar and salt and then the eggs, one at a time, beating very well after each addition. Pour into a shallow cake pan or casserole and set into a larger pan with hot water to halfway up the sides. Bake for 45 minutes, or until the center tests clean with a knife. It should be firm but soft in the center.

Macaroni and Cheese

What is more American than this? There are endless recipes and a multitude of variations, some good, some bad. The beauty of this recipe is that the macaroni does not have to be cooked separately and the dish is all cooked on top of the stove.

Serves 6

1/4 pound butter
8 ounces elbow macaroni
1/2 teaspoon dry mustard
Pinch oregano
Pinch freshly ground black pepper
1 teaspoon salt
2/3 cup chopped onion
1/3 cup chopped green bell pepper
2 cups water
1 tablespoon unbleached all-purpose flour
15-ounce can evaporated milk
2 tablespoons chopped pimiento
6 ounces sharp Cheddar cheese, shredded

Melt the butter in a 2-quart saucepan over low heat. Add the macaroni, mustard, oregano, pepper, salt, onion, and green pepper. Cook, stirring, until the onions are transparent. Add the water and bring to a boil. Cover and return to a low heat to simmer until the macaroni is done, about 25 minutes. Sprinkle the flour over the mixture and blend well. Stir in the milk, pimiento, and cheese and continue to cook, stirring occasionally, until the cheese is completely melted. Serve at once.

Welsh Rarebit

This has undergone many changes following its import from England to America. Also known as Welsh Rabbit, Welch Rarebit, Welsh Rare-bit, it is a favorite late-night snack and a chafing dish specialty in many homes.

Serves 6 as a first course

1 tablespoon butter
½ pound sharp Cheddar cheese, grated
1 egg, slightly beaten
1 cup light cream
¼ teaspoon salt
1 teaspoon dry mustard
Pinch cayenne pepper
Dash hot pepper sauce
1 tablespoon dry sherry

Melt the butter in a chafing dish or the top of a double boiler and add the cheese. As the cheese is melting, add the egg, cream, and seasonings. Add the sherry and continue to cook, stirring, about 3 minutes longer. Serve over lightly toasted English muffins or hamburger patties.

Fried Parmesan Cakes

These are great served with grilled fish or fried chicken, but they must be served as soon as they are fried.

Serves 6

3 egg yolks, beaten
⅔ cup Homemade Sour Cream *(see page 333)*
3 tablespoons unbleached all-purpose flour
1 teaspoon grated lemon rind
Dash freshly ground black pepper
¾ cup freshly grated Parmesan cheese

Mix all the ingredients together lightly and drop by tablespoons into a hot, well-greased skillet or onto a pancake griddle. Do not add salt. Fry until golden on both sides and serve immediately.

PASTA DISHES

Pasta dishes are popular entrées with almost everyone, although the weight-conscious tend to shy away from them. Actually, it is the butter sauce that goes on the pasta rather than the pasta itself that is the troublemaker. And speaking of sauces, the basic pasta recipes given here can be complemented by a number of the sauces that appear in the Sauces, Condiments, and Accompaniments Section (see page 309).

Homemade Pasta

I like to make my own pasta although I realize that many people don't have the time or inclination to do so. There really *is* a difference between the homemade and the commercial. Fresh pasta requires far less cooking time: allow about 1 minute in boiling water for fresh pasta that has had no drying time, and about 2 to 3 minutes for pasta that has. Commercial pasta takes 8 to 10 minutes in boiling water. In buying readymade pasta, select an imported Italian brand, one that is made from hard durum wheat, and by all means buy it where there is a large turnover. It lasts a long time but not forever. There are good American brands too, but don't expect any of them to taste like fresh homemade.

Although I don't think it makes a difference whether you use a hand or an electric pasta machine as far as taste and texture are concerned, I prefer the hand machine for kneading and cutting because I feel I have better control. By the same token, I never make pasta in a processor because I don't think the end result is nearly as rich or as good, but that doesn't mean you can't use one if that's your choice.

If you are going to the trouble of making pasta by hand, it pays to make enough so that there is some left to store. Once it is rolled and cut, use a portion fresh and dry the rest to store for another time. There are two ways to do this. The pasta can be cut into the desired widths and lengths and then hung on a laundry drying rack or over broom handles hooked to the backs of two kitchen chairs. When it is completely dry, it can be stored in a paper bag in a dry place in the cupboard until ready to use. Just be sure it is really dry before storing. In the other method, the pasta is loosely folded or twirled into serving-portion sizes and then allowed to dry on linen cloth, tea towels, or over a wire screen. Once it is completely dry, it can be stored as above.

Don't ever store fresh pasta in airless glass jars unless you know the pasta is *completely* dry. And, once dry, don't store it in the refrigerator because it will draw moisture and spoil. I have purposely avoided mention of freezing pasta because in my estimation it doesn't freeze well.

I have given several recipes for homemade pasta. All call for eggs, flour, salt, and oil, but in differing quantities. All can be doubled and tripled, although the dough can be hard to handle in volume.

Basic Pasta Dough

My friend and colleague Giuliano Bugialli taught me this method of making pasta, and it is the one that I always use. It produces the smoothest and most velvety pasta, and I think it has the best taste.

Enough for 2 generous servings

1 cup unbleached all-purpose flour
1 large whole egg
1 tablespoon olive or vegetable oil
1 teaspoon salt

Work on a flat surface—a cutting board or counter top. Place the flour in a heap; make a well in the center only slightly larger than the size of the egg. Break the egg into the well; add the oil and salt. Using a table fork, beat the egg in a circular motion to gradually incorporate flour from the edges of the well. Work the flour in slowly, only as much as the egg will absorb and still not be too sticky to the touch.

When you can move the egg-flour mixture in a loose ball, set it aside. Using a pastry scraper, clean the flour and egg from the work surface and sift it through a screen or sieve to remove loose particles, leaving only clean flour on the board.

Knead the ball of dough, working close to the edge of the cleaned flour; work in as much flour as the ball will hold without becoming stiff. The kneading process will continue as you work the dough through the roller of the pasta machine.

Most hand pasta machine rollers are marked with settings numbered 1 through 6. For most pastas, I usually roll the dough only through settings up to No. 5, simply because that is the thickness that I prefer.

Starting on setting No. 1, which is the widest setting, flatten the dough with your hands and roll it through the machine. Then drag the dough through the flour still on the work surface, adding flour only on the bottom side of the dough strip. Fold the dough one third over the center and fold the remaining third over the first third. Flatten with your hand, pushing toward the open ends, to remove any air bubbles, and process through the No. 1 setting again.

Repeat this process five or six times, or until the dough is satiny to the touch. You should then be ready to change your setting, dragging the dough through any remaining flour left on the work surface for further dusting. Do not be concerned that all the flour has not been used up; some eggs absorb more flour than others.

At setting No. 5, the dough should be about 5 to 6 feet long. Cut it into 12- to 15-inch lengths before continuing to the noodle-cutting attachment on the machine. Most hand machines have two cutting sizes, wide and narrow.

Note: Pasta does not have to be dried before it is cooked. Perfect pasta, for me, is straight from the work table and into a kettle of boiling water for about 1 minute. It should not be overcooked. Drain but do not rinse the pasta, and serve immediately, tossed with whatever sauce you choose.

Variations: Spinach Pasta—Add 1 tablespoon of cooked spinach,* pureed, and work in with the egg and oil.

Pink Pasta—Add 1 small, cooked beet,* pureed, and work in with the egg and oil. *Or*, add 1 medium-size tomato, peeled, seeded, and pureed,* and work in with the egg and oil.

* Extract as much moisture as possible before pureeing.

Egg Pasta, Roman Style

This recipe is for the hardy. It is made entirely by hand—kneaded, rolled, and cut. Any pasta can be made from start to finish by hand, but it's not often done today by other than a purist who doesn't want to use either a hand or electric pasta machine. Mostly it requires stamina, an extra-long rolling pin, and a very large table for the rolling.

Enough for 8 servings

5 cups unbleached all-purpose flour
1 teaspoon salt
5 eggs, slightly beaten
1 tablespoon olive oil

Sift the flour onto a board and make a well in the center. Put the salt, eggs, and oil into the well and work them into the flour by hand until a firm dough is formed. Continue kneading for about 20 minutes, or until the dough is smooth and elastic. During the kneading, flour both hands and board frequently.

Divide the dough into two or three parts. Roll out each part, one at a time, on a large floured surface with an extra-long rolling pin. After first rolling each part, wrap it around the rolling pin and stretch it a bit. Roll it out again, sprinkle with flour, roll over the pin again, and stretch a little more.

Repeat this process at least 10 times for each section of dough until all the pieces are very thin, smooth, and greatly enlarged.

Then roll each part two or three more times until it is thin enough to see the grain of the rolling surface through it and dry enough to pick up like a piece of material. When each piece of dough has been thoroughly rolled, place it over the back of a chair or on a clean cloth before proceeding with the next piece.

When all the pasta is rolled out, dry it out for about 20 minutes. It is now ready for cutting and cooking, or completely drying for storage.

Fresh Egg Noodles

Enough for 4 servings

1¾ cups unbleached all-purpose flour
Salt
1 whole egg plus 3 egg yolks
1 tablespoon olive oil

Combine the flour in a mixing bowl with the other ingredients. Work with a fork until thoroughly blended, adding a bit more flour if necessary; then knead with your knuckles just long enough to bring it all together in a firm mass. Roll into a ball and leave to rest, covered by a towel, for about 1 hour.

Divide the dough into two or three parts. Press one out flat on a lightly floured board and turn it through the roller of a noodle machine set at the widest notch. Fold it in thirds, and if it is sticky, drag the two sides over the floured board before passing it through again. Fold again, in half or thirds, and continue passing and folding until the sheet of dough is consistently smooth-textured, and its width equals that of the width of the rollers. Adjust the rollers to the next-to-finest thickness, pass the dough through, and hang it to dry while treating the other sections of dough in the same way.

Pass the sheets through the noodle-cutting rollers, sprinkle with a little flour to keep them from sticking together, and toss them lightly, using splayed fingers. Carefully place pasta strands on a screen or towel. The finished pasta is now ready to cook.

Cook the noodles in a large quantity of salted boiling water, to which a dribble of olive oil has been added. Gently shake them free of one another the moment they are added to the water. Allow 1 to 2 minutes' cooking time. Drain well and add the sauce or garnish you wish.

Noodles with Swiss Cheese and Sour Cream

This is a good accompaniment to grilled or broiled lamb, beef, or chicken, and takes very little preparation. Any kind of noodle will do, but I prefer thin noodles. To make individual servings, bake them in muffin tins. If a crusty top is wanted, bake uncovered; if the top is to be soft, cover the baking container with buttered foil or waxed paper.

Serves 6

½ pound Swiss cheese, grated
8-ounce package medium noodles, cooked, drained, and hot
1 tablespoon onion juice
1 teaspoon Worcestershire sauce
¼ pound butter, melted
1 pint sour cream
½ cup buttered bread crumbs

Preheat the oven to 350°F.

Add the cheese to the hot noodles. Then add the onion juice, Worcestershire sauce, and butter. Cool. Combine with sour cream and mix lightly. Place in a buttered 2-quart casserole, top with buttered crumbs, and bake for 1 hour.

For individual casseroles, use muffin tins and reduce the baking time to 45 to 50 minutes. Let sit for a few minutes before running a knife around the edges and unmolding.

Creamed Noodles with Ham and Vegetables

To taste the original, take a trip to Rome and stay at the Hassler. They don't call it one of their specialties, but it could well be.

Serves 4

3 ounces prosciutto
Handful chopped parsley
1 teaspoon finely chopped fresh marjoram or tarragon or ½ teaspoon dried
Salt
10 ounces mushrooms, sliced paper-thin
1 pound small zucchini, sliced paper-thin
3 tablespoons butter
2 garlic cloves, peeled and finely chopped
1 cup heavy cream
1 recipe Basic Pasta Dough, cooked (see page 197)
Freshly ground black pepper
⅔ cup freshly grated Parmesan cheese

Cut the ham into a 1-inch-long fine julienne. Mix with the parsley and marjoram or tarragon to keep the ham strips from sticking together, and set aside.

Salt the mushrooms and zucchini and sauté in butter over high heat until the liquid is evaporated, about 6 to 7 minutes, adding the garlic after 3 or 4 minutes. Add the ham-and-herb mixture and continue sautéing for another 2 or 3 minutes. Add the cream, reduce for a few minutes over high heat, and toss in the noodles. Remove from the heat, taste for salt, and add pepper over the top. Add the Parmesan cheese and toss, mixing thoroughly.

Baked Lasagne with Prosciutto and Mushrooms

Make the pasta filling first so that the flavors will have time to marry, then make the pasta dough. Once both are ready to assemble, there will only be a 20-minute baking wait for this great dish.

Serves 6 to 8

Sauce

¼ pound butter, divided
2 medium yellow onions, chopped
½ cup grated carrots
½ cup chopped celery
2 tablespoons chopped fresh parsley
1 pound ground beef
1 pound ground veal
1 teaspoon salt
¼ teaspoon freshly ground black pepper
¾ pound fresh mushrooms, finely chopped
1½ cups Tomato Pulp (see page 325)
1½ cups meat stock

---

1 recipe Basic Pasta Dough (page 197), doubled
8 quarts boiling water
2½ tablespoons salt

½ pound prosciutto, finely shredded, divided
1¾ cups freshly grated Parmesan cheese, divided

To prepare the sauce, melt half the butter in a large, heavy frying pan. Add the onions, carrots, celery, and parsley, and sauté lightly until the onions are golden. Add the beef, veal, salt, and pepper, and cook, stirring, over moderate heat for 15 minutes, or until the meats are browned. Add the mushrooms and cook, stirring, for 5 minutes. Add the tomato pulp and stock; cook for 30 minutes, uncovered, stirring occasionally. Remove from the heat and set aside.

Prepare and roll the pasta dough according to recipe directions (page 197). The pasta will be a little thinner than commercial lasagne. Cut the uncooked pasta into 4-inch squares. Plunge 6 to 8 pasta squares into boiling salted water. After the pasta squares have risen to the top, let them cook for about 2 to 3 minutes longer. Remove from the water, one at a time, with a slotted spoon and place, straightened out, on thick tea towels. Dry well.

Place a layer of pasta on the bottom of a well-buttered deep baking pan or casserole. Cover the pasta with a layer of the meat-mushroom sauce. Sprinkle with 2 tablespoons of the shredded prosciutto and 1 tablespoon of the Parmesan cheese; dot with 1 tablespoon of butter.

Repeat the process, boiling only enough pasta squares at a time to make one or two layers. Drain, add to the casserole, and top with sauce, shredded prosciutto, Parmesan, and butter.

Preheat the oven to 350°F.

Top with a final layer of pasta sprinkled with Parmesan and dotted with the remaining butter. Place in the oven for 15 to 20 minutes, or until the top is golden and the edges of the pasta are crisp and curly. Remove from the oven and serve accompanied by a bowl of the remaining Parmesan cheese.

Note: This recipe for lasagne may be prepared ahead of time and reheated thoroughly. If commercial lasagne is used, follow the instructions for cooking time suggested on the package and cook all the pasta at the same time. As soon as they are removed from the water, toss them with butter so that they do not stick together.

Fettuccini Alfredo Hotel Hassler

Gildo Concari of the Hassler Hotel in Rome gave me a lot of pointers about Italian cuisine. This remains my favorite pasta recipe.

Serves 6

1 pound imported fettucine noodles*
1 cup heavy cream
¼ pound butter
½ cup chopped ham
½ cup grated Parmesan cheese
1 egg yolk, beaten
Pinch nutmeg
Freshly ground black pepper

Cook the noodles in a large quantity of rapidly boiling salted water according to package directions, until just tender. Drain well.

Combine the cream, butter, and ham in a large pan. Add the noodles, cheese, egg yolk, nutmeg, and pepper. Toss gently.

Place in a large ovenproof serving dish and put under the broiler for a few seconds before serving.

* Or triple Basic Pasta Dough recipe (page 197); cook according to directions.

Spaghetti with Tuna and Anchovy Sauce

A one-dish meal, and like most casserole dishes, the ingredients can be used in varying amounts, depending on the cook's taste. The milk in this recipe draws the bitter flavor out of the anchovies, and this applies to any recipe that calls for anchovies; if you don't like anchovies full strength, soak them in milk.

Serves 6

2 anchovy fillets
¼ cup whole milk
2 tablespoons butter, softened
¼ cup olive oil, divided
2½ cups Tomato Pulp (see page 325)
1 teaspoon salt
¼ teaspoon freshly ground black pepper
½ cup flaked canned tuna fish
1 pound spaghetti, cooked al dente and drained
2 tablespoons chopped fresh parsley

Soak the anchovies in milk for 10 minutes. Drain and puree.

Mix the pureed anchovies with the butter and set aside. Heat 2 tablespoons of the olive oil in a saucepan. Add the tomato pulp, salt, and pepper. Cook for 15 minutes over moderate heat, stirring occasionally.

Heat the remaining 2 tablespoons of olive oil in a small saucepan. Add the tuna and sauté for 2 to 3 minutes on high heat. Remove from the heat and keep hot.

Place the hot spaghetti on a heated platter or bowl. Combine the anchovy butter, the tuna, and the tomato sauce and pour the mixture over the spaghetti. Sprinkle with chopped parsley before serving.

Cannelloni

My wonderful friend Mirella Panarello, who lives in Taormina, gave me this recipe. It is not Sicilian, but then neither is Mirella. She is a Florentine married to a Sicilian, and just lucky enough to live in Taormina. Don't worry about not having any white truffles for this dish; they are optional.

Serves 6 to 8

- *1/4 pound plus 4 tablespoons butter, divided*
- *2/3 cup finely chopped yellow onion*
- *2/3 cup finely chopped carrots*
- *2/3 cup finely chopped celery*
- *3 tablespoons finely chopped fresh parsley*
- *1 1/4 pounds lean ground beef*
- *3 ounces lean prosciutto, chopped*
- *2 ounces dried mushrooms, soaked in tepid water for 20 minutes, squeezed dry, and finely chopped*
- *2 tablespoons chopped fresh or canned white truffles (optional)*
- *1 teaspoon salt*
- *1/2 teaspoon freshly ground black pepper*
- *1/4 teaspoon freshly grated or ground nutmeg*
- *2 cups white wine*
- *2 tablespoons sifted, unbleached, all-purpose flour*
- *1 cup Tomato Pulp (see page 325)*
- *3 cups consommé, divided*
- *1 recipe for Basic Pasta Dough (page 197), doubled*
- *8 quarts boiling water*
- *2 1/2 tablespoons salt*
- *1 3/4 cups freshly grated Parmesan cheese, divided*

Melt 1/4 pound of the butter in a saucepan. Add the onion, carrots, celery, and parsley; sauté over very low heat until the onion is golden. Add the beef and cook, stirring, over moderate heat for 2 to 3 minutes. Add the prosciutto, mushrooms, and truffles (if used). Season with salt, pepper, and nutmeg. Mix well. Add the wine and cook until it has been completely reduced.

Sprinkle with the flour and mix well. Add the tomato pulp and 1/2 cup of the consommé. Cook over moderate heat until thickened to a pasty consistency, stirring frequently. Remove from heat; cool completely.

Prepare and roll the pasta dough according to recipe directions (page 197). Cut sheets of dough into 3 x 4-inch rectangles. Cook 6 at a time in boiling salted water for 5 minutes. Remove one at a time with a slotted spoon and place, straightened out, on damp towels. Continue the operation until all the squares are cooked.

Preheat the oven to 375°F.

Spread about 2 tablespoons of the beef mixture on half of each rectangle, across the width, leaving a ½-inch margin at one end. Starting from the spread end of the rectangles, roll each one tightly like a cigar.

Put a layer of stuffed cannelloni in a large, buttered rectangular baking pan. Pour 1½ cups of the consommé over them, sprinkle with ¾ cup of Parmesan cheese, and dot with the remaining butter. (Two layers may be necessary instead of one, in which case, use half the consommé, half the cheese, and half the butter for each layer.)

Bake, uncovered, for 15 to 20 minutes. Serve immediately, accompanied by the remaining consommé and Parmesan cheese in separate bowls.

RICE DISHES

This has to be as much American as Oriental, always the "if in doubt" side dish. Rice accompanies more foods than the potato and ranks with pasta. Both rice and pasta are now part of classic American cooking.

Oriental, or short-grain, rice has more body and taste than our long-grain variety but is not as popular here because of its sticky texture. The long-grain variety is much more adaptable to combinations and casseroles and is generally easier to work with.

The preparation of short-grain rice really requires a "rice cooker," made expressly for cooking this kind of rice. The instructions on all packages of long-grain rice are very explicit and have been tested thoroughly. If you follow the directions that come with the short-grain rice cooker or those on the packages of long-grain rice, you can't go wrong.

Rice Casserole

It takes less than 30 minutes to make this recipe, and the rice is guaranteed to be nice and fluffy. Just be sure to use long-grain rice.

Serves 8

3 tablespoons butter
2 teaspoons minced onion
½ teaspoon minced garlic
2 cups long-grain rice
½ bay leaf
5 cups chicken stock

Melt the butter in a saucepan and cook the onion and garlic, being careful not to let them burn. Add the rice and bay leaf and cook, stirring, for about 2 minutes. Meanwhile, bring the chicken stock to a boil and add to the rice. Cover and simmer for exactly 20 minutes. The rice should be cooked no more than 30 minutes before it is served.

Green Risotto

Risotto is a special rice cooked in a special way. Long-grain rice is always used to make this dish, and if you can find Arborio brand rice, that's the one to use; it's the one the Italians favor and it is the best. Risotto is served as a first course in Italy. It is very filling and should be used sparingly. In this recipe, the addition of finely chopped parsley lends the green color.

Serves 8

6 tablespoons butter, divided
1 cup finely chopped scallions, including the tender part of the green stalk
½ cup chopped fresh parsley
1½ cups finely chopped raw spinach
2 cups uncooked long-grain rice
4 cups chicken stock, divided
Salt and freshly ground white pepper
1 cup freshly grated Parmesan cheese

Melt 5 tablespoons of the butter in a large, heavy saucepan and add the scallions, parsley, and spinach. Sauté over low heat for about 5 minutes, stirring occasionally. Add the rice and cook, stirring, until thoroughly mixed with the vegetables.

Add 2 cups of the chicken stock, the salt, and pepper. Cook until absorbed, stirring occasionally. Continue adding the stock, a cup at a time, stirring almost constantly, until the rice is tender but still firm. Remove from the heat and mix in the remaining tablespoon of butter and the cheese and serve.

Ham and Tomato Risotto

Serves 4

1 white onion, finely chopped
4 tablespoons butter
¾ cup raw rice
1 cup diced boiled ham
1 tablespoon tomato puree, or ½ can condensed tomato soup
2 cups clear chicken stock
Salt and freshly ground black pepper
2 heaping tablespoons freshly grated Parmesan or Gruyère cheese
¼ cup butter, cut into small pieces

Preheat the oven to 350°F.

Cook the onion slowly in the butter until lightly browned. Add the raw rice and stir constantly over low heat until it begins to brown lightly. Add the ham; when it has heated through, add the tomato puree and the chicken stock, and bring gently to a boil. Cover tightly and bake in the oven for 25 minutes. (All the liquid should be absorbed.) Add salt and pepper to taste and stir in the cheese and butter before serving.

Rice with Champagne

As with any risotto, the liquid—in this case, champagne—is added a cup at a time, and allowed to be completely absorbed before any more is added. Add the fourth cup of champagne carefully—you may not need it all.

Serves 8

6 tablespoons butter, divided
1 small onion, peeled and very finely chopped
1½ cups Arborio or other long-grain rice
3 to 4 cups heated champagne,* divided
½ cup freshly grated Parmesan cheese

Melt 4 tablespoons of the butter in a heavy skillet; add the onion and cook over medium heat, stirring, until light golden. Add the remaining butter and, when it has melted, the rice. Stir the rice around in the butter with a fork until the grains have become coated and are almost translucent.

Keep the champagne hot in a pan on another burner. Because the champagne is added in stages, not all at once, it must be kept at a simmer or the rice will not cook properly. When the rice is coated with butter, add 1 cup of the champagne to the rice. Stir vigorously for a minute with a fork, then let the rice cook over medium-high heat until the liquid is almost absorbed, stirring now and then so it does not stick to the pan. Add another cup of champagne and continue to cook and stir until the liquid is almost absorbed.

The rice should bubble and gradually soften and become creamy. At this point, add the liquid more cautiously, ½ cup at a time, stirring until it is absorbed. You don't want to drown the rice with liquid, only add as much as it can absorb. You may find you need less, or possibly more, than the amount specified. As it cooks, taste a grain now and then.

When the risotto is done (after 25 to 30 minutes), the rice will be creamy and tender but still al dente, and all the liquid will be absorbed. Keep stirring during the final period of cooking to prevent the rice from sticking to the pan. When done, sprinkle with Parmesan cheese and stir it in with a fork. Serve at once on hot plates.

* It should be a drinkable champagne.

BEAN DISHES

Dried bean dishes have been a part of the American cuisine since our earliest days. The dried bean was here with the Indian when the first Europeans arrived, and it became a mainstay of our diet "way back when." The lentil was a later arrival and one that has a special place in my heart, perhaps because it is a product of the Pacific Northwest where I now live.

Vermont Baked Beans

These are not at all like Boston baked beans—the same principle maybe, but a different taste and slightly different texture.

Serves 6

3 cups dried pea beans
½ pound salt pork
¾ cup maple syrup
3 tablespoons sugar
2 teaspoons dry mustard
1 teaspoon salt
1 cup boiling water

Wash and soak the pea beans in cold water overnight.

Cut the salt pork into 2 pieces and scald in boiling water. Remove and score with two ½-inch-deep cuts the length of the rind.

Cover the beans with fresh water and bring slowly to a simmer. Cook for 1½ to 2 hours until the skins burst and the beans are swollen. Drain them well when done.

Preheat the oven to 300°F.

Place one piece of prepared salt pork in the bottom of a bean pot. Cover with the drained beans. Mix together the maple syrup, sugar, mustard, salt, and boiling water. Bury the second piece of salt pork, leaving just the surface of the rind exposed. Pour the maple syrup mixture over the rind and beans. Then pour enough boiling water into the pot to cover the beans. Cover and bake slowly for 8 hours, adding more boiling water if necessary.

Check the mixture occasionally. About 30 minutes before the time is up, remove the cover to let the mixture brown.

Oregon Baked Lima Beans

This is very similar to Boston baked beans, but the flavor of the lima bean is more delicate and has a taste all its own. The recipe came about because one of my students didn't know the difference between navy beans and lima beans, and bought the wrong ones. We went ahead and used lima beans and the dish was a winner. It is now standard picnic fare on the Oregon coast. Adjust the seasonings to suit yourself—that's the way Boston baked beans are made.

Serves 12

4 cups dried lima beans
1 pound thickly sliced bacon
2 teaspoons mustard
4 tablespoons brown sugar
3 teaspoons salt
1 teaspoon freshly ground black pepper
1 teaspoon ground ginger
6 tablespoons molasses

Cover the beans with cold water and soak overnight. In the morning, pour off the water, cover with fresh water in a saucepan, and simmer until the beans are tender (about 1 hour). Drain and put into a beanpot or earthen bowl with the bacon.

Preheat the oven to 250°F.

Mix the mustard, sugar, salt, pepper, and ginger with a little water. Add the molasses and mix. Pour over the beans to cover. Add about 1 cup of boiling water if there is not enough liquid. Bake, covered, for 4 hours. Stir in hot water occasionally if the beans seem too dry. At the end of 4 hours, uncover and raise the heat to 300°F.; bake until the beans are brown on top, approximately 2 more hours.

Cold White Bean Salad with Caviar

This first-course or luncheon dish is a real winner, but you can't cut corners: the black caviar is a must. Although a substitute would be nice, I have yet to find one. For the best taste, prepare the bean salad early in the day so that the flavors have a chance to develop.

Serves 8 to 10

1 pound dried white beans
1 garlic clove, peeled and slashed
2 shallots, minced
¼ red onion, finely minced
1 tablespoon chopped fresh dill
1 tablespoon chopped fresh parsley
Lemon Dressing (recipe follows)
1 small jar black caviar
Chopped chives
Chopped parsley

The night before, add the beans to a large pot of boiling salted water and cook for 45 minutes. Allow to cool overnight.

Drain the beans. Rub a bowl with garlic; add the beans, shallots, onion, dill, and parsley. Toss thoroughly with dressing until the beans are coated. When mixed, spread caviar lightly over the beans. Decorate with chopped chives and parsley and chill before serving.

Lemon Dressing

1 teaspoon salt
½ teaspoon freshly ground black pepper
¼ cup lemon juice
¾ cup olive oil

Prepare the dressing by placing the salt and pepper in a jar. Add the lemon juice slowly, stirring until well mixed. Add the olive oil; close the jar and shake well to mix.

Dakota Chili

With all the schools of chili, and all the official tasters, there's no agreement on a perfect chili. After judging a number of chili "cook-offs," I have concluded that one simply makes the chili one likes best, and that's the end of it. This recipe is one I grew up with, and I still like it, so I stick with it. The sugar used in the recipe is not for taste but to cut the acid of the tomato. It works.

Serves 20 to 24 (Makes 10 quarts)

- *2 pounds lean sliced bacon, cut into ½-inch pieces*
- *3 medium onions, cut into a large dice*
- *4 pounds lean ground beef*
- *4 16-ounce cans whole red kidney beans, including juice*
- *2 16-ounce cans garbanzo beans, drained*
- *3 16-ounce cans diced or whole tomatoes, including juice*
- *Salt and freshly ground black pepper*
- *½ teaspoon chili powder*
- *1 teaspoon sugar*
- *1 teaspoon cumin*
- *1 pound mushrooms, cleaned and quartered*

In a 12-inch skillet, fry the cut-up bacon until just crisp. Remove the bacon pieces to a paper towel to drain. Pour off all but 3 tablespoons of the bacon fat from the skillet; add the onion and sauté until just transparent. Set aside to use later.

In a 12-quart kettle or Dutch oven, fry the ground beef over high heat, stirring occasionally, until the pink color disappears. When the beef has cooked for about 10 minutes, add the drained bacon pieces and the sautéed onion, and mix together. Add the kidney beans and their juice, the garbanzo beans, and tomatoes.

Mix thoroughly and turn the heat to medium-high. When the mixture is heated through, add the seasonings: salt and pepper, chili powder, sugar, and cumin. Lower the heat and simmer, covered, for 3 hours. Taste and adjust the seasoning; continue to simmer and 30 minutes before serving add the mushrooms.

Note: If a thicker chili is desired, simmer with the lid ajar to reduce the liquid. This chili will freeze very well.

Lentils with Sausage

Lentils make a strong statement and this combination, served hot or cold, is great for luncheon or a Sunday supper. Any leftovers can be used as a base for a hearty vegetable or meat soup.

Serves 6

3 pounds tomatoes or 2 large cans whole tomatoes, drained
2 pounds cotechino sausage
2 medium yellow onions, quartered, divided
4 ribs celery, divided
2¾ cups consommé
¾ cup dry Marsala wine
2 tablespoons butter
1½ cups dried lentils
2 teaspoons salt
2 tablespoons olive oil
2 ounces lean salt pork, chopped
1 medium yellow onion, chopped
½ cup chopped celery
¼ teaspoon freshly ground black pepper

Prepare a tomato pulp by dipping the tomatoes in boiling water for 10 to 12 seconds. Remove, peel, and cut in half. Squeeze each half gently to get rid of seeds and water; if necessary, use the handle of a spoon to dig out any remaining seeds. Chop fine. Let stand in a bowl for about 20 minutes, then drain thoroughly.

Place the cotechino sausage in a kettle, cover with cold water, and let stand for 2 hours. Remove from the water, drain, prick all over with a fork, and wrap in cheesecloth. Sew it up carefully and tie all around with a string. Place it in a kettle and cover with cold water. Bring to a boil. Reduce the heat, add 1 quartered onion and 2 celery ribs, and cook over moderate heat for 3 hours. Remove from the heat and keep warm in the cooking water.

To make the Marsala sauce, dilute the consommé with Marsala and place in the top of a double boiler. Mix in the butter bit by bit, and cook, stirring with a wire whisk, until the butter is melted and the sauce is smooth and creamy. Remove from the heat and let stand for several hours.

Wash the lentils, cover with water, and bring to a boil. Remove from the heat and let soak for 1 hour. Drain. Add 3 cups of water and the remaining quartered onion, 4 celery ribs, and the salt. Bring to a boil; reduce the heat and simmer for 1 hour. Remove the onion and celery and drain the lentils. Reserve the water in which the lentils have cooked.

Heat the olive oil in a saucepan, add the salt pork and the chopped onion and chopped celery, and cook over very low heat until the onions are golden. Add the lentils, 1 cup of tomato pulp, 2 tablespoons of the reserved lentil water, and the pepper. Cook over low heat, stirring, for 10 to 15 minutes, or until the lentils have absorbed all the liquid. Remove from the heat and keep warm. Remove the sausage from the kettle, snip off the cheesecloth, drain, and cut into thin slices.

Place the sausage slices in the middle of a heated platter, surround with lentils, and pour the Marsala sauce over the cotechino slices.

Sautéed Lentils

Similar to Lentils with Sausage, but a bit more robust.

Serves 6

2 cups quick-cooking lentils
1 tablespoon salt
1 onion stuck with 2 cloves
1 bay leaf
½ pound slab bacon, cut into small dice
1 cup finely chopped onion
2 garlic cloves, finely chopped
Freshly ground black pepper
¼ cup chopped parsley

Bring the lentils to a boil in 1½ quarts of salted water to which the onion and bay leaf have been added. Simmer until the lentils are just tender, about 15 to 20 minutes (take care not to overcook them); drain, removing the onion and bay leaf.

Fry the bacon in a heavy skillet until crisp. Drain off some of the fat. Sauté the chopped onion and garlic in the remaining fat, then add the drained lentils, and toss well. Add the pepper and parsley.

Serve as a side dish with pork, beef, or lamb.

CORNMEAL DISHES

If I were told that I could only have one staple food from now on, I would choose cornmeal without a second thought. I've never been able to pass up cornmeal dishes, whether it's spoon bread soufflé, Indian pudding, or corn bread.

Cornmeal with Parmesan Cheese

My grandmother fixed cornmeal mush as far back as I can remember. She always made more than was needed and formed the leftover mush into a loaf, let it set, and then sliced it and fried it for another meal. The leftovers from this recipe can be treated the same way and served with some butter and maybe a little maple syrup.

Serves 8

1½ cups yellow cornmeal
4½ cups cold water
1 teaspoon salt
5 tablespoons butter
½ cup grated Parmesan cheese

Combine the cornmeal and water in a saucepan and bring to a boil, stirring constantly. Add the salt and butter and continue to stir until mixture has the consistency of a thick cream sauce.

Remove from the heat; transfer the cornmeal mixture to a cheesecloth-lined steamer or colander and place over boiling water, covered, to steam for about 1 hour. Transfer to a bowl and add the grated Parmesan. Serve hot.

Grits Parmesan

There are two ways of making this dish: you can follow the recipe, or you can simply make the mush, add the Parmesan, and bake in the oven for 10 or 15 minutes at 325°F.

Serves 8

1 cup quick-cooking grits
4 cups boiling water
1 teaspoon salt
6 tablespoons melted butter
½ cup freshly grated Parmesan cheese

Slowly stir the grits into the boiling water. Reduce the heat, cover the pan, and cook for 4 to 5 minutes, stirring occasionally.

Pour into a well-greased 9 x 5-inch loaf pan and allow to set in the refrigerator for a few hours.

Preheat the oven to 400°F.

Cut the grits into thin slices and arrange them overlapping in a shallow casserole. Pour the butter over the slices and sprinkle with Parmesan. Bake for 30 to 35 minutes until lightly browned.

Polenta

Polenta is a staple dish among Italian-Americans. It takes a long time to cook and needs lots of stirring and close attention, but it is worth the effort.

Serves 6

1½ cups yellow cornmeal
4½ cups cold water, divided
1 teaspoon salt
4 tablespoons butter
½ cup grated Parmesan cheese

Put the cornmeal in the top of a double boiler and stir in 1 cup of the water. Mix well. Bring the rest of the water to a boil in another pan and stir it into the cornmeal. Cook over very low heat, stirring constantly, until the mixture comes to a boil. Stir in the salt. Place over the bottom half of the double boiler filled with enough simmering water to come just below the top section. Cover and steam the polenta over the simmering water for 1 hour. Stir in the butter and cheese and serve.

Polenta with Pine Nuts and Raisins

The method I use here makes a lighter polenta and eliminates the constant stirring and watching. I am indebted to Shirley Sarvis, author and cooking colleague, for the basic recipe.

Serves 6 to 8

1 3/4 cups finely chopped onion
1/4 pound butter, divided
1 cup yellow cornmeal
4 cups cold water
1 teaspoon salt
1 pound Monterey Jack cheese, cut into 1/4-inch-thick slices, divided
1/2 cup toasted pine nuts, divided
*1/4 cup golden raisins**
2 tablespoons grated Parmesan cheese

Sauté the onion in half the butter until limp; set aside. Combine the cornmeal with the water and salt; cook over medium-high heat, whisking constantly, until the mixture has the consistency of a thick cream sauce. Remove from the heat; transfer the cornmeal to a cheesecloth-lined steamer or colander and place over boiling water, covered, to steam for at least an hour. Transfer to a mixing bowl; stir in the sautéed onion and the remaining butter.

Preheat the oven to 350°F.

Spread half the polenta mixture over the bottom of a buttered, shallow 2-quart baking dish. Top with half the Jack cheese, half the pine nuts, and all the raisins. Top with the remaining polenta and the rest of the Jack cheese and nuts. Melt the remaining butter and pour over the surface. Sprinkle with Parmesan cheese and bake for 50 minutes. Spoon out to serve.

* If necessary, steep in boiling water until plump.

Esther's Spoon Bread

This recipe was given to me by Esther Johnson, one of the best old-fashioned cooks ever. Her background was Minnesota Scandinavian, but her food was universal good.

Serves 6

2 tablespoons butter
1⅓ cups yellow cornmeal
½ cup sifted unbleached all-purpose flour
4 tablespoons sugar
1¼ teaspoons salt
1 teaspoon baking soda
1 teaspoon baking powder
1 cup whole milk
2 eggs
1 cup buttermilk
1 cup light cream

Preheat the oven to 400°F.

Melt the butter in a casserole. Sift together the cornmeal, flour, sugar, salt, baking soda, and baking powder. Stir in the milk, eggs, and buttermilk. Pour the batter into a buttered casserole and pour the cream over the top. Do not stir. Bake for 35 minutes.

Spoon Bread Soufflé

When I am asked what my favorite dish is, I don't have to think at all: this is it.

Serves 6

2 cups whole milk
½ cup white cornmeal
¼ pound butter
*5 ounces garlic cheese**
4 eggs, separated
1 teaspoon baking powder
1 teaspoon salt
1 teaspoon sugar

* Available commercially in 5-ounce jars, or make your own by mixing 1 teaspoon of Garlic Puree (see page 332) with ½ cup grated mild Cheddar. This is one time when store-bought works just as well as homemade—I've used both in this dish and can't tell the difference.

Preheat the oven to 325°F.

Combine the milk and cornmeal in a saucepan. Cook, stirring constantly, to the consistency of a thick cream sauce. Be careful not to burn. Remove from the heat and transfer to a large bowl; add the butter, stirring it in as it melts. Add the garlic cheese and stir until smooth. Cool. Add the well-beaten egg yolks, baking powder, salt, and sugar and mix well. Beat the egg whites to stiff peaks and fold into the cornmeal mixture.

Bake in a well-buttered 2-quart soufflé dish for 45 to 50 minutes, or until the top is puffed and golden.

Corn Chili Bread

You can vary this Southwest dish to suit your taste, adding more chilies for a spicy-hot version or leaving out the chilies altogether if you wish. Even without the chilies, it's an interesting variation of corn bread.

Serves 8

3 ears fresh uncooked corn or a 10-ounce package frozen corn
1 cup yellow cornmeal
2 teaspoons salt
3 tablespoons double-acting baking powder
1 cup sour cream
¼ pound plus 4 tablespoons melted butter
2 eggs, well beaten
¼ pound Gruyère or Monterey Jack cheese, finely diced
4-ounce can peeled green chilies, finely chopped

Preheat the oven to 350°F.

Scrape the kernels from the corn cobs and combine with the remaining ingredients. Pour into a well-buttered 9-inch square baking dish or a 2½-quart soufflé dish.

Bake for 1 hour (do not overbake). Serve with melted butter.

Sunday Supper Corn Bread with Sausage

Don't be limited by the title. This is a good winter brunch dish too. It's good anytime for that matter. Just be sure to leave enough of the drippings in the skillet to keep the cornmeal combination from sticking. It is good even if it sticks, but it won't look as nice.

Serves 6 to 8

1 pound link sausages
½ cup maple syrup
½ cup water
½ teaspoon cinnamon
Pinch freshly grated nutmeg
3 apples, peeled, cored, and sliced in eighths
1 cup unbleached all-purpose flour
1 cup yellow cornmeal
2 tablespoons sugar
1 tablespoon baking powder
1 teaspoon salt
1 egg
1 cup whole milk

Preheat the oven to 400°F.

Cook the sausage in a frying pan until browned on all sides; skim off the drippings and reserve.

Arrange the sausages in a pinwheel fashion in the bottom of a 9- or 10-inch cast-iron skillet.

Combine the maple syrup, water, cinnamon, and nutmeg in a 2-quart saucepan and bring to a boil. Reduce the heat to a simmer. Drop the apple slices into the simmering syrup and cook gently for about 2 minutes. Remove the apples, reserving the syrup, and arrange the slices, also in a pinwheel fashion, between the sausages.

To make the corn bread, mix together the flour, cornmeal, sugar, baking powder, and salt. In a separate bowl, beat together the egg, milk, and 3 tablespoons of the reserved sausage drippings. Pour this liquid mixture into the dry mixture and combine with a few rapid strokes.

Spoon the batter over the sausage and apples carefully, so as not to disturb the pinwheel design. Bake until the corn bread is a golden color, about 25 minutes. Invert on a serving plate. Heat the reserved syrup and pour over the top of the corn bread. Cut into wedges and serve warm.

VEGETABLES

WHEN someone tells me that there is only one way to cook a vegetable, or anything else for that matter, I bristle. There is no such thing as only one way to do anything. Asparagus does not have to be tied and standing to cook. Artichokes do not have to be cooked in oily lemon-water. Carrots do not have to be scraped before cooking. And beets do not have to be boiled; in fact, they are far better if they are baked.

I grew up eating vegetables that had been cooked to death, and I hated most of them until I learned that they could be treated far differently. I now like every vegetable I thought I hated. Oddly enough, root vegetables like turnips, rutabagas, and parsnips, which so many people refuse to eat, were the only ones I grew up liking. My maternal grandparents homesteaded in South Dakota and brought with them a knowledge of these vegetables which stemmed from their childhoods in Kentucky and Tennessee, so I had no need to develop a taste for them; it was already established, as was my love of "greens." Collard greens are still one of my favorite vegetables, next to beet greens. I used to volunteer to thin out the beets in the garden because that meant tender young beets with greens cooked in butter, salt, and pepper for dinner.

The early settlers "wintered" root vegetables and later canned the more perishable ones. From this home-canning came volume commercial canning as we know it today. While lots of canned stock is acceptable, some items should never be canned, among them, potatoes, carrots, and onions.

Today's frozen vegetables, other than those frozen in plastic packages with butter or sauce, are a good substitute when fresh are not available. Because they have already been partially cooked, it is important not to overcook them. In most cases, running boiling water over them for a few minutes after they have thawed is enough to heat them through; then add butter or whatever sauce or seasoning you want.

The techniques for cooking vegetables have probably gone through more modifications than for any other food we eat. At one time, vegetables were boiled in a lot of water; then the age of the pressure cooker reduced the amount of water. Today the trend is toward steaming. In the last analysis, it is up to the individual cook to select the method he or she wants. The method is less important than knowing the proper cooking time.

However one chooses to prepare vegetables, they should be selected carefully and handled gently. Vegetables bruise just like anything else, and this affects their texture and flavor. In buying vegetables, I usually select small- to medium-size ones because they are generally more tender and have a better flavor.

Our climate is so varied, and the soil so productive that almost every vegetable is available year round. What is not grown locally is grown somewhere else and shipped. Alas, for the most part, to meet the demand of the consumer, many items are picked too green and forced to ripen under refrigeration; the consequence is less than good. Vegetables need the sun for natural ripening. Happily, today I see more and more home vegetable gardens—not so much to save money as to ensure quality.

Artichoke Balls

This is a very rich mixture to serve with cocktails. Add additional seasonings to suit your taste.

Makes 24 canapés

2 garlic cloves, pureed
2 tablespoons olive oil
2 8-ounce cans artichoke hearts, drained and mashed
2 eggs, slightly beaten
½ cup toasted bread crumbs
½ cup grated Parmesan cheese

Sauté the garlic in oil. Add the artichoke hearts and eggs and cook over low heat for about 5 minutes, stirring constantly. Remove from heat and add the crumbs and cheese. Roll into individual balls, using about 1 teaspoon of the mixture for each ball. Chill until firm. Roll the balls in additional cheese and crumbs and bake for 10 to 15 minutes in a 350°F. oven. Serve with picks.

Asparagus with Wine Sauce

This sauce is elegant and is a welcome change from the usual hollandaise as well as being refreshing to the palate. I prefer to steam asparagus; 7 minutes is exactly the right length of time for tender, crisp results. Watch the timing; overcooked asparagus is no better than canned.

Serves 6 to 8

2 egg yolks
1 tablespoon water
1 cup dry white wine
2 tablespoons butter, softened
¼ cup heavy cream
¼ teaspoon freshly ground white pepper
3 pounds fresh young asparagus
1 quart boiling water
½ teaspoon salt

Combine the egg yolks, water, and wine in the top of a double boiler. Place over warm water and beat with a wire whisk, increasing the heat of the water, and continuing to beat until the mixture is thick and creamy. Do not allow to boil. Beat in the butter. Remove from hot water and mix in the cream and pepper. Keep the sauce hot.

Wash the asparagus carefully and steam over boiling salted water until tender-crisp (about 7 minutes). Remove from the steamer and arrange in a single layer on a platter. Cover with wine sauce.

Green Beans

Serves 4

1 pound fresh green beans
2 quarts boiling water
Dash salt
Dash soda
2 tablespoons butter

Prepare the beans by slicing down the center and cutting off both ends. Put the beans into boiling water with salt and soda. Bring again to a boil and cook for no more than 10 or 15 minutes. Check occasionally so as not to overcook. Drain thoroughly.

Melt a large lump of butter in a pan; add the drained beans and shake them in the butter until coated. Serve immediately.

Sauté of Green Beans

Refreshing and it takes very little time to complete. Fresh beans are best with this dish, but if frozen is all that is on hand, go ahead and use them. Just don't cook them very much because they are partially cooked to begin with.

Serves 4

1 large sweet onion (about 4 ounces), halved and finely sliced
4 tablespoons butter, divided
2 medium tomatoes, peeled, seeded, and coarsely chopped, or the equivalent amount of canned tomatoes, drained and chopped
Salt
½ teaspoon dried oregano
1½ pounds green beans, parboiled for 8 to 10 minutes until slightly firm, well drained
Freshly ground black pepper
Handful chopped parsley, divided

Cook the onion gently in half the butter in a large skillet for 15 to 20 minutes, stirring occasionally, until soft but not browned. In a separate pan, stew the tomatoes in the remaining butter with a pinch of salt and the oregano, tossing to prevent sticking, until nearly dry, about 10 to 15 minutes. Add the beans to the onion; add salt, turn the heat to medium, and toss regularly for about 15 minutes. Add the tomatoes, pepper, and half the parsley, toss all together for 5 minutes or so. Sprinkle with the remaining parsley and serve.

Creamed Broad Beans and Bacon

Savory is a must with this dish; use either fresh or dried, but preferably fresh. You can also add a pinch of sugar.

Serves 6 to 8

5 pounds fresh young broad beans
4 ounces lean bacon slices
1 tablespoon butter
1 branch fresh savory or a pinch of finely crumbled dried savory
Salt
½ cup water (approx.)
⅔ cup heavy cream
3 egg yolks
Pepper
Lemon juice
Chopped parsley
Finely chopped fresh savory leaves, if available

Shell the beans and remove the skins from all except the tiny bright green ones. Cut the bacon slices into ½-inch pieces; parboil in water for a few seconds and drain.

Cook the bacon in a heavy saucepan over very low heat for a few minutes (it should remain limp). Add the butter, beans, savory, and salt with just enough water to moisten lightly. Cover tightly. Turn the heat to high for a few seconds to launch the cooking; turn it to low again to allow the beans to "sweat" in their steam. Cook for 20 to 30 minutes, shaking the pan gently from time to time, until the beans are tender. Remove from the heat and cool for a few minutes.

Mix together the cream, egg yolks, and pepper. Stir gently into the beans. Cook over low heat, stirring, until the sauce is slightly thickened. Do not allow to boil. Squeeze in a few drops of lemon juice to taste. Sprinkle with chopped parsley and savory. Serve directly from the saucepan.

Baked Beets

I first found out that I could bake a beet when I read an old White House cookbook. I have no idea of the publication date because the book came to me coverless with the first ten pages missing, but it changed my life where beets are concerned. I guarantee that once you taste a baked beet, you'll never boil another one. The moisture is on the inside, not in the water, and everything about it is better: less mess, easier to handle, and a far superior taste.

Serves 6 to 8

6 to 8 medium to large unpeeled, unwashed beets
3 to 4 tablespoons melted butter or margarine
1 teaspoon sugar
Salt and freshly ground black pepper

Preheat the oven to 400°F.

Line a Dutch oven or casserole with foil. *Do not wash the beets;* remove any soil with a dry paper towel. Moisture will cause the beets to steam, and you do not want this to happen.

Leave ½ inch of the stem and the "tail" (root) on the beets. Place them in the foil-lined Dutch oven or casserole; cover and bake for 1 hour.

Remove the beets from the oven and the baking container, and allow them to cool for about 5 minutes. When they are cool enough to handle, remove the stems and skin. Leave the tails on if you are serving the beets whole; remove if you are dicing or slicing them. The skin is easily removed simply by slipping it off with the fingers.

Place the skinned beets, sliced, diced, or whole, in a saucepan or skillet. Add the melted butter and season with the sugar, salt, and pepper. Heat through and serve.

Variation: Baked Beets in Cream—Bake beets as directed above. Peel and cut them into thin slices. Pour ½ cup of thick cream over them and heat. Season to taste with salt and pepper, and just before serving add lemon juice.

Puree of Broccoli

Serves 4 to 6

2 10-ounce packages frozen broccoli
2 tablespoons butter
3 tablespoons unbleached all-purpose flour
1 teaspoon salt
½ teaspoon freshly ground black pepper
¼ teaspoon grated nutmeg
4 tablespoons sour cream
3 tablespoons melted butter

Cook the frozen broccoli according to package directions. Drain and put through the finest disk of a food mill. Melt the butter in a saucepan, stir in the flour, and cook, stirring, over high heat until the roux is slightly browned. Add the salt, pepper, and nutmeg. Add the pureed broccoli and stir in the sour cream and melted butter.

Brussels Sprouts Gratin

Too often sprouts are overcooked and soggy and consequently have a most disagreeable taste. Not so with this recipe.

Serves 4

1 pound small brussels sprouts, outer leaves removed
2 ounces lean bacon, cut into ½-inch widths
2 tablespoons butter
Salt and freshly ground black pepper
½ cup heavy cream
⅓ cup bread crumbs
Butter

Preheat the oven to 400°F.

Parboil the sprouts for 12 minutes, then drain them, refresh in cold water, and chop coarsely.

Cook the bacon lightly in butter until limp but not crisp. Add the sprouts, season, and toss over medium heat for a minute.

Spread into a buttered baking dish, spoon the cream over the surface, sprinkle with bread crumbs, and distribute paper-thin shavings of butter on top. Bake for 25 minutes.

I HAVE always been particularly fond of cabbage, raw or cooked, and deliberately have included a number of recipes because I feel that it has been misused and maligned. The crunch and fresh taste of the raw is delightful in coleslaw or other salads, and cooked it takes on an entirely different taste. Green cabbage is young or early cabbage, white is older and has a heavier head. Either can be used in recipes that call for green cabbage. However, if a recipe calls for red cabbage, be sure you use it. I prefer to use red cabbage raw, mixed with green or white cabbage in coleslaw, for the color that it lends; the recipe below is an exception.

Red Cabbage

Red (or purple) cabbage is quite different from the other varieties. Cooked, it tends to turn bluish and loses flavor; it is generally cooked with apples and either brown or white sugar. The addition of vinegar or chopped beets to the cooking water of red cabbage will help retain the color.

Serves 8

2 heads red cabbage, washed and finely sliced
2 tablespoons cider vinegar
1 onion, finely chopped
2 tablespoons bacon fat
3 tablespoons butter, divided
1 bay leaf
3 whole cloves
2 peppercorns
2 tart apples, peeled and finely sliced
1 teaspoon unbleached all-purpose flour
1 teaspoon sugar
Juice of ½ lemon

Marinate the sliced cabbage in water to cover, to which the vinegar has been added. Brown the onion in the bacon fat and 2 tablespoons of the butter. Add the cabbage to the browned onions with the bay leaf, cloves, peppercorns, and apples. Cook slowly until tender, about 15 to 20 minutes, stirring frequently.

Melt the remaining butter in a saucepan; add the flour, stir, and add to the cabbage mixture. Sprinkle with the sugar and lemon juice. Simmer for 1 to 2 minutes and serve.

Creamed Cabbage

Don't even consider this unless you are willing to take on a last-minute chore, which is when this must be cooked if it isn't to be overcooked.

Serves 6

1 large head green cabbage, shredded
¼ cup minced onion
2 tablespoons butter
3 ounces cream cheese, softened
2 teaspoons snipped fresh dillweed or 1 teaspoon dried dillseed
Salt and freshly ground black pepper

In a large saucepan, cook the shredded cabbage in salted water to cover for 3 minutes. Drain the cabbage, refresh it under running cold water, and drain it well again.

In a saucepan, sauté the onion in the butter until softened; add the cabbage and toss well. Cut the cream cheese into bits and add to the cabbage. Cook the mixture over low heat, stirring, until the cheese is melted. Add the dill, salt, and pepper and simmer for 2 minutes more.

Sautéed Cabbage

Pepper bacon is available in many butcher shops. If you can't find it, just pound some cracked pepper into thick slices of bacon to create the same effect. This dish is especially good with roast pork or grilled pork chops.

Serves 12 to 14

1¼ pounds pepper bacon, chopped
¼ pound plus 4 tablespoons butter
¼ cup (approx.) fat from pork roast, or bacon fat
2 heads green cabbage, chopped
1 large onion, minced
½ lemon, peeled and chopped
Salt and freshly ground black pepper

Cook the bacon in two skillets over medium heat until crisped. Remove with a slotted spoon, add the butter and any fat from pork roast (if available) and heat over medium-high heat. Add the cabbage and onion and cook quickly over high heat for about 5 minutes, or until tender-crisp. Stir in the lemon, bacon, salt, and pepper to taste.

Note: Depending on the size of the heads of green cabbage you may not need two skillets.

Savoy Cabbage

Savoy or curly cabbage is decorative and has a delicate texture and a bit stronger taste than either white or red cabbage.

Serves 6 to 8

2 heads savoy cabbage, washed, cut in quarters, and soaked in cold water for 30 minutes
1 small onion, finely chopped
2 tablespoons butter
1 tablespoon unbleached all-purpose flour
¼ cup meat stock, or 1 teaspoon beef extract dissolved in ¼ cup water and cabbage juice
Salt and freshly ground black pepper
Grated nutmeg

Cook the cabbage in salted boiling water for 10 minutes. Drain well and chop fine.

Brown the onion in the butter and sprinkle with flour. Add the chopped cabbage and the stock and season with salt and pepper to taste. Sprinkle with a little nutmeg, cook for 10 minutes, and serve.

Cabbage Casserole with Cheese

This is a nice accompaniment to a boiled brisket of beef. You can change the seasonings in this recipe to suit your palate. Clove and allspice are my choices because they remind me of a cabbage dish I used to have as a child.

Serves 8

3-pound green cabbage
6 tablespoons butter, divided
3 tablespoons unbleached all-purpose flour
2 cups whole milk
1½ cups grated sharp Cheddar cheese
Salt and freshly ground black pepper
½ cup finely chopped onion
1 garlic clove, minced
½ cup dry white wine
½ teaspoon ground cloves
½ teaspoon ground allspice
3 tablespoons grated Parmesan cheese

Pull off and discard the tough outer leaves of the cabbage. Discard any blemished leaves. Cut away and discard the core and cut the cabbage into eighths. Cut each eighth into 1-inch-thick pieces.

Bring a large quantity of salted water to a boil and add the cabbage pieces. Cook about 2 minutes; drain.

Melt 2 tablespoons of the butter in a saucepan and add the flour, stirring with wire whisk. When blended, add the milk, stirring rapidly. Remove from the heat, add the cheese and stir until melted and smooth. Reheat if necessary. Add the salt and pepper to taste; set aside.

Heat the remaining butter in a large, heavy skillet and add the onion and garlic. When wilted, add the drained cabbage, wine, cloves, and allspice. Sprinkle with salt and pepper. Partly cover and cook, stirring occasionally, until the liquid evaporates.

Preheat the oven to 400°F.

Add half the cheese sauce to the cabbage and blend, then spoon the mixture into an oval baking dish and smooth over. Add the remaining cheese sauce and level. Sprinkle with Parmesan cheese. Bake for 15 to 20 minutes, or until bubbling throughout and nicely browned on top.

Cabbage Loaf

This is good hot or cold. I use it as a side dish, but if you add ham and a sauce, as in the variation, it can serve as a main luncheon dish.

Serves 8

1 medium green cabbage (about 2½ pounds), quartered, with the core and ribs removed
½ cup unbleached all-purpose flour
Salt and freshly ground black pepper
3 eggs
⅔ cup whole milk
1 tablespoon olive oil
Butter for the mold

Parboil the cabbage for 30 minutes. Drain thoroughly, squeeze dry, and chop.

Combine the flour, seasonings, eggs, milk, and olive oil in a mixing bowl, working from the center out and whisking until smooth. Set aside for 30 minutes.

Preheat the oven to 400°F.

Add the chopped cabbage to the mixture and pour into a generously buttered baking dish. (If it is to be unmolded when done, press a piece of buttered parchment paper into the bottom of the mold before filling it.)

Bake for 30 to 40 minutes until the center of the loaf is firm to the touch. The loaf may be unmolded or served directly from the baking dish. If it is being unmolded, it should be allowed to stand for a few minutes after coming out of the oven so that it can set. Run a knife around the edges before unmolding.

Variations: Serve hot with a Béchamel or tomato sauce, to which a bit of butter has been added at the last minute. To serve cold, add cubes of boiled ham to the mixture before pouring into the mold.

Carrots in Orange Marmalade

When children refuse carrots, try this recipe and see if it doesn't make them change their minds. The sweetness of the marmalade does not obliterate the taste of the carrot. And, I am sure that whatever is in the carrot that is supposed to enable you to see in the dark will still be there.

Serves 8

6 cups peeled carrots, thinly sliced on the diagonal
2 tablespoons butter
¼ cup chicken stock
½ teaspoon salt
½ teaspoon freshly ground black pepper
1 cup orange marmalade
Dash Grand Marnier (optional)

Put the carrots, butter, and stock in a heavy saucepan. Cook, covered, over low heat for 3 minutes. Add the remaining ingredients and cook, uncovered, until the carrots are tender and the sauce has become a thick glaze. Stir often as the sauce thickens.

Carrot Pudding

This dish looks as good as it tastes. For an impressive presentation, it can be baked in a precooked pastry shell.

Serves 4 to 6

2 pounds carrots, peeled
6 tablespoons butter
Juice of ½ lemon or ½ orange
Salt and freshly ground black pepper
1 teaspoon sugar
1½ cups heavy cream
3 eggs
Butter for the baking dish

Peel and coarsely grate the carrots or pass them through the medium shredding blade of a food processor.

In a saucepan, combine the carrots, butter, lemon or orange juice, salt, pepper, and sugar. Add just enough water to barely cover. Bring to a boil and simmer, covered, for about 30 minutes. Then remove the cover and cook over high heat, stirring all the time, until the liquid has evaporated. Allow to cool for about 10 minutes.

Preheat the oven to 325°F.

Whisk together the cream, eggs, salt, and pepper, and stir into the carrots. Pour into a buttered baking dish and bake for about 35 minutes, or until the surface is puffed and brown.

Carrots Vichy

Properly cooked, carrots have a great deal of character, taste good, and give great color to the plate. They go with almost any menu because they don't make a strong statement. "Vichy" is a cooking method less elegantly known as "sweating." It is accomplished by pressing a piece of aluminum foil right down on the vegetable and then cooking with a lid on the pan.

Serves 6

½ pound butter
Salt
1 teaspoon sugar
*3 bunches young carrots, finely sliced**
⅓ cup cognac or brandy

Preheat the oven to 350°F.

Melt the butter in an enamel baking dish, add salt and sugar and mix well. Add the carrots and cognac. Cover with foil and the pan lid and bake for 1 hour.

Do not stir during the baking, but watch carefully to make sure that the carrots do not become hard or brown.

* If carrots have just been pulled from the garden, do not peel them; otherwise, do.

Carrots and Leeks Vichy

Carrots and peas have traditionally been linked and it's a bad marriage—they cannot be cooked together properly because their cooking times differ. However, carrots and leeks are a wonderful combination that complements every meat dish I can think of. Covering the saucepan tightly with foil means the vegetables will sweat, which keeps the flavor inside the dish and also cooks the vegetables very fast.

Serves 8

10 carrots, peeled (unless very fresh and young)
4 leeks, white part only, roots cut off, split and thoroughly rinsed
¼ pound butter, melted, divided
2 tablespoons cold water
2 teaspoons sugar
1 teaspoon salt
½ teaspoon freshly ground black pepper

Cut the carrots and leeks into very thin slivers. Place in a saucepan with 4 tablespoons of the butter, the water, sugar, salt, and pepper. Cover with foil, pressing it right down onto the vegetables inside the pan; put the lid on over the foil. Place over medium-high heat and cook for about 20 minutes; shake occasionally. Place the vegetables in a serving dish and pour the remaining melted butter over them.

Carrots in Cream Sauce

Serves 4

1 pound carrots, unpeeled
Coarse salt
2 tablespoons butter
Salt and freshly ground white pepper
½ cup heavy cream (approx.)

Cut off the tips of the carrots at both ends but do not scrape or peel them. Place in a large bowl of cold water and let them soak for about 15 minutes.

Fill a 6-quart kettle with water, add coarse salt, and heat. When the water reaches the boiling point, add the carrots and let them boil until cooked but still firm, about 15 minutes.

Drain the carrots and place in a large bowl of ice water to cool. When cooled, peel by gently pushing off the outer skin. Cut the carrots into small slices, about ⅛ inch. Heat the butter in a saucepan. Add the carrot slices and sauté for about 5 minutes.

Season with salt and pepper. Add the cream, 1 tablespoon at a time, stirring slowly until it is absorbed. Continue to add more cream whenever the cream in the pan is nearly absorbed. The carrots are ready to serve when all the cream is absorbed.

Cauliflower with Cream Sauce and Buttered Crumbs

A fresh head of cauliflower should be very compact and feel heavy for its size. If the florets are loose and spread apart it means the cauliflower is way past its prime. When cooking cauliflower, start checking for doneness after 10 minutes, using a sharp skewer and testing in the stalk. It usually takes about 20 to 25 minutes to cook; once overcooked, it becomes mushy and tasteless.

Serves 4

1 firm head cauliflower
3 tablespoons butter, divided
3 tablespoons unbleached all-purpose flour
2 cups whole milk, heated
Parsley bouquet
1 bay leaf
Salt and freshly ground black pepper
⅔ cup fresh bread crumbs

Remove the leaves and part of thick stem of the cauliflower. Soak the cauliflower, head down, for 20 minutes in salted water.

Plunge the cauliflower into boiling salted water and cook for 20 minutes. When done, place, head up, on a heated platter.

Make a sauce by melting 1 tablespoon of the butter in a saucepan, adding the flour, milk, parsley, bay leaf, salt, and pepper. Cook slowly until thickened. Pass through a fine sieve and pour over the cauliflower.

Fry the bread crumbs in the remaining 2 tablespoons of butter until crisp and brown, about 3 minutes. Sprinkle over the cauliflower before serving.

Cauliflower Mousse with Mornay Sauce

This is definitely a party dish. It can be cooked and served in individual ramekins, or in a mold to be unmolded and served at the table; the Mornay sauce can be poured on, or passed for individual helpings.

Serves 6

2 pounds cauliflower
1 tablespoon salt
1/8 teaspoon cayenne pepper
1/4 teaspoon freshly grated nutmeg
1 cup medium Béchamel Sauce (see page 310)
6 eggs
Butter to grease the soufflé dish
2 tablespoons bread crumbs
2 tablespoons chopped parsley
2 cups Mornay Sauce (see page 312)

Cut the cauliflower into large pieces. Cook in water to cover, with 1 tablespoon of salt, until tender. Drain. Add the cayenne pepper and nutmeg to the cauliflower and puree through a food mill, using the finest disk. *Do not put it in a blender.* Catch the puree in a large bowl. Mix the Béchamel sauce into the cauliflower puree. Beat the eggs just enough to mix them (they should not be frothy), then fold into the cauliflower mixture. Taste for salt and, if desired, add some. Pour into a 6- or 8-cup soufflé dish that has been greased and dusted with bread crumbs.

Preheat the oven to 350°F.

Set the dish in a pan of hot water and bake for 45 to 55 minutes, or until the mousse begins to pull away from the edge of the dish. Do not leave in the oven too long. The mousse will continue to cook after it is taken out of the oven, and if overcooked, it will tend to separate and become watery.

Serve in the soufflé dish or unmold onto a platter. Garnish with parsley, and serve with Mornay sauce.

Note: To unmold, let rest for 5 to 10 minutes after removing from the oven, then invert on a platter.

Celery Root Ring with Mushroom Sauce

Celery root and celeriac are one and the same. Don't pass it up when it's in the market—it isn't there very often. Because it tends to discolor, once peeled, celery root should be plunged into cold salted water immediately. Cooked, it is similar to a potato in texture but has more taste. It is great in soups, lending a nice celery flavor, and boiled and diced, it is wonderful in potato salad. Celery root is sometimes served in a herring salad with diced apples, potatoes, and beets. Cooked and pureed, it is especially good with game.

Serves 8

4 medium celery roots (about 3½ pounds)
1 teaspoon salt
Dash freshly ground black pepper
4 tablespoons butter
¼ cup heavy cream
2 eggs, separated
Mushroom Sauce (recipe follows)
Parsley for garnish

Peel and quarter the celery roots. Clean away any soft fiber from the centers; rinse. Cover with salted water in a saucepan. Bring to a boil, then lower the heat and cook until tender, about 30 to 45 minutes. Remove from the heat and drain in a colander.

Preheat the oven to 350°F.

Return the celery roots to the saucepan while still hot; add the salt, pepper, butter, cream, and egg yolks. Mash until smooth. Beat the egg whites in a bowl until stiff but not dry. Fold into the celery root mixture.

Put the mixture into a buttered 6-cup ring mold and bake for 45 minutes.

Remove the celery root ring from the oven. Put a platter or serving dish upside down on top of the ring mold. Turn the dish and the ring mold over and let stand for 2 minutes. Remove the ring mold, pour the Mushroom Sauce into the center of the celery root ring, and garnish with parsley.

Mushroom Sauce for Celery Root Ring

Makes 3 cups

½ pound fresh mushrooms
2 medium garlic cloves
7 tablespoons butter, divided
3 tablespoons unbleached all-purpose flour
1 teaspoon salt
2 cups light cream

Clean and cut the mushrooms into thin slices, then slice into thin strips. Peel the garlic cloves and put through a garlic press. Sauté the mushrooms and pressed garlic in 2 tablespoons of the butter for 8 minutes. Set aside.

Melt the remaining butter in a saucepan. Add the flour slowly; cook and stir over low heat for 4 minutes. Add the salt. Pour in the cream slowly, stirring constantly. Cook over low heat for 3 minutes. Add the mushroom mixture and keep warm.

Chard Timbales

Nutmeg is the contrasting complement for some foods, and chard is one of them. No other seasoning can take its place.

Serves 6

2 bunches chard, washed
½ cup whole milk
4 eggs plus 1 egg yolk
1 cup finely chopped onion
1 garlic clove, minced
Salt and freshly ground black pepper
Pinch freshly grated nutmeg
¾ cup Parmesan and Gruyère cheeses, grated

Preheat the oven to 350°F.

Chop the chard; cook it in the milk until tender. Combine the eggs and egg yolk with the onion, garlic, salt, and pepper, and add to the chard-milk mixture. Add the nutmeg and the grated cheeses and mix well. Fill individual molds three quarters full. Cover the molds with buttered parchment paper or waxed paper. Set the molds in a larger pan of hot water and bake in the oven for 35 minutes, or until the custard has set.

Puree of Chick-Peas

If too much liquid is added during the pureeing process, the puree becomes too loose or runny. If this happens, add a tablespoon of fresh bread crumbs to the puree, cook briefly to remove any taste of the bread, and the puree will return to the proper texture.

Serves 8

2 15-ounce cans chick-peas (garbanzo beans)
½ cup heavy cream
2 tablespoons butter
Pinch nutmeg

Drain the liquid from the chick-peas and discard. Rinse the chick-peas thoroughly.

Combine with the cream and puree in a food processor using the metal blade. Use an "on-off" motion with the processor to retain some texture. Add the butter and nutmeg and transfer to a saucepan. Heat on top of the stove to melt the butter.

Note: This can be served when you would serve any starch, like rice or potatoes. It is particularly good with roast beef, pork, and poultry.

Baked Corn

What is better than garden-fresh corn on the cob? Actually nothing. But this is a good second. If you grow your own corn or have fresh-picked at your disposal, try this recipe. It's a wonderful way to fix fresh corn.

Serves 6 to 8

24 large ears corn
1½ teaspoons salt
¼ teaspoon coarsely ground black pepper
1 tablespoon sugar
½ pound butter, melted

Preheat the oven to 375°F.

Husk the corn. With a sharp knife, score each row of kernels; then slice off in a thin layer. Scrape well with the dull side of the knife to extract all the remaining milky pulp. The yield will be about 8 cups. Season the corn pulp with salt, pepper, and sugar and mix with melted butter. Butter two 9-inch ovenproof glass pie plates and fill them with the corn pulp mixture.

Bake for 40 to 50 minutes, or until the sides and top are crusty and golden brown.

Corn Pudding

I have tried this recipe using fresh corn but like it better with canned. That wonderful fresh-picked taste isn't missed in a pudding recipe. This is the best corn pudding I have ever eaten, and I've tested enough of them to be able to make that statement with confidence.

Serves 8

16-ounce can whole-kernel corn, drained
16-ounce can cream-style corn
1 tablespoon melted butter
1 teaspoon salt
1 teaspoon sugar
5 eggs
1 cup whole milk
1 cup heavy cream
1½ cups Homemade Bread Crumbs (see page 335)

Preheat the oven to 300°F.

Combine the whole and creamed corn, butter, salt, and sugar.

Beat the eggs lightly, and beat in the milk and cream. Combine with the corn mixture.

Pour into a well-greased 7½ x 10½ x 2-inch baking dish. Bake for 40 minutes. Reduce the heat to 250°F. and bake an additional 20 minutes.

Sprinkle the crumbs over the top and serve.

Fried Cucumbers

Here's a recipe for those of you who have type-cast cucumbers in salads only.

Serves 4 to 6

2 medium cucumbers, peeled
2 scallions, trimmed and finely sliced
2 tablespoons butter, divided
Salt and freshly ground black pepper
4 tablespoons sour cream
2 tablespoons chopped fresh dill or chives, or 1 or 2 teaspoons dried

Use an apple corer to remove the cucumber seeds or halve them and scoop out the seeds. Cut into thin slices. Sauté the scallions gently in half the butter for about a minute. Add the remaining butter and the cucumber slices and sauté, shaking the pan occasionally. When the cucumber slices begin to give water, season generously, stir in the sour cream, and sprinkle with dill. Cook until the sour cream is warm.

Cucumbers in Cream

This is excellent with plain poached salmon and tiny boiled potatoes.

Serves 6 to 8

8 small cucumbers, peeled and sliced
2 tablespoons butter
2 tablespoons unbleached all-purpose flour
2 cups light cream, scalded
Salt and freshly ground black pepper
½ cup heavy cream
Chopped chives for garnish

Boil the cucumbers in salted water until tender (about 8 to 10 minutes). Drain and pour cold water over them. Spread on a dish towel to drain further.

Melt the butter, add the flour and light cream, and cook in a double boiler for 15 minutes. Season to taste. Add the cucumbers and heavy cream. Sprinkle with chives and serve.

Eggplant Custard I

Pick eggplant without bruises, and look for smaller ones which will be more tender. Japanese eggplants, which are small and narrow, are the most tender and flavorful (you would need 4 of them for this recipe). The more common, larger variety is bitter and needs to be salted before being used in anything. The best way to get rid of the bitter taste is to cut the eggplant, salt the slices or chunks, and let them rest for an hour or so. The bitter juice, a brownish liquid, will be extracted from the meat and can be discarded. Depending on how the eggplant is to be cooked, either wash the salt away or leave as it is. Just don't add salt if the recipe calls for it until you are tasting for a seasoning adjustment.

Serves 4

1 large eggplant, sliced
Salt
4 eggs, lightly beaten
1 quart light cream
Freshly ground black pepper
Nutmeg

Preheat the oven to 275°F.

Salt the eggplant slices; press them to remove excess moisture. Cut into cubes. Simmer in 2 cups of water for 3 minutes and drain. Mix the eggs and cream; season with salt, pepper, and nutmeg. Put into a 2-quart casserole with the eggplant. Bake for 1 hour, uncovered.

Eggplant Custard II

This more piquant Mediterranean version of eggplant custard goes very well with pork.

Serves 4

10 ounces mushrooms passed through medium blade of a vegetable mill or chopped in a food processor
Salt and freshly ground black pepper
Olive oil
½ lemon
2 large, firm, ripe tomatoes, peeled, seeded, and coarsely chopped, or 1 cup drained, canned tomatoes
1 garlic clove, crushed, peeled, and finely chopped
1½ pounds eggplant
2 eggs
1 cup whole milk
⅛ teaspoon (approx.) powdered saffron dissolved in 1 or 2 tablespoons boiling water

Preheat the oven to 375°F.

Season the mushroom pieces and sauté in a little olive oil over high heat until their liquid has evaporated. Squeeze in a few drops of lemon juice.

Season and stew the tomatoes in 2 tablespoons of olive oil until nearly dry, stirring in the garlic a minute before removing from the heat.

Cut the eggplant into ⅓- to ½-inch slices. Cook immediately in a skillet containing ½ inch of olive oil. When golden on both sides and tender, remove to drain on absorbent paper; sprinkle with salt and pepper.

Spread the mushrooms on the bottom of an oiled, shallow 2-quart casserole. Arrange half the eggplant slices on the mushrooms. Spread them with the stewed tomato mixture, and arrange the remaining eggplant slices on top. Beat the eggs with a whisk; add the milk, a little salt, and the saffron, and pour over the vegetables, lifting them gently around the sides to allow the liquid to penetrate.

Bake for about 30 minutes, until the custard has just set in the center.

Jerusalem Artichoke Soufflé

Jerusalem artichokes, or sun chokes, are very versatile, yet I hardly ever find them on a menu or served in private homes. My friend Mrs. Robert Pamplin, Sr., really made me aware of them some time ago when she gave me a jar of home-canned artichoke pickles, and followed it with the recipe. After that, I started growing them myself. I use them sliced raw in salads or steam them and serve them as a side vegetable seasoned with a bit of butter and salt and pepper, but my favorite is this soufflé recipe.

Serves 8

¾ pound Jerusalem artichokes
4 tablespoons butter
3 tablespoons unbleached all-purpose flour
Scant ½ cup whole milk
2 tablespoons finely chopped parsley
Salt and freshly ground black pepper
4 eggs, separated

Scrub the artichokes, cover with lightly salted water, and bring to a boil. Cook until just tender and drain, reserving a scant ½ cup of the cooking liquid. When cool enough to handle, peel and puree through the medium or coarse mesh of a vegetable mill. Dry out the puree by stirring over very low heat.

Preheat the oven to 400°F.

In another pan, melt the butter and stir in the flour. Heat the milk and reserved cooking water and pour into the butter and flour. Stir until smooth. Bring to the boiling point and simmer for 4 minutes. Stir in the puree and the parsley. Season with salt and pepper and remove from the heat. Beat the egg yolks into the sauce. Beat the egg whites to stiff peaks and fold into the slightly cooled mixture. Turn into a buttered soufflé dish and bake for 20 minutes.

Note: Turnips or carrots may be used instead of Jerusalem artichokes.

Jerusalem Artichokes with Cheese Sauce

A good cheese is essential in making this dish. I have chosen Gruyère for its taste, quality, and texture. Cheddars can be used too, although I think they make too strong a statement. This recipe takes less than 30 minutes to make, and is my favorite accompaniment to broiled venison chops.

Serves 4

1½ pounds Jerusalem artichokes

Cheese Sauce

⅔ cup whole milk
½ bay leaf
1 slice onion
2 cloves
4 tablespoons butter
3 tablespoons unbleached all-purpose flour
½ cup light cream
¼ pound Gruyère cheese, grated
Salt and freshly ground black pepper

Scrub the artichokes well and put in a pan of cold water. Add salt, bring to a boil, and cook until tender when pierced with a fork, about 5 to 7 minutes. Drain, reserving 1 cup of the cooking water. When cool enough to handle, peel the artichokes and cut into thick slices. Place in an ovenproof dish and keep warm while the sauce is made.

To make the sauce, heat the milk with the bay leaf, onion, and cloves. Just before it boils, cover and remove from the heat. Allow to stand for 15 minutes; then strain it. Melt the butter; stir in the flour and blend with the reserved cooking water, strained milk, and cream. Simmer until thickened and smooth. Reserve a little of the cheese; add the rest to the sauce and stir until blended. Pour over the artichokes, sprinkle with the reserved cheese, and brown under the broiler.

The dish may be prepared ahead and reheated for 20 to 25 minutes in a 400°F. oven.

Mushroom Roll

If you want to wow your guests, try this. It might seem difficult to do, but it isn't. Try it on the family first if you have doubts. It's very good no matter how it looks, and the second one you make should be perfect.

Serves 8

¾ cup dry bread crumbs (approx.), divided
1½ pounds mushrooms, washed and finely chopped
6 tablespoons butter, melted
5 eggs, separated
Salt, freshly ground black pepper, and nutmeg
Scrambled eggs or cooked asparagus tips

Grease an 11 x 15 x ½-inch jelly-roll pan and line it with waxed paper, leaving about a 1-inch overhang of paper at each end. Grease the paper and sprinkle with 2 to 3 tablespoons of bread crumbs. Set aside.

Preheat the oven to 350°F.

Put the mushrooms in a dish towel and twist very hard to squeeze out all the moisture. Transfer them to a bowl and mix in the butter, egg yolks, salt, pepper, and nutmeg with just enough bread crumbs to make the mixture hold together (about ¼ cup).

Beat the egg whites until they hold soft peaks, as for a soufflé, and fold quickly and thoroughly into the mushroom mixture. Turn into the prepared pan and smooth the top evenly with a rubber spatula. Bake for 12 to 16 minutes, or until the center feels barely firm when touched.

Put a sheet of buttered waxed paper or foil over the top of the roll and invert it onto a warm platter or long board. With the aid of the overhanging ends of waxed paper, carefully peel away the paper the roll was baked on, gently loosening it with the point of a knife where necessary. It does not matter if a little bit of the surface of the roll sticks to the paper, since this is the side you will fill.

Fill the roll with scrambled eggs, or with asparagus tips that have been cooked in boiling salted water until just done but still crisp. Roll up with the aid of the waxed paper or foil and serve as a luncheon or a supper dish.

Stuffed Mushrooms

Serve as a first course on buttered toast sprinkled with Parmesan cheese, or use as a garnish with meat or game.

Serves 6

3 dozen medium mushrooms
2 garlic cloves, finely chopped
1 cup Homemade Bread Crumbs (see page 335)
½ cup grated Parmesan cheese
1 egg, well beaten
Salt and freshly ground black pepper
2 tablespoons olive oil
6 tablespoons chopped parsley (approx.)
4 tablespoons butter
1 cup dry white wine

Preheat the oven to 400°F.

Wipe the mushrooms well with damp paper towels to remove any dirt. Dry thoroughly. Remove the stems and chop fine. Combine with the garlic, bread crumbs, cheese, egg, salt, pepper, and olive oil.

Stuff the mushroom caps with this mixture; sprinkle with parsley, dot with butter, and arrange in a baking dish. Pour in the white wine and bake for 15 minutes (if you are using very large mushrooms, they will have to cook longer).

Mushrooms with Garlic Butter

This can be a supper or luncheon main dish or a vegetable side dish.

Serves 4

4 slices firm-textured bread
Olive oil
3 garlic cloves, divided
16 large mushroom caps
Lemon juice
4 tablespoons butter
5 tablespoons finely chopped parsley, divided
Paprika

Fry the bread in oil flavored with 1 garlic clove until crisp and browned on both sides. Remove and keep hot.

Add a little more oil to the pan and sauté the mushroom caps, sprinkling with a little lemon juice until just cooked through but still firm. Remove to a hot dish.

Knead together the butter, 4 tablespoons of the parsley, and the remaining garlic cloves, crushed. When well blended and soft, spread the butter on the fried toast and arrange 4 mushrooms on each slice. Dot each mushroom with a little more of the garlic butter, sprinkle liberally with more chopped parsley, and dust with paprika. Put under the broiler for just a minute before serving.

Mushroom Casserole

Serve on toast rounds as a luncheon entrée or as a side dish with game meats. Of course, it can be served any time, but it is really special with game.

Serves 4

2 pounds mushrooms
½ cup chopped parsley leaves and stems
1 tablespoon fresh summer savory, or 1 teaspoon dried savory
Salt and freshly ground black pepper
¼ pound butter, melted
1 cup (4 ounces) grated Gruyère cheese

Preheat the oven to 400°F.

Wipe the mushrooms with a damp cloth; remove the stems and reserve. Cut the mushroom caps into quarters and put in a 1-quart casserole dish. Put the stems in the container of a food processor with the parsley, savory, salt, and pepper. Process until finely chopped. Spoon over the quartered mushrooms with the melted butter. Put in the oven and bake for 30 minutes. Remove, sprinkle with cheese, and return to the oven for about 15 minutes. Serve at once.

Puree of Mushrooms with Braised Endive

This is a great accompaniment to broiled or grilled steaks, and especially good with all wild game. Use either Belgian endive or curly endive.

Serves 6

3 pounds endive, washed and thoroughly dried
Few drops lemon juice
½ cup veal or chicken stock
4 tablespoons butter, divided
1 pound mushrooms, washed and wiped dry
1 small rib celery, finely chopped
1 small onion, finely chopped
1 small carrot, finely chopped
3 tablespoons unbleached all-purpose flour
1 pint whole milk, heated
Parsley bouquet
1 small bay leaf
Salt and freshly ground black pepper
1 tablespoon freshly grated Swiss cheese
1 tablespoon freshly grated Parmesan cheese
¼ cup heavy cream

Preheat the oven to 300°F.

Take the outer leaves of the endive and place them in a well-buttered dish. Sprinkle the lemon juice on them, season to taste, and dot with 2 tablespoons of the butter. Add the stock, cover with a buttered paper, and bring to a boil on top of the stove. Transfer to the oven and bake slowly for 2 hours.

Peel the mushrooms and puree them in a food processor. Melt 1 tablespoon of the butter in a frying pan and cook the puree over very high heat until all the juice has evaporated.

Make a sauce by melting the remaining butter in a saucepan, adding the celery, onion, and carrot, and browning lightly. Add the flour and cook for 5 minutes, then slowly add the hot milk. Add the parsley and bay leaf and reduce the sauce until quite thick. Season to taste and pass through a fine sieve. Add the mushroom puree, the Swiss and Parmesan cheeses, and the cream.

Spoon the puree of mushrooms into an oblong dish, place the endive on top, pour the juice from the endives over all, and serve very hot.

Baked Onions

Onions are used as bit players in lots of recipes but seldom get a chance for solo stardom, as they do in this recipe and some of the ones that follow.

Serves 12

24 small onions, peeled and washed
1 tablespoon butter, divided
1 teaspoon sugar
48 whole cloves
1 teaspoon unbleached all-purpose flour
1 cup light cream
Salt and freshly ground black pepper
2 tablespoons heavy cream

Preheat the oven to 375°F.

Parboil the onions for 10 minutes; drain well and sauté in a frying pan with half the butter and the sugar until glazed. Stick 2 whole cloves in each onion and arrange them in an oblong baking dish.

Make a very thin cream sauce with the remaining butter and the flour, light cream, salt, pepper, and heavy cream. Pour over the onions and bake for 15 minutes.

Sautéed Onion Rings

Liver means sautéed onion rings to me, and if you sauté the onions in bacon fat they are even better.

Makes 2 to 4 servings

2 medium yellow or white onions
3 tablespoons bacon fat or butter
Salt and freshly ground black pepper

Slice the onions to whatever thickness you like. Melt the bacon fat or butter over medium heat in a 2-quart saucepan or skillet and sauté the onions until transparent or limp. Add salt and pepper to taste. Serve over beef liver.

Onion Casserole

This dish may be prepared in two ways. One I describe below; in the other, the onions are sautéed first until they are brown. The difference between the two methods is quite noticeable. When the onions are cooked until brown, the dish makes a much stronger statement.

Serves 8

7 to 8 cups chopped onion
4 tablespoons butter
Salt and freshly ground black pepper
½ cup raw rice
5 cups boiling salted water
1 cup grated Swiss cheese
⅔ cup light cream

Preheat the oven to 325°F.

Sauté the onions in the butter until transparent; season with salt and pepper. Cook the rice in the water for 5 minutes. Drain and mix with the onions. Add the cheese and cream.

Bake uncovered for 1 hour. Serve hot as a vegetable side dish, or chill and serve with Basic Vinaigrette (see page 304) for a picnic.

Onion Soufflé

Serves 6

3 tablespoons butter
3 tablespoons unbleached all-purpose flour
Salt, freshly ground black pepper, and cayenne pepper
¼ teaspoon dry mustard
¾ cup whole milk
¼ cup freshly grated Parmesan cheese
4 egg yolks
3 medium white onions, chopped and sautéed in butter until brown
2 tablespoons sherry
5 egg whites, beaten stiff
Additional grated Parmesan cheese
Paprika

Preheat the oven to 350°F.

Melt the butter in a saucepan; stir in the flour and cook briefly. Season with salt, black and cayenne peppers, and mustard. Remove from the heat and gradually stir in the milk. Return to the heat and cook, stirring, until thickened; do not allow to boil. Add the grated cheese, egg yolks, onions, and sherry. Fold in the egg whites. Grease a 1½-quart soufflé dish and add an oiled collar. Fill with the mixture and bake for 30 minutes, or until firm to the touch. Sprinkle with a little cheese and paprika. Remove the collar and serve.

Onion Dumpling

My grandmother used to make this years ago and it has long been one of my standby favorites. It is good with any entrée, and it takes no effort to make. It puffs up a bit, like a soufflé, but there the similarity stops, for it is not delicate but hearty. If for any reason it cannot be served at the end of the baking time, turn off the oven, and leave it there, with the door open a crack, for up to 20 minutes. It may drop a bit, but it won't be noticeable or hurt the texture at all.

Serves 8

3 medium-size onions, diced
3 tablespoons butter
6 eggs, separated
½ cup bacon fat
4 tablespoons unbleached all-purpose flour
1 teaspoon salt
¼ teaspoon freshly ground black pepper

Preheat the oven to 350°F.

Sauté the onions in the butter until transparent. Transfer to a mixing bowl and add the egg yolks, fat, flour, and seasoning. Beat the egg whites to stiff peaks and fold them into the onion mixture. Bake in a greased baking dish for 30 to 40 minutes. Spoon out to serve.

Onion Pudding

In texture and flavor this dish is superb. It is excellent with roast beef, pork, or lamb, and can be made in under an hour.

Serves 4

1 pound sweet onions, halved and finely sliced
2 tablespoons butter
2 eggs
Salt and freshly ground black pepper
2/3 cup whole milk
1/4 cup unbleached all-purpose flour
1 tablespoon butter for the baking dish

Stew the onions gently in butter for about 30 minutes without browning. Add the eggs, seasonings, and milk to the flour, whisk until smooth, and stir into the onions. Preheat the oven to 450°F. Pour the onion mixture into a liberally buttered baking dish and bake for 20 to 25 minutes, or until puffed up and well browned.

Fried Parsley

A garnish that offers good taste as well as good looks, this is excellent with fish. Be sure to use only very crisp parsley.

36 small sprigs very green parsley
1 1/2 cups olive or vegetable oil
Salt

Wash the parsley sprigs well in cold water, drain thoroughly, and squeeze dry in paper towels. Lay in a wire basket or slotted spoon and plunge into very hot oil. The parsley will be crisp in just a second or two. Drain thoroughly on paper towels and sprinkle lightly with salt. Be careful not to break it; it is very fragile.

Lemon-Sweet Parsnips

Most parsnip dishes are so overcooked that the taste is lost and the texture almost that of a puree. If you let parsnips cook only until tender-crisp, I can assure you a taste treat. Carrot-size parsnips are the best; when they get too big they are often woody in the center and not edible. (A woody center means "last year's" parsnips in most cases; they should not even be on the market.) The sweetness of the parsnip is sometimes emphasized by adding ginger, spices, and honey, or lemon and sugar, as in the recipe that follows.

Serves 4 to 6

1 to 1¼ pounds parsnips
1 cup water
½ teaspoon salt
2 tablespoons butter or margarine
¼ cup fresh lemon juice
¼ cup sugar

Peel the parsnips and cut crosswise in ¼-inch slices. Heat the water to boiling; add the salt and parsnips. Cook until just barely fork-tender. Drain and keep warm.

In a saucepan on low heat, melt the butter and add the lemon juice and sugar. Stir until the sugar is dissolved.

Place the parsnips in a pan. Pour the lemon juice, butter, and sugar mixture over them and heat for 10 minutes to blend the flavors, stirring constantly. Serve hot.

Note: Try this recipe using carrots when parsnips are not available.

Parsnip and Potato Puree

Mashed potatoes and mashed parsnips mixed together are a good combination. This recipe calls for putting both vegetables through a medium-mesh sieve, but that's only if you want them pureed. There is nothing wrong with simply mashing both vegetables and combining them.

Serves 6

5 medium parsnips
5 medium baking potatoes
4 tablespoons butter
Salt and freshly ground black pepper
1/4 cup heavy cream (optional)

Peel the parsnips and cover with cold salted water. Bring to a boil and cook until just tender but not mushy. Drain well and dry out over gentle heat. Sieve through the medium mesh of a food mill.

Cook the potatoes in the same way; then sieve them through the same mill on top of the parsnips. Combine the two, stirring constantly over low heat, until dry and well mixed. Stir in the butter in small pieces and season well with salt and pepper. Add a little cream, if desired.

Puree of Parsnips and Madeira

This dish has become a Thanksgiving tradition at my house. Sometimes I sprinkle walnuts on top, sometimes I use toasted sesame seeds and orange slices as a garnish. Try the dish as given to appreciate its flavor, then make up your own variations.

Serves 8

5 to 6 pounds parsnips
1/4 pound butter, melted
1/2 cup Madeira wine
1/4 cup heavy cream
1/4 teaspoon nutmeg
Salt and freshly ground black pepper
Finely chopped walnuts
Butter

Wash and trim the parsnips and put them in a 6- to 8-quart pan with salted water to cover. Simmer until they can be pierced; drain and cool until they can be handled. Peel and cut them into 3- to 4-inch pieces. Put the pieces through a food mill.

Preheat the oven to 375°F.

Combine the puree with the butter, wine, cream, and seasonings. Beat well, adding more butter or cream if the puree seems too dry. Spoon the mixture into a 6-cup baking dish, sprinkle with finely chopped walnuts, and top with pieces of butter. Bake until heated and serve very hot.

Frozen Peas

Nothing beats sweet garden-fresh peas, but there are some tricks to cooking frozen peas so that their flavor is maximized. The main trick is not to cook frozen peas at all—simply pour boiling water over them after they have thawed. Let them stand for a minute and then drain them completely. Once they've had this boiling-water treatment, toss them into a hot skillet with melted butter and stir-fry them only long enough to heat them through completely—about 2 minutes. Then add some salt and pepper and a dash of sugar and serve.

Puree of Peas and Watercress

This is a really great combination of flavors but should be made with frozen peas. Don't waste fresh peas.

Serves 6

2 10-ounce packages frozen green peas
1 cup watercress
Chicken stock to cover
1 tablespoon butter

Cook the peas and watercress in the stock for 4 to 5 minutes. Drain and reserve the stock.

Let the mixture cool, then puree in a food processor with some of the stock and the butter. Transfer the puree to a saucepan to reheat for serving.

Note: This may be prepared well in advance of serving. For color, serve in a tomato cup: peel a tomato, slice it in half, and remove the seeds and fill with hot puree.

Peas and Prosciutto

A very nice combination, and if prosciutto is not available, use chopped ham or crumbled crisp bacon. The bacon will lose its crispness when combined with the peas and cooked further, but it is the taste of the bacon not its texture that you are after. If frozen peas are used, do not cook them—just pour boiling water over them after they have thawed and then combine them with the prosciutto; toss in butter for a couple of minutes to just heat everything through.

Serves 6

6 tablespoons butter
2 tablespoons finely chopped, small white onion
6 cups shelled, small fresh green peas
1 teaspoon salt
½ teaspoon freshly ground black pepper
¼ teaspoon sugar
3 tablespoons beef or chicken stock
6 ounces prosciutto, shredded

Melt the butter in a saucepan, add the onions and sauté until golden and soft. Add the shelled peas, salt, pepper, sugar, and stock, and cook, covered, over moderate heat for about 10 minutes, or until the peas are tender. Add the prosciutto and cook briskly for 2 minutes more, stirring constantly.

Sautéed Green Peppers

Peppers can be mild and sweet or fiery hot. The large green, red, or yellow peppers are called sweet or bell peppers; although these can be hot, generally only the mild varieties are sold in the markets. These peppers start out green, ripen to red, finally turn red-brown when dried. Red bell peppers are sweeter than the green; the yellow fall in between. Chili peppers are the hot peppers that you feel, rather than taste—although some of these can actually be quite mild. Generally, the smaller the pepper the hotter it is. To test, touch a piece of the broken pepper to your tongue.

Serves 16 as a first course

8 sweet green peppers
1 garlic clove, chopped
¼ cup olive oil
Salt and freshly ground black pepper

Wash and seed the peppers. Parboil in salted water for 5 to 7 minutes. Drain and dry thoroughly. Cut into quarters. Heat the garlic in the oil; remove and replace with the peppers. Cook until the peppers begin to brown. Season to taste and serve with Italian bread.

Pepper, Tomato, and Onion Stew

Sweet red peppers add color and taste to this dish, but if they are not available, you can use just green peppers. Fresh ripe tomatoes are essential, however, because the vegetables should have a bit of crispness when the dish is done. Prepare over medium-low heat in order to cook off the liquid without overcooking the vegetables. This dish is especially good with roast pork or chicken.

Serves 6

2 pounds green and red sweet peppers
2 pounds ripe tomatoes
1 teaspoon salt, divided
2 tablespoons butter
¼ cup olive oil
1 pound small white onions, peeled and thinly sliced
¼ teaspoon freshly ground black pepper

Wash the peppers; cut off the stem ends, remove the seeds, and slice coarsely.

Skin the tomatoes by dipping them briefly into boiling water; cut the peeled tomatoes in half, remove the seeds, and sprinkle the insides lightly with ½ teaspoon of the salt. Place upside down in a colander for 30 minutes to let the excess water drain out. Chop coarsely.

In a large, heavy skillet heat the butter and olive oil. Add the peppers and onions, and cook, stirring, until the onions are soft and translucent. Add the tomatoes; cover, reduce the heat, and cook for about 10 minutes more, stirring, until almost all the liquid has evaporated. Add the remaining salt and the pepper. Serve hot or cold.

Crusty Potatoes with Parmesan Cheese

Turning the dish out of the skillet and onto a plate takes a little practice and I suggest making it in a small quantity the first time so it isn't too cumbersome. Just make sure that the potatoes don't stick to the bottom—I avoid the problem by using a nonstick skillet.

Serves 6

6 large baking potatoes
¼ pound butter
2 tablespoons vegetable oil or bacon fat
1 cup freshly grated Parmesan cheese
2 teaspoons salt, divided
½ teaspoon freshly ground black pepper, divided
4 tablespoons melted butter, divided

Put the potatoes in a saucepan, cover with cold water, and bring to a boil; boil hard, uncovered, for about 10 minutes. Drain and peel the potatoes while still warm; then grate them.

Heat the ¼ pound butter with the oil in a large skillet over high heat until the foaming subsides, being careful not to let the butter brown. Put about half the grated potatoes into the skillet, pressing them down firmly with a spatula. Sprinkle with the cheese, half the salt and pepper, and drizzle with 2 tablespoons of the melted butter. Add the remaining potatoes; press firmly with a spatula.

Shake the pan to make sure the potato cake moves freely; if it is sticking, use the spatula to push the potatoes in from the edge of the pan. Drizzle with the remaining 2 tablespoons of butter and sprinkle with the remaining salt and pepper.

Cook over high heat for 5 minutes. Then press down hard on the potatoes, using a flat lid just a bit smaller than the skillet. Reduce the heat to medium and cook, keeping the lid on, for about 30 minutes, or until the potatoes are crusty on the sides and bottom. Shake the skillet every few minutes to insure that the potatoes stay "afloat." Unmold on a round serving plate, crusty-side up.

Potatoes in Beer

Beer gives an elusive flavor to the potatoes in this dish. You can vary the amounts and use milk instead of cream and margarine instead of butter.

Serves 4

5 medium potatoes, thinly sliced
1 large onion, finely sliced
Salt
1 cup beer
2 tablespoons butter
½ cup heavy cream

Preheat the oven to 400°F.

Press alternate, salted layers of potatoes and onion in a deep, buttered baking dish, beginning with a layer of onion on the bottom and finishing with a layer of potatoes; arrange neatly overlapping layers of potatoes so that they take up a minimum of space. Add the beer, distribute paper-thin shavings of butter over the entire surface, and bake for 10 minutes.

Reduce the temperature to 350°F. and continue baking for 50 minutes. Ten minutes before removing from the oven, pour the cream evenly over the surface.

Potato Custard

Ever since the first time I served it and could not come up with seconds, I have doubled it, although theoretically it's enough for six. I suggest you do the same. If prosciutto is not available, use chopped ham or chopped, cooked bacon.

Serves 6 sparingly

6 medium potatoes, peeled, sliced, rinsed, and dried
Salt
6 tablespoons butter, divided
1 large sweet onion, thinly sliced
2 ounces thinly sliced prosciutto, chopped
1½ cups heavy cream
3 eggs
Freshly ground black pepper
Nutmeg

Sauté the potatoes, seasoned with salt, in half the butter over medium-low heat, tossing them regularly every 7 or 8 minutes until they are lightly colored and just cooked, about 20 minutes. Sauté the onions in the remaining butter for 20 to 30 minutes until soft.

Preheat the oven to 425°F.

Spread the prosciutto over the bottom of a lightly buttered, shallow casserole. Spread the onions on top, then the potatoes. Beat together the cream, eggs, and seasonings (use only a suspicion of nutmeg). Pour over the potatoes. Bake for 20 minutes, or until the mixture has barely solidified at the center.

Dauphinoise Potatoes

A mandoline, the device traditionally used for slicing vegetables to make this dish, is not absolutely necessary. A good sharp knife that makes really thin slices will do the trick. A word of advice: don't stint on the cheese; the better the grade, the better the dish.

Serves 6

Butter
1 garlic clove, cut in half
*5 to 6 potatoes, peeled and sliced very thin**
Salt and freshly ground black pepper
1 cup shredded Gruyère or Swiss cheese
4 tablespoons soft butter
¾ cup grated Parmesan cheese
1 to 2 cups heavy cream

Preheat the oven to 350°F.

Butter a 2-quart oblong baking dish and rub with garlic. Line with half the potato slices. Sprinkle with salt and pepper. Cover with the shredded cheese. Add the remaining potato slices; season with salt and pepper. Dot with the butter and Parmesan cheese. Add enough cream to come halfway up the dish. Bake for 1 hour or longer, until the potatoes are soft and the top is nicely browned.

* Do not wash the potato slices—you want both the starch and sugar that would be lost if they were soaked.

Potatoes with Sage and Parmesan

Serves 6

6 large potatoes, peeled and cut into wedges
¼ pound butter
2 tablespoons chopped fresh sage or 2 teaspoons dried sage leaves, crumbled
1 cup freshly grated Parmesan cheese
½ teaspoon freshly ground black pepper

Boil the potatoes in 3 quarts salted boiling water for barely 5 minutes (they have to remain very firm). Drain.

Melt the butter in a heavy skillet, add the sage, and cook over low heat until the butter is almost brown. Add the potatoes and stir well until they have absorbed all the butter and are warmed through. Mix in the cheese and pepper, stir gently but thoroughly, remove from the heat, and serve.

Scalloped Potatoes

Serves 8

Butter
1 garlic clove, peeled and halved
1½ cups heavy cream, light cream, or whole milk, divided
2½ pounds (about 10 medium) potatoes, peeled and sliced ⅛ inch thick
1½ teaspoons salt
½ teaspoon freshly ground black pepper
2 tablespoons butter, divided
6 ounces Gruyère cheese, freshly grated (1½ cups)

Preheat the oven to 350°F.

Generously butter a gratin pan or 9 x 12-inch baking dish and rub with the garlic. Pour in enough of the cream to coat the bottom of the pan. Layer the potatoes, sprinkling each layer with salt, pepper, and dots of butter. Top with the cheese and the remaining butter. Pour in enough of the remaining cream to come halfway up the potato layers.

Bring to a simmer on top of the stove, then put in the oven for about 1 hour, or until the potatoes are browned and easily pierced with a knife.

Note: This dish will have a crisp crust and a rich, moist interior. For variety, omit the cream, place the dish directly in the oven after it is assembled, and bake until it is crisp throughout, about 1 hour.

Puree of Spinach and Peas

Have you ever had a puree of spinach that wasn't loose or on the runny side? Well, here's one that isn't, and the addition of peas takes nothing away from the spinach.

Serves 8

2 pounds fresh spinach
½ pound fresh or frozen peas
2 cups chicken stock
2 tablespoons heavy cream
3 tablespoons butter
Salt and freshly ground black pepper
Pinch nutmeg

Remove the stems and wash the spinach thoroughly. Combine the spinach and peas in a 2-quart saucepan; add the chicken stock and cook until tender. Drain thoroughly and reserve the chicken stock.

Puree the spinach and peas in a processor using the "on-off" method to retain some texture. Add the heavy cream and puree a bit more. Add several tablespoons of the reserved chicken stock only if the puree seems too stiff for your liking. Transfer to a saucepan and stir in the butter over medium heat. Add salt, pepper, and nutmeg, all to taste.

Note: For an elegant presentation, serve on slightly heated artichoke bottoms.

Spinach Casserole

I never liked spinach as a child—probably because it was always so bland and uninteresting, and also because the kind I was generally forced to eat came from a can. Fortunately, fresh spinach bears no resemblance to canned—nor, for that matter, does the frozen, which is made even better in this recipe by the addition of a cheese sauce. This dish can be prepared early in the day, to be baked as needed.

Serves 8

3 10-ounce packages frozen chopped spinach
1/3 pound fresh mushrooms, sliced
4 tablespoons butter or margarine, divided
3 tablespoons unbleached all-purpose flour
1 1/2 cups whole milk
1/2 cup grated Gruyère cheese

Preheat the oven to 350°F.

Cook the spinach just enough to separate, then drain thoroughly.* Place half the spinach in the bottom of a well-greased 1-quart casserole. Sauté the mushrooms in butter or margarine for 3 to 4 minutes, until limp. Place on top of the spinach and cover with the remaining spinach.

Make a sauce by melting the remaining 3 tablespoons of butter or margarine in a small saucepan over medium heat and adding the flour. Cook for 2 minutes to get rid of the raw taste of the flour. Add the milk and stir until the consistency of a medium cream sauce. Add the cheese and stir until completely melted, about 2 minutes.

Pour the cheese sauce over the spinach casserole and bake for 35 to 45 minutes.

* To drain the spinach, press out whatever water remains by using the flat of your hand or the back of a large spoon. Just letting it drain in a sieve is not enough.

Spinach Timbales

Seamless timbales or individual ovenproof glass baking cups can be used to prepare this dish. The main thing is to be sure to drain and squeeze the water from the spinach before adding the other ingredients and baking.

Makes 10 timbales

2 10-ounce packages frozen spinach
3 eggs
1 egg yolk
2 tablespoons grated onion
½ garlic clove, finely chopped
Salt and freshly ground black pepper
Pinch freshly ground nutmeg
2 cups whole milk
4 tablespoons freshly grated Parmesan cheese (optional)

Preheat the oven to 350°F.

Cook the spinach according to package directions. Drain and squeeze out the moisture. Chop fine and put into a bowl. Add the eggs and egg yolk, onion, garlic, salt, pepper, and nutmeg. Stir in the milk. For flavor, add the cheese if desired. Mix well.

Brush the timbale molds or glass cups with butter and fill almost to the top with the mixture. Cover the molds with buttered foil or parchment paper to prevent any crust from forming while they are baking. Set in a water bath and bake for about 35 minutes, or until the custard is set.

Squash in Cream

Summer or soft-skinned squash include zucchini, patty pan, crookneck, straightneck, and the lesser known cocozelle. All should be eaten when they are young and tender.

Serves 4

4 white summer squash, peeled, seeded, and sliced
Salt and freshly ground black pepper
3 tablespoons butter
½ pint heavy cream
Chopped parsley

Preheat the oven to 350°F.

Place the squash in a well-buttered baking dish; sprinkle with salt and pepper and dot with butter. Cover with a pie tin and bake for 45 minutes. Halfway through the baking, remove the pie-tin cover and add the cream. Finish baking covered.

Serve sprinkled with chopped parsley.

Hubbard Squash Custard

Any pureed winter squash—and even sweet potatoes and yams—will work in this recipe, but Hubbard squash is the best as far as I am concerned.

Serves 8

*3 10-ounce packages frozen Hubbard or other hard-skinned baking squash**
2 eggs, lightly beaten
1 cup light cream
1 teaspoon minced onion
4 to 6 parsley sprigs, finely chopped
Salt and freshly ground black pepper
Freshly grated Parmesan cheese
Paprika

* Fresh squash can also be used. It should be baked and then pureed first, however. Frozen is simpler to use.

Thaw the frozen squash at room temperature or over low heat. Preheat the oven to 300°F. Combine the thawed squash with the eggs and cream. Add the onion, parsley, salt, and pepper.

Pour into a lightly buttered 1½-quart soufflé dish or other casserole. Sprinkle with a liberal dusting of cheese and garnish with a light sprinkle of paprika. Bake for 1 hour.

The custard should be slightly raised and golden brown on top. It is done when a table knife inserted near the center comes out clean.

Sweet Potato Pudding

Although sweet potatoes and yams are related in the United States, they are actually two different families—the sweet potato is the tuberous root of a tropical vine, whereas the true yam belongs to a family of climbing plants that are not cultivated in North America. What we call a yam is actually an orange-fleshed sweet potato with a brown skin, a hybrid. It would be simpler if both were called sweet potatoes. Although there is a difference in taste and texture, they can be used interchangeably.

Serves 6

8 sweet potatoes, peeled, quartered, and boiled until tender
¼ pound butter, divided
Grated rind of 1 lemon
Salt and freshly ground black pepper
¼ cup brandy
½ pint heavy cream

Preheat the oven to 375°F.

Drain the sweet potatoes thoroughly. Mash them with half of the butter, add the lemon rind, salt, a touch of pepper, and the brandy. Gradually fold in the cream and the remaining butter. Beat until smooth and fluffy. Pour into a baking dish, top with additional butter, and bake in the oven for 30 minutes until brown.

WITH rare exceptions today, the only good tomato is one grown in the back yard. The market variety is tasteless and mealy in texture, the result of being picked too green and forced to ripen in chemically treated refrigeration. A rock-hard pinkish green tomato isn't worth carting home, let alone spending money on. It is often better to use canned tomatoes since they at least have flavor; adding a fresh tomato that's been peeled, seeded, and chopped to the canned gives an illusion of freshness.

Baked Tomatoes Stuffed with Mozzarella

Don't remove the peel from the tomatoes because they tend to soften too much after being in the oven and lose their shape. This can be served as a salad course or as a vegetable-cheese accompaniment with a lamb or beef entrée.

Serves 6

6 large, ripe but firm tomatoes
Salt and freshly ground black pepper
3 tablespoons olive oil
¼ to ½ pound mozzarella cheese (depending on the size of the tomatoes)
2 tablespoons minced fresh basil or 2 teaspoons dried basil

Preheat the oven to 375°F.

Cut a slice from the top of each tomato. Using a teaspoon, scoop out the pulp and seeds. Turn the tomatoes upside down on a platter and let them stand for 15 minutes to drain.

Place the tomatoes, cut-side up, in an oiled baking dish just large enough to hold them. Season each tomato cavity with salt and pepper. Drizzle 1 teaspoon of the oil into each tomato. Chop the mozzarella fine and mix it with the basil. Stuff the tomatoes with mozzarella.

With a pastry brush, brush the outside skin of tomatoes with the remaining olive oil. Bake for about 20 minutes, or until the mozzarella has melted. Serve hot.

Batter-Fried Green Tomatoes

Green tomatoes fried in batter have a very special flavor and texture. Incidentally, ripe tomatoes do not work; they must be green. Serve this as a side dish with chicken or ground beef and corn on the cob.

Serves 6

3 large green tomatoes
2 egg yolks
2 tablespoons unbleached all-purpose flour
¼ cup whole milk
2 egg whites, beaten to soft peaks
Corn or safflower oil
Salt and freshly ground black pepper
Sugar

Cut thin slices off the top and bottom of each tomato and discard. Cut the tomatoes into ¼- to ⅓-inch slices. Make a batter using the egg yolks, flour, and milk; fold in the egg whites.

Dip the tomato slices in the batter and deep-fry in a skillet with about 2 inches of heated oil. Drain on paper towels and serve hot, sprinkled with salt, pepper, and sugar.

Fried Tomatoes in Cream

You can use either green or ripe tomatoes for this side dish. It's good with beef or pork, and is a good breakfast or lunch entrée with bacon.

Serves 4

4 tomatoes, cut in ¾-inch slices
Salt and freshly ground black pepper
Sugar
Unbleached all-purpose flour
2 tablespoons hot butter
2 tablespoons hot bacon drippings
1 cup heavy cream
Finely chopped parsley for garnish

Sprinkle both sides of the tomato slices with the salt, pepper, and very little sugar, and dip them in flour. Transfer them, one by one, to a frying pan containing hot butter and bacon drippings. Fry them quickly to a golden brown, turning them to brown on both sides, and remove to a hot plate.

Pour the cream into the same frying pan, stirring until hot. Season to taste and pour over the tomatoes. Sprinkle with the parsley.

Casserole of Turnips and Mushrooms

The younger the turnip, the better this dish is. I try to find them the size of a golf ball, never any larger than a tennis ball. After that, the turnip is "over the hill."

Serves 6

8 turnips, washed but unpeeled
1½ pounds mushrooms, sliced
Butter
Chopped parsley
1½ cups Béchamel Sauce (see page 310)
Buttered bread crumbs

Preheat the oven to 325°F.

Dice the turnips and cook them in boiling salted water for 5 or 6 minutes at a rapid boil. The turnips should be only partially cooked. Drain the turnips and run cold water over them to stop cooking.

Sauté the mushrooms briefly in butter. Put the turnips in a buttered casserole with mushrooms. Stir together and sprinkle with chopped parsley.

Pour the sauce on top and sprinkle generously with bread crumbs. Bake for about 45 minutes.

Glazed Turnips

This recipe is good with wild game or pork.

Serves 6

18 small white turnips, washed but unpeeled
4 tablespoons butter
Salt and freshly ground black pepper
1 tablespoon sugar
¼ cup canned beef consommé
2 tablespoons finely chopped parsley

Boil the turnips in salted water for about 10 minutes and drain. Heat the butter in a skillet and brown the turnips carefully. Season with salt and pepper and sprinkle with sugar. Drain off the butter and add the consommé. Simmer until almost dry, or until the juice is reduced to a glaze. Sprinkle with the parsley.

Turnip and Egg Gratin

Gratin refers to a grated cheese or buttered bread crumb topping and also to a kind of shallow baking container in which "au gratin" dishes are made. A gratin dish is usually made of cast-iron or some other heavy metal. Even though the turnips in this recipe are grated, it is important that you use tender young ones.

Serves 4

1 pound young, nonfibrous turnips, washed, peeled, and coarsely grated
Salt
¼ pound butter, divided
2 tablespoons unbleached all-purpose flour
3 cups whole milk
1 cup day-old bread (not dried out), crusts removed and crumbled
6 hard-cooked eggs, halved
Freshly ground black pepper

Salt the turnips in layers and set aside for 30 minutes. Squeeze them in their liquid first; then drain them and squeeze thoroughly and repeatedly to extract all the juice. Cook gently in 4 tablespoons of the butter, stirring regularly, for 15 minutes, or until tender.

Sprinkle the flour over the turnips and continue cooking, stirring, for 3 to 4 minutes longer. Add the milk slowly, stirring all the time. Bring to a boil; reduce the heat and simmer, stirring occasionally, for 30 minutes.

Cook the soft bread crumbs gently in the remaining butter, tossing until lightly colored.

Preheat the oven to 375°F. Arrange the eggs in a lightly buttered baking dish. Adjust the seasoning of the turnip sauce and spoon it over the eggs. Sprinkle with the bread crumbs and bake for 15 to 20 minutes, or until the sauce is bubbling and the crust is colored.

Puree of Watercress

This is wonderful with broiled kidneys, lamb chops, and wild game. Thinned with a little cream, it can serve as a delicious sauce for fish. When buying or picking watercress, look for large leaves; the darker they are the more flavorful.

Serves 4 to 6

10 bunches watercress
3 tablespoons butter
1 tablespoon unbleached all-purpose flour
1¼ cups heavy cream
Salt and freshly ground black pepper
Fried croutons

Wash the watercress and remove the stems. Cook in boiling salted water for 12 minutes. Drain and rinse in cold water.

Pass the watercress through a fine sieve and set aside in the refrigerator until ready to use. (This may be done the day before.) Before using, pour off the water that has formed on the surface of the bowl of watercress puree.

Melt the butter in a saucepan; add the flour and cook for a minute without browning. Add the watercress puree to the butter-flour mixture with the cream. Season to taste. Heat slowly, stirring constantly, until very hot. Serve garnished with fried croutons.

Broiled Zucchini with Tomato and Cheese

There are more zucchini recipes than I want to know about. All too often it is served overcooked, and it is an overworked vegetable: too many breads, too many chutneys, and too many of a lot of things that people have wrongly put zucchini into. It is a nice vegetable, although it makes no strong statement. It should be picked young for best flavor, nutrition, and use, and then treated gently. It's hard to keep up with in the garden—beware of the 10-pound zucchini; it is spongy, pithy, and unattractive.

Serves 4

- *2 medium zucchini (about 1 pound)*
- *2 tablespoons melted butter, divided*
- *Salt and freshly ground black pepper*
- *½ teaspoon crumbled oregano*
- *4 ounces Port Salut, Danish Fontina or Havarti, freshly grated*
- *1 large tomato, thinly sliced*

Wash the zucchini and cook whole in a large pot of boiling salted water for 10 minutes. Drain, refresh under cold water, and dry. Cut off the ends, halve lengthwise, and arrange cut-side up on a broiler tray. Paint with half the butter. Sprinkle with salt, pepper, and oregano, and cover with grated cheese and tomato slices.

Paint the tomato with the remaining butter and sprinkle with salt and pepper. Place the tray 4 inches from broiler and cook for about 10 minutes, until the cheese has melted and the tomato has browned. Serve hot or cold.

Grated Sautéed Zucchini

Don't peel the zucchini—just wash it carefully, remove the stem and butt ends, and grate or shred it, using either a hand grater or the grating disk of a food processor. Less moisture is extracted if it is done by hand, but in this case, since the moisture needs to be wrung out anyway, use either method. I usually extract the moisture from grated zucchini by placing it by the handful into a dish towel and wringing out the moisture. This dish must be cooked very fast or it will become mushy.

Serves 6

8 medium zucchini
2 tablespoons butter
1 small onion, chopped (optional)
1 teaspoon Garlic Puree (optional) (see page 332)
Juice of 1 lemon
Salt and freshly ground black pepper
3 tablespoons buttered bread crumbs

Shred the zucchini; drain and press out the moisture.

Sauté quickly in the butter for 1 to 2 minutes, adding the onion and garlic puree, if desired. Squeeze the lemon juice over it; season with salt and pepper and top with bread crumbs.

Zucchini Custard

Serves 8

4 large zucchini, sliced into very thin rounds
¼ cup salt
6 to 8 eggs, beaten
2 to 3 cups heavy cream
1 teaspoon nutmeg
2 garlic cloves, mashed and chopped
Salt and freshly ground black pepper
1 tablespoon unbleached all-purpose flour
1½ cups grated Parmesan cheese

Place the zucchini rounds in a bowl with ¼ cup of salt and toss to coat the zucchini. Allow to stand for 1 hour, then rinse two or three times very thoroughly. Place the zucchini on a dry towel and squeeze to remove as much moisture as possible. The towel will have to be changed two or three times.

Preheat the oven to 350°F.

Distribute the "dried" zucchini evenly in a buttered baking dish and combine the eggs, cream, nutmeg, garlic, salt, and pepper. Sprinkle the zucchini with the flour and pour the egg mixture over it. Sprinkle cheese over the top and bake for 35 to 40 minutes.

SALADS AND SALAD DRESSINGS

IT'S hard to understand how cooks can concentrate their talents on slippery molded salads when so many nice greens are there for the taking—romaine, iceberg, red and green leaf lettuce, Bibb, Boston, curly, limestone, as well as spinach, cabbage, endive (French and curly), escarole, sorrel, watercress, rocket, and chicory.

Cabbage, the least-used green, is the one I probably favor most. I cannot change the world but do plan to do something about cabbage in this book. There are so many ways to use it, both raw and cooked. You will find a number of uses that you may not have been aware of, and some that you might have known about but not tried.

Whatever the leaf used in salads, it should not be cut with a scissors or knife but instead broken by hand—with the exception of cabbage and Belgian endive. Salad greens should never be broken into tiny pieces but rather into good-sized pieces so they don't all go flat on the plate and become impossible to spear with a salad fork. Greens should never be drowned in an overdose of dressing nor dressed until just a few minutes before serving—unless, of course, it is to be a marinated salad. Salad should be served close to room temperature, never ice cold.

Slaw-Stuffed Cabbage

The cooked dressing is what makes this coleslaw special. It is an old-fashioned dressing, and as far as I am concerned, no other coleslaw dressing can match it for taste. In addition to being a first-rate coleslaw, the presentation, using the outer leaves of the cabbage to form the salad bowl, makes it a dramatic salad as well.

Serves 6

1 large head green cabbage
½ cup chopped onion
1 cup finely diced carrot
2 tablespoons finely chopped green pepper
4 tablespoons chopped parsley

Dressing

½ cup vegetable oil
2 tablespoons unbleached all-purpose flour
2 teaspoons dry mustard
1 teaspoon salt
½ cup white wine vinegar
6 tablespoons sugar
Dash hot pepper sauce
1 cup heavy cream
2 egg yolks

Core the cabbage. Remove 5 or 6 outer leaves and reserve them, being careful not to tear them. If they are difficult to remove, run the head of cabbage under hot water for a few minutes. Halve the remainder of the cabbage and slice, crosswise or lengthwise into paper-thin slices. Combine with the onion, carrot, green pepper, and parsley.

To prepare the dressing, combine the oil and flour in a saucepan over medium heat, as you would for a roux. When completely blended and slightly thickened, add the mustard, salt, vinegar, sugar, and hot pepper sauce, stirring constantly. Combine the cream and egg yolks thoroughly and add to the mixture in the saucepan. Continue to cook, stirring, until slightly thickened. Remove from the heat and allow to cool for a few minutes. Then pour over the cabbage and mix thoroughly. Allow the slaw to marinate for 45 minutes, refrigerated, before stuffing the leaves.

To prepare the outer cabbage leaves for stuffing, place a piece of cheesecloth large enough to encase the original head in a bowl. (This will enable you to remove the stuffed cabbage when you are ready to serve it.) Place the reserved outer leaves, core end up, in the cheesecloth-lined bowl, overlapping until all 5 or 6 leaves are in place.

Drain the slaw in a colander to remove any excess dressing. Pick up the slaw, a handful at a time, pressing to extract more dressing, and fill the leaf-lined bowl. Pack down and continue until the leaves are filled up. Cover and refrigerate for 2 or 3 hours before serving. To serve, remove the slaw-stuffed cabbage from the bowl by lifting out with the cheesecloth. Carefully remove the cheesecloth after placing the cabbage on a serving platter.

Italian Cabbage Salad

This version of coleslaw should serve as an entrée rather than an accompaniment because the addition of ham, prosciutto, eggs, cheese, and walnuts makes it a meal in itself.

Serves 6

1 medium head green cabbage
3 hard-cooked eggs, peeled and halved
¼ pound cooked ham, cubed
¼ pound prosciutto, cut into strips
½ pound imported Swiss cheese, cubed
½ cup coarsely broken walnuts

Dressing

1 tablespoon Dijon mustard
2 tablespoons vinegar
3 tablespoons heavy cream
½ teaspoon each salt and freshly ground black pepper
2 tablespoons finely chopped fresh herbs (tarragon, parsley, or chives, or a combination) or 1 tablespoon dried herbs
1 shallot, finely chopped

Remove and discard any wilted outer leaves. Core the cabbage and reserve 1 cabbage leaf for each serving. Shred the remainder of the cabbage coarsely. Sprinkle generously with salt and let stand for 1 hour. Rinse to remove the salt; drain and dry.

To make the dressing, combine the mustard and vinegar, then stir in the remaining dressing ingredients. Pour over the shredded cabbage; mix and let stand for at least 30 minutes. Line a bowl with the reserved cabbage leaves and add the dressed, shredded cabbage. Combine the eggs, ham, prosciutto, cheese, and nuts and place on top. Toss together just before serving.

Hot Slaw with Seafood

Without the seafood, this is a slaw side dish; with the addition of cooked seafood, it becomes a salad main dish. Baby to medium-size shrimp or sea scallops are the best choice of seafood, but cooked halibut is a good substitute if the others are not available. Allow ½ pound of whatever seafood is selected if the dish is to be a first course; if it is to be a main dish, use 1 pound of seafood.

Serves 10 to 12

2- to 3-pound head green cabbage
4 tablespoons butter
1 tablespoon unbleached all-purpose flour
½ cup water
2 eggs
6 tablespoons sugar
1 teaspoon dry mustard
1 teaspoon salt
½ cup vinegar
½ to 1 pound cooked shrimp, scallops, or halibut

Halve and core the cabbage; slice crosswise or lengthwise into paper-thin slices. Heat water in the bottom of a double boiler. Melt the butter in the top and stir in the flour until it is bubbling and lightly colored and the raw flour taste has cooked away. Add the water and continue stirring until the mixture is smooth and slightly thickened. Beat the eggs with the sugar, mustard, and salt. Spoon a little of the hot sauce into the egg mixture to temper it. Then add the egg mixture into the hot base and continue stirring until blended and thickened. Gradually add the vinegar and blend well. Remove from the heat.

Add the seafood to the shredded cabbage and toss to mix. Stir in the heated dressing. The cabbage will become limp and pungent.

Note: The dressing may also be cooled and stirred into the salad, producing a salad with an entirely different character since the slaw will remain crisp.

Red Cabbage Salad

This salad makes an excellent main-course dish for lunch. Just be sure to adjust the seasoning before serving it, because red cabbage absorbs a lot of salt. If this salad is not seasoned properly, it tastes like a lot of nothing.

Serves 8

2 pounds red cabbage
1 cup tarragon vinegar
Salt and freshly ground black pepper
10 hard-cooked eggs, divided
1 cup heavy cream
Juice of 1 lemon
1 teaspoon chopped shallots
1 teaspoon chopped fennel tops
1 teaspoon chopped fresh tarragon leaves
Thinly slivered radishes

Core the cabbage. Remove and discard the outer leaves; shred the remainder.

Parboil the cabbage in salted water for about 2 minutes; pour cold water over it and drain well. Put in a bowl and pour the vinegar over it. Season with salt and pepper, and marinate for 1 hour.

Run the yolks of 6 of the eggs through a potato ricer into a bowl. Reserve whites. Stir the cream into them and add salt and pepper. Add the lemon juice and the chopped herbs. Drain the marinated cabbage thoroughly and add it to the egg-cream dressing.

Slice the remaining eggs. Pile the cabbage salad in the center of a chilled bowl, decorate with reserved chopped egg whites, a wreath of egg slices, and polka-dot the top with slivers of radish.

Wilted Cabbage Salad

This makes a nice first course. If you want to dress it up more, add a poached egg just before serving and call it lunch.

Serves 6

2-pound head green cabbage
12 ounces lean slab or packaged bacon
½ cup olive oil
Salt and freshly ground black pepper
¼ cup wine vinegar

Remove the damaged or discolored outer leaves of the cabbage and slice off the ribs of the remaining leaves; wash, cut in half vertically, remove the core, picking out and discarding the thick sections, or ribs. Shred the two halves as for coleslaw. Pack the shredded cabbage into a salad bowl, pour on boiling water, and let stand, covered, to steep for 10 minutes.

Remove and discard the rind from the bacon; cut into ¼-inch wedges. (Cut packaged sliced bacon into wedges.) Add a spoonful of olive oil to a skillet and cook the bacon wedges over moderate heat, tossing regularly until lightly crisp.

Drain the cabbage, pressing to extract as much liquid as possible. Return to the warm salad bowl. Season with salt and freshly ground pepper. Pour over it the bacon and its fat, the vinegar and oil. Toss rapidly but thoroughly. Serve on hot plates.

Wilted Lettuce Salad

This is a common Midwest salad. It should be eaten right away before the bacon fat can change its character and become a turn-off.

Field salad refers to purslane, watercress, dandelion greens, and any edible green not a market product and can include greens taken from the tops of young vegetables when thinning the rows.

Serves 4

1 head leaf lettuce or any field salad
Salt and freshly ground black pepper
6 slices fat bacon, cut into small squares
1 teaspoon vinegar

Prepare the greens and place in a heated bowl. Sprinkle with salt and pepper. Fry the bacon until crisp. Pour the hot grease and the bacon directly onto the greens. Pour the vinegar into the hot pan and then pour over the salad. Mix well and serve at once.

Celery Salad with Mustard Dressing

Use the center ribs of the heads of celery and cut them in slivers about 2 inches long. The dressing is best if made with slightly sweet, hot German mustard.

Serves 4

4 bunches celery
1 tablespoon German mustard
Salt and freshly ground black pepper
Juice of 1 small lemon
¾ cup light cream

Use only the tender center ribs of the celery, removing as many strings as possible. Cut into 2-inch pieces and split each piece several times almost to the end. Curl by soaking in ice water for several hours. Wipe thoroughly dry and pile in a cold bowl.

Combine the mustard with salt, pepper, and lemon juice. Stir well and add the cream.

Pour the dressing over the celery and chill. Serve very cold.

Cucumber, Tomato, and Radish Salad

The French dressing in this recipe enhances this selection of the very freshest produce.

Serves 6

Dressing

1 teaspoon salt
Dash freshly ground black pepper
3 tablespoons olive oil
1 tablespoon vinegar

Salad

1 cucumber, peeled, finely sliced, and soaked in ice water (without salt)
6 tomatoes, peeled, sliced and thoroughly chilled
12 small radishes, soaked in ice water

Combine the salt, pepper, oil and vinegar. Remove the cucumber slices from the ice water, dry thoroughly, and mix well in a bowl with the dressing. Drain and transfer to a shallow chilled dish. Surround with thinly sliced tomatoes and add the dressing left in the bowl.

Cut the radishes into extremely thin slices and sprinkle over the top.

Leek Salad

This is a great accompaniment to pork, chicken, and beef. It should be served with, not after, the meal. Clean the leeks, large or small, by cutting off the root end and all but a half inch of the green tops. Remove any discolored outer leaves and, if there are traces of dirt, remove the leaves until all are clean, or split the leek in half and wash under running water. If only extremely large leeks are available, be wary that the core isn't so woody that it is not usable. When the core is so tough that you cannot cut through it easily, it is either last year's or has stayed in the ground too long.

Serves 6

3 pounds small leeks, cleaned
3 hard-cooked eggs
½ teaspoon Dijon mustard
Salt and freshly ground black pepper
1 tablespoon wine vinegar
½ cup olive oil
Handful chopped parsley

Use only the white and very light-green parts of the leeks. Tie them into bundles, as for asparagus; plunge them into salted boiling water and cook, covered, at a simmer for 10 minutes. Drain well and transfer to a serving platter. Remove the strings and spread the leeks to cool.

Remove the egg yolks and mash them; chop the whites fine.

Mix the mustard with the salt and pepper. Add the vinegar, stirring until the mustard is completely combined. Add the egg yolks, stir in the oil, and add half the egg whites. Adjust the seasoning, if necessary. Pour the dressing over the leeks.

Mix the remaining chopped egg whites with the parsley and sprinkle on the top of the salad. Serve tepid.

Fennel Salad

Fennel, which is also known as finocchio and anise, is seasonal and not always plentiful, so if you find it on the market be sure to buy it and try this recipe. Do not add the oil until just before serving because it will wilt the fennel. A good salad for pork or broiled fish.

Serves 6

1 fennel bulb
Juice of 1 lemon
Salt and freshly ground black pepper
1 tablespoon olive oil
Chopped watercress or parsley

Remove the stem completely from the fennel bulb and discard the outer layer. Slice the bulb into julienne strips. Add the lemon juice, salt, and pepper. Mix and let stand for at least 45 minutes. Just before serving, add the olive oil and toss. Use a generous amount of chopped watercress or parsley as a garnish.

Lettuce, Orange, and Fennel Salad

A wonderful, tangy salad to serve as a luncheon main course with sesame sticks or slices of French or sourdough bread. The textures and flavors of each are distinct, yet together they form a good combination.

Serves 6

1 large fennel bulb
2 medium carrots
6 lettuce hearts
2 seedless oranges

Dressing

⅓ cup red wine vinegar
1 teaspoon salt
¼ teaspoon freshly ground black pepper
¼ teaspoon dry mustard
⅔ cup olive oil
1 tablespoon lemon juice
3 drops hot pepper sauce

Remove the tough outer leaves and cut off the ends of the fennel. Cut the bulb into thin slices. Clean, scrape, and thinly slice the carrots. Shred the lettuce hearts coarsely. Peel and cut the oranges into thin slices.

Prepare the dressing by mixing the vinegar with salt, pepper, and mustard. Then add the olive oil, lemon juice, and hot pepper sauce, and stir or shake well.

Place the fennel and carrot slices in a large salad bowl. Add the dressing, toss, and let marinate for 30 minutes. Add the lettuce hearts and toss. Top with orange slices and serve.

Mushroom Salad

Don't dress this salad until just before serving. The oil will discolor and wilt the mushrooms if left on too long.

Serves 6

2 pounds white mushrooms, sliced thin
½ cup Parmesan cheese slivers
¼ cup chopped parsley
2 tablespoons light olive oil, or a combination of olive oil and vegetable oil
1 teaspoon wine vinegar
Salt and freshly ground black pepper

Put the mushrooms on a serving dish or in a salad bowl. Add the Parmesan slivers and sprinkle with chopped parsley. Just before serving, dress with oil and vinegar and season with salt and pepper, tossing to combine.

Pea and Mushroom Salad

This salad is a good side dish with cold roast chicken or cold poached fish.

Serves 6

1½ pounds fresh peas or 2 10-ounce packages frozen tiny peas
1½ teaspoons sugar
2 tablespoons Basic Vinaigrette (see page 304)
1 tablespoon chopped fresh basil or 1 teaspoon dried basil
¼ pound mushrooms, sliced
Romaine or butter lettuce

Shell the peas and cook for a minute or two in boiling salted water to which the sugar has been added. When just tender, drain and add the vinaigrette. Allow to cool. Add the basil to the mushrooms and toss with the peas. Serve on a bed of romaine or butter lettuce.

Endive, Mushroom, and Cucumber Salad

Ideally, this recipe should be made with Belgian endive, but if it isn't available, curly endive will do.

Serves 6

6 heads Belgian endive
1 pound white mushrooms
2 cucumbers
2 tablespoons finely chopped parsley
2 tablespoons finely chopped shallots
Basic Vinaigrette (see page 304)

Trim the root ends of the endive, removing any discolored leaves. Wash and drain. Cut into julienne pieces with a sharp knife. Clean the mushrooms in acidulated water (1 tablespoon lemon juice to 1 quart water), trim the stems, and cut into thin slices. Peel the cucumbers with a potato peeler and cut into thin slices. Put the vegetables in a chilled bowl and sprinkle with parsley. Add the shallots to the dressing. Just before serving, pour the dressing over the vegetables and toss to mix.

Hot Chick-Pea Salad

I have purposely left out some of the quantities on the ingredient list because each guest should season this salad to suit his or her taste. This is a hearty salad and, as such, a good luncheon entrée.

Serves 6

*2 cups dried chick-peas**
Pinch baking soda
1 onion stuck with 2 whole cloves
1 carrot
Pinch thyme
1 bay leaf
Salt
Olive oil
Vinegar
Pepper in a pepper mill
Finely chopped onion
Chopped parsley

* Canned chick-peas can also be used; just be sure to rinse and drain them.

Soak the chick-peas overnight in water with a pinch of baking soda. Drain and rinse thoroughly. Cover with cold water and add the onion stuck with cloves, the carrot, thyme, and bay leaf. Bring to a boil; cover and simmer for 2 hours, or until done. Add salt only toward the end of the cooking.

Drain the chick-peas and serve hot, accompanied by olive oil, vinegar, salt, pepper, onion, and parsley. Guests then prepare their own salads.

Note: The water in which spinach has been cooked is good for cooking chick-peas. It gives a nice flavor. Just add a little salt.

Cold Dilled Peas

Although the curry powder is optional, without it this salad is nothing special. You can vary the amounts of all the ingredients to suit your taste.

Serves 8

2 cups fresh peas or 2 10-ounce packages frozen tiny peas
1 cup fresh pea pods or 10-ounce package frozen pods
½ cup sour cream
½ cup chopped fresh dill or chives (or a combination of the two)
½ to 1 teaspoon curry powder (optional)
Salt and freshly ground black pepper
Leaf lettuce leaves

If frozen peas and/or pea pods are used, defrost them and be sure to drain off as much moisture as possible. Combine the sour cream, herbs, curry powder, salt, and pepper, and mix thoroughly. Add to the peas and pea pods, mixing lightly so as not to break or mash the peas. Place in a glass bowl and garnish with additional dill and/or chives. Chill for 10 to 15 minutes, if desired. Serve on leaf lettuce.

Cheese and Olive Salad

Good cheese, chopped scallions, green olives, and a strong, mustard-flavored dressing make this hearty salad refreshing and filling. A perfect summer luncheon.

Serves 6 to 8

2 pounds imported Emmentaler or Gruyère cheese, finely shredded
2 cups finely chopped green onions or scallions
1½ cups sliced stuffed green olives
1 cup olive oil
¼ cup wine vinegar
4 teaspoons Dijon mustard
1 teaspoon salt
½ teaspoon freshly ground black pepper
Fresh salad greens: Bibb, Boston, butter, leaf, or romaine lettuce
Stuffed green olives, whole

Combine the cheese, onions or scallions, and olives, and mix well. Toss with a dressing made from the olive oil, vinegar, mustard, salt, and pepper. Arrange on a nest of fresh salad greens in a salad bowl and garnish with stuffed green olives.

Orange, Cheese, and Onion Salad

An excellent salad to accompany a rich entrée.

Serves 6

6 seedless oranges
1 medium red onion
½ pound Gruyère cheese cut into julienne strips
⅓ cup red wine vinegar
1 teaspoon salt
¼ teaspoon freshly ground black pepper
¼ teaspoon dry mustard
⅔ cup olive oil
1 tablespoon lemon juice
3 drops hot pepper sauce

Peel the oranges and remove the pith and as much of the white fiber as possible. Separate into sections; remove the skin and cut each large section into thirds. Peel the onion and slice into thin rings. Mix the orange sections, onion rings, and cheese strips together.

Prepare the dressing by mixing the vinegar with salt, pepper, and mustard. Add the olive oil, lemon juice, and hot pepper sauce, and stir or shake well. Add to the orange-cheese-onion mixture and toss.

Orange, Onion, and Walnut Salad

This very Italian salad is a natural with a pasta main course.

Serves 8

6 seedless oranges, peeled and sliced
1 onion, thinly sliced
Juice of 1 orange
Salt and freshly ground black pepper
1 tablespoon walnut oil or vegetable oil
2 heads romaine lettuce, broken into bite-size pieces
½ cup walnut pieces

Combine the orange and onion slices; marinate in the orange juice and add salt and pepper. Dress with the oil. Add to the romaine and toss. Top the salad with the walnuts.

Lentil Salad

The robust flavor of lentils goes very well with barbecued meats such as beef or pork ribs.

Serves 6

1 cup dried lentils, rinsed and picked over
2 tablespoons finely chopped parsley
3 scallions, finely chopped
½ cup French Dressing (see page 304)

Put the lentils in a pot with 2 quarts of cold water. Bring to a boil, reduce the heat, and simmer for 10 to 15 minutes, or until the lentils are cooked but still firm. Drain immediately and put into a bowl. Add the remaining ingredients while the lentils are still hot. Combine all the ingredients by lifting lightly from below with two forks in order not to mash the lentils. Serve cool or at room temperature.

Potato Salad

What is more American than potato salad? And what picnic is complete without it? It is the ideal companion to cold fried chicken, to hamburgers or hot dogs. For a perfect potato salad, the potatoes should be fork-tender, not soft or mashed. In fact, everything in the salad should have some texture.

Serves 6

2 pounds tiny (quarter-size) new potatoes
4 hard-cooked eggs, chopped
½ cup finely chopped celery
¼ cup thinly sliced scallions
½ cup Homemade Mayonnaise (see page 307)
½ teaspoon Dijon mustard
1½ teaspoons sugar
Salt and freshly ground black pepper

Scrub the potatoes and leave them unpeeled. Start them in cold water and bring to a boil. Remove from the heat after 2 or 3 minutes of boiling. Drain and refresh with cold water. They should be slightly underdone.

Cut the potatoes in half. Add the eggs, celery, and scallions. Combine the mayonnaise, mustard, sugar, salt, and pepper and add to the potato mixture. Mix thoroughly and serve at room temperature.

Curried Rice Salad

This is a salad entrée. It can be served chilled or hot (see Variation below), although I prefer it chilled.

Serves 6 to 8

2 cups cooked rice (al dente)
¼ cup coarsely diced fennel or celery
1 canned, roasted pimiento, diced (about ⅓ cup)
½ cup cooked fish, shrimp, or drained canned tuna, cut into pieces
4 pitted black olives, halved
4 uncooked mushroom caps, broken into pieces
1 tablespoon dried currants or raisins
2 tablespoons finely chopped parsley
2 tablespoons finely chopped chives
2 teaspoons curry powder
½ teaspoon cinnamon
1 teaspoon Pernod

Dressing

3 tablespoons oil
1 tablespoon lemon juice or vinegar
1-inch ribbon anchovy paste
Freshly ground black pepper

Put all the ingredients except those for the dressing in a serving bowl. In a separate bowl, beat together the oil, lemon juice, anchovy paste, and pepper. Pour the sauce over the salad ingredients and mix thoroughly but lightly, tossing with two forks.

Variation: Cut slices off the tops of eight ripe tomatoes and save them to use as lids. Remove and discard the tomato pulp. Fill each tomato with Curried Rice Salad and cover with the reserved tops. Dribble olive oil, to which a pinch of sugar has been added, over the tomatoes. Bake in a 350°F. oven for 15 minutes. Serve at room temperature.

Potato and Watercress Salad

Serves 8

3 pounds new potatoes
1 cup dry white wine
1 teaspoon salt
Dash freshly ground black pepper
3 tablespoons olive oil
1 tablespoon vinegar
1 bunch watercress, washed and dried
2 hard-cooked eggs, finely chopped
Chopped chervil

Scrub the potatoes and cook them unpeeled in salted water until just fork-tender—if small, about 8 to 10 minutes.

Peel and slice the potatoes while they are still hot. Add the white wine to them and let them marinate in the refrigerator for 1 hour.

Combine the salt, pepper, olive oil, and vinegar and mix well. Before serving, add the watercress and the dressing to the marinated potatoes and toss to combine. Top with the chopped eggs and chervil.

Roasted Pepper Salad

I consider this a condiment as well as a salad. As a condiment, it goes well with grilled meats, fish, or chicken, and it can be transformed into a salad with the addition of shredded lettuce or chopped spinach.

Serves 6

4 sweet red or green peppers
1 or 2 garlic cloves, thinly sliced
1½ tablespoons red wine vinegar
4 tablespoons olive oil
Salt and freshly ground black pepper
2 tablespoons finely chopped parsley

Preheat the broiler. Set the broiler rack so that the tops of the peppers will be about 4 inches from the heat source. Spread foil over the oven rack and place the whole peppers on it. Roast, turning occasionally, until the skin is charred and almost black all over. Remove the peppers, wrap them in a dish towel, and allow them to steam for about 5 minutes.

Transfer the peppers from the towel to a colander and run cold water over them until they are cool enough to handle. The skins should slip off easily under running water. Remove the core and seeds and slice the peppers into strips.

Place the pepper strips in a serving dish; add the garlic, vinegar, and oil, and season with plenty of salt and pepper. Toss together, and check the seasoning (roasted peppers seem to need quite a bit of salt). Add the parsley and allow to stand at room temperature for an hour or two before serving.

Note: If possible, use sweet red peppers; they are more succulent than the green.

Tomato Salad with Mozzarella

Fresh mozzarella, fresh basil, and ripe red tomatoes are an absolute necessity with this combination for both flavor and texture. If you don't want to scoop out the tomatoes, simply slice them and alternate layers of cheese and tomato.

Serves 6

6 large, ripe tomatoes
1½ pounds mozzarella cheese (as fresh as possible)
¾ cup olive oil
1 teaspoon salt or to taste
Freshly ground black pepper
1 cup shredded or coarsely chopped fresh basil*

Halve the tomatoes crosswise. Squeeze gently to remove the juice and seeds; if necessary, use the handle of a spoon to remove excess seeds. Salt and let stand, cut-side down, before cutting into wedges. Cut the cheese into 1-inch cubes. Place the tomato wedges, cheese cubes, olive oil, salt, and pepper in a salad bowl and toss. Top the salad with the basil leaves and toss gently at the table.

* If fresh basil is not available, add 1 tablespoon of dry basil and 2 tablespoons of lemon juice to the olive oil and let stand to soften before adding to the salad.

Spinach Salad

This old-fashioned spinach salad is unusual both because the spinach is cooked and because it is adorned only with dressing.

Serves 4

3 pounds fresh spinach, washed and stems removed
1 teaspoon Dijon mustard
Salt and freshly ground black pepper
3 tablespoons olive oil
1 tablespoon red wine vinegar

Place the spinach in a pan with a little cold water and bring quickly to a boil. Remove immediately, drain well, and chill thoroughly.

Combine the mustard, salt, pepper, oil, and vinegar in the bottom of a salad bowl. Add the spinach and toss gently several times until it is well coated with dressing. Serve very cold.

Spinach-Mushroom-Bacon Salad

Although this is a more familiar spinach salad, in this version the chopped egg is mixed with the dressing and tossed with the other ingredients as opposed to being sprinkled on top as a garnish. The mixture of egg with the dressing ingredients makes a stronger statement, which is needed in order to compete with the bacon and mushrooms.

Serves 6

2 pounds spinach
½ pound mushrooms
6 to 8 bacon slices, chopped
½ cup Egg Vinaigrette (see page 305)

Wash the spinach carefully. Remove the coarse stems and tear the leaves into bite-size pieces. Slice the mushrooms. Fry the bacon until crisp; drain on paper towels.

In a salad bowl, toss the spinach, mushrooms, and bacon with the vinaigrette.

Russian Salad

This hearty entrée salad is a meal in itself.

Serves 8

4 medium potatoes, cooked, peeled, and diced
1½ cups diced cooked carrots, divided
6 cauliflower florets, cooked and diced
8 green beans, cooked and diced
1 small zucchini, cooked 5 minutes in boiling salted water and diced
1 cup cooked fresh peas, divided
1 small head crisp lettuce, shredded, divided
1½ cups Basic Vinaigrette (see page 304)
1 teaspoon tarragon vinegar
½ teaspoon dry mustard
8 anchovy fillets, soaked in milk for 10 minutes, then drained and finely chopped
6 hard-cooked eggs, divided
8 sour gherkins, divided
4 tablespoons small capers, divided
2 cups mayonnaise, divided

Place the potatoes, 1¼ cups of the carrots, the cauliflower, green beans, zucchini, ¾ cup of the peas, and the lettuce into a large bowl.

Mix together the vinaigrette, tarragon vinegar, mustard, and anchovies, and add to the vegetables. Toss gently. Cube 4 of the hard-cooked eggs and chop 4 of the gherkins; add with 2 tablespoons of the capers to the vegetable mixture. Mix in 1 cup of the mayonnaise and toss gently but thoroughly. Place the salad on a platter and mold into a mound. Coat with the remaining 1 cup of mayonnaise. Decorate the salad with the remaining carrots, peas, hard-cooked egg slices, gherkins, and capers.

Vegetable Salad

This wonderful marinated vegetable salad is a meal in itself. The marinade and the dressing enhance the salad without taking it over. Try it my way and if you decide to increase the amounts, be my guest.

Serves 12

Marinade

1 teaspoon salt
Dash freshly ground black pepper
3 tablespoons olive oil
1 tablespoon cider vinegar
Chopped chives or onion

Vegetables

1 pound cooked green peas
½ pound cooked green beans
1 pound cooked lima beans
6 cooked beets, diced
6 carrots, cut in small cubes and cooked
1 bunch cooked asparagus (use only the tips)
2 pounds new potatoes, boiled in their skins, peeled, and chopped

Dressing

2 tablespoons sugar
1 tablespoon unbleached all-purpose flour
1 teaspoon salt
Freshly ground black pepper
¾ cup wine vinegar
¼ cup water
6 tablespoons butter
2 egg yolks, well beaten
½ cup heavy cream
Chopped chives for garnish

To make the marinade combine the salt, pepper, olive oil, vinegar, and chives or onion, and mix well.

Combine all the cooked vegetables except the potatoes in a large bowl. Pour the marinade over the vegetables and toss until all the pieces are thoroughly coated. Let marinate for 1 hour. Reserve the potatoes for use later.

To make the dressing, combine the sugar, flour, salt, pepper, vinegar, and water in the insert of a double boiler over hot water. Add the butter and egg yolks and bring to a boil, stirring constantly until thick. Remove from the heat and chill in the refrigerator. When ready to serve, add the cream. Pour over the reserved potatoes and sprinkle with chopped chives; arrange the marinated vegetables in small mounds around the potato salad and serve.

Romaine Salad with Hard-Cooked Egg Dressing

The crisp crunch of the romaine combined with hard-cooked egg and tarragon makes this a hard salad to beat.

Serves 4

1 head romaine
3 hard-cooked eggs, separated
1 teaspoon Dijon mustard
Salt and freshly ground black pepper
3 tablespoons olive oil
3 tablespoons tarragon vinegar
Fresh tarragon, chopped

Wash the romaine and dry it thoroughly.

Pass the egg yolks through a fine sieve and place in the bottom of a chilled salad bowl. Chop the whites and reserve them. Add the mustard, salt, and pepper to the yolks; mix in the olive oil gradually and stir in the vinegar.

Place the romaine in the bowl and toss. Serve sprinkled with finely chopped egg whites.

Marinated Vegetable Salad

This combination can be mixed and tossed or kept separate and composed just before serving. Add or delete vegetables as you choose, and by all means taste the marinade before the final assembly and adjust the seasonings as you see fit.

Serves 12

1 head cauliflower, divided into florets
1½ green peppers, cut into thin slices
3 zucchini, cut into thin slices
1 bunch broccoli, divided into florets and thinly sliced stems
4 medium carrots, cut into julienne strips
1 small rib celery, cut into julienne strips
½ pound green beans, left whole or cut in half
2 cucumbers, peeled, halved, seeds removed, and cut into julienne strips
12 whole cherry tomatoes
1 avocado, peeled and sliced
½ pound fresh mushrooms, cleaned and sliced

Marinade

¼ cup vegetable oil
1½ cups tarragon vinegar
½ cup sugar
2 garlic cloves, crushed
1½ teaspoons salt
1 tablespoon Dijon mustard
2 teaspoons fresh tarragon, chopped, or 1 teaspoon dried
1 tablespoon lemon juice
Coarsely ground black pepper

Steam the cauliflower, green pepper, zucchini, and broccoli for 2 minutes. Then plunge them into cold water. Drain.

Steam the carrots, celery, green beans, and broccoli stems for 4 minutes. Then plunge them into cold water. Drain.

Combine all the cooked vegetables with the cucumbers, cherry tomatoes, avocado slices, and mushrooms in a large bowl, and pour the marinade over all; toss well and refrigerate for 2 hours before serving.

SALAD DRESSINGS

There was a time when one could tell from the name what a dressing consisted of, but in the last fifty years so many variations have been concocted that it is impossible to be anything but confused and often horrified. Among the dressings that I cannot accept are any that include catsup, meat sauce, pickle juice or chopped pickles, pineapple or orange juice, and powdered garlic or powdered onion.

A basic vinaigrette or French dressing is really all that anyone needs. The classic formula is 5 parts oil to 1 part vinegar, with a pinch of salt and ground pepper, and a little Dijon mustard; sometimes lemon juice replaces the vinegar. A vinaigrette should enhance a salad, not detract from it. Start with a good olive or vegetable oil, or a combination of the two. Don't economize on the oil; it should be a good brand and not too strong. I avoid Greek or Italian "extra" virgin oils because they are too strong for my taste. However, you have to consider the salad in every case. A "strong" salad—radish, cucumber, cabbage, endive, or watercress—can take a stronger oil.

As to vinegars, I stick to red wine, white wine, tarragon, and champagne vinegars and stay clear of the "fruit" varieties. As far as I am concerned, there have been enough raspberry, pear, strawberry, or "homemade" vinegars to last the world a lifetime.

There are only three herbs that I ever use in a vinaigrette—tarragon, basil, or parsley—and never together but always separately. Never combine herbs in a vinaigrette; they simply kill each other. I do add a pinch of sugar now and again because it cuts the acid.

Homemade mayonnaise is easily made and is certainly preferable to the commercial variety. You do not need a blender or processor to produce good mayonnaise. My grandmother always made hers on a platter using only a fork to beat the egg and oil together, and the result was perfect. Generally, I make mayonnaise in batches, never seasoning it to start with, other than giving it a squeeze of lemon and a dash of salt. Later I add whatever herb or spice I want to this "all-purpose" dressing. I give several recipes here for seasoned mayonnaise—you can begin to branch out on your own once you master the basic recipe. Other mayonnaise recipes appear in the Sauces section (page 309).

Basic Vinaigrette

Makes about ½ cup

2 tablespoons red or white wine vinegar
6 tablespoons vegetable or olive oil
1 teaspoon salt
½ teaspoon freshly ground black pepper

Whisk all the ingredients together and pour over the salad just before serving.

Variations: Add a pinch of sugar and/or 1 teaspoon of Dijon mustard; chopped shallots and/or fresh herbs.

French Dressing

Makes about ¼ cup

½ garlic clove
Salt
½ tablespoon red wine vinegar
½ teaspoon Dijon mustard
Pinch sugar
3 tablespoons olive oil or a combination of olive oil and vegetable oil

In a bowl, mash the garlic with the salt until it is almost a paste. Stir in the remaining ingredients, using a wire whisk, until well blended.

Mustard Vinaigrette

Makes about ½ cup

⅓ cup vegetable or olive oil
1 tablespoon white wine vinegar
1 teaspoon sugar
1 garlic clove, minced
2 tablespoons Dijon mustard

Combine all the ingredients and whisk together to form an emulsion.

Celery Seed Dressing

This is especially good on fruit salads like papaya and avocado. It should be thoroughly chilled and poured over room-temperature fruits, and is best used the same day it is made.

Makes about 1½ cups

½ cup sugar
1 teaspoon dry mustard
1 teaspoon salt
1 teaspoon celery seeds
2 tablespoons grated onion
⅓ cup cider vinegar
1 cup vegetable oil

Combine the sugar, mustard, salt, celery seeds, onion, and vinegar. Slowly add the oil, beating with rotary beater.

Chill before serving. This should not be kept for very long—2 days, refrigerated, at the most—because the onion flavor becomes too strong.

Egg Vinaigrette

Makes about 1 cup

3 hard-cooked eggs, chopped
¼ cup vegetable oil
2 tablespoons olive oil
1 tablespoon red or white wine vinegar
1 teaspoon sugar
Salt
Freshly ground black pepper
½ teaspoon dry mustard
1 tablespoon lemon juice

Combine all the ingredients thoroughly and allow to marinate for 1 hour. This is particularly good on spinach salad.

Blue Cheese Salad Dressing I

Good on a chef's salad or on a combination of greens and vegetables.

Makes 4 to 6 servings

1 ounce blue cheese
4 tablespoons sour cream
2 tablespoons heavy cream
Salt and freshly ground black pepper

In a small bowl, crumble the blue cheese with a fork. Mash in the sour cream and heavy cream and stir together until the mixture forms a smooth paste. Season with salt and pepper.

Blue Cheese Salad Dressing II

This dressing is sensational with an endive and walnut salad as well as on any green salad that accompanies grilled meat.

Makes 4 to 6 servings

1 ounce blue cheese
1½ tablespoons red wine vinegar
½ teaspoon Dijon mustard
4 tablespoons olive oil
1 small garlic clove, minced
Salt and freshly ground black pepper

In a small bowl, crumble the blue cheese with a fork. Mash with the vinegar and mustard and stir in the oil, a drop at a time. Add the garlic and season with salt and pepper.

Homemade Mayonnaise

Today commercial mayonnaise has all but replaced homemade. There are several good brands, and although I often use them, I prefer to make my own. Unlike commercial mayonnaise, which will keep under refrigeration, the homemade kind will spoil in a very short time. The answer is to make it in small amounts and use it within a day or two. I generally make it in 2- to 3-cup quantities and doctor it according to what it will be used on. If it is for a slaw, I add Dijon mustard and tend to go heavy on the seasonings because I know that cabbage absorbs a lot of flavors. When it is to be used on fruit salads, I add a combination of sugar and additional lemon juice to bring out the flavors and sweeten them at the same time. Whatever you add—curry powder, dill, garlic, mustard, tarragon, anchovy, or anything else—wait until the mayonnaise is bound before incorporating it. However, if a liquid is to be added, include it with the egg yolks at the very beginning. The recipe that follows is the traditional one.

Makes about 2 cups

3 egg yolks
½ teaspoon salt
¼ teaspoon freshly ground black pepper
1⅓ cups olive oil or vegetable oil
2 tablespoons white wine vinegar or lemon juice

Place the egg yolks in a bowl and add the salt and pepper. Beat thoroughly with a wire whisk, a hand beater, or an electric beater at high speed.

Add the oil, 1 tablespoon at a time, beating thoroughly after each addition, until ½ cup has been added and the sauce is thick. Then add the remaining oil in larger quantities and, last, the vinegar or lemon juice.

Note: Should the mayonnaise curdle, immediately beat the curdled mixture into another egg yolk and continue adding the rest of the oil.

Tart Mayonnaise

A good base for salad dressings, this can be made tarter by adding more wine vinegar.

Makes about 1¼ cups

1 egg
1 teaspoon dry mustard
1 tablespoon wine vinegar
½ teaspoon salt
¼ teaspoon lemon pepper
1 cup vegetable oil

Place all the ingredients, except the oil, in a food processor or blender. Blend for about 10 seconds. Add the oil slowly in a steady stream. The mixture will begin to thicken in a few minutes. For a thicker mayonnaise, blend the mixture longer.

Mayonnaise Dijon

Makes about 2½ cups

2 egg yolks
1 whole egg
1 teaspoon Dijon mustard
Salt
½ teaspoon lemon juice
1 cup olive oil
1 cup vegetable oil
Freshly ground black pepper

Place the egg yolks, egg, mustard, and salt in a food processor or blender. Process for about 10 seconds. Add the lemon juice and then add the oil slowly in a steady stream while processing. Check the flavor of the mayonnaise after adding half the oil. Correct the seasoning. Continue processing until the mixture thickens.

SAUCES, CONDIMENTS, AND ACCOMPANIMENTS

INCLUDED here are recipes for some nice "finishing touches": various sauces, from the classic Béchamel (or white sauce) and Hollandaise, with their many variations, to special sauces for meats, poultry, seafood, and pasta. I have also added some recipes for seasoning agents and spice combinations as well as some accompaniments that provide a taste contrast that lends interest to the meal.

Unlike gravies, which are made from the pan drippings of the food they will accompany, sauces are intended to be lighter, creamier accompaniments that enhance the flavor. And "enhance" is the operative word, for they should neither mask nor overwhelm the dish they are used with.

Two words about sauces: their base and seasoning should be appropriate to the dish they are to accompany, and they should be light. Although cornstarch and arrowroot are sometimes used to thicken sauces, to my way of thinking these agents are a last resort; I do not like the texture they produce. Properly handled, egg yolks will do the trick very nicely, producing a velvet-smooth sauce that is neither gelatinous nor glue-like.

Sauces

Béchamel Sauce

This is a basic white or cream sauce and, as the recipe states, it can be thin, medium thick, or thick. The base of the sauce is a combination of butter and flour, called a roux, plus any one of a number of liquids. The finished sauce is the foundation for many other sauces, among them Velouté, Soubise, Supreme, Curry, Cheese, Mornay, Mustard, Herb, and Tarragon Sauces (recipes appear on pages 311–313).

Makes about 1 cup

Thin Sauce

1 tablespoon butter
1 tablespoon unbleached all-purpose flour
Salt and freshly ground black pepper
1 cup liquid (see list below)

Medium Sauce

2 tablespoons butter
2 tablespoons unbleached all-purpose flour
Salt and freshly ground black pepper
1 cup liquid (see list below)

Thick Sauce

3 tablespoons butter
3 tablespoons unbleached all-purpose flour
Salt and freshly ground black pepper
1 cup liquid (see list below)

Liquids

chicken stock/ veal stock/ beef stock/ lamb stock/ pork stock/ turkey stock/ game stock/ mushroom stock/ vegetable stock/ clam broth/ fish stock/ shellfish stock/ a mixture of white wine and stock/ whole milk/ light cream

Melt the butter in a saucepan and combine with the flour. Cook the two together over medium heat, stirring constantly, until the raw taste of the flour is gone. This takes about 2 or 3 minutes of cooking with the contents bubbling and frothy. Stir in the liquid, either hot or cold. Using a wire whisk, stir constantly at a simmer until the desired consistency is reached. If the liquid is hot when added, the mixture will come together immediately and it is imperative that it be whisked fast to prevent lumps from forming. If lumps do form, remove the pan from the heat and whisk the mixture until they disappear. This will not happen if cold liquid is added, but be sure to stir all the time so that the sauce remains creamy.

Velouté Sauce

A very rich sauce that can be used on meat or fish. If the sauce is to be used on meats, a meat stock should be the liquid used in making the Béchamel. If it is for fish, use fish stock.

Add ½ cup of heavy cream to 1 recipe Béchamel Sauce and season with a few grains of nutmeg. Simmer for a few minutes, and just before serving, beat in 3 to 4 tablespoons of butter, a spoonful at a time. Makes about 1½ cups of sauce.

Soubise Sauce

A slightly thicker sauce good with meat or fish. If the sauce is to be used on meat, use beef broth to make the Béchamel; on fish, use fish stock.

To 1 recipe Béchamel Sauce, add 1 cup of pureed, cooked onions and ⅓ cup of freshly grated Parmesan cheese. Just before serving, beat in about 2 tablespoons of butter, a spoonful at a time. Makes about 3 cups of sauce.

Supreme Sauce

Chicken or veal stock should be the liquid, as this sauce is generally used with chicken or veal dishes.

Prepare 1 recipe Béchamel Sauce. Beat 3 egg yolks slightly and stir in 1 cup of heavy cream. Temper the egg-cream combination with a little of the Béchamel, then stir the mixture back into the sauce. Reheat, but do not allow to boil. Makes about 2½ cups of sauce.

Curry Sauce

This is a mild curry sauce appropriate for eggs, mushrooms, veal, or chicken.

Following the recipe for Béchamel Sauce, cook 2 teaspoons of mild curry powder in the butter for 2 minutes before adding the flour. Use either light cream or chicken broth for the liquid. Makes about 1 cup of sauce.

Cheese Sauce

You can use sharp or mild Cheddar, Gruyère, Swiss or Emmentaler, Monterey Jack, or Fontina, depending on what the sauce is to accompany.

Following the basic Béchamel recipe, add milk to the roux, then add ½ cup of grated cheese and a dash of hot pepper sauce or a pinch of dry mustard. Let the grated cheese melt in the hot sauce. Do not stir too much after melting or the cheese may become stringy. Makes about 1½ cups of sauce.

Mornay Sauce

This sauce is great with any dish that is to be broiled or oven-baked, especially veal dishes.

Stir ¼ to ½ cup of grated Parmesan cheese and 1 to 2 tablespoons of butter into the finished Béchamel. Simmer for 3 to 4 minutes and correct the seasoning. Makes about 1½ cups of sauce.

Mustard Sauce

This is best with fish dishes, particularly salmon or halibut. Be sure to use a good brand of Dijon mustard; the strength is up to you.

Add 2 tablespoons or more of Dijon mustard to the finished Béchamel. Stir in well and simmer for 2 to 3 minutes. This makes a fairly hot sauce. For a milder sauce, use less mustard. Makes about 1 cup of sauce.

Herb Sauce

A good sauce for fish, veal, or chicken dishes. The choice of herb can be varied, but it should complement the dish the sauce will accompany.

For *Parsley Sauce,* stir ¼ cup or more of chopped parsley into the finished sauce. Makes about 1¼ cups of sauce.

For *Dill Sauce,* stir in chopped fresh dill or dillweed to taste, and add a few drops of lemon juice. Makes about 1 cup of sauce.

Tarragon Sauce

An excellent sauce with roast, broiled, fried, or poached chicken.

Make 1 recipe Béchamel, using chicken stock for the liquid. Add about 2 tablespoons of chopped fresh tarragon to the finished sauce and stir. Then stir in 2 egg yolks mixed with ½ cup of light cream. Heat but do not allow to boil. Makes about 1½ cups of sauce.

Hollandaise Sauce

This is one of the most popular sauces used in America today. The canned varieties are terrible and do not compare in any way to the real thing. The most successful way to make hollandaise is in the blender or processor. It can also be made in a double boiler or in a stainless-steel saucepot over direct low heat, but these two methods are more difficult to master.

Hollandaise is used over eggs benedict, steamed leeks, asparagus, hot and cold fish, broccoli, cauliflower, and for that matter on anything you wish in the way of vegetables, fish, or eggs. Add anything you like in the way of seasoning, but take into consideration what the sauce is to be served with or on, and make sure the seasonings are complementary.

Basic Hollandaise—Blender Method

Makes about 1 cup

4 egg yolks
½ teaspoon salt
Dash of hot pepper sauce
1 tablespoon lemon juice
¼ pound butter

Combine the egg yolks, salt, hot pepper sauce, and lemon juice in a food processor or blender. Melt the butter until it is bubbling but has not yet turned color. Gradually pour a thin stream of hot butter into the egg yolk mixture. It will thicken and become golden in color. If the sauce becomes curdled, pour about 1 tablespoon of boiling water into the sauce while the processor is turned on. Keep the finished sauce over warm water until ready to serve.

Basic Hollandaise—Stove-Top Method

Makes about 1 cup

4 egg yolks
½ teaspoon salt
Dash hot pepper sauce
1 tablespoon lemon juice
¼ pound butter

In the top of a flameproof glass double boiler over warm, not boiling, water or in a stainless-steel saucepan over low heat, thoroughly combine all the ingredients except the butter. In a separate pan heat the butter to very hot. Slowly pour the hot butter into the egg mixture, whisking all the time with a loose metal whisk, until the sauce thickens. Remove from the heat and continue stirring until it has cooled a little. If it curdles, beat in 1 tablespoon of light cream or boiling water and continue to whisk until it is smooth again.

Variations:

Anchovy Hollandaise—This is a good accompaniment to fish and lamb. Prepare 1 recipe Basic Hollandaise and add 5 anchovy fillets to the finished sauce. If you are using a processor, use whole anchovies; if you are making the hollandaise by hand, finely chop or mash the fillets before adding. Makes about 1 cup.

Caper Hollandaise—For broiled and poached fish and boiled meats. Prepare 1 recipe Basic Hollandaise and add 2 tablespoons of capers to the finished sauce. Mix well. Makes about 1 cup.

Hollandaise-Mousseline Sauce

This is a basic hollandaise to which whipped cream is added. It is used on poached or baked fish.

Makes about 1½ cups

¼ cup vinegar
Salt and freshly ground black pepper
2 tablespoons cold water
4 egg yolks
2 teaspoons plus ½ pound softened butter, divided
Juice of ½ lemon, strained
½ cup heavy cream, beaten until stiff

Pour the vinegar in an enamel pan with a big pinch of salt and a little pepper. Reduce by simmering until only 2 teaspoonsful are left. Add the water, egg yolks, and 2 teaspoons of the butter. Place the pan directly on very low heat and beat constantly with a wire whisk until the mixture thickens slightly.

Remove from the heat and place over hot water in a double boiler. Add the remaining butter little by little, beating continuously. Before it thickens, add 1 tablespoon of cold water. When the sauce thickens, stir in the lemon juice, season to taste, remove from the heat, and fold in the cream. Continue beating with the whisk for a few seconds. Serve in a warm bowl.

Note: The ingredients may be doubled.

Quick Brown Sauce

A good sauce for meat, it is also the base for Madeira Sauce, Piquante Sauce, Currant Jelly Sauce, and Bordelaise Sauce, all of which follow.

Makes about 1½ cups

2 tablespoons butter
2 tablespoons unbleached all-purpose flour
1½ cups canned beef bouillon or beef stock
Pinch thyme
Parsley sprig
Salt and freshly ground black pepper

Melt the butter in a heavy saucepan over low heat. Add the flour and blend well over medium heat. Reduce the heat and simmer for a couple of minutes. Add the liquid, heated or cold, and whisk constantly over medium heat until the sauce thickens. Add the herbs; reduce the heat and simmer for a few minutes. Adjust the seasoning, if necessary. (Canned bouillon or beef stock often contains enough salt so that no more is needed.)

Madeira Sauce

Makes about 1½ cups

Combine 1½ cups of Quick Brown Sauce with ½ cup of dry Madeira wine; simmer until it is reduced by almost a third. Correct the seasoning and serve. This is especially good with baked ham or a fresh leg of pork.

Piquante Sauce

Makes about 1½ cups

1 cup Quick Brown Sauce (page 315)
¼ cup dry red wine
1 teaspoon Dijon mustard
1 tablespoon finely chopped sour pickles
1 tablespoon chopped capers
½ teaspoon hot pepper sauce
2 tablespoons chopped parsley

In a saucepan combine all the ingredients except the parsley. Heat and simmer for 5 minutes, stirring constantly. Add the parsley. Good on rib eye steak or eye of rib roast.

Currant Jelly Sauce

Makes about 1½ cups

1 cup Quick Brown Sauce
½ cup currant jelly
1 tablespoon dry mustard
Juice of ½ lemon

Combine all the ingredients and simmer for 5 minutes. This is excellent with game or turkey.

Bordelaise Sauce

Makes about 1½ cups

1 cup red wine
¼ cup chopped shallots
1 teaspoon thyme
1 cup Quick Brown Sauce
1 tablespoon cognac
1 tablespoon lemon juice
1 tablespoon chopped parsley

Combine the wine with the shallots and thyme in a saucepan. Reduce over high heat to about ⅓ cup. Strain into the brown sauce and add the cognac and lemon juice. Simmer for a few minutes and add the parsley. This is especially good with steaks, roast beef, and grilled lamb.

Béarnaise Sauce

This is a natural for grilled or sautéed meat and grilled fish.

Makes about 1½ cups

1 pound butter
1 teaspoon whole peppercorns
2 tablespoons finely chopped shallots
2 tablespoons chopped fresh tarragon, or 1 tablespoon dried tarragon
2 tablespoons white wine vinegar
2 egg yolks
2 tablespoons water
Salt
⅛ teaspoon (or less) cayenne pepper
⅛ teaspoon chopped fresh tarragon (optional)

Clarify the butter by placing it in a saucepan and letting it melt slowly either over low heat or in a slow oven. (You may use a 1-quart heatproof glass measuring cup in the oven to facilitate pouring.) When the butter melts, remove it from the heat and carefully skim off and discard the foam that has risen to the surface. Pour off the clear golden liquid into a measuring cup, leaving the thin milky liquid at the bottom. One pound of butter should yield about 1½ cups of clarified butter.

Crush the peppercorns, using a mallet or the bottom of a heavy skillet.

Put the peppercorns, shallots, tarragon, and vinegar in a saucepan (do not use aluminum) and bring to a boil. Simmer until the vinegar has completely evaporated. Remove from the heat.

Add the egg yolks and water to the saucepan with the peppercorn-shallot-tarragon mixture and beat vigorously with a wire whisk over low heat. Continue beating while gradually adding the clarified butter. It should thicken like mayonnaise. Add the salt and cayenne pepper.

At this point, the sauce may be strained through a fine sieve, but it is not essential. If fresh tarragon is available, stir it into the sauce. The sauce may be heated, stirring gently, but it must not be allowed to become too hot or it will separate.

Variation: Choron Sauce—add 2 tablespoons of tomato puree to 1 cup of béarnaise. Good on grilled fish.

Hunter's Sauce

For Hunter's Stew (see page 41) and for all game meats as well as for any meats where a bordelaise sauce is called for.

Makes 3 cups

4 shallots, finely diced
9 medium mushrooms, finely diced
6 tablespoons butter, divided
4 ounces white wine
4 ounces red wine
1 tablespoon tomato catsup
2 cups consommé
1½ tablespoons bottled brown gravy sauce
3 tablespoons unbleached all-purpose flour
Salt and freshly ground black pepper
1 teaspoon sugar
¼ cup chopped parsley

Sauté the shallots and mushrooms in 3 tablespoons of the butter. Add the wines. Over medium heat, reduce to half the original amount of liquid; add the catsup. Add the consommé and cook at a slow boil for 10 minutes; add the brown gravy sauce. Make a roux of the remaining butter and the flour; whip into the consommé mixture. Add the salt, pepper, sugar, and parsley. Simmer on the back of the stove for as long as you like.

Herbed Butter

A noncooked type of béarnaise sauce for use on meat and fish.

Makes ¼ pound

¼ pound butter at room temperature
1 teaspoon finely chopped shallots
½ teaspoon salt
½ teaspoon freshly ground black pepper
2 teaspoons tarragon vinegar
1 teaspoon finely chopped fresh tarragon

Mash all the ingredients together until blended. Form into a cube and chill for 20 minutes. Slice into tablespoon-size pieces and serve on steaks, etc.

Herbed Butter Sauce

Good with all boiled, broiled, baked, grilled, or fried meats, especially lamb.

Makes 2½ cups

1 tablespoon chopped shallots
½ cup tarragon vinegar
1 tablespoon dried tarragon
3 egg yolks
3 tablespoons cold water
¼ pound butter, melted
Salt and freshly ground black pepper
1 teaspoon chopped parsley

Cook the shallots, vinegar, and dried tarragon over medium heat until no liquid remains. Add the egg yolks and cold water. Whisk over medium heat until thick. Add the butter and whisk until the sauce reaches light, creamy, medium consistency. Season with salt, pepper, and parsley.

Cumberland Sauce with Cherries

For baked ham or any pork dish.

Makes about 2 cups

1⅓ cups pitted sour cherries
½ cup Port wine
¼ cup red currant jelly
1 tablespoon Dijon mustard
⅓ cup lemon juice
¼ cup orange juice
1 tablespoon grated orange rind

In a saucepan, simmer the cherries in the wine for 10 minutes. Let the mixture cool completely. In a small saucepan set over hot water, soften (do not melt) the currant jelly. Transfer the jelly to a small bowl and combine it with the mustard, lemon juice, orange juice, and orange rind. Stir in the cherries and wine.

Marinade for Butterflied Leg of Lamb

Good for other broiled meats but tailor-made for lamb.

Makes 4½ cups

3 to 4 cups vegetable oil
¼ cup vinegar
1 garlic clove
½ onion, chopped
2 teaspoons Dijon mustard
2 teaspoons salt
½ teaspoon oregano
½ teaspoon basil
¼ teaspoon freshly ground black pepper
1 bay leaf, crushed

Combine all the ingredients and pour the mixture over the butterflied leg of lamb. Cover and refrigerate overnight, turning occasionally.

Mustard Sauce

For ham, pork, or brisket of beef.

Makes 2 cups

1 cup light cream, divided
¼ cup sugar
2 tablespoons dry mustard
1 tablespoon unbleached all-purpose flour
¼ teaspoon salt
1 egg yolk, slightly beaten
¼ cup red or white wine vinegar, heated

Heat ¾ cup of the cream in a heavy saucepan, adding the sugar gradually. Combine the mustard, flour, and salt; stir in the remaining ¼ cup of cream. Add this to the hot mixture and simmer, stirring, until thickened.

Add a little of the hot mixture to the egg yolk, stirring constantly; then return this to the hot mixture and blend well. Simmer, stirring constantly, until thickened and smooth. Gradually stir in the vinegar.

Serve warm or cold. The flavor improves if the sauce is refrigerated tightly covered for a day.

Parsley Sauce

Serve with broiled or boiled meats.

Makes 3 cups

4 tablespoons butter
4 tablespoons unbleached all-purpose flour
1 cup light cream
1 cup chicken stock
½ cup chopped parsley
Salt and freshly ground black pepper

Melt the butter in a saucepan; add the flour to make a roux. Allow the roux to cook for 2 to 3 minutes, stirring constantly. Add the cream and chicken stock.

The liquid may be added cold or hot, but if it is hot, remove the roux from the heat when adding and stir briskly with a wire whisk. If the liquid is added cold, do not remove from the heat, but stir with a wire whisk constantly to the desired consistency. Add the chopped parsley and season with salt and pepper.

Simple Steak Sauce

For grilled or broiled beef, lamb, and pork.

Serves 4

2 tablespoons drained capers
6 anchovy fillets
4 tablespoons butter
1 tablespoon sour cream
Freshly ground black pepper
1 teaspoon chopped parsley

Chop the capers and anchovies together until very fine. Melt the butter in a saucepan over medium heat until sizzling. Add the caper-anchovy mixture; reduce the heat and cook for 1 or 2 minutes until the anchovies dissolve a little. Remove from the heat and stir in the remaining ingredients.

Shrimp Sauce

This is good with any poached, grilled, baked, or sautéed fish as well as with cheese soufflés.

Makes 2½ cups

4 quarts fish stock
½ pound cooked shrimp, peeled, deveined, and mashed or pureed
½ cup heavy cream
4 tablespoons cold butter
Salt and freshly ground white pepper

Reduce the fish stock to approximately 1 cup. Do not salt the stock until it is fully reduced to avoid oversalting. (If this should occur, slices of raw potato added to the stock will draw out the excess salt.)

When the stock is reduced, add the shrimp and whisk in. Add the cream and bring to a boil. Take off the heat and whisk in the cold butter. Taste before adjusting the seasoning.

Egg Sauce

For Salmon-Crab Loaf or as a topping on Spoon Bread Soufflé or any cheese soufflé, or on vegetable dishes.

Makes 3 cups

3 hard-cooked eggs
3 tablespoons butter
3 tablespoons unbleached all-purpose flour
2 cups whole milk, or 1 cup whole milk and 1 cup chicken stock
Salt and freshly ground black pepper

Chop the eggs in a large dice and set aside. Melt the butter in a 1-quart saucepan over medium heat. Add the flour and mix completely; allow to cook for 1 or 2 minutes, stirring constantly; do not allow to burn. Add the liquid, beating with a wire whisk, and continue to stir until the mixture thickens to the desired consistency.

Remove from the heat and add the eggs. Season with salt and pepper. Taste the sauce to be sure there is no uncooked flour taste. If there is, return the sauce to medium heat and cook a bit longer. Do not allow the sauce to boil, just simmer.

Green Sauce

Use on any poached fish.

Makes about 2 cups

½ pound chard leaves, carefully washed
½ pound spinach, carefully washed
2 or 3 slices stale bread without crusts
1 tablespoon capers, rinsed and drained
Salt and freshly ground black pepper
6 anchovy fillets
1 teaspoon finely chopped fresh tarragon
2 tablespoons finely chopped parsley
3 hard-cooked egg yolks
⅓ cup olive oil
1 teaspoon vinegar or lemon juice

Add the chard to boiling water; cook for 5 minutes. Add the spinach and cook for 2 or 3 minutes longer. Drain, squeeze dry, and chop the greens.

Soak the bread in warm water; squeeze thoroughly.

Pound the capers to a paste in a large mortar or bowl. Add the salt, pepper, anchovies, tarragon, parsley, and the greens, and pound until the mixture has the consistency of a puree. Pound and stir in the soaked bread and the egg yolks. When the mixture is smooth, begin dribbling in the olive oil, stirring vigorously and uniformly with the pestle as if making a mayonnaise. Adjust the seasoning and stir in the vinegar or the lemon juice.

If the emulsion is prepared ahead of time, the oil may separate; to recombine it, give it a rapid beating with the pestle just before serving.

Cucumber Sauce

For any fish, especially salmon.

Makes 3 cups

3 to 4 medium-size cucumbers, peeled and seeded
1 cup sour cream
Pinch sugar
½ teaspoon Garlic Puree (see page 332)
Pinch salt and freshly ground black pepper

Coarsely grate half the cucumber and pulverize the remainder. Add the sour cream, sugar, garlic puree, salt, and pepper. Refrigerate until ready to use.

For the hot version, follow the recipe above, but substitute 1 cup Béchamel Sauce (see page 310) for the sour cream. Add the cucumbers and spices and keep the sauce hot until ready to use.

White Butter Sauce

Serve with any poached, baked, or grilled fish.

Makes about 2½ cups

¼ to ½ cup fish stock
½ cup chopped shallots
1 cup dry white wine
½ cup heavy cream
½ pound soft butter

Combine the fish stock, shallots, and wine in a saucepan. Reduce by half over high heat. When reduced, add the cream and cook over high heat until the mixture coats a spoon.

Set aside; allow to settle and cool slightly. Add the butter, a tablespoon at a time, whisking constantly until the sauce thickens like mayonnaise. If the sauce separates, add small chunks of cold butter and continue to whisk until it emulsifies again.

Tomato Pulp

This may be made in large quantities and frozen for later use.

Makes about 4½ cups

3 pounds firm, ripe tomatoes

Dip the tomatoes in boiling water for 10 to 12 seconds. Remove, peel, and cut in half crosswise.

Squeeze each half gently to get rid of the seeds and juice; if necessary, use the handle of a spoon to dig out any remaining seeds. Chop fine and let stand in a bowl for about 20 minutes. Drain thoroughly.

Note: Canned tomatoes may be substituted; they must be thoroughly drained, seeded, chopped, and redrained.

Tomato Puree

This is more concentrated than the tomato pulp and is used in smaller quantities for soup bases and for other tomato sauces.

Makes about 2 cups

4 pounds firm, ripe tomatoes
2 teaspoons salt
3 tablespoons finely chopped yellow onion
1 large bay leaf

Dip the tomatoes in boiling water for 10 to 12 seconds. Remove, peel, and cut in half. Squeeze each half gently to get rid of the seeds and juice, using the handle of a spoon to dig out remaining seeds, if necessary. Sprinkle the interiors with the salt, which will draw out even more juice; invert in a colander; let drain for about 20 minutes.

Chop the tomatoes and let stand in a bowl for about 20 minutes more. Drain the tomatoes thoroughly and place in a 2-quart saucepan with the onion and bay leaf. Bring to a boil, then cook over moderate heat for 30 minutes, or until thickened. Stir occasionally; as the sauce thickens, stir more frequently. Remove from the heat, discard the bay leaf, and puree the mixture in a blender or food mill.

Cold Tomato Sauce

This can be used in any recipe that calls for cooked tomatoes.

Makes about 4 cups

3 cups Tomato Pulp (see page 325) or 3 cups canned tomatoes, drained, seeded, and finely chopped
1 garlic clove
¼ teaspoon dried sage
1 teaspoon salt
¼ teaspoon freshly ground black pepper
2 tablespoons butter, softened

Place the pulp or canned tomatoes, garlic, sage, salt, and pepper in a 3-quart saucepan and cook without boiling, stirring until all the ingredients are well mixed. Add the butter, bit by bit, and stir until well mixed. Remove from the heat and discard the garlic; chill.

Taste for seasoning and puree in a blender briefly.

Easy Tomato Sauce

Makes about 5 cups

6 tablespoons butter, divided
1 medium onion, coarsely chopped
½ cup coarsely chopped celery
½ cup coarsely chopped carrots
4 cups Tomato Pulp (see page 325) or canned tomatoes, drained, seeded, and chopped
1 teaspoon salt
Freshly ground black pepper
2 tablespoons chopped parsley
2 tablespoons chopped fresh basil or 1 teaspoon dried basil

Melt 4 tablespoons of the butter in a 2-quart saucepan. Add the onion, celery, and carrots. Sauté, stirring over low heat, until the onion is almost golden.

Add the tomato pulp or the canned tomatoes, salt, and pepper to the sautéed mixture. Bring to a boil; lower the heat and simmer, stirring occasionally, for 20 minutes. Add the parsley, basil, and the remaining 2 tablespoons of butter. Stir and cook briefly until the butter is dissolved.

Note: For a richer sauce, add ½ cup of heavy cream at the end of the cooking time.

Bolognese Sauce

This may be used over pasta, rice, gnocchi and cornmeal dishes, and is sometimes an ingredient in other Italian dishes. It is a meat sauce with mushrooms that probably originated in Bologna, hence the name.

Makes 5 cups

3 tablespoons butter
2 ounces salt pork or prosciutto, diced
½ cup chopped onions
¼ cup grated carrots
¼ cup chopped celery
¾ pound mixed meats (beef, pork, and veal in equal amounts)
¼ pound fresh mushrooms, chopped
1½ cups dry red wine
1 tablespoon chopped parsley
½ teaspoon dried marjoram
1 teaspoon salt
Freshly ground black pepper
Pinch ground nutmeg
1½ teaspoons unbleached all-purpose flour
3 cups chopped tomato, peeled and seeded
1½ cups beef stock
¼ cup heavy cream

Combine the butter and salt pork or prosciutto in a saucepan and cook slowly until browned. Add the onions, carrots, and celery and cook over low heat until the onions brown, about 10 minutes. Add the meats and mushrooms and continue to cook, raising the heat to moderate, for 5 minutes. Add the wine, parsley, and seasonings and cook until wine is nearly evaporated.

Remove from the heat and mix in the flour, then return to the heat and cook. Add the tomato pulp. Turn the heat to very low and allow to cook for 1 hour, adding the stock and stirring occasionally. Add the heavy cream during the last 10 minutes of cooking.

Clam Sauce

When you use a clam sauce on pasta, please don't use any cheese with the dish. Sprinkle on chives or parsley instead.

Makes 2¼ cups

2 7-ounce cans minced clams
4 tablespoons olive oil
2 garlic cloves, minced
Salt and freshly ground black pepper
Chopped parsley or chives

Drain the clams, reserving the liquid. Heat the olive oil in a small skillet; add the garlic and cook over medium-low heat for 5 minutes. Add the clam liquid and reduce by about a third over high heat. Heat the drained clams in this garlic broth for only a couple of minutes, then add some parsley or chives.

To serve, spoon the clam sauce over cooked, drained pasta and add more parsley or chives.

Walnut Sauce for Noodles

Adjust the quantity of walnut halves to suit your palate. This is what I like, but that isn't gospel. This is best served with broad noodles.

Makes about 2 cups

2 tablespoons olive oil
24 shelled walnut halves, crushed
1 teaspoon salt
½ teaspoon freshly ground black pepper
3 tablespoons Tomato Puree (see page 325)
¼ pound butter
½ cup chicken stock
1¼ cups freshly grated Parmesan cheese, divided

Heat the oil in a small saucepan or skillet. Add the walnuts, salt, and pepper. Sauté, stirring, over low heat for 2 minutes. Mix in the tomato puree and butter. Add the chicken stock and cook over low heat for 10 minutes, or until reduced and thickened. Pour over cooked noodles tossed with ¼ cup Parmesan cheese and mix until they are well coated. Serve with the remaining Parmesan cheese.

Pesto, Genoa Style

This distinctive sauce is very versatile. It can be served with pasta, on vegetables, or added to bean and vegetable soups.

Makes 1 cup

- *½ cup pine nuts*
- *¼ cup chopped fresh basil or 1 tablespoon dried basil*
- *1 cup chopped raw spinach leaves*
- *2 teaspoons finely minced garlic*
- *½ cup freshly grated Fiore Sardo cheese or ¼ cup freshly grated Romano cheese*
- *¼ cup freshly grated Parmesan cheese*
- *6 tablespoons softened butter*
- *½ cup olive oil*
- *¼ teaspoon salt*
- *⅛ teaspoon freshly ground black pepper*

Mash the pine nuts, basil, spinach, and garlic to a smooth paste with a mortar and pestle. Slowly stir in the cheese and butter. Add the olive oil slowly, a little at a time. Season with salt and pepper.

Note: This may be made in a blender, but mix all the ingredients together before blending. If made in larger quantities, pesto may be covered with a layer of olive oil, placed in a jar, and stored in the refrigerator.

Special Accompaniments, Seasonings, and Condiments

Aioli Sauce

This is much more potent than plain garlic mayonnaise. The French use it with any boiled or baked fish and on all fresh vegetables. Aioli is a good accompaniment to boiled salt cod, potatoes, carrots, green beans, artichokes, chick-peas, beets, hard-cooked eggs, snails, or squid stew.

Makes about 2 cups

16 garlic cloves, peeled (allow 2 cloves per person)
Pinch salt
1 or 2 egg yolks, at room temperature
1 cup virgin olive oil
Juice of 1 lemon
1 teaspoon tepid water

Pound the garlic to a paste in a mortar with a pestle. Add the salt and egg yolks and mix until the yellow of the eggs becomes pale. Add the oil in a thin thread while turning with the pestle; pour the oil extremely slowly and stir constantly in the same direction to obtain a thick, smooth cream. After about 3 or 4 tablespoons of oil have been added, add the lemon juice and water. Continue to add the oil, little by little. When the cream becomes too thick again, add another few drops of water.

Should the oil separate from the rest of the ingredients, empty the mortar completely, put another egg yolk with a few drops of lemon juice into it, and, spoonful by spoonful, add the separated aioli.

Note: Aioli may also be made in a blender. The result will be lighter and have a drier, flatter flavor.

Jellied Mayonnaise

Use to decorate cold meats, fish, or poultry. It may also be chilled briefly, put in a pastry tube, and piped on cold foods as a decoration.

Makes 1¼ cups

1 envelope (1 tablespoon) unflavored gelatin
¼ cup cold water
1 cup Homemade Mayonnaise (see page 307)

Soften the gelatin in cold water for 5 minutes. Stir over hot water until the gelatin is dissolved. Add to the mayonnaise and blend well. Allow to thicken slightly.

Garlic Mayonnaise

Excellent with hot or cold poached fish, cold vegetables, and hot boiled beef or lamb.

Makes 4 cups

3 garlic cloves
4 egg yolks
1½ teaspoons salt
3 cups virgin olive oil

Place the garlic and egg yolks in the blender with the salt and run at high speed for 30 seconds. Pour the oil in very slowly, until the sauce is thick and thoroughly blended. Should it curdle, remove the mixture to a bowl, start with another egg yolk and a tiny bit of oil in the blender, then slowly pour it into the curdled mixture. The finished product will emerge as a dense, highly fragrant mayonnaise flavored with garlic.

Note: Although the recipe calls for a blender, this mayonnaise can very easily be whisked by hand; mash the garlic first.

Garlic Puree

No cook should be without garlic puree, which can be used instead of fresh garlic. Like duxelles, it is good on just about everything. It will keep for weeks in the refrigerator, ready to use when you want it. A teaspoon is the equivalent of 2 garlic cloves.

Makes about 2 cups

20 to 24 whole heads garlic

2 to 3 tablespoons olive or vegetable oil

Preheat the oven to 425°F.

Wrap the garlic in aluminum foil and bake for 1 hour. Remove the foil-wrapped garlic, and when it is cool enough to handle, break up the heads and discard the outer covering. Using your fingers simply squeeze the cooked garlic, which has become very soft, out of the skin and into a jar. Cover with the olive oil to preserve and store in the refrigerator.

Variation: Garlic Cream Sauce—Blend 3 tablespoons of garlic puree with 2 tablespoons of pan juices and 1½ cups of heavy cream to make a cream gravy for roast capon, chicken, or lamb.

Homemade Peanut Butter

This homemade peanut butter is the base for the peanut sauce that follows.

Makes 2 cups

4 cups roasted peanuts, shelled and skinned

Salt (optional)

Place the peanuts in the food processor and process, using the steel blade, until they are a smooth paste. Turn the machine on and off and scrape the mixture down from the sides of the bowl. The mixture will form a ball. Add salt to taste, if desired.

If the peanut butter seems too stiff, continue processing until it softens.

Peanut Sauce

Especially good with roast, broiled, or grilled lamb as well as with beef and chicken.

Makes 4½ cups

1¾ cups Homemade Peanut Butter (see page 332) or use commercial smooth peanut butter
1¾ cups coconut cream
¼ cup lemon juice
¼ cup soy sauce
¾ ounce Worcestershire sauce
2 dashes hot pepper sauce
½ teaspoon salt

Combine all the ingredients and mix together, blending well.

Homemade Sour Cream

I make my own. It is far more delicate than the commercial and does not separate when added to something hot. It will last as long as the cream used to make it (check the date on the cream container). When dolloped on top of a bowl of soup, it will dissolve instead of remaining a solid lump. Once you try this, you will never again use commercial sour cream.

Makes about 1 quart

3½ cups whipping cream, divided
4 tablespoons buttermilk, divided

Pour 2 cups of the whipping cream in a 1-quart jar with a tight-fitting lid. Add 2 tablespoons of the buttermilk; cover and shake vigorously. Add the remaining whipping cream and buttermilk and stir with a spoon. Leave at room temperature, uncovered, for 3 to 4 hours. Cover the jar and shake again. Pour out the desired amount and whip as for any whipping cream. Store the remainder in the refrigerator until ready to use. Shake vigorously and whip each time it is used.

Sour Cream-Dill Sauce with Cucumber

Serve with fish dishes, or with chilled vegetables as a dip.

Makes about 3 cups

1 egg
1 teaspoon salt
Pinch freshly ground black pepper
Pinch sugar
4 teaspoons lemon juice
½ teaspoon grated onion
2 tablespoons finely chopped fresh dill or 1 tablespoon dried
1 cucumber, seeded and chopped
1½ cups Homemade Sour Cream ***(see page 333)***

Beat the egg until fluffy and lemon-colored. Add the remaining ingredients, mixing in the sour cream last. Blend well and chill thoroughly.

Crème Fraîche

This cream is used to enrich sauces in the manner of heavy cream and is wonderful served with fresh fruits or over any dessert that you might put whipped cream on. In Europe it is readily available in the markets, but in America it must generally be made at home. There is nothing difficult about making it, but it takes about 24 hours to be really satisfactory.

Makes 1 quart

2 cups Homemade Sour Cream ***(see page 333)***
2 cups whipping cream

In a 1-quart jar, combine both ingredients; cover and shake thoroughly for a minute or two. Uncover and leave on a counter for 5 to 6 hours. Cover and refrigerate for 12 hours, or overnight. When ready to use, pour out the amount you want to use, whip with a wire whisk to the consistency of pourable whipped cream, and use. Will keep up to 2 weeks refrigerated.

Homemade Bread Crumbs

Bread crumbs should not be pulverized to a sandlike texture, for they will become a sticky cement when mixed with liquids in cooking. (The same holds true for finely powdered cracker crumbs added to a casserole or loaf.) Leave some texture; they are meant to open up rather than seal, especially when added to a meat mixture, as for example, a meat loaf. Added to a casserole, they should be toasty and have a bit of crunch, not form a pastelike covering.

This recipe makes a 6-month supply, but it should be kept in an airtight container on a kitchen shelf, not stored in the refrigerator where the crumbs will absorb moisture and turn rancid.

2 loaves any firm-textured fresh bread
½ pound butter
Salt and freshly ground black pepper

Crumb the bread evenly in either a processor or blender. Melt the butter in a pan large enough to hold the crumbs and add them to the melted butter. Stir to distribute the butter evenly throughout. Cook over medium heat until all the moisture is gone and the butter is absorbed. Toss and stir the crumbs to prevent them from burning on the bottom. They are done when the tossed crumbs sound like sand dropping to the bottom of the pan.

Remove from the heat and allow to come to room temperature before storing. They must be completely cooled; otherwise they will form a condensation when sealed for storage and will not keep.

Four Spices

An excellent combination of spices to use in sauces for vegetables and game birds. You can make your own combinations for other dishes. The only guideline is that the spices complement the food they are to accompany.

Makes about ¾ cup

8 tablespoons freshly ground white pepper
2 tablespoons freshly ground nutmeg
2 tablespoons freshly ground juniper berries
2 teaspoons ground cloves

Mix all the ingredients thoroughly and put in a jar on the spice shelf.

Homemade Curry Powder

There is only one way to have a curry powder that suits you and that's to make it yourself. If there is a commercial blend that you like, stick to it, but if there is not, here is a recipe that gives you a base to make your own. If there is an ingredient that you don't like, just leave it out, and if there is something that you want more of, simply blend it in.

Makes 3 cups

1 tablespoon cayenne pepper
2 tablespoons powdered cloves
2 tablespoons Jamaica ginger
¼ cup freshly ground black pepper
¼ cup cardamom seeds, freshly ground
1 cup ground turmeric
¼ cup caraway seeds, freshly ground
¼ cup red chili powder
¾ cup coriander seeds, freshly ground

Mix all the ingredients thoroughly and store in a glass container with a tight screw top.

Note: Most whole spices will keep for a long time, but smell them to make sure they retain their distinctive odor. Once ground, they keep less well. Perfectionists grind curry powder only as needed, but in fact, it will keep for months.

Condiments to Serve with Curries

A curry dish does not require condiments, but they help. The condiments to serve with curries are as important as the blend for the curry powder, and to have a really fine curry, don't use yesterday's leftovers. Buy fresh and start from scratch.

Condiments should be served in small bowls and passed. Never serve the curry dish with the condiments already sprinkled on top. The choice of condiments should be left to each individual.

Major Grey's, Bengal Club, or Tamarind chutneys
Sweet pickled pineapple
Sweet pickled watermelon rind
Sweet pickled onions
Sweet and sour pickles
Mustard pickles
Pickled walnuts
Grated fresh coconut
Sieved hard-cooked eggs
Chopped peanuts
Grated white radish
Sliced fresh tomatoes
Fresh green onions
Fried bananas
Flaked fresh cooked crab or shrimp
Sardines

Chutney Sauce

The simplest kind of sauce to serve over baked ham or roast pork.

Makes 3 cups

1 cup bottled chutney, chopped
1 cup sugar
4 tablespoons lemon juice
¼ cup water
1 cup currants

Mix all the ingredients and simmer until syrupy.

Duxelles

Jim Beard always says that this cooked mushroom mixture is good on everything but ice cream, and he is right. Although duxelles can certainly be made with onions instead of shallots, I must confess that they aren't as good. Try duxelles on scrambled eggs, or add them to any sauce for meats.

Makes about ¼ cup

½ pound mushrooms
4 shallots, finely chopped
1 tablespoon butter
Salt and freshly ground black pepper
1 tablespoon chopped parsley
Few drops lemon juice

Trim the mushrooms, rinse quickly, and pass through the medium blade of a vegetable mill, or chop fine.

Stew the shallots in butter over very low heat for 20 to 25 minutes, stirring occasionally, until soft and slightly browned. Add the mushrooms and the seasoning; lower the heat, and toss regularly until the mushrooms have lost all their liquid and the mixture is dry. Stir in the parsley and cook for another minute over low heat. Remove from the heat and stir in the lemon juice.

Onion Marmalade

My grandmother had onions cooking on the back of the stove all the time, making this savory marmalade, and, true to family tradition, I always keep a supply on hand. It is good on practically everything. Add 2 or 3 tablespoons to the next onion soup you make, or serve it as a relish with hamburgers. Store refrigerated in a lidded jar.

Makes 1½ cups

8 onions, sliced
3 tablespoons butter
1 tablespoon Dijon mustard
Salt and freshly ground black pepper

Place the onions in a large, dry, cast-iron skillet and cook over medium-low heat until the moisture has evaporated. When it has, add the butter and continue cooking until the onions have turned a dark golden brown. The skillet will be very full when you start, and, as the cooking progresses, the onions will cook down. Season with the mustard, salt, and pepper.

Frozen Cranberry Mold

I only make this once a year—for Thanksgiving. I have never found any other cranberry recipe that I like as much.

Serves 12

16-ounce can jellied cranberry sauce
3 tablespoons lemon juice
1 cup heavy cream, whipped
¼ cup mayonnaise
¼ cup confectioners' sugar
1 cup chopped walnuts or macadamia nuts

Crush the cranberry sauce and add the lemon juice. Pour into a mold (or molds) that has been lightly coated with mayonnaise.

Combine the whipped cream, mayonnaise, sugar, and nuts. Pour over the cranberry mixture in the mold and freeze. Unmold to serve.

Note: This can be prepared 3 to 4 weeks in advance.

Sautéed Apples

I prefer this dish to applesauce to serve with roast pork. It is quick to make and has a better texture and a more pronounced apple taste. Just don't cook the apples too much; they should be slightly crisp.

Serves 6

4 Granny Smith or Newtown apples
4 tablespoons butter
1½ tablespoons Vanilla Sugar (below)
⅛ teaspoon cinnamon

Peel and slice the apples. Put them in salted water to keep them from turning brown until you are ready to use them. Drain and sauté the apples in the butter. Sprinkle with the vanilla sugar mixed with cinnamon. Cook the apples, turning carefully with a spatula, until they are delicately golden. It should take about 30 minutes. (It is best to cook them over medium heat to achieve the color without turning the apples to mush.)

Note: For an easy dessert, serve with Crème Fraîche.

Vanilla Sugar

This is simply a sugar that is vanilla-flavored. There are commercial brands available, but they usually come in 4-ounce containers and are hardly worth bothering with. Make your own.

5 pounds white sugar
1 vanilla bean

Add the vanilla bean to the sugar. It will absorb the vanilla flavor. Store in a glass container with a tight lid. When you need vanilla sugar, take out what you need, and keep the rest for future use.

BREADS, PASTRIES, AND BATTERS

I AM a pushover for homemade bread, or any bread for that matter as long as it's good. Today there are so many really fine bakeries everywhere that one has no trouble finding good bread, as opposed to mass-produced "balloon" bread.

Exact measurements of flour are next to impossible to give because some mixtures absorb more flour than others and some flours absorb more liquid than others. Atmospheric conditions make a difference too. Flours vary considerably from one region to the next. My best recommendation is to find a flour that suits you and stick to it. However, I prefer unbleached all-purpose flour and call for it in the recipes in this book. Even then, you cannot be sure exactly how much flour you will need to use until you have made the dough.

I prefer to use cake yeast in baking breads; however, it is not as readily available as the active dry yeast, which keeps longer. One thing is certain: in using the granular variety it is imperative that the yeast be "proofed." Proofing is making sure the yeast is active. To do this, add warm water to the yeast to begin the fermentation. The water should be 100° to 110°, just the far side of lukewarm. Lukewarm water will work, as will cold water for that matter, but it takes longer. Too hot water, however, will kill the yeast and it won't proof at all. You know the yeast is proofed when the mixture begins to bubble. Be sure to warm the water and add it to the yeast. Don't combine the two and heat over the stove—it doesn't work that way.

Sugar added to warm milk will hasten the proofing, and salt added to the yeast will slow it down. Salt should always be added to the yeast with the flour. Iodized salt works better than kosher or sea salt. In general, sugar in any large quantity should only be added to dessert-type breads. However, a few tablespoons are fine for regular bread baking, if the recipe calls for it.

Once a bread dough is made, the next problem comes in trying to tell anyone how long to let it rise. The conditions have to be just so or it will rise too fast. In cold locations, rising will take twice as long as normal. In high altitude baking—6,000 feet above sea level—where rising is always a problem, breads can be placed outside in the snow to rise, and they will do it.

Bread making and baking is a science and an art in itself, and I am not writing a book on this subject, but the few recipes I give here are ones I like and are almost no trouble to make.

Basic Homemade Bread

This is as easy as any bread can be and a good recipe for the beginner. It isn't fancy, but it tastes awfully good, and you can be proud of the finished loaves.

Makes 2 loaves

2½ cups warm water
2 packages active dry yeast
½ cup instant nonfat dry milk
2 tablespoons sugar
2 tablespoons salt
½ cup vegetable oil
7 to 7½ cups unbleached all-purpose flour, divided

Preheat the oven to 375°F.

Measure the water into a large mixing bowl. Sprinkle the yeast over the water and wait a few minutes for the combination to bubble—that means the yeast is active. Add the dry milk, sugar, salt, oil, and 3¼ cups of the flour to make a thick batter. Blend well using a wooden spoon. Beat for 5 minutes.

Gradually add the remaining flour to form a very stiff dough (it will be very difficult to work in with the spoon). Turn out onto a floured surface. Knead until smooth; this can take 10 minutes. Place in a cloth-covered, greased bowl and let rise until doubled in bulk. Divide in half and shape into 2 loaves and put into 9 x 5-inch bread baking pans. Cover with a cloth and let rise in a warm place until at least doubled in bulk. Bake for 35 to 45 minutes. Remove from the pans immediately and cool on a wire rack.

R. N. Fry Bread

This is one of my favorite things to eat, especially when there is homemade butter and blackberry jam to go with it. It is related to a skillet bread that I remember as a kid in South Dakota, but this version can be cooked in a deep fryer or an electric skillet.

Makes 10 to 12 rounds

3½ cups unbleached all-purpose flour, divided
½ cup yellow cornmeal
2 tablespoons baking powder
1 tablespoon sugar
1 teaspoon salt
1 tablespoon lard
2 cups buttermilk
Oil for deep frying

Heat the oil to 350°.

Mix 2½ cups of the flour, the cornmeal, baking powder, sugar, and salt together. Work in the lard, using your fingertips. Mix thoroughly to the consistency of gravel. Add the buttermilk and make a thick dough. Place on a floured board and incorporate the remaining flour, about ½ cup at a time, and knead well.

Place in an oiled bowl and allow to rest for 30 minutes. Break off small handfuls. Oil your hands before working with the dough. Flatten and stretch the dough with your fingers, then pierce the center with a sharp knife.

Drop in deep fat to cook. Allow about 1 minute per side. Turn only once, then remove to drain on paper towels. Serve hot.

Note: Can be made ahead and kept warm in the oven until serving time.

Batter Bread

This is a sticky quick bread best eaten fresh, although it makes wonderful toast and croutons.

Makes 2 loaves

- *3 cups sour milk*
- *1 tablespoon (1 envelope) dry yeast*
- *2 tablespoons white sugar*
- *4 tablespoons brown sugar*
- *2 cups whole-wheat flour*
- *4 cups unbleached all-purpose flour*
- *4 teaspoons salt*
- *3 tablespoons shortening*

Heat the sour milk until it is warm to the touch. Add the yeast and allow it to dissolve. While the milk is heating, mix the dry ingredients and combine with the shortening.

Combine the milk and yeast with half the flour mixture. Add the remainder of the flour mixture and beat until smooth. Cover with a cloth and let rise in a warm place until doubled in size (1 to 1½ hours).

Stir down and place in 2 well-greased 9⅝ x 5½ x 2¾-inch pans. Cover with a cloth and let rise to the top of the pans.

Preheat the oven to 350°F.

When the dough has risen, bake for 40 to 45 minutes.

Beer Batter Bread

Probably the best bread I know for breakfast toast. Self-rising flour is essential to this recipe, and useless to any other except biscuits. This is my kind of baking—just put everything together and bake it.

Makes 1 loaf

- *3 cups self-rising flour*
- *3 tablespoons sugar*
- *12 ounces beer*
- *¼ pound butter, divided*

Preheat the oven to 350°F.

Mix together all the ingredients except the butter and place in a 9 x 5-inch greased bread pan. Melt the butter and pour 4 tablespoons over the top of the dough.

Bake for 20 minutes, then pour the remaining 4 tablespoons of butter over the top of the dough. Continue to bake for another 40 minutes. Remove from the oven to a wire rack to cool.

Hot Cinnamon Bread

This is a batter bread that only needs to be mixed together and baked.

Makes 8 servings

¼ pound butter
2 cups brown sugar
2 teaspoons cinnamon
¼ teaspoon ground cloves
2½ cups unbleached all-purpose flour
1 egg, beaten
¾ cup buttermilk
½ teaspoon baking soda
½ teaspoon baking powder

Preheat the oven to 350°F.

Cream the butter and sugar; add the spices and mix in the flour well. Reserve ¾ cup of this crumbly mixture for the top. Add the beaten egg and the buttermilk mixed with the soda and baking powder to the rest.

Pour into a greased, floured 1½-quart ovenproof glass baking dish. Cover the top with the reserved crumbly mixture. Bake for 30 to 35 minutes. Serve hot with butter.

Spice Bread

This is more like cake than bread, but is still wonderful spread with butter and honey.

Makes 1 loaf

1 cup sugar
1¼ cups boiling water
¾ cup honey
2½ teaspoons baking soda
¼ teaspoon salt
3 tablespoons rum
2 teaspoons anise flavor
2 teaspoons cinnamon
4 cups unbleached all-purpose flour

Preheat the oven to 450°F.

Dissolve the sugar in the water with the honey, baking soda, and salt. Stir in the rum, anise, and cinnamon. Sift the flour and add to the liquid to form a smooth batter. If lumps form, strain through a sieve.

Pour the batter into a buttered 9 x 5-inch bread tin and bake for 10 minutes. Reduce the heat to 350°F. and bake for 1 hour longer.

Cool and wrap in waxed paper to store. To serve, slice very thin.

Apple-Nut Bread

A tea bread that is delicious, requires no rising or resting period, and doesn't last long enough.

Makes 1 loaf

1 tablespoon butter
3 tablespoons vegetable oil
½ cup honey
2 eggs
1 teaspoon vanilla
½ cup plain yogurt
1 cup whole wheat flour
1 cup unbleached all-purpose flour
1 teaspoon salt
2 teaspoons baking powder
2 cups peeled, chopped apples
1 cup chopped walnuts or macadamia nuts
½ teaspoon cinnamon
¼ teaspoon mace
¼ teaspoon nutmeg

Preheat the oven to 350°F. Grease a 9 x 5 x 3-inch loaf pan with the butter.

In a medium-sized bowl, beat together the oil, honey, eggs, vanilla, and yogurt. In a large mixing bowl, combine the flours, salt, baking powder, apples, nuts, and spices. Add the honey-oil mixture to the dry ingredients; mix well. Spoon into buttered loaf pan; bake for 1 hour.

Zucchini Bread

This moist, well-seasoned bread is best only when absolutely fresh. If kept in plastic wrap and refrigerated it will keep for about a week.

Makes 2 large loaves

3 eggs
1 cup peanut oil
2 cups sugar
2 cups coarsely shredded zucchini (peeled, if desired)
3 teaspoons vanilla
3 cups unbleached all-purpose flour
1 teaspoon salt
1 teaspoon baking soda
1 teaspoon cinnamon
¼ teaspoon baking powder
1 cup chopped nuts

Preheat the oven to 325°F.

Beat the eggs and add the oil, sugar, zucchini, and vanilla, beating until blended. Sift together all the dry ingredients. Add the egg-oil mixture and the nuts. Pour into 2 buttered 9 x 5-inch loaf pans and bake for 1 hour.

Corn Batter Cakes

This old-fashioned corn cake recipe that comes from the hills of Kentucky is simple to make and tastes wonderful.

Makes 10 to 15 cakes

2 cups corn kernels cut from the cob and boiled for a few minutes, or canned whole-kernel corn, drained
1 cup whole milk
2 tablespoons butter, melted
2 egg yolks, beaten
¾ cup unbleached all-purpose flour
1 teaspoon baking powder
1 teaspoon salt
2 egg whites, lightly beaten

Combine the corn, milk, butter, and egg yolks. Add the flour, baking powder, and salt. If too thick, add a little more milk. When the flour, corn, and liquid are well combined, fold in the egg whites. Fry on a hot griddle or in a heavy skillet with plenty of butter.

Serve with maple syrup or chicken gravy.

Texas Skillet Corn Bread

If you don't have a 10-inch cast-iron skillet, buy one to make this. It doesn't taste the same made in anything else. This is the best corn bread recipe I have ever come across.

Serves 6

1 cup yellow cornmeal
1 scant teaspoon salt
2 heaping teaspoons baking powder
1 tablespoon whole wheat flour
1 cup buttermilk
1 egg
2 tablespoons vegetable oil

Preheat the oven to 425°F.

Mix the cornmeal, salt, baking powder, and flour. Add the buttermilk and egg; beat briefly. Put the oil into a 10-inch skillet and heat to very hot. Quickly pour the oil into the batter, then pour the batter into the skillet. (This method makes the cornbread very crusty.)

Bake for 25 minutes. Turn out and serve.

Johnny Cakes

These white cornmeal cakes were popular during the Civil War and still are. I grew up on them, and I suggest if you have never tried them, you should. This method of preparation dates back a long time, but I know it to be good and tend to stick with it. There are short-cut recipes, but not for me.

Serves 6

2 cups white cornmeal
1 teaspoon salt
Boiling water
Whole milk
Beef drippings or bacon fat

Preheat the oven to 325°F.

Put the cornmeal in a cast-iron skillet and bake in the oven for 10 to 15 minutes, or until really heated through but not changed in color. Remove from the oven and stir in the salt and enough boiling water to make a very stiff paste. (It usually takes about 1½ cups.) Add a little milk and beat hard to get a smooth, lump-free texture.

Grease a griddle or frying pan with beef drippings or bacon fat, and drop the paste by spoonfuls to make 3-inch-diameter cakes about ¾ inch thick; cook for about 15 minutes. They should be golden brown in color and crusty.

Serve with butter and jelly or maple syrup.

Robert Pamplin Biscuits

This recipe is just right for two people—4 biscuits apiece, because that's how many you'll want. They are great with sweet butter and honey any time of the day.

Makes 8 biscuits

1 cup unbleached all-purpose flour
¼ teaspoon salt
1 teaspoon baking powder
2 heaping tablespoons vegetable shortening
⅓ cup whole milk

Preheat the oven to 400° F.

Sift the flour, salt, and baking powder together in a bowl. Cut the shortening into the flour mixture. Add the milk gradually while forming the mixture into a dough. The dough should hold together but not be sticky.

Roll out the dough about ¼ to ½ inch thick on a floured surface.

Cut into rounds, using a floured biscuit cutter. Place on a greased baking sheet and bake on the middle rack of the oven for about 12 to 15 minutes, or until brown on top.

Chive Drop Biscuits

If you don't have any chives, finely chopped scallions can be used as a substitute. These are excellent served with brunch eggs or with fried chicken and pan gravy.

Makes 12 biscuits

1½ cups sifted, unbleached all-purpose flour
2 teaspoons baking powder
1 teaspoon salt
1 cup heavy cream
1 egg, lightly beaten
2 tablespoons freshly chopped chives

Preheat the oven to 450° F.

Sift the dry ingredients together in a bowl. In a separate bowl whip the cream to form stiff peaks, then fold into the flour mixture with the egg and chives.

Drop the batter by rounded tablespoons 3 inches apart on a greased baking sheet. Bake for 15 minutes.

Bran Muffins

Covered, this batter will keep for up to a month in the refrigerator, enabling you to produce breakfast muffins in 15 to 18 minutes. The recipe as written makes 84 muffins, but it can be halved or quartered.

Makes 84 muffins

- *2 cups bran cereal "buds"*
- *2 cups boiling water*
- *½ pound plus 4 tablespoons margarine or butter*
- *3 cups granulated or brown sugar (or a combination)*
- *4 eggs, beaten*
- *1 quart buttermilk*
- *5 teaspoons baking soda*
- *5 cups unbleached all-purpose flour*
- *1 teaspoon salt*
- *4 cups bran flakes*

Preheat the oven to 400°F.

In a large mixing bowl, combine the cereal "buds" with boiling water; set aside. Cream the margarine or butter and sugar; add the eggs and buttermilk. Add this mixture to the bowl containing the bran and water. Mix the soda and salt with the flour and stir into the bran mixture. Add the bran flakes and stir lightly. Bake in muffin tins with paper liners for 15 to 18 minutes. Test for doneness and remove.

Variations: Add 2 tablespoons of grated lemon or orange rind, or 2 cups of raisins, or 2 cups of chopped pecans to the batter.

Note: If the batter is refrigerated, simply remove the quantity desired and return the remainder to the refrigerator, but *do not stir.*

Popovers

You do not preheat the oven for this recipe—a great boon for the forgetful. I recommend glass baking cups that measure 3½ inches wide by 2 inches deep. Coat them heavily with room-temperature butter, using your fingers.

Makes 6 large popovers

1 cup unbleached all-purpose flour
¼ teaspoon salt
2 eggs
1 cup whole milk
1 tablespoon butter, melted
Additional butter at room temperature

Sift together the flour and salt. Slightly beat the eggs, adding the milk and melted butter. Add the liquid to the dry ingredients and mix thoroughly. Pour into heavily buttered custard cups. Place in a cold oven, turn on heat to 425°, and bake for 45 minutes.

Pecan Popovers with Lemon-Honey Butter

Unlike the previous recipe, this one works best in a preheated 425°F. oven. Don't crowd the baking containers because the popovers don't "pop" if they are too close together, and by all means grease the containers generously. Nothing is as disappointing as a stuck popover.

Makes 6 popovers

2 eggs
1 cup whole milk
½ teaspoon salt
1 cup unbleached all-purpose flour
3 tablespoons finely chopped pecans
6 tablespoons softened butter or margarine
6 tablespoons honey
¾ teaspoon grated lemon peel

Preheat the oven to 425°F.

With a wire whisk, beat together the eggs, milk, and salt. Add the flour and beat until smooth; do not overbeat. Stir in the pecans. Pour into 6 well-greased 5- or 6-ounce custard cups.

Bake until puffed and golden brown, 30 to 35 minutes.

Meanwhile, stir together the butter or margarine, honey, and lemon peel. Serve the popovers at once with the lemon-honey butter.

Yorkshire Pudding

Just about everyone has a recipe for this popover-like pudding. This one is as foolproof as any I have ever tried, and it tastes a lot better than many I have eaten.

Serves 8

2 eggs
1 cup whole milk
1 cup sifted, unbleached all-purpose flour
½ teaspoon salt
½ teaspoon freshly ground black pepper
¼ cup beef drippings, heated

Preheat the oven to 450°F.

Beat the eggs with a whisk or electric hand beater until quite light, then gradually beat in the milk and flour. Season with salt and pepper.

Put an 11 x 14 x 2½-inch baking pan in the oven and let it get very hot. Remove from the oven; pour in the hot drippings and then the batter. Put on the center shelf of the oven and bake for 10 minutes. Reduce the heat to 375°F. and continue to bake for 15 to 20 minutes, or until the pudding has risen and is puffed and brown. Do not open the oven door during the first 20 minutes of baking.

Cut into squares and serve immediately with roast beef.

Fast Puff Paste

The word "fast" is relative here: it just means that this version takes a little less time than the classic one.

Makes 2 pounds dough

1 pound very cold butter
4½ cups unbleached all-purpose flour
1 teaspoon salt
1 cup cold water
Additional unbleached all-purpose flour

Dice the butter into ⅜-inch cubes. Put the flour on a pastry board or work table. Make a well in the flour and place the butter and salt in the center.

Using a pastry scraper, "cut" the butter into the flour.

Add the water and combine all the ingredients into a mass rapidly. Do not knead the dough.

At this point, the dough will look very lumpy (the butter is still in pieces), but it should hold together. Flour the work table generously. (This dough requires more flour during the rolling than does conventional dough.) Roll the dough into a ⅜-inch thick rectangle.

Brush the flour from the surface and fold one end into the center of the rectangle. Fold the other end in. Both ends should meet in the center. Brush again to remove any excess flour. Fold the dough in half.

You now have one double turn that gives you four layers of dough. Give two more double turns—a total of three altogether. This is the equivalent of four to five turns and is enough for a fast puff paste. If the dough does not become too elastic, the three turns can be given consecutively. Cover and refrigerate to thoroughly chill before using.

Cocktail Puff Pastries

These are made using Fast Puff Paste and any one of seven fillings. Once you master this, you can improvise, using other fillings that appeal to you. The pastries are best eaten the day they are baked, but they can be kept a day or two in an airtight container. They can also be frozen, either baked or unbaked.

1 recipe Fast Puff Paste (see page 354)
1 egg, beaten
½ teaspoon salt
Filling of choice (recipes follow)

Shape the pastry according to the directions in the recipes below. Combine the egg and salt to make an egg glaze. When assembled according to the directions in the following recipes, set the pastries on a baking sheet and chill for 15 minutes.

Preheat the oven to 425°F. Bake the pastries for 8 to 12 minutes, or until puffed and brown. Transfer to a rack to cool.

Anchovy Fingers

Roll out the pastry dough into a 6-inch-wide strip; cut in half lengthwise and trim the edges. Brush 1 rectangle with egg glaze and lay drained anchovy fillets crosswise on it at 1½-inch intervals. Place the second rectangle on top and press down gently with a fingertip to outline the anchovies. Brush with egg glaze and cut down between each fillet to form fingers. Decorate each finger in a lattice pattern with the back of a knife and bake as directed above. Makes about 30 fingers.

Cheese Fingers

Roll out the pastry dough into a 6-inch-wide strip and brush with the egg glaze. Sprinkle generously with grated Parmesan cheese. Cut in half lengthwise, trim the edges, and cut crosswise into rectangles 1 inch wide.

Bake as directed above. Makes about 80 fingers.

Chicken Liver Fingers

Melt 2 tablespoons of butter in a frying pan and fry 1 chopped onion until soft. Add 1 cup of chicken livers and sauté until brown on all sides but still pink in the center. Add 2 tablespoons of brandy, a pinch of cayenne, and plenty of salt and pepper, and continue cooking for 1 minute. Let cool, then chop fine. Roll out the pastry dough into a 6-inch-wide strip and spoon the chicken liver mixture to one side of the center, but not to the edge. Brush the edge of the pastry with egg glaze; fold over one side to meet the other, covering the chicken liver mixture, and press the edges to seal. Trim the edges, brush with egg glaze, and cut into 1-inch fingers. Bake as directed in the basic recipe (page 355). Makes about 40 fingers.

Foie Gras Fingers

Follow the recipe for Chicken Liver Fingers, but replace the chicken liver mixture with canned pâté de foie gras cut into sticks. Do not try to substitute a less expensive mousse of foie gras or liver pâté because it will melt during cooking, resulting in disaster.

Ham Crescents

Roll the pastry dough into a 6-inch-wide strip. Trim the edges and cut in half lengthwise. Then cut crosswise to form 3-inch squares. Cut each square into two triangles. Put 1 scant teaspoon of finely chopped prosciutto or finely chopped cooked ham mixed with a little Worcestershire sauce in the center of each triangle. Roll up the triangles, starting at the long edge. Elongate each roll slightly by rolling it on the table with your hand. Seal each roll and shape into a crescent on a dampened baking sheet. Brush crescents with egg glaze and bake as directed in the basic recipe. Makes about 50 crescents.

Anchovy Diamonds

Roll the dough into a 10 x 12-inch rectangle. Trim the edges and cut in half to form two smaller rectangles. Spread one rectangle with anchovy paste. Set the other rectangle on top and press lightly. Chill the dough for 15 minutes. Brush with egg glaze, cut into 1½-inch strips, then cut each strip diagonally into diamonds. Bake as directed in the basic recipe. Makes about 40 diamonds.

Brioche Loaf

Brioche is first and foremost a kind of dough, although the name has come to be associated with a French breakfast bread. Brioche can be baked "free," in a loaf pan, or even wrapped around a sausage. If you have never made brioche, it is time to start. First, you have to develop a feel for the dough. It is rarely perfect the first time, but once you have made it, the second time is a snap.

Makes 2 loaves

2 packages active dry yeast
½ cup lukewarm water
4 cups lightly spooned, unbleached all-purpose flour, divided
¾ pound butter
6 eggs
1 tablespoon sugar
1 teaspoon salt

Sprinkle the yeast into the water and stir until dissolved. Measure 1 cup of the flour into a small bowl; add the yeast mixture, stir to make a stiff dough, and knead until smooth. Form a ball; cut a cross or X in the top with a knife (to help the dough rise), and drop the ball into a bowl of lukewarm water. The ball of yeast sponge should rise to the top of the water in about 7 minutes. If it doesn't, the yeast isn't working; throw it out and start over.

While the yeast sponge is rising, whip the butter until smooth and creamy (if you have a heavy-duty mixer, use the dough paddle throughout the recipe) and set aside. In another bowl, beat together the eggs, the remaining 3 cups of flour, the sugar and salt. (Use the electric mixer and flat beater or beat by hand with a wooden spoon.) The dough should become shiny, sticky, wet-looking, and elastic. If it's very sticky and hard to get off the sides of the bowl, beat in another egg.

Remove the yeast sponge from the water, letting the water run off. Add the yeast sponge and creamed butter to the egg dough and beat until thoroughly mixed, using the flat beater or a wooden spoon. Grease and lightly flour a large bowl. Place the dough in the bowl, cover with plastic wrap, and let rise in a warm place, free from drafts, for about 1 hour. The dough does not have to double in bulk, but indentations should remain when you press a fingertip into the dough. When it's risen, stir it down; re-cover with plastic wrap and refrigerate overnight. Put a weighted dinner plate on top to prevent the dough from rising too high and crusting. The next day, punch the dough down and shape the brioche loaf. Let the dough rise again (about 1 hour).

Preheat the oven to 375°F. Bake for 35 to 45 minutes, or until nicely browned.

Pita Bread

Like making brioche, success with pita the first time it is made is rare. A feel for the dough is necessary, and there is no way to get that except by trial and error.

Makes 8 or 9 pitas

2 envelopes (2 tablespoons) active dry yeast
¼ teaspoon sugar
2 cups lukewarm water, divided
¼ cup olive oil
1½ tablespoons salt
6 cups unbleached all-purpose flour (approx.), divided
Cornmeal

Dissolve the yeast and sugar in ½ cup of the warm water in a large mixing bowl and allow to proof (see page 341). Then add the remaining 1½ cups of water along with the oil, salt, and 5 cups of the flour, mixing it in vigorously, 1 cup at a time. (The dough will be rather sticky.) Turn out on a floured board and work in the remaining cup of flour (more if the dough is too sticky).

Knead for a good 10 minutes or more, until the dough is smooth and elastic. Shape into a ball; place in a buttered bowl, and turn to coat with butter on all sides. Cover with a cloth and let rise in a warm, draft-free place for 1½ to 2 hours, or until doubled in bulk.

Punch down the dough, turn out on a floured board, and allow to rest for 10 minutes. Divide into 8 or 9 equal pieces and shape each piece into a ball. Cover the balls with a cloth or foil and let rest for 30 minutes.

Flatten each ball with a well-floured rolling pin and roll to ⅛-inch thickness in approximately 8-inch circles. Dust 2 baking sheets with cornmeal, place 2 circles on each sheet, cover, and let rest again for 30 minutes. (Leave the 4 remaining circles on a lightly floured work surface and transfer them to the baking sheets, dusted again with cornmeal, after the first 4 are baked.)

Preheat the oven to 500°F. Put one of the baking sheets on the lowest rack of the oven for 5 minutes. Do not open the oven door until the 5 minutes are up. Transfer the sheet to a higher shelf and continue baking for 3 to 5 minutes longer, until the loaves are puffed like balloons and just very lightly browned.

Repeat the procedure with the second baking sheet. Remove to prevent a crisp crust from forming and to ensure the familiar spongy pita texture. The loaves should deflate as they cool.

Milk Toast with Parmesan

This is what my mother always fixed for my brother and me when we were sick as children. Actually any bread will do in this recipe, but I happen to like French rolls, so I use them.

Serves 2 healthy appetites, 4 convalescents

1 quart whole milk
½ pint (1 cup) light cream
4 French rolls, sliced and toasted
Butter
Salt and freshly ground black pepper
Grated Parmesan cheese

Heat the milk and cream to the scalding point. Place a layer of toasted rolls in a hot soup tureen. Dot generously with butter and sprinkle with salt, pepper, and cheese. Add another layer of toasted rolls and repeat the process. Just before serving, pour on the scalded milk and serve very hot, accompanied by more grated Parmesan.

THE basic variation in pancakes lies in the thickness of the batter, which is a matter of personal preference.

As a rule of thumb, allow 2 teaspoons of baking powder and 1 egg for each cup of flour. This amount of batter makes about 9 pancakes.

If sour milk or buttermilk is used instead of sweet milk, allow an additional ¼ teaspoon of baking soda per cup of liquid.

For a richer pancake, add an extra egg.

To make pancakes more delicate, beat the egg yolks and whites separately and fold in the whites last.

To cook, grease the griddle or pan with vegetable oil—*not* butter. Always do a test pancake to make sure the griddle is hot enough. The pancake should start to bubble in 30 seconds; when the bubbles break and become holes, turn the pancake. Turn pancakes only once—flipping them back and forth makes them rubbery.

Old-Fashioned Buckwheat Pancakes

Buckwheat makes a heavier pancake, but one that is very flavorful. Look for buckwheat in bulk because it is better than the packaged variety.

Makes about 18 pancakes

1 envelope active dry yeast
⅓ cup lukewarm water
¾ cup boiling water
½ cup cornmeal
1½ cups water-ground buckwheat flour
1 cup (or more) buttermilk
½ teaspoon baking soda
½ teaspoon salt
1 tablespoon molasses
Whole milk

Dissolve the yeast in the lukewarm water. In a bowl, pour the boiling water over the cornmeal. Add the buckwheat flour and buttermilk. Combine with the yeast mixture. The batter should be rather thick; add more buttermilk if it is too thick. Cover and let stand in a warm place overnight.*

When ready to use, add the baking soda, salt, molasses, and enough milk to make a batter the consistency of heavy cream. Heat and grease the griddle and add the batter by ladlefuls; cook according to the directions above.

* Reserve ½ cup of this starter for another day's pancakes, if desired.

Buttermilk Pancakes

This is the recipe that I grew up with, and I have not changed it one iota because it is perfect as is.

Makes about 22 pancakes

2½ cups buttermilk
2½ cups unbleached all-purpose flour
¾ teaspoon baking soda
1 tablespoon hot water
3 eggs, beaten
1 teaspoon salt
2 teaspoons corn syrup or sugar syrup

Mix the buttermilk and flour. Cover and let stand in the refrigerator for 12 hours, or overnight.

Grease and heat the skillet or griddle.

Dissolve the baking soda in the hot water. To the flour mixture add the eggs, salt, baking soda, and syrup. Cook according to the directions on page 360.

Plain Waffles

Makes 6 round waffles

1½ cups unbleached all-purpose flour
3 teaspoons baking powder
½ teaspoon salt
6 egg yolks
1½ cups whole milk
6 tablespoons melted butter
6 egg whites, stiffly beaten

Preheat the waffle iron.

Sift the flour with the baking powder and salt. Beat the egg yolks well and add them to the flour with the milk. Add the melted butter and fold in the beaten egg whites.

When the waffle iron is good and hot, pour 2 to 3 tablespoons of batter in the center and close immediately. Cook until the iron stops steaming and the waffle is golden brown and crisp. If the test waffle sticks, add 2 tablespoons of oil or melted butter to the iron. (The cook always gets to eat the test waffle.)

French Waffles

Folding in the egg whites after the rest of the batter is assembled makes a great difference in waffles. They are lighter, crisper, and much better.

Makes 8 waffles

¼ pound butter
4 egg yolks
4 teaspoons sugar
1 teaspoon vanilla
½ teaspoon salt
4 tablespoons heavy cream
1 cup sifted unbleached all-purpose flour
4 egg whites, stiffly beaten
½ cup heavy cream, whipped
Vanilla Sugar ***(see page 340)***

Cream the butter and add the egg yolks, one at a time. Beat until very smooth. Add the sugar, vanilla, and salt, and gradually incorporate the cream alternately with the flour. Stir or beat until smooth.

Fold in the egg whites until well blended and then fold in the whipped cream. Refrigerate to chill thoroughly.

Cook in a hot waffle iron (see page 361). Remove the cooked waffles to a hot plate and immediately sprinkle generously with Vanilla Sugar.

Bran Waffles

These are heavier than the usual waffle and especially good with sweetened cream and fresh berries.

Makes 6 round waffles

1½ cups heavy cream
4 egg yolks
¾ cup unbleached all-purpose flour
¾ cup ground bran
2½ teaspoons salt
2 tablespoons ground nuts
4 egg whites, stiffly beaten

Preheat the waffle iron.

Mix the cream with the well-beaten egg yolks. Sift the dry ingredients and combine with the liquid ingredients and the nuts. (Add a little milk if necessary.) Fold in the egg whites. Cook in a hot waffle iron (see page 361).

Sour Cream Waffles

These are best made with homemade sour cream. It holds up better than the commercial kind and has a better flavor.

Makes 6 round waffles

3 tablespoons butter
4 egg yolks
1 cup unbleached all-purpose flour
½ teaspoon salt
1 cup Homemade Sour Cream (see page 333)
4 egg whites, stiffly beaten

Preheat the waffle iron.

Soften the butter and beat in the egg yolks, one at a time. Sift the flour and salt and add alternately with the sour cream. Fold in the beaten egg whites. Cook in a hot waffle iron (see page 361).

Note: These waffles must be baked a little longer to be crisp.

DESSERTS

AMERICANS come by a love of dessert quite naturally—puddings and pies were brought to the New World by the Pilgrims and some of them were considered standard breakfast fare. In the area where I grew up, desserts were part of the morning meal: I remember my mother, aunt, and grandmother frosting cakes that were to be served for breakfast to the men when they came in from their chores on the ranch. Nowhere has the American love of desserts been celebrated so gloriously as at the county fairs and church socials where the competition is fierce and the results marvelous.

The secret of a good dessert is that it properly complements the entrée that went before it. As will become evident, I tend to favor lighter desserts—fruit combinations, soufflés, ices, and ice creams, but I have tried to include something for every taste with a special nod to chocolate lovers. So take your pick from the selection here.

Crepes with Apricots

A bit of advice about crepes: Don't overbeat the batter—stop as soon as it is smooth; remember to refrigerate the batter—time is needed not only to chill but also to blend the ingredients; never overcook crepes—they become tough if you do. Now, let none of this deter you from making crepes; they are not difficult, especially if you follow instructions. A crepe pan is helpful because it controls the size of the crepe, which for desserts should be 6 or 7 inches in diameter.

Serves 8

Crepes

1 cup unbleached all-purpose flour
2 whole eggs
Pinch salt
1 teaspoon sugar
1 cup whole milk, divided
1 teaspoon kirsch or vanilla extract
1 teaspoon maraschino liqueur or almond extract

Filling

3 tablespoons butter
3 tablespoons apricot jam
½ cup finely chopped walnuts

Sauce

20-ounce can apricot halves, drained
1 cup sugar
½ cup water
2 to 3 tablespoons Grand Marnier

Prepare the crepe batter several hours in advance. Sift the flour into a bowl and make a hole in the center. Break the eggs into it, add the salt, sugar, and a little milk. Beat with a spoon until smooth. Add the remaining milk gradually, then the kirsch and maraschino liqueur. Refrigerate for 2 hours or more.

To make the filling, cream the butter and stir into it the apricot jam and nuts.

Heat a crepe pan, sprinkle it with salt, scour it out with a piece of paper towel, and wipe clean. Add a small piece of butter, melting it to coat the pan. Pour in a small quantity of the crepe batter and tilt the pan immediately so that the batter barely covers the bottom of the pan. When the crepe is brown on one side, flip it over on the other side. When the crepe is done, place it on a hot plate in a 200°F. oven to keep warm. Repeat the process to make 16 crepes.

Spread some of the jam-and-nut mixture on each crepe and roll it up. Place the crepes side by side in a well-buttered oblong glass baking dish. Spread a little soft butter over each one and place the dish in the oven while the sauce is being prepared.

To make the sauce, puree the apricots in a blender or food processor. Pour the puree into an enamel pan and add the sugar and water and simmer gently for a few minutes to melt the sugar. Add the Grand Marnier to flavor the sauce and continue to simmer for 5 minutes. Pour some of the sauce over the crepes and increase the oven heat to 325°F. As soon as the sauce bubbles over the crepes, remove them from the oven and serve with the remaining sauce passed separately.

Note: Crepes can be made in advance and frozen. Place a sheet of waxed paper between each crepe before freezing so that they are easy to separate.

Apricot-Rice Ring

Made with fresh or canned apricots, this dish is extremely good. At home it was served with plenty of heavy cream if anyone wanted it—and I always did.

Serves 8 to 10

2 cups uncooked rice
5 cups whole milk
1½ cups sugar
8 egg yolks
1 teaspoon vanilla
10 to 12 poached* fresh apricot halves or canned apricots
1 recipe Apricot Glaze (see page 419)
Glacéed, brandied, or maraschino cherries (optional)

Preheat the oven to 350°F.

Blanch the rice in boiling salted water for about 10 minutes; drain. Add the milk and sugar to the rice and bring the mixture to a boil, taking care not to scorch it.

Place the pan, covered, in the oven and bake until very tender, about 40 to 50 minutes. Remove from the oven and add the egg yolks and vanilla carefully to the hot rice to avoid curdling. Pour the mixture into a buttered ring mold and chill until well set. Unmold and fill the center with poached apricot halves and coat with the glaze. Decorate with cherries, if desired.

* To poach, cook gently in a syrup made of *sugar and water* for about 10 minutes, being careful to keep the fruit intact.

Chocolate Mousse

I use Grand Marnier or dark rum when I make this, but any sweet liqueur will do as long as it's drinkable. And no matter what is in it, this mousse must be thoroughly chilled to be good.

Serves 8

8 ounces sweet chocolate
6 large eggs, separated
3 tablespoons water
¼ cup Grand Marnier or dark rum
2 cups heavy cream
6 tablespoons sugar, divided
1 cup whipped cream for garnish

Cut the chocolate into ½-inch pieces; place in a saucepan. Set the pan in hot, almost boiling water, cover, and let the chocolate melt over low heat.

Put the egg yolks in a heavy saucepan and add the water. Place the saucepan over very low heat while beating vigorously and constantly with a wire whisk. When the yolks start to thicken, add the liqueur, beating constantly. Cook until the sauce reaches the consistency of a hollandaise. Remove from the heat. Add the melted chocolate to the sauce and fold it in. Scrape the sauce into a mixing bowl.

Beat the cream until stiff, adding 2 tablespoons of the sugar toward the end of the beating. Fold this into the chocolate mixture.

Beat the egg whites until soft peaks start to form. Beat in the remaining sugar and continue beating until stiff. Fold this into the mousse. Spoon the mousse into a crystal bowl and chill until ready to serve. To serve, garnish with whipped cream.

Sabayon Meringue

This is so good that I make it about once a month and never tire of it. There is no trick to it; just follow the directions for a really great dessert that takes little or no effort.

Serves 8 to 10

18 dry almond macaroons, crushed
6 eggs, separated
2 tablespoons plus 1 scant cup confectioners' sugar, divided
⅓ cup Madeira wine
Pinch salt
½ teaspoon vanilla extract
Blanched almonds

Butter a shallow baking dish and cover the bottom with the macaroon crumbs. Beat the egg yolks well with 2 tablespoons of confectioners' sugar and the Madeira. Cook this mixture over hot water, beating it constantly with a rotary beater until it is hot and foamy. Do not allow the mixture to boil. Pour the hot custard over the macaroon crumbs in the baking dish.

Preheat the oven to 350°F.

Beat the egg whites with the salt until soft peaks form. Beat in the remaining 1 cup of confectioners' sugar and the vanilla, and continue to beat until the meringue mixture is very stiff. Spread the meringue evenly over the custard in the baking dish, making sure that it touches the edges of the dish all around. Decorate the meringue with the almonds. Bake until the meringue and nuts are lightly browned (about 10 minutes). Serve at once.

COOKIES

Cinnamon Cookies

These are party cookies and have an exceptional flavor and texture. I only make them for special occasions. The number of cookies made depends on the size of the cookie cutter.

Makes 24 to 36

1 pound unblanched, shelled almonds
9 egg whites
1 pound confectioners' sugar
2 teaspoons cinnamon
Grated rind and juice of ½ lemon
½ cup sugar

Grind the almonds fine. Beat the egg whites until stiff; add the confectioners' sugar and beat until very stiff. Reserve 6 tablespoons of this meringue in a separate bowl for later use.

To the remaining meringue, add the cinnamon, lemon rind and juice, powdered almonds, and sugar. Refrigerate for 1 hour.

Preheat the oven to 325°F.

When ready to make the cookies, take out a little of the batter at a time and place it on a board sprinkled with additional granulated sugar. Pat or roll out gently to ⅜-inch thickness, sprinkling the top lightly with more sugar. Cut out with a cookie cutter and place on lightly buttered and floured cookie sheets, dipping the cutter each time in sugar to avoid sticking.

Bake for 1 hour, or until the cookies lift off easily. Remove from the oven and cool slightly. Ice the cookies with the reserved meringue and return to the oven just long enough to dry out the meringue without browning it.

Almond Macaroons

Macaroons will keep a long time if they are put in airtight tins, but be sure they are completely cooled before storing. While they are not difficult to make, don't attempt them on a rainy day, for just like other meringues, they won't work if the air is full of humidity.

Makes 16

¼ teaspoon salt
2 egg whites
1 cup sugar
1 cup chopped, blanched almonds
¾ teaspoon almond extract

Add the salt to the egg whites and beat until frothy. Add the sugar gradually, beating until the mixture is stiff but not dry. Add the almonds and almond extract and fold in gently.

Drop the mixture by teaspoonfuls onto a buttered, floured baking sheet. Shape into ovals, leaving about 1 inch between each mound. Let stand for about 2 hours.

Preheat the oven to 375°F. Bake the macaroons for about 12 minutes, or until delicately brown.

Macadamia Nut Tuiles

Tuile is the French word for tile; the cookie originated in France and the finished shape resembles a curved roofing tile.

Makes about 18

6 tablespoons soft butter
½ cup sugar
2 egg whites
⅓ cup unbleached all-purpose flour
Pinch salt
1 cup ground macadamia nuts

Preheat the oven to 400°F.

Cream the butter and sugar together until well blended. Stir in the egg whites, flour, salt, and nuts. Butter a heavy cookie sheet and drop the batter by teaspoonfuls, leaving enough space to allow for spreading.

Bake for about 10 minutes, or until golden brown around the edges and slightly yellow in the center. Remove each cookie from the sheet with a spatula and, while still hot, lay it over a rolling pin. Work quickly in forming them over the rolling pin or they will stick. Leave for a few minutes and remove to a cake rack to cool completely.

Store in an airtight tin but be sure cookies are completely cooled or they will turn soft and sticky.

FRUIT DESSERTS

Blueberry Slump

My grandfather's favorite dessert. He always ate it in a large drinking glass and poured fresh milk on top to fill the glass. He claimed it was the only way to eat slump because it never came out even and you could always add more of it to the milk. He had a point.

Serves 12

2 pints (4 cups) fresh blueberries
1 cup sugar
2 teaspoons cinnamon
¾ teaspoon salt, divided
½ cup water
2 cups unbleached all-purpose flour
4 teaspoons baking powder
1 cup light cream

Wash the berries thoroughly in a colander and remove all the stems. Mix the sugar, cinnamon, ¼ teaspoon of the salt, and water in a 6-quart Dutch oven with a tight lid. Add the blueberries to this mixture and bring to a boil over low heat.

Meanwhile, in a mixing bowl, combine the flour, baking powder, the remaining ½ teaspoon of salt, and the cream to form a biscuit dough. When the blueberry mixture starts to boil, drop the biscuit dough onto the hot liquid, a tablespoonful at a time, making sure the biscuits do not touch one another until they solidify.

When all the batter is in the pot, cover and cook for about 20 minutes. Do not remove the lid during this cooking period. (You may need to lower the heat somewhat so that the pot does not overflow.)

Serve at once with heavy cream spooned over each helping.

Note: You may substitute two 1-pound packages of frozen berries for the 2 pints of fresh. Just be sure to reduce the "juice" when cooking to enhance the flavor and insure that the consistency is not too liquid.

Oranges with Caramel and Pecans

Be sure to make this in a deep saucepan because when the hot water is added to the sugar-and-water mixture it will bubble up and spatter. It is best to remove the saucepan from the heat just before adding the hot water and return it to the heat as soon as the mixture calms down.

Serves 6

6 to 8 large navel oranges
1 cup sugar
½ cup cold water
1 cup hot water
Chopped pecans

Peel the oranges and refrigerate them.

In a saucepan, mix the sugar with the cold water. Cook without stirring until a light golden brown. Add the hot water and cook until thick and syrupy. Cool.

Remove the oranges from the refrigerator and cut out the pulp of each section with a sharp knife. Place in a shallow dish and pour half the caramel sauce over the oranges. Return to the refrigerator. Just before serving, pour on the remaining caramel sauce and sprinkle with the pecans. Serve on chilled dessert plates.

Oranges with Glazed Peel

If you like more peel, add that of another orange or two. This is a very refreshing dessert, tart and sweet at the same time.

Serves 8

6 large navel oranges
1½ cups sugar
½ cup water
2 tablespoons honey
½ cup Cointreau or Grand Marnier

Remove the outer peel from one orange and cut the peel into very thin julienne strips. Barely cover with water and simmer for 10 minutes. Drain. Run cold water over the peel and drain again thoroughly.

Place the sugar, water, and honey in a saucepan and heat, stirring, until the sugar dissolves. Boil to 230°F. on a candy thermometer. Remove from the heat; add the peel and stir gently. Let stand for about 30 minutes; then add the liqueur.

Peel the remaining oranges. Cut each one into 3 or more slices. Spoon the syrup over the orange slices and top with the glazed peel. Chill before serving.

St. Vincent Pears

This is a festive way to make use of the gift pears that arrive at Christmas. It is impossible to eat them all before they spoil, so I use them in various dishes, and this is one of my favorites. It's a great dessert and can be made way ahead of time; it keeps under refrigeration for as long as four days without deteriorating.

Serves 6

8 tart apples, washed, peeled, and cored
Confectioners' sugar
Powdered cinnamon
1 tablespoon butter
½ cup broken walnuts plus several extra for the sauce
2 cups dry red wine
1 cup sugar
Small piece cinnamon stick
Rind of 1 lemon
8 medium-size cooking pears, peeled, cut in half, and cored

Slice the apples and put them in a saucepan with just enough water to prevent them from sticking while cooking. Cook until tender. Add a little confectioners' sugar and cinnamon and cook a few minutes longer. Pass through a fine sieve, or puree in a processor or blender. While the applesauce is still hot, stir in the butter and the nuts and set aside to cool.

Make a syrup by boiling the wine, sugar, cinnamon stick, and lemon rind for 5 minutes. Add the pears and simmer until just tender. Cool slightly.

Spread the applesauce on a large shallow platter. Place the drained pears symmetrically on top.

Reduce the wine syrup by boiling rapidly until only a scant cup is left. Add a few broken walnuts to the sauce.

The fruit and the sauce are served separately, and both should be well chilled before serving.

Peaches in Red Wine

This colorful and tasty dish is best made with fresh peaches. If you use canned whole peaches, be sure they are the water-packed variety, not the ones canned in syrup, and poach them only long enough to heat through—about 5 minutes.

Serves 6

12 fresh peaches
1 quart red wine
1 cup sugar
6-ounce jar red raspberry jelly
6-ounce jar red currant jelly

Plunge the peaches into boiling water, then into cold water, and slip off the skins. Arrange the peeled peaches in one layer in a shallow enamel pan. Make a syrup by boiling the red wine with sugar for 5 minutes. Pour over the peaches. Place the pan over medium-low heat and poach the peaches gently for about 10 minutes, until they can easily be pierced with a fork. (They should be firm, not mushy.) Let them cool in the syrup.

When cool, remove peaches from the syrup and place on a platter. Reduce the syrup by boiling rapidly until only 1 cup is left. Remove from the heat and add the raspberry and currant jellies. Stir until melted; let the sauce become quite cold before pouring it over the peaches. Chill and serve.

Plums in Vodka

Fresh plums in season are preferable for this recipe, but a good grade of canned plums will do in a pinch. If you use canned plums, discard the canning liquid and heat the plums in the sugar syrup for only 2 minutes. They are already cooked and any additional cooking will make them too soft. The flaming vodka adds flavor to the plums, drama to the dessert, and a bit of excitement at the table. If you don't want to go through the flaming process, cook the vodka over high heat for a few minutes to burn off the alcohol; allow it to cool before pouring over the plums.

Serves 6

1 cup sugar
½ cup water
½ teaspoon powdered ginger, or 1 teaspoon finely minced fresh ginger root
2 pounds red, yellow, or blue plums
2 tablespoons vodka
1 teaspoon almond extract
1 teaspoon vanilla extract

Put the sugar, water, and ginger in a saucepan large enough to hold the plums. Bring to a boil. Lower the heat and cook for 10 minutes, stirring occasionally, until the sugar is completely dissolved.

Stem the plums, cut in half lengthwise, and remove the pits. Add the plums to the sugar syrup and cook until tender but still fairly firm (6 to 12 minutes, depending on the ripeness of the fruit). With a slotted spoon, remove the plums to a heat-resistant dish, such as a soufflé dish. Boil down the syrup until it is reduced to about two thirds of its original volume. Pour it over the plums and allow to cool to room temperature. Do not refrigerate.

When ready to serve, put the vodka and almond and vanilla extracts in a very small saucepan. Heat almost to the boiling point. Light the simmering liquid with a match, pour the mixture over the plums, and serve flaming.

Basic Cobbler

I grew up on peach, berry, cherry, and plum cobbler—a fresh one every day during the summer as the fruits became available. Topped with heavy cream, whipped or plain, nothing is better than a cobbler just out of the oven. And fresh fruit isn't essential; frozen or canned fruit can also be used.

Serves 6 to 8

For the Cobbler

1 cup unbleached all-purpose flour
½ cup sugar
1 tablespoon baking powder
¼ teaspoon salt
⅓ cup shortening
½ cup whole milk
2 cups prepared fruit (fresh, frozen, or canned)

For the Syrup

1 cup sugar
1 cup water

Preheat the oven to 375°F.

Sift the dry ingredients and cut in the shortening. Add the milk to make a soft dough. Spread evenly on a well-greased 13 x 9 x 2½-inch ovenproof dish. Spread the fruit over the dough. Bring the syrup ingredients to a boil in a small saucepan and cook for 3 or 4 minutes. Pour over the fruit and bake for 45 minutes. Serve hot or at room temperature.

Blueberry Fool

Serves 6 to 8

- *6 cups fresh, frozen or thawed blueberries*
- *3 large strips lemon rind*
- *1 cup sugar*
- *2 tablespoons Grand Marnier*
- *2 cups reduced cream (see page 380)*

Combine the blueberries, lemon rind, and sugar in a heavy saucepan and cook, covered, over moderately low heat for 5 minutes. Uncover the pan and boil gently until the mixture is thick and sticky, about 15 minutes. Stir occasionally.

Remove the lemon rind and force the berries through the fine disc of a food mill. The consistency should be that of a thick fruit sauce. If it is not thick enough, boil the puree a little more, stirring, but do not let it thicken to a jamlike consistency, as it will thicken when chilled. Chill for 2 to 3 hours. Add the Grand Marnier.

Whip the reduced cream to form soft peaks. Partly fold the cream into the fruit, leaving a slightly striated appearance. Turn into a serving dish or into individual parfait glasses. Serve at once. (May be chilled for several hours prior to serving.)

Blackberry Fool

This is one time when the frozen berry is preferable to the fresh—or just as good anyway. For my money, fresh blackberries should be eaten "as is" with some heavy cream and a sprinkle of sugar. Actually, they are best if you just eat them as you pick them.

Serves 8

5 cups fresh or thawed frozen blackberries
¾ cup sugar
1 tablespoon rosewater, or to taste
2½ cups heavy cream

Combine the blackberries and sugar in a saucepan and cook, covered, over moderately low heat until the sugar melts and the berry juice begins to run. Stir once or twice.

Pour the berries into a sieve over a bowl; press them—but do not mash them—through the sieve to extract the juice. Return the berry syrup to the saucepan and boil it until it is thick and sticky.

Mash the berries, or press them through the medium disc of a food mill, in a bowl. Stir in the thickened syrup and chill. Add the rosewater.

To make reduced cream, pour the cream into a saucepan and boil it very gently for about 10 minutes, stirring often, for as long as necessary to reduce it in volume to 2 cups. Pour the cream into a clean jar and let it cool. Chill, covered, for 2 to 3 hours in the freezer. Before using, whisk in the solid layer on top.

Using an ice-cold bowl and a whisk, whip the reduced cream to soft peaks. Gently fold the cream and fruit together to partly mix them, leaving streaks of color. Turn the "fool" into a glass serving dish and chill for 2 to 3 hours before serving.

Glazed Pineapple with Chocolate Sauce

The days of poking and smelling pineapple to find a ripe one are gone, for today all pineapple is picked ripe for the market. Just hunt for the biggest one you can find and then be sure to squeeze all the juice from the outer shell, because that's where the sweetest juice is.

Serves 8 to 10

Chocolate Sauce

6 ounces unsweetened chocolate
¼ pound butter
2 tablespoons dark rum
2 tablespoons strong, freshly brewed coffee
2 cups unsifted confectioners' sugar
2 scant cups evaporated milk
1 teaspoon vanilla extract

Glazed Pineapple and Topping

1 fresh ripe pineapple
2 cups confectioners' sugar
½ cup dark rum
3 tablespoons Grand Marnier
2 pints vanilla ice cream
1½ cups heavy cream, whipped
2 tablespoons slivered almonds

To make the sauce, melt the chocolate and butter with the rum and coffee in the top of a double boiler over hot water. Remove from the heat and stir in the sugar alternately with the evaporated milk. Return the double boiler to the heat and cook, stirring constantly, until the mixture is thick, smooth, and creamy. Remove from the heat and stir in the vanilla.

Peel and core the pineapple, and cut it into chunks. Place in a chafing dish over medium heat and add the confectioners' sugar and rum bit by bit, until the pineapple is glazed. Remove from the chafing dish and place in chilled, individual dessert bowls.

Sprinkle a little Grand Marnier over each serving. Top with heaping tablespoons of vanilla ice cream and whipped cream, and sprinkle with slivered almonds.

Serve with the chocolate sauce.

Strawberry Shortcake

This is Jim Beard's recipe, and the only one I ever use. Jim is the only person I know who can manage this dough with just one hand.

Serves 6

4 cups unbleached all-purpose flour
6 tablespoons sugar
2 teaspoons salt
5 teaspoons baking powder
¼ pound plus 4 tablespoons butter, chilled and cut into bits
1½ cups heavy cream
2 tablespoons butter, melted and cooled

Topping

2 pints fresh, ripe strawberries, washed and stemmed, divided
2 tablespoons sugar, or to taste
1 pint heavy cream

Preheat the oven to 425°F.

Sift the flour, sugar, salt, and baking powder into a large bowl. Add the butter and, with your fingertips, rub it into the dry ingredients until most of the lumps disappear and the mixture resembles coarse meal. Add the cream and mix thoroughly until a soft dough is formed. Gather it into a compact ball and place on a lightly floured board. Knead the dough for a minute, then divide it into two pieces, one of which should be a third larger than the other.

On a greased cookie sheet, press the larger piece of dough into a circle 1 inch thick. On another sheet, press the second piece into a slightly smaller circle. Brush each with melted butter and bake for 12 to 15 minutes. The layers should be firm to the touch and golden brown.

Coarsely chop half the strawberries, leaving the most attractive ones whole for the top. Spread a layer of chopped strawberries on the larger baked layer and sprinkle with sugar. Gently slide the smaller layer on top of the strawberries and garnish with the whole strawberries. The cream may be poured over the cake just before serving, or it may be whipped and passed separately.

Fresh Strawberries with Sour Cream

Use homemade sour cream and whip it until it is very thick but still pourable. The brown sugar must be free of lumps; since the moisture in brown sugar makes it difficult to sprinkle by hand or spoon, it should go through a medium sieve right onto the sour cream.

Serves 6

4 cups fresh strawberries
3/4 cup Homemade Sour Cream (see page 333)
1/4 cup sieved brown sugar

Wash and hull the berries; divide among 6 dessert dishes. Mix the sour cream and brown sugar and top each dish of berries with about 2 tablespoons of the mixture.

Note: To keep brown sugar soft, place a slice of fresh bread in the bag with the sugar.

Fresh Strawberries and Cream

Another no-cook dessert, but one that is seasonally limited, since it is only good with fresh strawberries.

Serves 6

4 cups fresh strawberries
3 tablespoons sugar
2 cups heavy cream, whipped
2 tablespoons confectioners' sugar
1/2 teaspoon vanilla extract

Wash and hull the berries. Slice and sprinkle with the granulated sugar. Combine the whipped cream, confectioners' sugar, and vanilla; fold into the strawberries. Turn into a freezer tray and place in the freezer until very cold—but not frozen (from 30 to 40 minutes). Serve at once.

CREAMS AND CUSTARDS

Crème Brulée

Despite the name, this is not French but English. It means "burnt cream" and originally the sugar on top was glazed with a special device called a salamander. Today the dish is simply put under the broiler for a few minutes, but the timing is tricky—a moment too long and the sugar will be too burned and the custard may curdle. The custard must be ice cold before glazing. After the glaze is set, allow the dish to cool before returning it to the refrigerator, or it will draw moisture and "weep." The sugar glaze, or caramel, should crack when lightly tapped with a serving spoon. When strawberries are in season, they can be served as an accompaniment or can be placed on the glaze as soon as the dish is removed from the broiler. The strawberries will seal into place as the glaze hardens.

Serves 8

1 quart heavy cream
2 tablespoons sugar
8 egg yolks, well beaten
2 teaspoons vanilla extract
Light brown sugar for the glaze

Preheat the oven to 275°F.

Heat the heavy cream in the top of a double boiler over hot water until hot but not scalding. Add the sugar and stir until completely dissolved. Then add the egg yolks and vanilla. Mix well and pour into a shallow 12 x 7½-inch glass baking dish (the custard should be about 1½ inches deep). Place the dish in a larger pan of hot water and bake in the oven until set, about 1½ hours. Cool and place the dish in the refrigerator for several hours to chill thoroughly.

Remove from refrigerator and cover the surface of the custard with ¼ inch of soft, lump-free light brown sugar. (Do not use dark brown sugar.) Place the dish under a heated broiler and watch carefully. The sugar should melt and run together, leaving a shiny caramel top. When the surface is glazed, remove and allow to cool. Return to the refrigerator to chill thoroughly (it must be served ice cold).

Lemon Curd

Both the English and the Scots claim this as their own. It is used as a spread for bread or toast, as a breakfast treat or afternoon snack, but is best as a dessert. The tartness suits any after-taste of whatever the main course was. A topping of whipped cream helps cut the richness of the custard, and chopped walnuts make a good garnish.

Serves 8

4 lemons
2 cups sugar
1 pound butter
6 eggs, beaten
½ teaspoon salt
1 cup heavy cream, whipped
2 tablespoons confectioners' sugar

Grate the peel from the lemons and squeeze out the juice. Put the peel, juice, sugar, butter, eggs, and salt in the top of a double boiler. Cook the mixture over boiling water, stirring constantly, for about 30 minutes until it is the consistency of a thick cream sauce. Remove from the heat and pour into a serving dish or dishes. Refrigerate for several hours before serving.

Top with whipped cream sweetened with confectioners' sugar.

Lemon Bay Custard

Don't use more than two bay leaves for the baking "garnish." Any more takes away from the delicate lemon flavor. If you don't believe me, try three.

Serves 8

6 egg yolks
½ cup sugar
Pinch salt
3 bay leaves, divided
3 cups heavy cream
Zest of 1 lemon

Preheat the oven to 275°F.

Beat the egg yolks thoroughly and add the sugar and salt. Continue to beat until well blended.

In a saucepan add 1 bay leaf to the cream; heat until bubbles form around the edge. Stir a small amount of the scalded cream into the egg mixture; when well blended, add the remaining cream. Strain the mixture through a sieve into a greased baking dish and add the lemon zest. Garnish with the remaining bay leaves. Put the baking dish in a larger pan of hot water and bake in the oven for about an hour, or until slightly firm in the center. If the custard starts to color, cover loosely with aluminum foil or waxed paper.

The custard is best served warm and should have a loose texture.

Custard Cream

A simple, everyday dessert with no pretensions.

Makes about 1¼ cups

1¼ cups whole milk
2 tablespoons sugar
2 strips lemon rind
1 strip orange rind
3 egg yolks
2 tablespoons cornstarch
1 tablespoon heavy cream

Heat the milk, sugar, and lemon and orange rind in a saucepan over medium heat until bubbles form around the sides of the pan. Cover the pan and set it aside.

Whisk the egg yolks, cornstarch, and heavy cream together in a bowl until thoroughly blended. Slowly whisk in the heated milk mixture.

Strain the combination back into the saucepan through a fine sieve and cook it over low heat, stirring constantly. Cook the custard until it is so thick you can cut a path through it with a spoon; keep the heat low and continue stirring and scraping vigorously until it reaches this point. The process will take up to 10 minutes. Strain the custard through a fine sieve into a bowl and cool it completely, uncovered.

When it is cool, cover with plastic wrap and chill in the refrigerator.

Fresh Peach Bavarian Cream

A no-cook recipe that has all the fresh taste one could want.

Serves 10 to 12

2 cups peeled, chopped fresh peaches
1 cup peaches pureed in a blender
1 cup confectioners' sugar
2 tablespoons lemon juice
2 tablespoons brandy
2 envelopes unflavored gelatin
½ cup cold water
2 cups heavy cream
Fresh or frozen sieved raspberries, sweetened if desired

Combine the chopped peaches and the peach puree in a large bowl (you should have a total of 3 cups). Add the sugar, lemon juice, and brandy.

Soak the gelatin in the water for 5 minutes. Dissolve over hot water and stir into the peach mixture. Allow to cool.

Whip the cream to stiff peaks and fold into the cooled peach mixture. Secure a collar of parchment or foil around the rim of a 1½-quart soufflé dish greased with mayonnaise, extending it about 3 inches above the rim (see page 388). Be sure to grease the collar with mayonnaise as well. Turn the mixture into the soufflé dish and chill overnight.

Serve with sieved raspberries.

SOUFFLÉS

Here are a few tips on making soufflés. The height of the soufflé depends on the treatment of the ingredients and the size of the baking dish.

1. Use jumbo eggs rather than small to average ones—it will help the soufflé reach new heights.

2. For guaranteed success, use a smaller container than the recipe suggests. The soufflé has to go somewhere, and since the top opening is the only escape available, that is where the soufflé is going to go.

The following specific techniques for egg whites are useful.

1. The volume of beaten egg whites depends on the eggs being at room temperature before one starts and on the way in which the whites are beaten.

2. Use a hand whisk. Electric processors are too fast and produce a dense texture, whereas a hand whisk will produce an airy froth. It might take more time and energy, but the result is worth it.

3. To lighten the mixture when folding in the beaten egg whites, first fold in only a quarter of the egg whites, then lightly fold in the rest.

4. If you put some sugar into the egg whites as they are being beaten, it will help to hold the height when the soufflé rises.

Of course, one runs the risk of having a hollow soufflé if height is the only goal. Personally, I am more interested in taste and texture than height.

To prepare a cold soufflé dish, I use a light coating of mayonnaise—it is tasteless, disappears on cooking or refrigerating, and works. Oil shows, as does butter. However, when called for, I do butter a hot soufflé dish.

Because soufflés usually rise well above the top of the baking dish, they need to have a collar to hold them as they rise. I prefer a foil collar because of the high oven temperatures. Waxed paper or parchment will sometimes scorch or burn and that tends to give the crust an unpleasant taste. By the same token, it is best to tie the collar with heavy string rather than tape because heat can loosen the tape, allowing the collar to drop. Remember to grease the inside of the collar so that the soufflé does not stick and *always be sure the oven is thoroughly preheated.*

Cold Lemon-Lime Soufflé

Ideally this should be prepared in the morning and refrigerated until evening. A great buffet dessert, it will feed 12 generously or 24 sparingly, and can be served directly from the soufflé dish or turned out carefully and garnished.

Serves 12 generously

10 eggs, separated
2 cups sugar
½ cup lemon juice
½ cup lime juice
Grated rind of 2 lemons and 2 limes
Pinch salt
2 envelopes (2 tablespoons) unflavored gelatin
½ cup light rum
3 cups heavy cream, divided

Beat the egg yolks until fluffy. Add the sugar slowly and beat until smooth. Add the lemon and lime juices, grated rinds, and salt; mix thoroughly. Stir constantly over low heat in the top of a double boiler over hot water until the consistency of a cream sauce. Dissolve the gelatin in the rum and stir into the custard. Cool.

Grease a 6-cup soufflé dish with mayonnaise and add a collar on top (see page 388), or use individual cups with collars. (Be sure to grease the collar.) Beat the egg whites until stiff. Whip 2 cups of the cream. Fold the egg whites into the custard, then fold in the whipped cream. Pour into the prepared soufflé dish and refrigerate for 6 to 8 hours, or overnight. Just before serving, unmold onto a serving plate and top with the reserved cup of whipped cream. Add chopped walnuts to the whipped cream for variation, if desired.

Note: Do not refrigerate for more than 24 hours to avoid a rubbery texture.

Chocolate Soufflé

If I have to pick a favorite chocolate soufflé recipe, this is it. It can be made with either semisweet or bittersweet chocolate, depending on how "chocolatey" the cook wants it.

Serves 6

To Prepare the Soufflé Dish

1 teaspoon butter
2 teaspoons sugar

For the Soufflé

6 eggs
½ cup sugar
¼ teaspoon salt
6 ounces semisweet or bittersweet chocolate
1 teaspoon vanilla extract
¼ teaspoon cream of tartar (optional)

For the Whipped Cream

1 cup heavy cream, chilled
2 tablespoons sifted confectioners' sugar
1 tablespoon cognac, Grand Marnier, or dark rum, or 2 tablespoons kirsch

Butter a 1-quart soufflé dish and add a buttered collar; sprinkle with the sugar. Chill the bowl in which the cream will be whipped. Separate the eggs, putting the yolks in a mixing bowl and the whites in the bowl in which they will be beaten. Beat the yolks until light and lemon-colored, then gradually beat in the sugar and salt until the mixture is very thick, pale yellow, and ribbony.

Meanwhile, melt the chocolate in the top of a double boiler over hot water or in a small pan in a 300°F. oven. Stir the chocolate and vanilla into the egg yolk-and-sugar mixture and beat until well mixed.

Preheat the oven to 375°F.

Beat the egg whites until foamy; add the cream of tartar (unless you are using a copper bowl) and continue to beat until they hold soft, unwavering peaks. Fold into the chocolate mixture. Pour into the buttered, collared soufflé dish and bake for 45 minutes. (This soufflé needs a longer baking time than most because of the density of the chocolate.)

Just before the soufflé is ready to come out of the oven, put the chilled cream in the chilled bowl and beat with a rotary beater until it has doubled in volume. Gently fold in the sugar and cognac or other flavoring. Serve as a sauce with the soufflé.

Hot Grand Marnier Soufflé

My friend Julie Dannenbaum gave me this recipe. I have never had it fail and you won't either if you follow the directions.

Serves 4 to 6

8 egg yolks
⅔ cup sugar
½ cup Grand Marnier
10 egg whites
¼ teaspoon cream of tartar

Butter a 4-cup soufflé dish and add a buttered 6-inch collar.

Place the baking rack in the lower third of the oven and preheat the oven to 450°F. In a large bowl whisk together the egg yolks and sugar. Place a pan of simmering water over medium-low heat and set the bowl in it. Continue whisking the yolk mixture until it mounds slightly. Add the Grand Marnier and continue whisking another 4 to 5 minutes, then remove from the heat.

Beat the egg whites and cream of tartar until stiff. Fold into the yolk mixture and pour into the buttered and collared soufflé dish. Put the soufflé in the hot oven and immediately turn the temperature down to 425°F.

Bake for 30 minutes. *Do not open oven door during the baking.* When the 30 minutes are up, the soufflé will be a dark golden color and very high. Remove the collar carefully and serve immediately.

Note: The soufflé may be served as is, or with Rich Vanilla Sauce (page 424).

Strawberry Soufflé

This wonderful dessert should be made only during strawberry season, for it is best with only the ripest of berries.

Serves 4

- *1 quart fresh strawberries, washed and stemmed*
- *2 cups sugar*
- *6 egg whites*
- *4 tablespoons confectioners' sugar, divided*
- *1 cup heavy cream*
- *Kirsch*

Set aside 8 of the berries and mash the rest thoroughly. Add the sugar, mix well, and refrigerate.

An hour before serving, drain off 1 cup of the juice that has accumulated on the berries. Slice the 8 reserved whole berries into the juice, cutting them into thin slivers. Set aside. This will be part of the sauce for the soufflé.

Preheat the oven to 325°F.

Beat the egg whites until very stiff; with a wire whisk, fold in 2 tablespoons of the confectioners' sugar. Fold in the strawberry pulp very carefully. Spoon gently into a well-buttered 8 x 3-inch soufflé dish. Place the dish in a pan of hot water and set immediately in the oven. Bake for 25 minutes. The soufflé should be firm to the touch and well risen.

Remove from the oven and sprinkle with the remaining 2 tablespoons of confectioners' sugar. Serve immediately with a sauce made by whipping the cream slightly and stirring in the reserved sliced strawberry syrup and kirsch to taste.

ICE CREAM

As far as I am concerned, ice cream should only be made in an old-fashioned hand-crank machine or one of the newer electric machines. Ice creams made in ice trays or containers in the freezer sections of the refrigerator are never as creamy as they should be. In fact, most of them have a rather unfortunate texture. Granted, those who choose to make ice cream in their refrigerator freezer sections probably know they won't be up to snuff, but for the amount of trouble involved, it seems cheaper to buy a machine. Most brands are relatively inexpensive and work very well. All you have to do then is follow the manufacturer's instructions to produce some really good ice cream.

Six Threes Ice Cream

The name comes from the fact there are six ingredients and all in quantities of three. It is one of the best ice creams I've come across, and one of the simplest to make. No cooking, just put it together according to the instructions, freeze it, pack it away for a couple of hours, and it's ready to eat. I found the recipe in an instruction manual when I bought an attachment for my Kitchen Aid, and have used it ever since.

Makes 3½ quarts

3 cups whole milk
3 cups heavy cream
3 cups sugar
Juice of 3 lemons
Juice of 3 oranges
3 bananas, mashed

Combine the milk, cream, and sugar, and stir until the sugar is dissolved. Place in an ice cream freezer and freeze according to manufacturer's directions until it is thoroughly chilled and has a mushy consistency. Add the fruit juices and mashed bananas and continue freezing until firm. Remove the dasher and pack the container in salt and ice for several hours.

Note: This recipe can be doubled or cut in half.

Blackberry Ice Cream

Maybe I should call this just plain "berry" ice cream because other berries can be substituted without making any other changes in the ingredient list. Marion berries, boysenberries, or raspberries all work equally well and are all delicious.

Makes 3 to 3½ quarts

1 quart blackberries
2¾ cups sugar, divided
1½ cups water
1 quart heavy cream
1 tablespoon lemon juice

Wash, drain, and crush the berries.

Make a syrup by boiling 2 cups of the sugar and the water for 5 minutes. Pour over the crushed berries and let stand for 1 hour. Press through a fine sieve and add the lemon juice.

Scald the cream and add the remaining ¾ cup of sugar. Stir until melted; cool and chill. Freeze to a mush, following ice cream freezer directions. Add the blackberry pulp and continue freezing until stiff. Remove the dasher; pack for 3 hours before serving.

Coffee Ice Cream with Grated Chocolate

This is a coffee-flavored ice cream with a real kick. It should only be made in an electric or old-fashioned hand-crank ice cream freezer.

Serves 8

2 cups sugar
1½ cups water
1 pint (2 cups) heavy cream
1 pint (2 cups) whole milk
8 egg yolks, beaten
*1 cup strong black coffee extract**
1 cup grated sweet chocolate

* To make a coffee extract, place 1½ cups freshly roasted coffee, ground to a powder, in a glass jar. Pour over it enough cold water to moisten it well. Cover tightly and place in the refrigerator overnight. Strain well before using.

In a saucepan, boil the sugar with the water for 5 minutes. Mix the cream with the milk in a double boiler. Add the syrup and scald. Add the egg yolks very gradually and continue cooking until the mixture coats the spoon. Remove from the heat and, when cold, add the coffee extract.

Freeze in an ice cream freezer, following the manufacturer's instructions. When frozen, remove the dasher, and pack the ice cream in a melon mold that has been thoroughly coated with the grated chocolate. Return to the freezer for 2 to 3 hours; turn out and serve immediately.

Note: The grated chocolate may be served in a separate bowl, if preferred, rather than frozen with the ice cream.

Frozen Yogurt Cream

This is far from diet food, but eaten in moderation it won't hurt. It is not as rich as ice cream, and has a tart, refreshing flavor, especially when made with fresh peaches or apricots. You can use any fresh or frozen fruit you like.

Makes 2 quarts

2 cups sliced fresh peaches or apricots, peeled
1 cup sugar
1 teaspoon vanilla extract
1 quart plain yogurt
1 pint heavy cream, lightly whipped

Combine the fruit and sugar in a pan and cook over low heat, stirring, until the sugar dissolves. Puree the mixture in a processor or blender. Cool.

Fold the vanilla and the yogurt into the whipped cream. Add the cooled fruit, and pour into an ice cream freezer. Churn until firm, following the manufacturer's instructions. The mixture may also be frozen in a bowl set in the freezer. When the edges are firm, remove, beat smooth, and return to the freezer for 1 hour, until firm but not hard. Remove, beat smooth again, and store tightly covered in the freezer until ready to serve.

PUDDINGS

Puddings were long-time favorites until all the "instant" versions came on the market and gave puddings a bad reputation. However, they have taken a back seat long enough. Nothing is more American than pudding, and no dessert is better. I offer a few of my favorites here.

Baked Chocolate Pudding

Here's one for the chocolate lover. This simple dessert, which tastes like a lot more than it really is, should be served warm or hot. However, you can make it in the afternoon (it takes 1 hour and 10 minutes from initial mixing to finished product) and simply reheat it at 325°F. for 15 minutes before serving. When you invert it on a serving platter, don't be surprised to find that the sauce, or frosting, is on the bottom of the pudding. Serve with sweetened whipped cream or vanilla ice cream.

Serves 8

1 cup sifted unbleached all-purpose flour
1¼ cups sugar, divided
2 teaspoons baking powder
¼ teaspoon salt
4 tablespoons unsweetened cocoa, divided
½ cup chopped walnuts or macadamia nuts
2 tablespoons melted butter
½ cup whole milk
1 teaspoon vanilla extract
½ cup brown sugar
1 cup cold water

Preheat the oven to 325°F.

Combine the flour, ¾ cup of the sugar, the baking powder, salt, and 2 tablespoons of the cocoa. Add the nuts and butter. Stir in the milk and vanilla. The batter will be quite thick. Pour the mixture into a greased 8-inch round by 3-inch deep baking dish.

Mix together the brown sugar, the remaining ½ cup of white sugar, and the remaining cocoa, and sprinkle over the batter. Pour on the cold water and bake for 1 hour.

Apple and Bread Pudding with Sabayon Sauce

Bread and apple puddings have always been favorites, so why not combine them? The sauce should be made at the last minute but will hold for 10 minutes. Just beat the mixture hard and be sure to use a stainless-steel whisk—*not aluminum,* unless you want the eggs to turn green.

Serves 6

1 pound tart apples, quartered, cored, peeled, and sliced
¼ pound butter, divided
Large handful (3 to 4 ounces) fresh bread crumbs (no crusts)
Cinnamon
1 cup whole milk or light cream
2 eggs
⅓ cup sugar
Pinch salt
Sabayon Sauce (recipe follows)

Cook the apples in 3 tablespoons of the butter, tossing occasionally, until tender, about 25 minutes. Cook the bread crumbs in the remaining 5 tablespoons of butter over low heat until golden and crisp (add more butter if necessary).

Preheat the oven to 325°F.

Spread the crumbs in the bottom of a lightly buttered 1½-quart casserole or baking dish. Arrange the apple slices on the bed of bread crumbs. Sprinkle lightly with cinnamon.

Whisk together the milk or cream, eggs, sugar, and salt, and pour over the apples, being careful not to displace the apples. Bake for 30 minutes. Serve warm with Sabayon Sauce.

Sabayon Sauce

½ cup sugar
3 egg yolks
⅔ cup white wine
Grated lemon peel

Combine the sugar, egg yolks, wine, and lemon peel in a small, heavy saucepan set in a larger pan of nearly boiling water. Be sure that the water does not boil. Whisk constantly over low heat until thick (about 20 to 25 minutes). Serve warm.

Bread Pudding

Just plain old-fashioned bread pudding is great as far as I am concerned, but this is a good "company" version.

Serves 4

3 ounces day-old bread, crusts removed and cut in cubes
1 cup whole milk
⅓ cup sugar
1 tablespoon kirsch
4 ounces chopped pecans
4 egg yolks
2 egg whites
1 tablespoon butter
1 recipe Apricot Sauce (page 427)

Preheat the oven to 400°F.

Put the bread to soak with the milk in a mixing bowl. Add the sugar, kirsch, pecans, and egg yolks, combining thoroughly. Beat the egg whites until they stand in peaks; fold them gently into the bread mixture. Pour into a liberally buttered baking dish and bake for 25 to 30 minutes, or until puffed, browned, and firm in the center. Serve immediately with Apricot Sauce.

Tombstone Pudding

This is good after a heavy meal when a dessert seems called for, but you don't want one that is too filling.

Serves 8

18 dry Almond Macaroons (see page 371), crushed
6 eggs, separated
1 cup plus 2 tablespoons confectioners' sugar, divided
½ cup sherry, heated
Pinch salt
½ teaspoon vanilla extract
Blanched, dried almonds

Preheat the oven to 350°F.

Place the macaroons in the bottom of a large glass baking dish. Beat the egg yolks with 2 tablespoons of the confectioners' sugar and add the sherry. Pour this sauce in the top of a large double boiler over hot water and beat with a rotary beater until the mixture foams up and is slightly warmed through. Pour the sauce over the macaroons.

Beat the egg whites and salt until very stiff; beat in the remaining 1 cup of confectioners' sugar and add the vanilla. Spread this meringue evenly over the surface of the pudding, making sure that it touches the rim of the baking dish to avoid shrinking. Stick the whole almonds upright evenly into the meringue to simulate tombstones in a graveyard.

Bake just long enough to lightly brown the meringue and the nuts. Serve hot with cream.

Almond and Rice Pudding

Although this recipe calls for espresso coffee beans, any coffee bean is all right, just not as flavorful. This pudding can be served hot from the oven, cold, or with heavy cream—but not whipped cream.

Serves 6 to 8

1 quart whole milk, heated
¾ teaspoon salt
1 cup uncooked long-grain rice
1 large slice lemon peel
2 large slices orange peel
3 or 4 espresso coffee beans
½ cup sugar
¼ teaspoon vanilla extract
1½ cups crushed blanched almonds
2 eggs, lightly beaten
2 egg yolks, lightly beaten
½ cup cognac, divided
½ heaping teaspoon grated orange rind
½ heaping teaspoon grated lemon rind
3 teaspoons Aurum or Grand Marnier

Preheat the oven to 375°F.

Mix the hot milk and salt in the top of a large double boiler and place over moderately boiling water. Add the rice, lemon and orange peels, and coffee beans. Cover loosely and steam, stirring very frequently with a fork, for approximately 30 minutes, or until the rice is tender and the milk absorbed. Remove from the heat and let cool completely.

When the rice is cool, remove and discard the lemon and orange peels and coffee beans. Add the sugar, vanilla, almonds, beaten eggs, and egg yolks, ¼ cup of the cognac, and the grated lemon and orange rinds. Mix thoroughly.

Pour the mixture into a well-buttered baking pan or individual cups to a depth of no more than 1¼ inches. Bake for 30 to 45 minutes, or until the top is golden brown and a knife inserted in the center comes out clean. Remove from the oven. Prick the top all over with a fork and pour on a mixture of the remaining cognac and Aurum or Grand Marnier. Chill completely before serving.

Pumpkin-Pecan Flan with Vanilla Sauce

This was my grandmother's favorite pumpkin recipe and it's now a Thanksgiving dinner tradition at my house. I still have her handwritten recipe, which listed the ingredients but gave no measurements. That's the way she cooked everything. After some experimentation, I came up with this version.

Serves 16

1¼ cups dark brown sugar
1¼ cups light brown sugar
3 tablespoons butter
¼ cup water
4 cups cooked or canned pumpkin, mashed
3 to 4 teaspoons salt
1½ teaspoons ground cloves
4 teaspoons ground cinnamon
2 teaspoons ground ginger
½ teaspoon allspice
Grated rind of 1 lemon
6 eggs, well beaten
3 cups evaporated milk
1½ cups chopped pecans
Pecan halves for garnish
Vanilla Sauce (recipe follows)

Mix the sugars together. Put ¾ cup of the sugar mixture and the butter in a saucepan and cook over medium heat, stirring constantly, until the mixture has come to a boil. Let boil for 1 minute, still stirring; add the water and boil for 4 minutes. Place a 3½-quart round stainless-steel mold in a pan of hot water and pour in the sugar mixture. Tilt the dish immediately in all directions to coat the bottom and sides with caramel. Set the mold aside.

Preheat the oven to 350°F.

Mix the remaining sugar mixture, the pumpkin, salt, spices, and lemon rind. Add the eggs to the mixture; then add the evaporated milk and pecans. Stir until well mixed. Pour into the caramelized mold. Return the mold to the pan of hot water, making sure that the water comes to within an inch of the top of the mold. Bake for 2 hours, or until the center is firm. Remove from hot water; cool. Refrigerate overnight.

Unmold the pudding by setting the dish in warm water and loosening with a spatula. Invert onto a platter and decorate the top and sides with pecan halves. Serve with Vanilla Sauce.

Vanilla Sauce

Makes 2 cups

2 cups heavy cream
6 tablespoons sugar
3 egg yolks
¼ teaspoon salt
1½ teaspoons vanilla extract

To make the sauce, heat the cream to a simmer. Combine the sugar with the egg yolks and salt. Pour some of the heated cream into the sugar-egg mixture, blend, and stir into the hot cream. Add the vanilla. Heat in a double boiler over hot water, stirring constantly, until the mixture is thick enough to coat a spoon.

Pumpkin Pudding

This is a dessert that must be served well chilled.

Serves 12 (makes 2 puddings)

4 cups steamed, mashed fresh pumpkin (or canned pumpkin)
1 cup light brown sugar
2 tablespoons molasses
1 cup sugar
3 teaspoons cinnamon
3 teaspoons ground ginger
Dash nutmeg
2 teaspoons salt
2 teaspoons butter, melted
2 tablespoons brandy
6 eggs, well beaten
4 cups heavy cream

For the Caramel

2 cups sugar
3 tablespoons butter
1 cup water

In a large bowl combine the pumpkin with the remaining ingredients, except those for the caramel. Mix well and set aside.

To make the caramel, melt the sugar in a small, heavy skillet over low heat, stirring all the time with a wooden spoon. Remove from the heat and add the butter and water; return the skillet to very low heat and simmer until the syrup is slightly thick and smooth.

Preheat the oven to 325°F.

Divide the caramel between two 1½-quart soufflé dishes and spoon the pumpkin mixture into them. Set the dishes in a large pan of hot water in the oven and bake until set, about 2 hours.

Remove from the oven, cool, and chill in the refrigerator until ready to serve. Turn out on dessert platters and serve with kirsch and heavy cream.

Plum Pudding with Cumberland Rum Butter

This version of the traditional Christmas pudding is made even more gala by the addition of the rum sauce. It's a bit of a production to make but well worth it—and fortunately there's absolutely no reason to make it at the last minute. The longer this pudding is stored, the better it becomes, which is why I usually make it six months in advance and store it in sealed tins.

Serves 8 to 10

½ cup unbleached all-purpose flour
Pinch salt
½ teaspoon ground cinnamon
½ teaspoon grated nutmeg
½ pound beef suet, shredded
8 ounces fresh white bread crumbs
Grated rind of 1 lemon
½ carrot, grated
1½ cups dark brown sugar
¼ cup chopped blanched almonds
1 cup seedless raisins
1 cup currants
1 cup sultanas
4 ounces, candied peel (orange, lemon, or grapefruit), chopped
4 ounces pitted prunes, finely chopped
3 tablespoons dark molasses
½ cup rum
Juice of 1 lemon, strained
3 eggs
1 cup or more Guinness stout

Sift the flour, salt, and spices into a large bowl. Add the suet, bread crumbs, lemon rind, carrot, brown sugar, almonds, raisins, currants, sultanas, mixed peel, and prunes. Mix thoroughly and make a well in the center.

Warm the molasses a little to make it thin and runny. Remove from the heat; add the rum and lemon juice. Beat the eggs and stir into the molasses mixture. Pour this, together with the stout, into the dry ingredients. With a large spoon, stir all the ingredients together until they are moist and well mixed. Cover the bowl with a napkin and let stand overnight. Next day, stir up the mixture and, if it seems at all dry, add more stout.

Thoroughly grease a 1-quart and a 1-pint pudding bowl with butter. (A charlotte mold or a tall-sided mixing bowl will do.) Fill each bowl to within 1 inch of the top with the pudding mixture. Cover each with a round of waxed paper, then with a cloth, and tie securely with string. Place each pudding in a large saucepan with boiling water that reaches one third the way up the side of the bowl. Cover the saucepan and steam for 5 hours, adding more boiling water if necessary.

When the puddings have cooled, remove the damp waxed paper, replace with a layer of fresh paper, cover with a clean cloth, tie securely, and store in a cool but light place. *Be sure the cover is not airtight, or mold may develop.*

On the day the puddings are to be served, re-cover with buttered waxed paper and aluminum foil and steam briskly for 2 hours. Turn each pudding out onto a warm platter and pour over each a little warm rum or brandy. Ignite and serve with Cumberland Rum Butter (recipe follows) or with Hard Sauce (page 428).

Cumberland Rum Butter

¼ pound butter, softened
½ cup superfine sugar
2 tablespoons rum
¼ teaspoon each lemon and orange extract
Dash nutmeg
Dash cinnamon

Beat the butter and sugar together until well blended. Add the remaining ingredients and mix in. Chill and serve.

Holiday Pudding

This can be a holiday pudding, although I use it all year long. If you like ginger and nuts, you will love this. Make it in a 9-cup mold.

Serves 12

1 cup light brown sugar
½ pound butter
½ cup molasses
2 tablespoons brandy
5 large eggs
2½ cups unbleached all-purpose flour
2 tablespoons ground ginger
1¼ teaspoons baking soda
1 cup chopped crystallized ginger
½ cup chopped walnuts or macadamia nuts
1 recipe Brandy Sauce (see page 428)

Cream the sugar and butter together; add the molasses and brandy. Beat the eggs lightly, add to the mixture, and beat well. Sift the flour, ginger, and soda together; add the crystallized ginger and nuts. Combine with the butter-and-egg mixture and beat until well mixed.

Spoon into a buttered pudding mold with a cover. Put into a large pot with boiling water two-thirds of the way up the mold; cover and simmer for 1½ hours. Turn the pudding out onto a serving dish and serve warm or cold with Brandy Sauce.

Note: To assure even cooking, you need a pudding mold with an inner hollow tube. It should hold at least 9 cups of liquid and be about 6 inches high, with a domed lid that clips in place and a handle for easy lifting. In a pinch, you can use a 1-pound coffee can, but the lid has to be a good snug fit so that moisture won't seep in during the steaming.

CAKES

A cake is not something that can be "thrown together" unless you are using a commercially prepared packaged mix. The ingredients must be measured carefully and accurately and should be at room temperature when you start, and proper pans should be selected and prepared. Of equal importance is the oven that is used in baking. It pays to know your oven. Make sure it is calibrated, that is, tested for correct temperatures.

When I refer to testing for doneness, I mean you should insert a broom straw, long toothpick, or other implement that can easily be inserted and withdrawn without making a big hole in the baked goods. If the insert comes out clean and dry, the cake is done, and if the insert comes out with anything gummy, it is not.

Most baked items should be removed from the oven to a cake rack and allowed to cool somewhat before being removed from the baking container. If the baked product is taken out of the container too soon, it may fall apart. Give it a chance to solidify. Anything that is to be frosted should be almost at room temperature first. If frosting goes on a cake that is still hot, it will not stay in place.

Pound Cake

Pound cake gets its name because it uses a pound of flour, a pound of butter, a pound of sugar—even a pound of eggs. This recipe is an old one, and it really does work best if the tins are lined in onionskin typewriter paper. Waxed paper will do, but not as well.

Makes 2 loaves

*4½ cups sifted cake flour**
½ teaspoon salt
1 pound butter
2 cups sugar
*10 eggs (approx.), separated**
1 teaspoon vanilla extract
½ teaspoon lemon extract, or 1 teaspoon lemon juice

* Weigh to make sure you have 1 pound.

Preheat the oven to 300°F.

Line two buttered 9 x 5 x 2½-inch loaf-cake tins with buttered onion-skin typewriter paper. Sift the cake flour twice more with the salt. Place in the sifter ready to sift into the batter.

Cream the butter until very soft, then gradually work in the sugar. When very fluffy and light, add the well-beaten egg yolks and beat again until very light. Sift in the flour gradually. When well mixed, flavor with the vanilla and lemon extracts.

Beat the egg whites until very stiff and fold them into the batter. Pour the batter into the prepared loaf-cake tins, dividing it equally. Bake slowly for about 70 to 85 minutes, or until the cake tests done.

Pineapple Upside-Down Cake

You can eat this hot, warm, or cold, just as long as you eat it soon after it has been made. This is a cake that is better on the first day.

Serves 8

½ pound butter, divided
2 cups light brown sugar
1 tablespoon brandy
10 pineapple slices, cut in half
4 ounces pecan halves
1 cup sugar
3 eggs, well beaten
2½ cups sifted, unbleached all-purpose flour
4 teaspoons baking powder
½ teaspoon salt
¾ cup whole milk
2 teaspoons vanilla extract
Heated brandy
Light cream (optional)

Preheat the oven to 350°F.

Melt half the butter in a large, oblong cake tin (14 x 9 x 2 inches). Add the brown sugar and brandy; stir over low heat until melted.

Arrange the pineapple slices evenly, in rows, over the bottom of the pan and scatter the nuts here and there.

Cream the remaining butter with the sugar until light and fluffy. Beat the eggs into the mixture. Sift the flour, baking powder and salt; add it alternately with the milk to the butter mixture. Add the vanilla and beat well.

Pour over the pineapple and bake for 45 minutes. Turn out onto a hot platter, pour a little heated brandy over the cake, and ignite. Serve with plenty of light cream.

Old-Fashioned Date-Nut Cake

This should probably be called a torte rather than a cake, but it was given to me as a cake, and cake it shall remain. Eggs provide the only moisture, and it is not a cake that rises; it remains about the same height as when it went into the baking container, which can be a pie tin or any flat rectangular cake pan. The recipe was given to me many years ago by a neighbor who was 80 at the time. She said the recipe had been given to her as a young girl by her mother—that puts age behind the recipe and lends weight to the term "old-fashioned."

Serves 6

16 ounces seeded dates, chopped
1 pound English walnuts, broken or cut
1 cup sugar
1 cup unbleached all-purpose flour, sifted
1 teaspoon baking powder
½ teaspoon salt
4 eggs, separated
½ teaspoon vanilla extract

Preheat the oven to 300° F.

Combine the fruit and nuts with the sugar; then add the flour, baking powder, and salt. Add the beaten egg yolks and the vanilla and mix well. Then add the beaten egg whites.

Pour the batter into a flat pan and bake for 45 minutes, or until done when tested.

Apple-Nut Cake

This is my favorite cake, hands down. Jim Beard introduced me to this addictive number about five years ago, and I have all but overdosed on it. It's changed a bit over the years, but Jim's basic idea is still there. A wonderful combination of textures and flavors, this cake goes on every picnic that I plan. It's even good for breakfast.

Serves 12

1½ cups vegetable oil
1½ cups sugar
½ cup light brown sugar
3 large eggs
3 cups unbleached all-purpose flour
1 teaspoon baking soda
2 teaspoons cinnamon
½ teaspoon freshly grated nutmeg
½ teaspoon salt
3½ cups tart, raw apples, peeled and cut into a large dice
2 cups chopped nuts (English walnuts, black walnuts, or macadamia nuts)
2 teaspoons vanilla extract

Glaze

3 tablespoons butter
3 tablespoons light brown sugar
3 tablespoons granulated sugar
3 tablespoons heavy cream
¼ teaspoon vanilla extract

Preheat the oven to 325°F.

Combine the vegetable oil with the sugars and blend well. Add the eggs, one at a time, beating thoroughly all the time. An electric mixer is recommended but not essential. Sift together the flour, baking soda, cinnamon, nutmeg, and salt, and add to the oil-egg mixture. Blend thoroughly. Add the apples, nuts, and vanilla, and mix well by hand, using a spoon or spatula. Pour the batter into a buttered, floured 10-inch tube pan with a removable tube and bottom. Bake for 1½ hours, or until it tests clean. Remove from the oven and let the cake rest in the pan until cool before turning it out on a wire rack or platter.

Combine all the ingredients for the glaze in a heavy saucepan, stirring constantly, and bring to a boil over medium heat; continue boiling for 1 minute, then remove from the heat and spoon over the cake.

WHOLE books have been devoted to cheesecake and everyone has a recipe that is better than anyone else's. Cheesecakes are as personal as chili recipes and just as diverse. I don't like most of the chili recipes and I don't like most of the cheesecake recipes, but the ones that I do like, I like a lot. The two cheesecake recipes that follow are very good in my estimation, and quite different from one another.

Cheesecake must be handled carefully in the making and the baking. Proper-size springform pans should always be used, and the baking instructions should be followed closely. Always turn the oven off at the end of the baking time, always leave the cheesecake in the oven with the door ajar until the oven has cooled, always allow the cake to reach room temperature before refrigerating, and never remove the cake from the baking pan until it is thoroughly chilled.

Great Cheesecake

The name says it all. It is super-rich, but not tricky. It should be made and handled with care, and once served, there will be no leftovers.

Serves 10 to 12

32 ounces cream cheese
16 ounces sour cream
¼ pound butter
2 tablespoons cornstarch
1¼ cups sugar
1 teaspoon vanilla extract
1 teaspoon lemon juice
5 eggs

Preheat the oven to 375°F.

All the ingredients must be at room temperature before starting. Blend the cream cheese, sour cream, and butter in a mixer. Add the cornstarch, sugar, vanilla, and lemon juice. Beat until well blended. Beat in 1 egg at a time and continue beating until the mixture is very smooth and light.

Pour into a well-greased 9-inch springform pan that has been encased in foil to prevent water from seeping in during the baking. Place in a pan of warm water that comes halfway up the sides of the springform pan. Bake for 1 hour, or until the top is golden and the center fairly firm.

Turn off the oven and let the cake cool, with the door open, for at least an hour. Allow to stand at room temperature until completely cool, about 2 hours, then cover and refrigerate for several hours before serving.

German Cheesecake

This old German-style recipe is not nearly so rich as most, and the zweiback–sugar–butter mixture forms a wonderful crust on the bottom and around the sides of the cake, so that it will hold when sliced.

Serves 12

6-ounce package unsweetened zweiback
2 cups sugar, divided
1 teaspoon cinnamon
½ pound butter, melted
4 eggs
Pinch salt
Juice and grated rind of ½ lemon
1 cup light cream
1½ pounds small-curd cottage cheese
¼ cup unbleached all-purpose flour

Preheat the oven to 325°F.

Roll the zweiback on waxed paper with a rolling pin until it is reduced to fine crumbs (or put it in a blender or processor). Mix the crumbs with 1 cup of the sugar, the cinnamon, and butter. Set aside ¾ cup of the mixture to be used on top of the cake.

Grease a 9-inch springform pan heavily with butter. Spread and press the crumb mixture (except for the reserved ¾ cup) thickly on the bottom and sides of the pan. (The pan must be well buttered so the zweiback will adhere.)

Beat the eggs thoroughly with the remaining cup of sugar. Add the salt, lemon juice, and rind. Stir in the cream, then the cheese and flour. Mix well and strain through a fine sieve. (The mixture may be whirled in a blender or processor, a portion at a time, before straining.) Pour into the zweiback-lined pan; sprinkle the reserved crumbs on top.

Place the pan on a large square of aluminum foil; bring the foil up around the sides, unless the springform is absolutely leakproof. Bake for 1 hour. Turn off the heat and let the cake stand in the oven for another hour with the door ajar. This will help keep the cheesecake from sinking, as it sometimes does with a sudden change in temperature.

When completely cooled, refrigerate. When chilled, remove the ring, but not the bottom, from the form. Place the cheesecake on a cake platter and return to the refrigerator. Before serving, let the cake stand outside the refrigerator for about 20 minutes.

Filbert Torte with Mocha Frosting

This recipe was given to me years ago by one of the best cooks I have ever known. It is so light it is more like a soufflé than a torte. Follow the directions to the letter and you will have a wonderful dessert. The Mocha Frosting is a "sometimes" addition. More often, I use lots of flavored whipped cream as a topping.

Serves 6 to 8

8 eggs, separated
1 cup sugar
½ pound filberts, ground
6 tablespoons dry bread crumbs or ladyfinger crumbs
1¼ teaspoons baking powder
⅛ teaspoon salt
Juice and zest of 1 lemon
½ pint whipping cream, for filling
Mocha Frosting (recipe follows)

Preheat the oven to 325°F.

Using a rotary beater, beat the egg yolks until thick. Add the sugar and continue beating until very thick. Add the nuts, crumbs, baking powder, salt, and lemon juice and zest; mix thoroughly.

Beat the egg whites into stiff peaks and fold into the egg yolk mixture. Bake in a lightly buttered 8½- or 9-inch springform pan for 1 hour. Remove from the oven and allow to cool upside down. When cool, remove the springform, cut into two layers, and fill with lightly sweetened whipped cream. Frost if desired.

Mocha Frosting

⅓ cup butter
4 tablespoons unsweetened cocoa
4 cups confectioners' sugar
½ teaspoon salt
⅓ cup strong freshly brewed coffee
1 teaspoon vanilla extract

Cream the butter until very smooth. Sift together the cocoa, sugar, and salt, and add gradually to the butter. Add the coffee until the frosting has reached the right consistency to spread. Stir in the vanilla.

Sourdough Chocolate Cake

Chocolate "anything" generally wins first place in desserts, but the all-time favorite seems to be chocolate cake—and the richer the better. The same sourdough starter you keep on hand for breads is the base for this breadlike cake. These starters are available commercially.

Serves 8

1 cup thick sourdough starter
1 cup water
1½ cups unbleached all-purpose flour
¼ cup nonfat dry milk

Mix the ingredients and let them ferment for 2 to 3 hours in a warm place until the mixture is bubbly and emits a clean, sour milk odor. Then mix the following:

¼ pound shortening
1 cup sugar
½ teaspoon salt
1½ teaspoons baking soda
1 teaspoon cinnamon (optional)
2 eggs
1 teaspoon vanilla extract
3 squares unsweetened chocolate, melted

Preheat the oven to 350°F.

Cream the shortening, sugar, salt, soda, and cinnamon. Beat in the eggs one at a time. Add the vanilla and chocolate and stir into the sourdough mixture. Blend in an electric mixer on low speed. Pour into two greased, floured 8-inch round cake pans or one large cake pan. Bake for 30 to 35 minutes. Test with a toothpick for doneness and remove to a wire rack to cool.

When the cake is cool enough to handle with bare hands, remove from the pan to a serving plate. When completely cooled, or at room temperature, cover but do not refrigerate. Serve with sweetened whipped cream or frost with your favorite frosting.

PIES AND TARTS

You need to develop a "feel" for pie crust. The secret is generally all in the handling of the dough. If the dough isn't chilled enough, the crust won't be a great success, and if the dough is overworked in the making, the crust will be anything but flaky.

In almost all recipes, flour is sifted before measuring, particularly in making pie crusts or pastries. It makes no difference how many times the flour is resifted after it is once measured. Sometimes it is necessary to sift two or three times, especially if other ingredients, such as baking powder, soda, salt, etc., are being mixed into the flour.

Pie crusts are often baked blind—i.e., baked before the filling goes in. The best way to do this is to line the crust in the baking tin with aluminum foil and fill the foil with dried beans or rice to hold the crust down during the baking. (Crusts have a tendency to puff up in the middle unless they are weighted.) Bake the crust for 15 minutes at 425°F., then remove the baking weight and the foil, reduce the heat to 400°F. and bake for another 10 minutes. Remove from the oven and cool on a wire rack until ready to use.

Flaky Pie Crust

I like this recipe because it makes what I consider a flaky crust, although flaky is a subjective word: what is flaky to one person isn't necessarily flaky to another.

Makes a 9-inch pie crust

1¼ cups sifted unbleached all-purpose flour
½ teaspoon salt
6 tablespoons chilled butter, divided
3 tablespoons ice water

Sift together the flour and salt. Sift again into a chilled bowl. Using a pastry cutter or two knives, cut in 3 tablespoons of the butter until the mixture resembles fine cornmeal. Add the remaining butter and cut into the mixture until it is the consistency of gravel.

Sprinkle the ice water on the flour mixture, a little at a time, stirring lightly with a fork. When the dough is moistened enough to form small lumps, press together to form a ball. (The dough may be either refrigerated until ready to use or rolled out at once.)

Roll the dough on a lightly floured board until it is 3 inches larger than the pie plate all around. Fit into the pie plate and flute the rim. For an especially thin crust, sprinkle a little superfine granulated sugar over the dough as you roll it out.

Either bake blind or follow the instructions on the specific recipe.

Plain Pie Crust

I suppose I would call this my basic pie crust recipe, since it produces successful results even when used by a beginner. It is one that I often use for a two-crust pie because this recipe makes enough for a double crust. If I am only making one pie, and it does not call for a top crust, I roll out the second half of the dough, line a pie tin with it, and freeze it for another time. Always cover dough that is to be frozen with plastic wrap to keep moisture out.

Makes 2 single large pie shells, or 1 large 2-crust pie

2½ cups sifted pastry flour* or all-purpose flour
1 level teaspoon salt
6 level tablespoons vegetable shortening
6 level tablespoons butter
3 to 6 tablespoons ice water

Sift together the flour and salt. Work into it the shortening and butter, using a pastry cutter, two knives, or your fingertips—if they are cold and you have a light touch. When the mixture is the consistency of cornmeal, add the ice water, a little at a time (do not exceed 6 tablespoons). Divide the dough into two flat balls, wrap each in waxed paper, and refrigerate for 15 to 20 minutes before using.

Remove the dough from the refrigerator and place one ball of pastry on a floured pastry board; press into a flat cake, using a rolling pin, then roll out to ⅛-inch thickness, keeping the dough in a circular form and using light pressure. Placing the rolling pin crosswise at the top of the circle of dough, lift the pastry by holding it against the rolling pin.

* A lighter flour that is to pies what cake flour is to cakes.

Then roll the pin toward you, rolling the pastry up onto the pin as you go. Unroll onto the pie plate, completely covering it, and gently press the dough to conform to the shape of the dish.

Trim off any excess pastry with floured scissors, leaving about a ½-inch overhang, which should be rolled under to form a double edge; crimp with your fingers as you roll the dough under itself. Place the shell back into the refrigerator while you prepare the second pie shell.

Bake blind or follow the instructions on the specific recipe.

Pâté Brisée Dough

This tart dough is foolproof if the directions are followed to the letter. My friend Gino Cofacci, the best pastry chef I know, developed the recipe and I have used it over and over with excellent results. This is often baked before the filling goes in (called baking blind, see page 413).

Makes an 8- to 10-inch crust

1⅔ cups (7 ounces) sifted unbleached all-purpose flour
¼ pound very cold butter, cut in pieces
1 egg yolk
4 tablespoons water
1 tablespoon vegetable oil
Pinch salt

Measure the flour and put it in a mixer bowl. With the machine on low speed, add the butter bit by bit to the flour. Mix to a gravel-like consistency. Beat together the egg yolk, water, oil, and salt; add gradually to the flour mixture. Continue mixing until the dough comes away from the sides of the bowl.

Remove the dough and work briefly with the hands until smooth, keeping the dough in a ball. Wrap in waxed paper and refrigerate for 30 to 45 minutes before rolling out.

Bake blind or follow the recipe directions for uncooked fillings.

Old-Fashioned Mincemeat

Until I was 21 years old, I didn't know you could have Christmas without mincemeat pies. My grandmother never did find out. I grew up with her pies and this is the mincemeat recipe she used; it's one of the best that I have come across. She baked her pies with a double crust, and I think that is a "must" with mincemeat because it cuts the heaviness of the filling. I use the Plain Pie Crust recipe (page 414) when making the pie because it has just the right amount of flakiness for the filling.

Many cooks now use commercially prepared mincemeats. Some of these are quite good, and need only an additional bit of apple, fruit juice, grated rind, almonds, and brandy to doctor them up.

Makes about 10 pints

2 pounds chopped beef
1 pound finely chopped suet
4 pounds tart apples, peeled, cored, and finely chopped
*1 cup chopped citron**
1 teaspoon salt
1 teaspoon grated nutmeg
1 teaspoon ground cloves
1½ teaspoons powdered mace
1½ pounds sugar
1½ pounds currants
2 pounds seedless raisins
1 quart apple cider
Juice of 2 oranges
Juice of 1 lemon
Grated rind of 1 orange
½ cup chopped candied orange peel
½ cup chopped candied lemon peel
1 cup candied cherries
1 pound chopped blanched almonds
1 cup brandy

Simmer the beef in a little water until tender. Cool and combine with the suet and apples in a large bowl. Add the citron to the beef, suet, and apple mixture.

Mix well and transfer to a large kettle. Add the salt, nutmeg, cloves, mace, sugar, currants, raisins, and cider. Simmer for 1 hour, stirring often. Add the orange and lemon juice and the grated orange rind.

Remove from the stove; add the candied orange and lemon peel, almonds, candied cherries, and brandy. Fill about 10 pint jars ½ inch from the top with the mincemeat, adjust lids, and process in a pressure cooker for 25 minutes at 10 pounds pressure. Store until ready to use, either on the shelf or in the freezer. It will keep for 2 or 3 years.

* Use a knife that has been dipped in boiling water.

All-American Apple Pie

Although the apple pie originated in England, it has become the traditional American dessert. The expression "as American as apple pie" has validity, for this homey dessert is a favorite across the country. There are undoubtedly almost as many recipes for apple pie as there are good cooks making it.

Serves 8

1 recipe Plain Pie Crust (see page 414)
2½ pounds tart cooking apples
1 cup plus 2 tablespoons sugar, divided
¼ cup unbleached all-purpose flour
1½ teaspoons ground cinnamon
½ teaspoon ground nutmeg
1 tablespoon unsalted butter
1 tablespoon lightly beaten egg white

Preheat the oven to 425°F.

Roll out half the pastry on a lightly floured board and fit it into a 9-inch pie plate.

Peel, quarter, and core the apples. Cut the quarters into thick wedges. Mix 1 cup of the sugar, the flour, cinnamon, and nutmeg in a medium-size bowl; add the apples and toss to coat them all over. Spoon them into the bottom crust, mounding in the center, and dot the top of the apples with butter.

Roll out the top crust on a lightly floured board. Moisten the edge of the bottom crust with cold water and place the top crust over the apples. Trim the overhang of both crusts even to ½ inch. Turn the excess pastry at the rim and seal the edges by crimping them. Cut two or three steam vents in the top crust, using the tip of a small knife. Lightly brush the pastry with the egg white and sprinkle the remaining 2 tablespoons of sugar evenly over the top.

Bake the pie for 35 to 40 minutes, or until the top is golden brown and the apples are tender when pierced with a knife through a vent. Place the pie on a rack to cool before serving.

Pumpkin-Macadamia Pie with Apricot Glaze

Don't buy a canned mix that has already been seasoned with pie spices. Pumpkin is labeled as pre-spiced or plain. If you are going to use pre-spiced canned pumpkin, omit the salt, ginger, and nutmeg that are called for in this recipe and proceed from there, but don't expect the finished pie to taste the same as this recipe, because it won't. If you chill this in the refrigerator after glazing, the glaze will "sweat," or weep, and run. It won't hurt the taste, but it does nothing for the appearance.

Serves 8

2 cups unseasoned canned pumpkin
¼ cup sugar
½ teaspoon salt
½ teaspoon ginger
½ teaspoon nutmeg
3 eggs
½ cup whole milk
¼ cup plus 2 tablespoons bourbon, divided
1¼ cups plus 1 tablespoon whipping cream, divided
10-inch pastry shell, unbaked (see Plain Pie Crust, page 414)
2 tablespoons Apricot Glaze (recipe follows)
⅔ cup firmly packed brown sugar
3 tablespoons melted butter
⅛ teaspoon salt
1 cup chopped macadamia nuts plus extra nuts for garnish

Preheat the oven to 425°F.

Combine the pumpkin, sugar, ½ teaspoon salt, ginger, nutmeg, eggs, milk, ¼ cup of the bourbon, and ¼ cup of the whipping cream in a large mixing bowl. Mix until well blended.

Paint the pastry shell with the apricot glaze. Pour in the pumpkin mixture and bake for 15 minutes. Reduce the heat to 350°F. and bake for 30 to 40 minutes longer, until the filling has set. Cool to lukewarm.

Combine the brown sugar, butter, 1 tablespoon of the whipping cream, ⅛ teaspoon salt, and the nuts in a saucepan; heat to a spreading consistency.

Spread this mixture evenly on top of the pumpkin filling and decorate with macadamia nuts. Broil 3 inches from a low flame until the top begins to bubble—about 3 minutes with a gas broiler, 5 minutes with an electric one. Watch carefully to avoid scorching. Whip the remaining 1 cup of cream, fold in the 2 tablespoons of bourbon, and serve with the pie at room temperature.

Note: If you care about appearances, do not chill in refrigerator after glazing the pie shell.

Apricot Glaze

11-ounce jar apricot preserves
4 tablespoons apricot brandy

To make the glaze, loosen the top of the preserves jar and place in a pan of hot water over low heat until the preserves have liquefied. Combine the preserves and the brandy in a blender or food processor. (Store excess in the refrigerator.)

Pumpkin Chiffon Pie

For best taste and texture, this should be eaten the same day it is made.

Serves 8

1 recipe Flaky Pie Crust, baked (see page 413)
1 envelope (1 tablespoon) unflavored gelatin
¼ cup cold water
3 eggs, separated
1 cup sugar, divided
1¼ cups canned unseasoned pumpkin
½ cup whole milk
¼ teaspoon salt
½ teaspoon cinnamon
½ teaspoon nutmeg

Soak the gelatin in the cold water. Beat the egg yolks slightly and add ½ cup of the sugar, the pumpkin, milk, salt, cinnamon, and nutmeg.

Cook, stirring, in the top of a double boiler over hot water until thickened. Add the gelatin mixture and stir until dissolved. Chill. Whip the egg whites with a pinch of salt until stiff. When the pumpkin mixture begins to set, stir in the remaining ½ cup of sugar and fold in the egg whites. Heap in the pie shell and chill for several hours before serving.

Pear Upside-Down Tart

I recommend a 10-inch cast-iron skillet in making this good old-fashioned dessert. The pastry is not rolled out or fluted but is more a biscuit base, like the shortcake in strawberry shortcake.

Serves 6

¾ cup unbleached all-purpose flour
Salt
7 tablespoons cold butter, cut into small pieces
¼ cup cold water
7 slightly underripe eating pears, cut in half, cored, and peeled
2½ cups (approx.) red wine, divided
½ cup sugar
½ teaspoon powdered cinnamon

Put the flour in a large mixing bowl, sprinkle with salt, add the butter, and mix with a pastry cutter. Gather the flour and the butter pieces back to the center of the bowl and work for no more than a minute or so. Add the water, a little at a time, stirring with a fork and mashing as little as possible to begin bringing the mass together. Finish rapidly, working with the fingertips to form the dough into a ball. Wrap in plastic and refrigerate for at least 2 hours.

Dust a board with flour, flatten the dough with your hand, and give it a few raps with a rolling pin to flatten. Turn it over. It may be cut to the exact inside dimension of the pan or can be rolled out slightly larger, the edges rolled up and crimped either with your thumb or with fork tines.

Pour about 1¼ cups of red wine into a 10-inch frying pan. Arrange the pear halves in the pan, cored surface facing up, the wide end of each pressed against the side of the pan and the elongated tips pointing in toward the center of the pan so that the "empty" areas form a fairly symmetrical star shape. Split the remaining pear halves and use them to fill the empty spaces, slender tips pointing out, wide ends meeting in the center, so that the bottom of the pan has a complete layer of pears in a neat geometric pattern.

Sprinkle the sugar and cinnamon on top and add enough of the remaining red wine to cover. Bring to a boil and cook, covered, at barely a simmer for 1 hour, or until the pears are tender. Holding a lid firmly against the pears' surface to prevent displacing them, drain all the liquid into a saucepan. Reduce this cooking liquid over high heat until only about ½ cup remains; the liquid will be the consistency of syrup. Dribble the syrup over the pears' surface.

Preheat the oven to 375°F.

Lay the pie crust upside down over the pears and bake for about 40 minutes, or until the pastry is golden and crisp.

Unmold carefully by placing a platter upside down over the pan. Turn both platter and pan in one swift movement and ease the tart into the middle of the platter. If the pears spread slightly in the unmolding, push them gently into place by pressing all around the outside with a spatula.

Note: The tart may be served hot, at room temperature, or cold but should not be unmolded until just before serving to prevent the cooking juices from soaking the pastry.

Poached Pear Tart

Serves 8

9-inch baked tart shell (see Pâte Brisée recipe, page 415)

6 ounces semisweet chocolate
2 tablespoons butter
2 cups water
1 cup sugar
1 tablespoon vanilla extract
4 to 6 fresh pears, peeled, halved, and cored
16 ounces apricot preserves
2 tablespoons cognac
⅔ cup macadamia nut pieces

Melt the chocolate in the top of a double boiler over hot water and stir in the butter. Brush the inside of the tart shell with the chocolate mixture and let it cool for 30 minutes. Boil the water with the sugar, add the vanilla, and continue to boil for 5 minutes longer. Reduce the heat and add the pears. Poach the pears in the syrup at a simmer for about 15 minutes. Test for doneness with a toothpick; when it slips in easily, the pear is poached. Drain the pears.

Melt the apricot preserves and add the cognac. Simmer for 4 minutes, then strain through a sieve. Arrange the pears in the bottom of the tart shell and brush them with the apricot mixture. Top with macadamia nuts. Cool for 2 hours at room temperature before serving.

Green Tomato Pie

This is definitely a dessert pie, not a savory, and a great way to use all those green tomatoes in the garden. It's not unlike an apple pie; once you taste it, you will be looking for green tomatoes. Red ones don't work because they're not firm enough.

Serves 8

1 recipe Plain Pie Crust (see page 414)
4 cups peeled and thinly sliced green tomatoes
1½ cups sugar
¼ teaspoon salt
3 tablespoons unbleached all-purpose flour
2 tablespoons minute tapioca
Grated rind of 1 lemon
⅓ cup fresh lemon juice
2 tablespoons melted butter

Preheat the oven to 425°F.

Arrange the tomatoes in a pastry-lined pie plate. Combine the sugar, salt, flour, and tapioca, and cover the tomatoes with the mixture. Sprinkle the lemon rind over the top and add the lemon juice and butter. Add the top crust or make a top of lattice pastry strips.

Bake for 15 minutes, then reduce the heat to 350°F. and bake for 30 minutes longer. When the pie starts to bubble, turn down the oven to 325°F. to prevent dripping.

Serve with whipped cream or ice cream, if desired.

Note: This pie should sit for several hours before being cut in order to give the filling time to set. It can even be refrigerated as soon as it cools down and chilled overnight—just be sure to let it stand at room temperature for a good 20 minutes before serving.

Filbert Pie

This is a Pacific Northwest version of Georgia's pecan pie. It's every bit as rich but has a different taste because filberts are used instead of pecans.

Serves 8

1 recipe Plain Pie Crust (see page 414), unbaked
5 eggs, beaten
1¼ cups sugar
½ cup dark corn syrup
½ cup light corn syrup
2 tablespoons melted butter
1 cup coarsely ground, roasted filberts

Preheat the oven to 400°F.

Combine the eggs and sugar and whisk to mix thoroughly. Continue whisking while adding the corn syrups and butter. Add the filberts and mix well.

Pour into the pie shell and bake for 10 minutes, then lower the heat to 300°F. and continue to bake for 1 hour, or until the custard is firm to the touch. Remove from the oven and place on a wire rack to cool.

Serve with a dollop of sweetened whipped cream or some vanilla ice cream.

SAUCES

Soufflé Sauce

Makes 1 cup

1 egg
3 egg yolks
5 tablespoons sugar
½ cup Grand Marnier (or any suitable liqueur)
Pinch salt

Combine all the ingredients in a heatproof bowl set in a pan of hot water over low heat. Beat with a rotary whisk until the sauce thickens to the desired consistency. Serve at once.

Rich Vanilla Sauce

Good on any pudding or soufflé.

Makes 1½ cups

3 egg yolks
⅓ cup sugar
1¼ cups whole milk, heated
2 teaspoons vanilla extract
1 tablespoon rum (optional)
1 tablespoon softened butter (optional)

Beat the egg yolks in a heavy saucepan until thick and sticky (about 1 minute). Gradually stir in the sugar, then beat in the hot milk by droplets. Stir over moderately low heat with a wooden spoon until the sauce thickens enough to coat the spoon. Do not let the sauce approach a simmer or the egg yolks will curdle. Remove from the heat and stir in the vanilla, then the rum and butter, if desired. Serve warm or cool.

Note: I do not suggest the "optional rum and butter" if the sauce is to be served with a liqueur-flavored soufflé.

Lemon and Vanilla Sauce

Adds a nice touch to rice pudding.

Makes about 2 cups

1 cup sugar
2 tablespoons cornstarch
2 cups boiling water
1/4 pound butter
Juice and grated rind of 1 lemon
1 teaspoon vanilla extract

In a heavy saucepan, mix together the sugar and cornstarch. Add the boiling water gradually, stirring constantly. Cook for 5 minutes. Remove from the heat, add the butter, and stir until melted. Add the lemon juice and rind and the vanilla and mix thoroughly.

Lemon Sauce

This tart sauce is good as a dessert by itself or on bread puddings, sliced pound cake, or ice cream.

Makes about 3 cups

3/4 cup sugar
3 tablespoons sifted unbleached all-purpose flour
3 egg yolks
3/4 cup cold water
2 tablespoons butter
3/4 cup lemon juice
Grated rind of 1 lemon
1 teaspoon grated orange rind
1 teaspoon grated lime rind

Mix the sugar and flour in the top of a double boiler over hot water. Add the egg yolks. Mix in the cold water and stir for 10 minutes. Add the butter, bit by bit. Add the lemon juice and grated rinds and mix well. Serve hot or cold.

Lemon-Whipped Cream Sauce

This is marvelous over strawberries.

Makes about 3½ cups

1 cup sugar
½ cup lemon juice
2 teaspoons grated lemon peel
3 eggs
1 cup (½ pint) whipping cream

Put sugar, lemon juice, and lemon peel in the top of a double boiler and place over direct heat. Cook, stirring, until blended, then stir eggs into the hot sugar mixture in the top of the double boiler. Place over simmering water and cook, stirring, until thickened. Chill in the refrigerator.

Whip the cream until almost stiff and fold into the chilled lemon custard. Cover and chill until ready to use.

Strawberry-Raspberry Sauce

Good on ice cream, soufflés, plain cake, or fresh fruit.

Makes 2 cups

1 pint (2 cups) strawberries, washed and hulled
10-ounce package frozen raspberries, thawed and drained
1 tablespoon kirsch

Reserve some strawberries for a garnish. Combine the remaining strawberries and the raspberries and kirsch in a blender or processor and puree. Slice the reserved strawberries and gently stir into the sauce.

Bitter Chocolate Sauce

Good on everything.

Makes 1 cup

3 ounces unsweetened chocolate
4 tablespoons butter
1 tablespoon dark rum
1 tablespoon strong freshly brewed coffee
1 cup unsifted confectioners' sugar
1 scant cup evaporated milk
½ teaspoon vanilla extract

Melt the chocolate and butter with the rum and coffee in the top of a double boiler over hot water. Remove from the heat and stir in the sugar alternately with the evaporated milk. Replace the double boiler on the heat and cook, stirring constantly, until the mixture is thick, smooth, and creamy. Remove from the heat and stir in the vanilla.

Apricot Sauce

Good over bread or rice puddings and Grand Marnier soufflés.

Makes about 2 cups

1 cup apricot jam
½ cup water
½ cup kirsch

Combine all the ingredients in a small saucepan and heat to the boiling point. Stir to mix thoroughly and remove from the heat after the mixture has boiled for 1 or 2 minutes. May be used hot or at room temperature.

Note: If refrigerated, warm before using or the mixture will be too stiff to pour.

Brandy Sauce

Makes about 2 cups

¼ pound softened butter
1⅓ cups sifted confectioners' sugar
Pinch salt
1 egg, separated
2 tablespoons cognac
½ cup heavy cream

Blend the butter with the sugar, adding the sugar a little at a time, until smooth. Add the salt and egg yolk and beat well. Cook over hot but not boiling water, stirring constantly, until the mixture is light and fluffy. This takes 8 or 9 minutes. Remove from the heat and blend in the cognac. Let the mixture come to room temperature; then chill. When chilled, beat the egg white to soft peaks and fold in. Whip the cream and fold in just before serving.

Hard Sauce

This is not the usual hard sauce, in that it should not be chilled but should stay at room temperature. It's wonderful on mincemeat pies, apple pies, even vanilla ice cream.

Makes about 2½ cups

¼ pound butter
1¼ cups confectioners' sugar
¼ cup brandy

Cream the butter and gradually add the sugar. Add the brandy when the butter and sugar are well creamed, and continue beating until the mixture is very light and fluffy. Spread over room-temperature or warm (not chilled) pies just before serving.

Index

Aioli Sauce, 330
All-American Apple Pie, 417
Almond and Rice Pudding, 399
Almond Macaroons, 371
Anchovies
  Anchovy Diamonds, 356
  Anchovy Fingers, 355
  Anchovy Hollandaise, 314
  Spaghetti with Tuna and Anchovy Sauce, 204
Appetizers
  Artichoke Balls, 224
  Baked Oysters, 165
  Chicken Liver–Walnut Pâté, 86
  Clam Fritters, 151
  Cocktail Puff Pastries, 355–356
  Crab Pâté, 158
  Crab Puffs, 159
  Crustless Crab Quiche, 162
  Eggs Stuffed with Sorrel, 183
  Gingered Scallops, 163
  Green Pepper and Tortilla Cheese Dip, 188
  Hot Olive-Cheese Appetizers, 189
  Seviche, 129
  Stuffed Mushrooms, 250
  Terrine of Pork and Veal, 73
Apples
  All-American Apple Pie, 417
  Apple and Bread Pudding with Sabayon Sauce, 397
  Apple-Nut Bread, 346
  Apple-Nut Cake, 408
  Sautéed Apples, 340
Apricots
  Apricot Glaze, 419
  Apricot-Rice Ring, 367
  Apricot Sauce, 366, 427
Artichoke Balls, 224
Asparagus with Wine Sauce, 225
Baked Beets, 228
Baked Chicken with Cabbage, 101
Baked Chocolate Pudding, 396
Baked Corn, 242
Baked Eggs in Cream and Bacon, 182
Baked Eggs with Onions, 184
Baked Halibut, 134
Baked Ham in a Crust, 70
Baked Lasagne with Prosciutto and Mushrooms, 202
Baked Onions, 253
Baked Ox Tongue, 77
Baked Oysters, 165
Baked Tomatoes Stuffed with Mozzarella, 272
Baked Tuna, 132
Baltimore Lobster Stew, 149
Barley soup, *see* Rassolnik (kidney and barley soup), 22
Basic Cobbler, 378
Basic Homemade Bread, 342
Basic Pasta Dough, 197
Basic Roast Turkey, 115
Basic Vinaigrette, 304
Batter Bread, 344
Batter-Fried Green Tomatoes, 273
Beans, 211–216
  Black Bean Soup, 6
  Cold White Bean Salad with Caviar, 213
  Creamed Broad Beans and Bacon, 227
  Dakota Chili, 214
  Lamb, Pork, and Beans, 62
  Lentils with Sausage, 215
  Mexican Bean Soup, 7
  Oregon Baked Lima Beans, 212
  Sautéed Lentils, 216
  Vermont Baked Beans, 211
  White Bean Soup, 5
  See also Green beans, Chick-peas

Béarnaise Sauce, 317
Béchamel Sauce, 310
  variations, 310–313
Beef, 31–44
  Baked Ox Tongue, 77
  Beef and Onions in Beer, 39
  Beef Stroganoff, 40
  Beef Tongue with Ham Mousse and Mayonnaise Collée, 76
  Brisket of Beef, 34
  Calf's Liver in Red Wine Vinegar, 80
  Casserole of Beef, 42
  Chicken-Beef Pie, 110
  cooking methods, 30
  Dakota Chili, 214
  Hunter's Stew, 41
  Marinated Eye of Rib Roast, 32
  Meat Loaf, 43
  New York Steak with Mushrooms, 33
  Oxtail Stew, 78
  Pan-Fried Liver, 79
  Pot Roast of Beef, 35
  Pot Roast with Ginger, 36
  Puchero (Argentine boiled beef), 44
  Rib Roast of Beef, 31
  Short Ribs of Beef, 37
  Short Ribs of Beef with Cornmeal Dumplings, 38
  Stock, 4
Beer Batter Bread, 344
Beets
  Baked Beets, 228
  Baked Beets in Cream, 228
Biscuits, *see* Bread, biscuits, and muffins
Bitter Chocolate Sauce, 427
Black Bean Soup, 6
Blackberry Fool, 380
Blackberry Ice Cream, 394
Blue Cheese Salad Dressing I, 306
Blue Cheese Salad Dressing II, 306
Blueberry Fool, 379
Blueberry Slump, 373
Boiled Turkey with Butter Sauce, 114
Bolognese Sauce, 327
Bordelaise Sauce, 316
Braised Lamb Shanks, 57
Braised Loin of Pork, 66
Bran Muffins, 351
Bran Waffles, 363
Brandy Sauce, 428
Bread, biscuits, and muffins, 341–363
  Apple-Nut Bread, 346
  Basic Homemade Bread, 342
  Batter Bread, 344
  Beer Batter Bread, 344
  Bran Muffins, 351
  Brioche Loaf, 357
  Chive Drop Biscuits, 350
  Cocktail Puff Pastries, 355
  Corn Batter Cakes, 348
  Cornmeal Dumplings, 38
  Esther's Spoon Bread, 220
  Fast Puff Paste, 354
  Homemade Bread Crumbs, 335
  Hot Cinnamon Bread, 345
  Johnny Cakes, 349
  Milk Toast with Parmesan, 359
  pancakes and waffles, *see* Pancakes and Waffles
  Pecan Popovers with Lemon-Honey Butter, 352
  Pita Bread, 358
  Popovers, 352
  R.N. Fry Bread, 343
  Robert Pamplin Biscuits, 350
  Spice Bread, 346
  Spoon Bread Soufflé, 220
  Sunday Supper Corn Bread with Sausage, 222
  Texas Skillet Corn Bread, 348
  Yorkshire Pudding, 353
  Zucchini Bread, 347
Bread Pudding, 398
Bread and Squash Soup, 9
Brioche Loaf, 357
Brisket of Beef, 34
Brittany Chowder, 28
Broccoli
  Chicken and Broccoli, 95
  Puree of Broccoli, 229
Broiled Leg of Lamb with Orange Butter, 55
Broiled Marinated Leg of Lamb, 56
Broiled Scrod, 134
Broiled Shrimp, 154
Broiled Zucchini with Tomato and Cheese, 277
Broths, *see* Stocks and broths
Brunswick Stew, 111
Brussels Sprouts Gratin, 229

Butter, clarifying, 105, 317
Buttermilk Pancakes, 361
Butters
  Cumberland Rum Butter, 403
  Fennel Butter, 133
  Herbed Butter, 133
  Herbed Butter Sauce, 319
  Lemon Butter, 133
  Tarragon Butter, 133
  White Butter Sauce, 324

Cabbage
  Cabbage Casserole with Cheese, 233
  Cabbage Loaf, 234
  Creamed Cabbage, 231
  Hot Slaw with Seafood, 282
  Italian Cabbage Salad, 281
  Red Cabbage, 230
  Red Cabbage Salad, 283
  Sautéed Cabbage, 231
  Savoy Cabbage, 232
  Slaw-Stuffed Cabbage, 280
  Wilted Cabbage Salad, 284
Cakes, 405–412
  Apple-Nut Cake, 408
  Filbert Torte with Mocha Frosting, 411
  German Cheesecake, 410
  Great Cheesecake, 409
  Old-Fashioned Date-Nut Cake, 407
  Pineapple Upside-Down Cake, 406
  Pound Cake, 405
  Sourdough Chocolate Cake, 412
Calf's Liver in Red Wine Vinegar, 80
Calf's Liver with Cream, 80
Calvados, Chicken with, 90
"Canadian Rule" for cooking fish, 127, 136
Cannelloni, 205
Caper Hollandaise, 314
Carla's Tamale Pie, 173
Carrots, 235–237
  Carrot Pudding, 235
  Carrots and Leeks Vichy, 237
  Carrots in Cream Sauce, 237
  Carrots in Orange Marmalade, 235
  Carrots Vichy, 236
Casseroles
  Cabbage Casserole with Cheese, 233
  Carla's Tamale Pie, 173
  Casserole of Beef, 42
  Casserole of Hard-Cooked Eggs in Creamed Sorrel, 185
  Casserole of Turnips and Mushrooms, 274
  Chicken and Broccoli, 95
  Chicken Casserole, 107
  Lamb, Pork, and Beans, 62
  Lamb Casserole, 63
  Lamb Stew, 60
  Lamb with Sour Cream and Dill, 59
  Mushroom Casserole, 251
  Onion Casserole, 254
  Rice Casserole, 207
  Seafood Casserole, 146
  Smoked Cod Casserole, 145
  Spinach Casserole, 268
  Veal Casserole, 53
Cauliflower Mousse with Mornay Sauce, 239
Cauliflower with Cream Sauce and Buttered Crumbs, 238
Caviar, Cold White Bean Salad with, 213
Celery Root Ring with Mushroom Sauce, 240
Celery Salad with Mustard Dressing, 285
Celery Seed Dressing, 305
Chard Timbales, 241
Cheddar Cheese Pudding with Mushroom Sauce, 192
Cheese and cheese dishes, 188–195
  Blue Cheese Salad Dressing I, 306
  Blue Cheese Salad Dressing II, 306
  Cheddar Cheese Pudding with Mushroom Sauce, 192
  Cheese and Olive Salad, 292
  Cheese Custard for Chicken Casserole, 107
  Cheese Fingers, 355
  Cheese Sauce, 312
  Cheese-Scrambled Brunch Eggs, 179
  Cheese Soufflé, 190
  Easter Cheese, 193
  Fried Parmesan Cakes, 195
  Green Pepper and Tortilla Cheese Dip, 188
  Hot Olive-Cheese Appetizers, 189
  Macaroni and Cheese, 194
  Mornay Sauce, 312
  Orange, Cheese, and Onion Salad, 292

Cheese and cheese dishes (*Cont.*)
Quiche Lorraine, 191
Soufflé of Cheese and Chicken, 189
Welsh Rarebit, 195
Cheesecakes
German Cheesecake, 410
Great Cheesecake, 409
Cherries, Cumberland Sauce with, 319
Chick-Peas (Garbanzo Beans)
Hot Chick-Pea Salad, 290
Mexican Bean Soup, 7
Puree of Chick-Peas, 242
Chicken, 83–113
Baked Chicken with Cabbage, 101
Brunswick Stew, 111
Chicken and Broccoli, 95
Chicken and Mushrooms in Sour Cream, 90
Chicken Baked in Madeira, 100
Chicken-Beef Pie, 110
Chicken Breasts with Cornmeal Mush, 94
Chicken Breasts with Grapes and Wine, 92
Chicken Breasts with Tomato Sauce, 93
Chicken Casserole, 107
Chicken Crepes, 108
Chicken Curry I, 105
Chicken Curry II, 106
Chicken in Consommé, 103
Chicken in Mushroom and Truffle Sauce, 91
Chicken Liver Custard, 87
Chicken Liver Fingers, 356
Chicken Liver Terrine, 85
Chicken Liver-Walnut Pâté, 86
Chicken Paprika with Sour Cream, 97
Chicken Pot Pie, 109
Chicken Stew with Vinegar, 113
Chicken Stock, 3
Chicken with Calvados, 90
Chicken with Fresh Noodles, 96
Cinnamon Fried Chicken, 89
Cold Boiled Chicken, 102
cooking methods, 83–84
freezing and thawing, 83
Mexican Chicken Stew, 112
Plain Fried Chicken, 88
Roast Chicken, 98
Roast Chicken with Cognac Cream Sauce, 99
Sautéed Chicken, 104
Chilies
Chili Relleno Omelet, 180
Corn Chili Bread, 221
Dakota Chili, 214
Chilled Cucumber Soup, 17
Chive Drop Biscuits, 350
Chocolate
Baked Chocolate Pudding, 396
Bitter Chocolate Sauce, 427
Chocolate Mousse, 368
Chocolate Sauce, 381, 427
Chocolate Soufflé, 390
Coffee Ice Cream with Grated Chocolate, 394
Glazed Pineapple with Chocolate Sauce, 381
Sourdough Chocolate Cake, 412
Choron Sauce, 317
Chowders
Brittany Chowder, 28
Clam Chowder-New England Style, 27
Corn Chowder, 26
Chutney Sauce, 338
Cinnamon
Cinnamon Cookies, 370
Cinnamon Fried Chicken, 89
Hot Cinnamon Bread, 345
Cioppino (fish stew), 131
Clams
Clam Chowder-New England Style, 27
Clam Fritters, 151
Clam Loaf, 152
Clam Sauce, 328
Fried Razor Clams, 150
Hot Clam Pie, 152
cooking methods, 128
Scalloped Clams, 150
Cobbler, Basic Fruit, 378
Cocktail Puff Pastries, 355–356
Codfish
Cod, Potatoes, and Eggs, 142
Codfish Balls, 142
Codfish Soufflé, 144
Codfish Stew, 141
Smoked Cod Casserole, 145

Coffee Ice Cream with Grated Chocolate, 394
Cognac Cream Sauce with Roast Chicken, 99
Cold Boiled Chicken, 102
Cold Dilled Peas, 291
Cold Lemon-Lime Soufflé, 389
Cold Poached Salmon, 138
Cold Tomato Sauce, 326
Cold White Bean Salad with Caviar, 213
Coleslaw
  Dressing for, 280
  Hot Slaw with Seafood, 282
  Slaw-Stuffed Cabbage, 280
  See also Cabbage
Condiments and seasonings
  Chutney Sauce, 338
  condiments to serve with curries, 337
  Duxelles, 338
  Four Spices, 336
  Frozen Cranberry Mold, 339
  Homemade Bread Crumbs, 335
  Homemade Curry Powder, 336
  Onion Marmalade, 339
  Roasted Pepper Salad, 296
  Sautéed Apples, 340
  Vanilla Sugar, 340
Consommé, 2
  Chicken in Consommé, 103
Cookies
  Almond Macaroons, 371
  Cinnamon Cookies, 370
  Macademia Nut Tuiles, 371
Corn
  Baked Corn, 242
  Carla's Tamale Pie, 173
  Corn Batter Cakes, 348
  Corn Chili Bread, 221
  Corn Chowder, 26
  Corn Pudding, 243
Cornmeal dishes, 217–222
  Carla's Tamale Pie, 173
  Chicken Breasts with Cornmeal Mush, 94
  Corn Chili Bread, 221
  Cornmeal Dumplings, 38
  Cornmeal with Parmesan Cheese, 217
  Esther's Spoon Bread, 220
  Grits Parmesan, 218
  Johnny Cakes, 349
  Polenta, 218
  Polenta with Pine Nuts and Raisins, 219
  Spoon Bread Soufflé, 220
  Sunday Supper Corn Bread with Sausage, 222
  Texas Skillet Corn Bread, 348
Cotechino Sausage, 74
Court Bouillon for Poached Fish and Shellfish, 136
Court Bouillon with Red Wine, 138
Court Bouillon with White Wine, 137
Crab meat
  cooking methods, 128
  Crab and Mushroom Sandwich, 160
  Crab Pâté, 158
  Crab Puffs, 159
  Crustless Crab Quiche, 162
  Deviled Crab, 161
  Salmon-Crab Loaf, 148
  Seafood Casserole, 146
Cranberry Mold, Frozen, 339
Cream of Pumpkin Soup, 13
Cream of Rutabaga and Watercress Soup, 11
Cream of Sorrel Soup, 14
Cream of Turtle Soup, 23
Creamed Broad Beans and Bacon, 227
Creamed Cabbage, 231
Creamed Noodles with Ham and Vegetables, 201
Creams and custards, 384–387
  Cheese Custard for Chicken Casserole, 107
  Chicken Liver Custard, 87
  Crême Brulée, 384
  Custard Cream, 386
  Fresh Peach Bavarian Cream, 387
  Lemon Bay Custard, 385
  Lemon Curd, 385
Crème Brulée, 384
Crème Fraîche, 334
Crepes
  Chicken Crepes, 108
  Crepes with Apricots, 365
Crown Roast of Pork with Sausage-Apple Stuffing, 67
Crustless Crab Quiche, 162

Crusty Potatoes with Parmesan Cheese, 263
Cucumbers
  Chilled Cucumber Soup, 17
  Cucumber, Tomato, and Radish Salad, 286
  Cucumber Sauce, 324
  Cucumbers in Cream, 244
  Endive, Mushroom, and Cucumber Salad, 290
  Fried Cucumbers, 244
  Sour Cream–Dill Sauce with Cucumbers, 334
Cumberland Rum Butter, Plum Pudding with, 402
Cumberland Sauce with Cherries, 319
Currant Jelly Sauce, 316
Curried dishes
  Chicken Curry I, 105
  Chicken Curry II, 106
  condiments to serve with, 337
  Curried Eggs in Brown Rice, 184
  Curried Rice Salad, 295
  Curried Shrimp Soufflé, 156
  Curry Sauce, 312
  Homemade Curry Powder, 336
Custards
  Cheese Custard for Chicken Casserole, 107
  Chicken Liver Custard, 87
  Custard Cream, 386
  Eggplant Custard I, 245
  Eggplant Custard II, 246
  Hubbard Squash Custard, 270
  Lemon Bay Custard, 385
  Zucchini Custard, 278

Dakota Chili, 214
Dauphinoise Potatoes, 265
Desserts, 365–428
  Apricot-Rice Ring, 367
  cakes, *see* Cakes
  Chocolate Mousse, 368
  cookies, *see* Cookies
  creams and custards, *see* Creams and custards
  Crepes with Apricots, 365
  fruit, *see* Fruit desserts
  Ice cream, *see* Ice cream
  Pies and tarts, *see* Pies and tarts
  puddings, *see* Puddings
  Sabayon Meringue, 369
  sauces, 424–428
    Apricot Sauce, 427
    Bitter Chocolate Sauce, 427
    Brandy Sauce, 428
    Chocolate Sauce, 381, 427
    Cumberland Rum Butter, 402
    Hard Sauce, 428
    Lemon and Vanilla Sauce, 425
    Lemon Sauce, 425
    Lemon-Whipped Cream Sauce, 426
    Rich Vanilla Sauce, 424
    Sabayon Sauce, 397
    Soufflé Sauce, 424
    Strawberry-Raspberry Sauce, 426
    Vanilla Sauce, 401
  soufflés, 388–392
    Chocolate Soufflé, 390
    Cold Lemon-Lime Soufflé, 389
    Hot Grand Marnier Soufflé, 391
    Strawberry Soufflé, 392
Deviled Crab, 161
Dumplings
  Cornmeal Dumplings, 38
  Onion Dumpling, 255
Duxelles, 338

Easter Cheese, 193
Easy Tomato Sauce, 326
Egg-Lemon Sauce, 65
Egg Pasta, Roman Style, 198
Egg Soup, 20
Eggplant
  Eggplant Custard I, 245
  Eggplant Custard II, 246
  Eggplant Soup, 10
  Pizza with Eggplant Crust, 174
Eggs and egg dishes, 175–187
  Baked Eggs in Cream and Bacon, 182
  Baked Eggs with Onions, 184
  Casserole of Hard-Cooked Eggs in Creamed Sorrel, 185
  Cheese-Scrambled Brunch Eggs, 179
  Cheese Soufflé, 190
  Chili Relleno Omelet, 180
  Cod, Potatoes, and Eggs, 142
  Curried Eggs in Brown Rice, 184
  Egg Sauce, 322
  Egg Vinaigrette, 305
  Eggs in Spinach, 186
  Eggs in Tomatoes, 181

Eggs Scrambled with Cheese and White Wine, 178
Eggs Scrambled with Tomato and Basil, 177
Eggs Stuffed with Sorrel, 183
Eggs Surprise, 175
Hard-Cooked Eggs, 183
Hard-Cooked Eggs with Potatoes, 187
omelets
Chili Relleno Omelet, 180
directions for making, 180
Quiche Lorraine, 191
Romaine Salad with Hard-Cooked Egg Dressing, 301
Spanish Eggs, 178
Tabasco Eggs, 182
Turnip and Egg Gratin, 275
Endive
Endive, Mushroom, and Cucumber Salad, 290
Puree of Mushrooms with Braised Endive, 252
Esther's Spoon Bread, 220

Fast Puff Paste, 354
Fennel
Fennel Butter, 133
Fennel Salad, 287
Lettuce, Orange, and Fennel Salad, 288
Fettuccini Alfredo Hotel Hassler, 203
Filbert Pie, 423
Filbert Torte with Mocha Frosting, 411
Fillet of Sole in Herbed Butter, 133
Fish and shellfish, 127–170
Baked Halibut, 134
Baked Oysters, 165
Baked Tuna, 132
Baltimore Lobster Stew, 149
Brittany Chowder, 28
Broiled Scrod, 134
Broiled Shrimp, 154
Cioppino (fish stew), 131
Clam Chowder—New England Style, 27
Clam Fritters, 151
Clam Loaf, 152
Clam Sauce, 328
Cod, Potatoes, and Eggs, 142
Codfish Balls, 142
Codfish Soufflé, 144
Codfish Stew, 141
Cold Poached Salmon, 138
cooking methods, 127, 136
"Canadian Rule," 127, 136
for crayfish, 137
for frozen lobster, 137
Court Bouillon for Poached Fish and Shellfish, 136
Court Bouillon with Red Wine, 138
Court Bouillon with White Wine, 137
Crab and Mushroom Sandwich, 160
Crab Pâte, 158
Crab Puffs, 159
Crustless Crab Quiche, 162
Curried Shrimp Soufflé, 156
Deviled Crab, 161
Fillet of Sole in Herbed Butter, 133
Fish Rolls Florentine, 140
French-Fried Butterfly Shrimp, 153
Fried Oysters, 167
Fried Razor Clams, 150
Gingered Scallops, 163
Gingered Shrimp, 154
Greek Fish Soup, 25
Hot Clam Pie, 152
Hot Slaw with Seafood, 282
Marinated Salmon, 130
Mousseline of Scallops and Sole, 147
Oyster Pie, 168
Oyster Soufflé, 169
Oyster Stew, 166
Oysters Casino, 166
Oysters in Cream, 170
Oysters Rockefeller, 164
poaching technique, 136
Salmon-Crab Loaf, 148
Salmon Fillets with Sorrel or Spinach Sauce, 135
Salmon Mousse, 148
Salmon Soup, 24
Sautéed Tuna with Tarragon, 132
sautéeing, 128
Scalloped Clams, 150
Scallops in Heavy Cream, 163
Seafood Casserole, 146
Seviche, 129
Shrimp Steamed in Vermouth, 155
Shrimp-Stuffed Petrale Sole, 139
Skewered Shrimp and Ham, 157
Smoked Cod Casserole, 145
Smoked Salmon Soufflé, 144

Fish and Shellfish (*Cont.*)
  Turban of Salmon and Sole, 143
  Whole Shrimp à la Nage, 158
  See also under name of fish or shellfish
Flaky Pie Crust, 413
Foie Gras Fingers, 356
Four Spices, 336
French Dressing, 304
French-Fried Butterfly Shrimp, 153
French Waffles, 362
Fresh Egg Noodles, 199
Fresh Ham (Leg of Pork), 69
Fresh Peach Bavarian Cream, 387
Fried Cucumbers, 244
Fried Oysters, 167
Fried Parmesan Cakes, 195
Fried Parsley, 256
Fried Razor Clams, 150
Fried Tomatoes in Cream, 273
Frozen Cranberry Mold, 339
Frozen Peas, 259
Frozen Yogurt Cream, 395
Fruit desserts
  Basic Cobbler, 378
  Blackberry Fool, 380
  Blueberry Fool, 379
  Blueberry Slump, 373
  Fresh Peach Bavarian Cream, 387
  Fresh Strawberries and Cream, 383
  Fresh Strawberries with Sour Cream, 383
  Glazed Pineapple with Chocolate Sauce, 381
  Oranges with Caramel and Pecans, 374
  Oranges with Glazed Peel, 374
  Peaches in Red Wine, 376
  Plums in Vodka, 377
  St. Vincent Pears, 375
  Strawberry Shortcake, 382

Garlic
  Aioli Sauce, 330
  Garlic Cream Sauce, 332
  Garlic Mayonnaise, 331
  Garlic Puree, 332
German Cheesecake, 410
Gingered Scallops, 163
Gingered Shrimp, 154
Glazed Pineapple with Chocolate Sauce, 381
Glazed Turnips, 275
Gnocchi
  Gnocchi Bolognese, 172
  Gnocchi Buongustaio, 172
  Gnocchi Piedmontese, 172
  Gnocchi Salvia, 172
  Potato Gnocchi, 171
Goose with Onion and Sage Stuffing, 124
Grapes, Chicken Breasts with Wine and, 92
Grated Sautéed Zucchini, 277
Great Cheesecake, 409
Greek Fish Soup, 25
Green Beans, 226
  Sauté of Green Beans, 226
Green peppers
  Green Pepper and Tortilla Cheese Dip, 188
  Pepper, Tomato, and Onion Stew, 262
  Roasted Pepper Salad, 296
  Sautéed Green Peppers, 261
Green Risotto, 208
Green Sauce, 323
Green Tomato Pie, 422
Greens, salad, 279
Grits Parmesan, 218

Halibut, Baked, 134
Ham
  Baked Ham in a Crust, 70
  Fresh Ham (Leg of Pork), 69
  Ham and Tomato Risotto, 209
  Ham Crescents, 356
  Ham Mousse with Beef Tongue, 76
  Skewered Shrimp and Ham, 157
Hard-Cooked Eggs, 183
Hard-Cooked Eggs with Potatoes, 187
Hard Sauce, 428
Herb Sauce, 312
Herbed Butter Sauce, 319
Herbed Butters, 133, 318
Holiday Pudding, 404
Hollandaise Sauce, 313–314
  Anchovy Hollandaise, 314
  Blender Method, 313
  Caper Hollandaise, 314
  Hollandaise-Mousseline Sauce, 314
  Stove-Top Method, 314

Homemade Bread, 342
Homemade Bread Crumbs, 335
Homemade Curry Powder, 336
Homemade Mayonnaise, 307
Homemade Pasta, 196
Homemade Peanut Butter, 332
Homemade Sour Cream, 333
Hot Chick-Pea Salad, 290
Hot Cinnamon Bread, 345
Hot Clam Pie, 152
Hot Grand Marnier Soufflé, 391
Hot Olive-Cheese Appetizers, 189
Hot Slaw with Seafood, 282
Hubbard Squash Custard, 270
Hunter's Sauce, 318
Hunter's Stew, 41

Ice cream, 393–395
  Blackberry Ice Cream, 394
  Coffee Ice Cream with Grated Chocolate, 394
  Frozen Yogurt Cream, 395
  Six Threes Ice Cream, 393
Irish Stew, 61
Italian Cabbage Salad, 281

Jellied Mayonnaise, 331
Jerusalem Artichoke Soufflé, 247
Jerusalem Artichokes with Cheese Sauce, 248
Johnny Cakes, 349

Lamb, 54–63
  Braised Lamb Shanks, 57
  Broiled Leg of Lamb with Orange Butter, 55
  Broiled Marinated Leg of Lamb, 56
  butterflying leg of lamb, 55
  cooking methods, 30, 54
  Irish Stew, 61
  Lamb, Pork, and Beans, 62
  Lamb Casserole, 63
  Lamb Chops with Shallots, 58
  Lamb Kidneys and Mushrooms, 75
  Lamb Shanks with Garlic, 57
  Lamb Stew, 60
  Lamb with Sour Cream and Dill, 59
  Marinade for Butterflied Leg of Lamb, 320
  marinades, 56, 320
  Rack of Lamb, 54
Lasagne with Prosciutto and Mushrooms, 202
Leeks
  Carrots and Leeks Vichy, 237
  Leek, Carrot, and Cheese Soup, 16
  Leek and Potato Soup, 16
  Leek Salad, 286
  Vichyssoise, 17
Lemons
  Cold Lemon-Lime Soufflé, 389
  Lemon and Meatball Soup, 20
  Lemon and Vanilla Sauce, 425
  Lemon Bay Custard, 385
  Lemon Butter, 133
  Lemon Curd, 385
  Lemon Dressing, 213
  Lemon Sauce, 425
  Lemon-Sweet Parsnips, 257
  Lemon-Whipped Cream Sauce, 426
  Turkey Fillets in Lemon Sauce, 122
Lentils
  Lentil Salad, 294
  Lentils with Sausage, 215
  Sautéed Lentils, 216
Lettuce, 279
  Lettuce, Orange, and Fennel Salad, 288
  Wilted Lettuce Salad, 285
Lima Beans, Oregon Baked, 212
Liver
  Calf's Liver in Red Wine Vinegar, 80
  Calf's Liver with Cream, 80
  Pan-Fried Liver, 79
Lobster
  Baltimore Lobster Stew, 149
  cooking methods, 128, 137
  Court bouillon for poaching lobster, 136

Macadamia Nut Tuiles, 371
Macaroni and Cheese, 194
Madeira Sauce, 315
Marinade for Butterflied Leg of Lamb, 320
Marinated Salmon, 130
Marinated Vegetable Salad, 302
Mayonnaise
  Beef Tongue with Ham Mousse and Mayonnaise Collée, 76
  Garlic Mayonnaise, 331

Mayonnaise (*Cont.*)
  Homemade Mayonnaise, 307
  Jellied Mayonnaise, 331
  Mayonnaise Dijon, 308
  Tart Mayonnaise, 308
Meat Loaf, 43
Meats, 29–81
  cooking methods, 29–30
    high-heat, 30
    low-heat, 30
  roasting chart, 30
  meat and fish soups, *see* Soups, meat and fish
  See also Beef; Lamb; Pork; Variety meats; Veal
Meringue, Sabayon, 369
Mexican Bean Soup, 7
Milk Toast with Parmesan, 359
Mincemeat, Old-Fashioned, 416
Minestrone, Genoa Style, 8
Mornay Sauce, 312
Mousseline of Scallops and Sole, 147
Mousses and molded dishes
  Apricot-Rice Ring, 367
  Cabbage Loaf, 234
  Cauliflower Mousse with Mornay Sauce, 239
  Celery Root Ring with Mushroom Sauce, 240
  Chard Timbales, 241
  Cheddar Cheese Pudding with Mushroom Sauce, 192
  Chocolate Mousse, 368
  Frozen Cranberry Mold, 339
  Ham Mousse with Beef Tongue and Mayonnaise Collée, 76
  Holiday Pudding, 404
  Mousseline of Scallops and Sole, 147
  Pumpkin-Pecan Flan with Vanilla Sauce, 400
  Salmon Mousse, 148
  Turban of Salmon and Sole, 143
Muffins, *see* Breads, biscuits and muffins
Mushrooms
  Casserole of Turnips and Mushrooms, 274
  Duxelles, 338
  Endive, Mushroom, and Cucumber Salad, 290
  Mushroom Casserole, 251
  Mushroom Roll, 249
  Mushroom Salad, 289
  Mushroom Sauce for Cheddar Cheese Pudding, 192
  Mushrooms with Garlic Butter, 250
  Pea and Mushroom Salad, 289
  Puree of Mushrooms with Braised Endive, 252
  Spinach-Mushroom-Bacon Salad, 298
  Stuffed Mushrooms, 250
Mustard Sauce, 312, 320
Mustard Vinaigrette, 304

New York Steak with Mushrooms, 33
Noodles
  Chicken with Fresh Noodles, 96
  Creamed Noodles with Ham and Vegetables, 201
  Fettuccini Alfredo Hotel Hassler, 203
  Fresh Egg Noodles, 199
  Noodles with Swiss Cheese and Sour Cream, 200
  Walnut Sauce for Noodles, 328

Old-Fashioned Buckwheat Pancakes, 360
Old-Fashioned Date-Nut Cake, 407
Old-Fashioned Mincemeat, 416
Omelets
  Chili Relleno Omelet, 180
  directions for making, 180
Onions
  Baked Onions, 253
  Onion Casserole, 254
  Onion Dumpling, 255
  Onion Marmalade, 339
  Onion Pudding, 256
  Onion Soufflé, 254
  Sautéed Onion Rings, 253
  White Wine Onion Soup, 15
Oranges
  Broiled Leg of Lamb with Orange Butter, 55
  Lettuce, Orange, and Fennel Salad, 288
  Orange, Cheese, and Onion Salad, 292
  Orange, Onion, and Walnut Salad, 293
  Orange-Sweet Potato Stuffing, 120

Oranges with Caramel and Pecans, 374
Oranges with Glazed Peel, 374
Oregon Baked Lima Beans, 212
Ox Tongue, Baked, 77
Oxtail Stew, 78
Oysters
Baked Oysters, 165
Fried Oysters, 167
Oyster Pie, 168
Oyster Soufflé, 169
Oyster Stew, 166
Oysters Casino, 166
Oysters in Cream, 170
Oysters Rockefeller, 164
Sautéed Oyster Stew, 167

Pancakes and waffles
Bran Waffles, 363
Buttermilk Pancakes, 361
French Waffles, 362
notes on pancake making, 360
Old-Fashioned Buckwheat Pancakes, 360
Plain Waffles, 361
Sour Cream Waffles, 363
Pan-Fried Liver, 79
Parsley, Fried, 256
Parsley Sauce, 312, 321
Parsnips
Lemon-Sweet Parsnips, 257
Parsnip and Potato Puree, 258
Puree of Parsnips and Madeira, 258
Pasta dishes, 197–206
Baked Lasagne with Prosciutto and Mushrooms, 202
Basic Pasta Dough, 197
Cannelloni, 205
Chicken with Fresh Noodles, 96
Creamed Noodles with Ham and Vegetables, 201
Egg Pasta, Roman Style, 198
Fettucini Alfredo Hotel Hassler, 203
Fresh Egg Noodles, 199
Homemade Pasta, 196
Noodles with Swiss Cheese and Sour Cream, 200
Pink Pasta, 198
sauces
Bolognese Sauce, 327
Clam Sauce, 328
Cold Tomato Sauce, 326
Easy Tomato Sauce, 326
Pesto, Genoa Style, 329
Tomato Pulp, 325
Tomato Puree, 325
Walnut Sauce for Noodles, 328
Spaghetti with Tuna and Anchovy Sauce, 204
Spinach Pasta, 198
Pastry, *see* Pies and tarts
Pâte Brisé Dough, 415
Pâtés
Chicken Liver Terrine, 85
Crab Pâté, 158
Terrine of Pork and Veal, 73
Peaches
Fresh Peach Bavarian Cream, 387
Peaches in Red Wine, 376
Peanut Butter, Homemade, 332
Peanut Sauce, 333
Pears
Pear Upside-Down Tart, 420
Poached Pear Tart, 421
St. Vincent Pears, 375
Peas, green
Cold Dilled Peas, 291
Frozen Peas, 259
Pea and Mushroom Salad, 289
Peas and Prosciutto, 260
Puree of Peas and Watercress, 259
Puree of Spinach and Peas, 267
Pecan Popovers with Lemon-Honey Butter, 352
Pepper, Tomato, and Onion Stew, 262
Pesto, Genoa Style, 329
Pies and tarts, 413–423
All-American Apple Pie, 417
Fast Puff Paste, 354
Filbert Pie, 423
Flaky Pie Crust, 413
Green Tomato Pie, 422
Old-Fashioned Mincemeat, 416
Pâte Brisé Dough, 415
Pear Upside-Down Tart, 420
Pie Crust, 413–414
for Baked Ham in a Crust, 70
for Chicken Pot Pie, 109
Plain Pie Crust, 414
Poached Pear Tart, 421
Pumpkin Chiffon Pie, 419
Pumpkin-Macadamia Pie with Apricot Glaze, 418

Pineapple
  Glazed Pineapple with Chocolate Sauce, 381
  Pineapple Upside-Down Cake, 406
Piquante Sauce, 316
Pita Bread, 358
Pizza with Eggplant Crust, 174
Plain Fried Chicken, 88
Plain Pie Crust, 414
Plain Waffles, 361
Plum Pudding with Cumberland Rum Butter, 402
Plums in Vodka, 377
Polenta, 218
Polenta with Pine Nuts and Raisins, 219
Popovers, 352
  Pecan Popovers with Lemon-Honey Butter, 352
Pork, 64–74
  Baked Ham in a Crust, 70
  Braised Loin of Pork, 66
  cooking methods, 30, 64
  Cotechino Sausage, 74
  Crown Roast of Pork with Sausage-Apple Stuffing, 67
  Fresh Ham (Leg of Pork), 69
  Lamb, Pork, and Beans, 62
  Meat Loaf, 43
  Pork Chops and Apples in Mustard Sauce, 71
  Pork Chops with Beer Sauce, 72
  Pork Loin in Egg-Lemon Sauce, 65
  Pork Pot Roast, 68
  Roast Loin of Pork with Pepper and Thyme, 64
  Terrine of Pork and Veal, 73
Pork Pot Roast, 68
Pot Roast of Beef, 35
Pot Roast with Ginger, 36
Potatoes
  Crusty Potatoes with Parmesan Cheese, 263
  Dauphinoise Potatoes, 265
  Hard-Cooked Eggs with Potatoes, 187
  Leek and Potato Soup, 16
  Parsnip and Potato Puree, 258
  Potato and Watercress Salad, 296
  Potato Custard, 264
  Potato Gnocchi, 171
  Potato Salad, 294
  Potato Stuffing, 120
  Potatoes in Beer, 264
  Potatoes with Sage and Parmesan, 266
  Scalloped Potatoes, 266
  Vichyssoise, 17
Poultry, 83–125
  cooking methods, 83–84
  freezing and thawing, 83
  See also Chicken; Turkey
Pound Cake, 405
Puchero (Argentine boiled beef), 44
Puddings
  Almond and Rice Pudding, 399
  Apple and Bread Pudding with Sabayon Sauce, 397
  Baked Chocolate Pudding, 396
  Bread Pudding, 398
  Carrot Pudding, 235
  Corn Pudding, 243
  Holiday Pudding, 404
  Plum Pudding with Cumberland Rum Butter, 402
  Pumpkin-Pecan Flan with Vanilla Sauce, 400
  Pumpkin Pudding, 401
  Sweet Potato Pudding, 271
  Tombstone Pudding, 398
Puff pastry
  Cocktail Puff Pastries, 355–356
  Fast Puff Paste, 354
Pumpkin
  Cream of Pumpkin Soup, 13
  Pumpkin Chiffon Pie, 419
  Pumpkin-Macadamia Pie with Apricot Glaze, 418
  Pumpkin-Pecan Flan with Vanilla Sauce, 400
  Pumpkin Pudding, 401
  Pumpkin Soup, 12
Purees
  Garlic Puree, 332
  Parsnip and Potato Puree, 258
  Puree of Broccoli, 229
  Puree of Chick-Peas, 242
  Puree of Mushrooms with Braised Endive, 252
  Puree of Parsnips and Madeira, 258
  Puree of Peas and Watercress, 259
  Puree of Spinach and Peas, 267
  Puree of Watercress, 276
  Tomato Puree, 325

Quiches
Crustless Crab Quiche, 162
Quiche Lorraine, 191
Quick Brown Sauce, 315

Rack of Lamb, 54
Radish, Cucumber and Tomato Salad, 286
Raisins, Polenta with Pine Nuts and, 219
Raspberry-Strawberry Sauce, 426
Rassolnik (kidney and barley soup), 22
Red Cabbage, 230
Red Cabbage Salad, 283
Rib Roast of Beef, 31
Rice dishes, 207–210
Almond and Rice Pudding, 399
Apricot-Rice Ring, 367
Curried Eggs in Brown Rice, 184
Curried Rice Salad, 295
Green Risotto, 208
Ham and Tomato Risotto, 209
Rice Casserole, 207
Rice with Champagne, 210
Wild Rice Stuffing, 119
Rich Vanilla Sauce, 424
R. N. Fry Bread, 343
Roast Chicken, 98
Roast Chicken with Cognac Cream Sauce, 99
Roast Turkey, Basic, 115
Roasted Pepper Salad, 296
Robert Pamplin Biscuits, 350
Romaine Salad with Hard-Cooked Egg Dressing, 301
Russian Salad, 299
Rutabaga and Watercress Soup, Cream of, 11

Sabayon Meringue, 369
Sabayon Sauce, 397
St. Vincent Pears, 375
Salad dressings, 303–308
Basic Vinaigrette, 304
Blue Cheese Salad Dressing I, 306
Blue Cheese Salad Dressing II, 306
Celery Seed Dressing, 305
Dressing for Slaw-Stuffed Cabbage, 280
Egg Vinaigrette, 305
French Dressing, 286, 304
Homemade Mayonnaise, 307
Lemon Dressing, 213
Mayonnaise Dijon, 308
Mustard Vinaigrette, 304
Tart Mayonnaise, 308
Vinaigrette Dressings, 288, 304
Salads, 279–302
Celery Salad with Mustard Dressing, 285
Cheese and Olive Salad, 292
Cold Dilled Peas, 291
Cucumber, Tomato, and Radish Salad, 286
Curried Rice Salad, 295
Endive, Mushroom, and Cucumber Salad, 290
Fennel Salad, 287
greens, 279
Hard-Cooked Eggs with Potatoes, 187
Hot Chick-Pea Salad, 290
Hot Slaw with Seafood, 282
Italian Cabbage Salad, 281
Leek Salad, 286
Lentil Salad, 294
Lettuce, Orange, and Fennel Salad, 288
Marinated Vegetable Salad, 302
Mushroom Salad, 289
Orange, Cheese, and Onion Salad, 292
Orange, Onion, and Walnut Salad, 293
Pea and Mushroom Salad, 289
Potato and Watercress Salad, 296
Potato Salad, 294
Red Cabbage Salad, 283
Roasted Pepper Salad, 296
Romaine Salad with Hard-Cooked Egg Dressing, 301
Russian Salad, 299
Slaw-Stuffed Cabbage, 280
Spinach-Mushroom-Bacon Salad, 298
Spinach Salad, 298
Tomato Salad with Mozzarella, 297
Vegetable Salad, 300
White Bean Salad with Caviar, 213
Wilted Cabbage Salad, 284
Wilted Lettuce Salad, 285

Salmon
  Cold Poached Salmon, 138
  Marinated Salmon, 130
  Salmon-Crab Loaf, 148
  Salmon Fillets with Sorrel or Spinach Sauce, 135
  Salmon Mousse, 148
  Salmon Soup, 24
  Smoked Salmon Soufflé, 144
Sandwiches
  Crab and Mushroom, 160
Sauces, 309–334
  Chutney Sauce, 338
  classic, 310–316
    Anchovy Hollandaise, 314
    Béarnaise Sauce, 317
    Béchamel Sauce, 310
    Bordelaise Sauce, 316
    Caper Hollandaise, 314
    Cheese Sauce, 312
    Choron Sauce, 317
    Currant Jelly Sauce, 316
    Curry Sauce, 312
    Dill Sauce, 312
    Herb Sauce, 312
    Hollandaise Sauce, 313
    Hollandaise-Mousseline Sauce, 314
    Madeira Sauce, 315
    Mornay Sauce, 312
    Mustard Sauce, 312
    Parsley Sauce, 312
    Piquante Sauce, 316
    Quick Brown Sauce, 315
    Soubise Sauce, 311
    Supreme Sauce, 311
    Tarragon Sauce, 313
    Velouté Sauce, 311
  dessert, *see* Desserts, sauces
  meat and poultry, 318–321
    Cumberland Sauce with Cherries, 319
    Herbed Butter, 318
    Herbed Butter Sauce, 319
    Hunter's Sauce, 318
    Marinade for Butterflied Leg of Lamb, 320
    Mustard Sauce, 320
    Parsley Sauce, 321
    Simple Steak Sauce, 321
  seafood, 322–324
    Cucumber Sauce, 324
    Egg Sauce, 322
    Green Sauce, 323
    Shrimp Sauce, 322
    White Butter Sauce, 324
  special accompaniments, 330–334
    Aioli Sauce, 330
    Crème Fraîche, 334
    Garlic Mayonnaise, 331
    Garlic Puree, 332
    Homemade Peanut Butter, 332
    Homemade Sour Cream, 333
    Jellied Mayonnaise, 331
    Peanut Sauce, 333
    Sour Cream-Dill Sauce with Cucumber, 334
  tomato and pasta sauces, 325–329
    Bolognese Sauce, 327
    Clam Sauce, 328
    Cold Tomato Sauce, 326
    Easy Tomato Sauce, 326
    Pesto, Genoa Style, 329
    Tomato Pulp, 325
    Tomato Puree, 325
    Walnut Sauce for Noodles, 328
Sausage
  Cotechino Sausage, 74
  Lentils with Sausage, 215
  Sausage Paste Stuffing for Boned and Rolled Turkey, 116
  Sausage with Vegetable Puree, 172
Sauté of Green Beans, 226
Sautéed Apples, 340
Sautéed Cabbage, 231
Sautéed Chicken, 104
Sautéed Green Peppers, 261
Sautéed Lentils, 216
Sautéed Onion Rings, 253
Sautéed Oyster Stew, 167
Sautéed Sweetbreads, 81
Sautéed Tuna with Tarragon, 132
Sautéeing technique, 104
Savoy Cabbage, 232
Scalloped Clams, 150
Scalloped Potatoes, 266
Scallops
  cooking methods, 128
  Gingered Scallops, 163
  Hot Slaw with Seafood, 282

Scallops in Heavy Cream, 163
Seafood Casserole, 146
Scrod, Broiled, 134
Seafood, *see* Fish and Shellfish
Seasonings, *see* Condiments and seasonings
Seviche (raw fish in lime juice), 129
Short Ribs of Beef, 37
Short Ribs of Beef with Cornmeal Dumplings, 38
Shrimp
Broiled Shrimp, 154
cleaning, 154
cooking methods, 128
Curried Shrimp Soufflé, 156
French-Fried Butterfly Shrimp, 153
Gingered Shrimp, 154
Hot Slaw with Seafood, 282
Seafood Casserole, 146
Shrimp Sauce, 322
Shrimp Steamed in Vermouth, 155
Shrimp-Stuffed Petrale Sole, 139
Skewered Shrimp and Ham, 157
Whole Shrimp à la Nage, 158
Simple Steak Sauce, 321
Six Threes Ice Cream, 393
Skewered Shrimp and Ham, 157
Slaw-Stuffed Cabbage, 280
Smoked Cod Casserole, 145
Smoked Salmon Soufflé, 144
Sole, fillet of
Fillet of Sole in Herbed Butter, 133
Mousseline of Scallops and Sole, 147
Shrimp-Stuffed Petrale Sole, 139
Turban of Salmon and Sole, 143
Sorrel
Casserole of Hard-Cooked Eggs in Creamed Sorrel, 185
Cream of Sorrel Soup, 14
Eggs Stuffed with Sorrel, 183
Salmon Fillets with Sorrel Sauce, 135
Sorrel Soup, 13
Soubise Sauce, 311
Soufflé Sauce, 424
Soufflés
Cheese Soufflé, 190
Chocolate Soufflé, 390
Codfish Soufflé, 144
Cold Lemon-Lime Soufflé, 389
Curried Shrimp Soufflé, 156
Hot Grand Marnier Soufflé, 391
Jerusalem Artichoke Soufflé, 247
Onion Soufflé, 254
Oyster Soufflé, 169
Smoked Salmon Soufflé, 144
Soufflé of Cheese and Chicken, 189
Spoon Bread Soufflé, 220
Strawberry Soufflé, 392
Soups and chowders, 1–28
Beef Stock, 4
Black Bean Soup, 6
Bread and Squash Soup, 9
Brittany Chowder, 28
Chicken Stock, 3
Chilled Cucumber Soup, 17
Cioppino (fish stew), 131
Clam Chowder–New England Style, 27
clarifying, 3
cold soups
Chilled Cucumber Soup, 17
Spinach Soup, 18
Vichyssoise, 17
Corn Chowder, 26
Cream of Pumpkin Soup, 13
Cream of Rutabaga and Watercress Soup, 11
Cream of Sorrel Soup, 14
Cream of Turtle Soup, 23
Egg Soup, 20
Eggplant Soup, 10
freezing, 2
Greek Fish Soup, 25
Leek, Carrot, and Cheese Soup, 16
Leek and Potato Soup, 16
Lemon and Meatball Soup, 20
Mexican Bean Soup, 7
Minestrone, Genoa Style, 8
Pumpkin Soup, 12
Rassolnik, 22
Salmon Soup, 24
Sorrel Soup, 13
Spinach Soup, 18
Stock, 2–5
Tex-Mex Soup with Meatballs, 21
Tomato Soup, 19
Turnip Soup, 10
Vegetable soups, 8–19
Vegetable Stock, 5
Vichyssoise, 17
White Bean Soup, 5
White Wine Onion Soup, 15
See also Stocks and broths

Sour Cream
  Chicken and Mushrooms with Sour Cream, 90
  Chicken Paprika with Sour Cream, 97
  Fresh Strawberries with Sour Cream, 383
  Homemade Sour Cream, 333
  Lamb with Sour Cream and Dill, 59
  Noodles with Swiss Cheese and Sour Cream, 200
  Sour Cream-Dill Sauce with Cucumber, 334
  Sour Cream Waffles, 363
Sourdough Chocolate Cake, 412
Spaghetti with Tuna and Anchovy Sauce, 204
Spanish Eggs, 178
Special dishes, 171–222
  bean dishes, 211–216
  Carla's Tamale Pie, 173
  cheeese dishes, 188–195
    See also Cheese and cheese dishes
  cornmeal dishes, 217–222
    See also Cornmeal dishes
  egg dishes, 175–187
    See also Eggs and egg dishes
  pasta dishes, 196–206
    See also Pasta dishes
  Pizza with Eggplant Crust, 174
  Potato Gnocchi, 171
  rice dishes, 207–210
    See also Rice dishes
  Sausages with Vegetable Puree, 172
Spice Bread, 346
Spices, Four, 336
Spinach
  Eggs in Spinach, 186
  Green Risotto, 208
  Puree of Spinach and Peas, 267
  Salmon Fillets with Spinach Sauce, 135
  Spinach Casserole, 268
  Spinach-Mushroom-Bacon Salad, 298
  Spinach Pasta, 198
  Spinach Salad, 298
  Spinach Soup, 18
  Spinach Timbales, 269
Spoon Bread Soufflé, 220
Squash
  Bread and Squash Soup, 9
  Hubbard Squash Custard, 270
  Squash in Cream, 270
  See also Zucchini
Steak
  New York Steak with Mushrooms, 33
Stews
  Baltimore Lobster Stew, 149
  Brunswick Stew, 111
  Cioppino (fish stew), 131
  Codfish Stew, 141
  Lamb Stew, 60
  Mexican Chicken Stew, 112
  Oxtail Stew, 78
  Oyster Stew, 166
  Pepper, Tomato, and Onion Stew, 262
  reheating, 51
  Sautéed Oyster Stew, 167
  Veal Stew, 51
  Veal with Herbed Vegetables, 50
Stocks and broths, 2–5
  Beef Stock, 4
  Chicken Stock, 3
  Court Bouillon for Poached Fish and Shellfish, 136
  Court Bouillon with Red Wine, 138
  Court Bouillon with White Wine, 137
  Vegetable Stock, 5
  See also Soups
Strawberries
  Fresh Strawberries and Cream, 383
  Fresh Strawberries with Sour Cream, 383
  Strawberry-Raspberry Sauce, 426
  Strawberry Shortcake, 382
  Strawberry Soufflé, 392
String beans, *see* Green beans
Stuffed Mushrooms, 250
Stuffing
  Crown Roast of Pork with Sausage-Apple Stuffing, 67
  Onion and Sage Stuffing, 124
  Orange-Sweet Potato Stuffing, 120
  Potato Stuffing, 120
  Sausage Paste Stuffing, 116
  Whole Wheat-Pecan Stuffing, 121
  Wild Rice Stuffing, 119

Sunday Supper Corn Bread with Sausage, 222
Supreme Sauce, 311
Sweet Potatoes
  Orange-Sweet Potato Stuffing, 120
  Sweet Potato Pudding, 271
Sweetbreads
  Sautéed Sweetbreads, 81
  Sweeetbreads with Bacon, 81
  Sweetbreads with Madeira, 81
  Sweetbreads with White Wine and Ham, 81

Tabasco Eggs, 182
Tamale Pie, Carla's, 173
Tarragon, Sautéed Tuna with, 132
Tarragon Butter, 133
Tarragon Sauce, 313
Tart Mayonnaise, 308
Tarts, *see* Pies and tarts
Terrines
  Chicken Liver Terrine, 85
  Terrine of Pork and Veal, 73
Texas Skillet Corn Bread, 348
Tex-Mex Soup with Meatballs, 21
Timbales
  Chard Timbales, 241
  Spinach Timbales, 269
Tomatoes
  Baked Tomatoes Stuffed with Mozzarella, 272
  Batter-Fried Green Tomatoes, 273
  Cucumber, Tomato, and Radish Salad, 286
  Eggs in Tomatoes, 181
  Fried Tomatoes in Cream, 273
  Green Tomato Pie, 422
  Tomato Pulp, 325
  Tomato Puree, 325
  Tomato Salad with Mozzarella, 297
  Tomato Sauces, 325–327
    Bolognese Sauce, 327
    Cold Tomato Sauce, 326
    Easy Tomato Sauce, 326
  Tomato Soup, 19
Tombstone Pudding, 398
Tongue
  Baked Ox Tongue, 77
  Beef Tongue with Ham Mousse and Mayonnaise Collée, 76
Tuna
  Baked Tuna, 132
  Sautéed Tuna with Tarragon, 132
  Spaghetti with Tuna and Anchovy Sauce, 204
  Turkey with Tuna Sauce, 123
Turban of Salmon and Sole, 143
Turkey, 114–123
  Basic Roast Turkey, 115
  Boiled Turkey with Butter Sauce, 114
  Boned, Rolled Turkey with Sausage Paste Stuffing, 116
  boning and rolling, 117
  cooking methods, 83–84, 114–116
  stuffings
    Orange-Sweet Potato Stuffing, 120
    Potato Stuffing, 120
    Sausage Paste Stuffing, 116
    Whole Wheat-Pecan Stuffing, 121
    Wild Rice Stuffing, 119
  Turkey Fillets in Lemon Sauce, 122
  Turkey with Tuna Sauce, 123
Turnips
  Casserole of Turnips and Mushrooms, 274
  Glazed Turnips, 275
  Turnip and Egg Gratin, 275
  Turnip Soup, 10
Turtle Soup, Cream of, 23

Vanilla Sauce, 401
  Lemon and Vanilla Sauce, 425
  Rich Vanilla Sauce, 424
Vanilla Sugar, 340
Variety meats, 75–81
  Baked Ox Tongue, 77
  Beef Tongue with Ham Mousse and Mayonnaise Collée, 76
  Calf's Liver in Red Wine Vinegar, 80
  Calf's Liver with Cream, 80
  Lamb Kidneys and Mushrooms, 75
  Oxtail Stew, 78
  Pan-Fried Liver, 79
  Sautéed Sweetbreads, 81
Veal, 45–53
  Chops with Fresh Herbs, 49
  cooking methods, 30, 45
  Meat Loaf, 43
  Sautéed Sweetbreads, 81

Veal (*Cont.*)
Terrine of Pork and Veal, 73
Veal Casserole, 53
Veal Orloff, 48
Veal Scallops, 45
Veal Scallops in Cream Sauce, 47
Veal Scallops with Lemon, 46
Veal Stew, 51
Veal Stew with Olives, 52
Veal with Herbed Vegetables, 50
Vegetables, 223–278
cooking methods, 223–224
frozen, 223
home-canning, 223
Marinated Vegetable Salad, 302
preparing, 224
root vegetables, 223
Russian Salad, 299
Vegetable soups, 5–19
Vegetable Stock, 5
Vegetable Salad, 300
See also under name of Vegetable
Velouté Sauce, 311
Vermont Baked Beans, 211
Vichyssoise, 17
Vinaigrette Dressing, 303
Basic Vinaigrette, 304
Egg Vinaigrette, 305
French Dressing, 304
Mustard Vinaigrette, 304

Waffles, *see* Pancakes and waffles
Walnut Sauce for Noodles, 328
Watercress
Cream of Rutabaga and Watercress Soup, 11
Potato and Watercress Salad, 296
Puree of Peas and Watercress, 259
Puree of Watercress, 276
Welsh Rarebit, 195
White Bean Salad with Caviar, 213
White Bean Soup, 5
White Butter Sauce, 324
White Wine Onion Soup, 15
Whole Shrimp à la Nage, 158
Whole Wheat-Pecan Stuffing, 121
Wild Rice Stuffing, 119
Wilted Cabbage Salad, 284
Wilted Lettuce Salad, 285

Yorkshire Pudding, 353

Zucchini
Broiled Zucchini with Tomato and Cheese, 277
Grated Sautéed Zucchini, 277
Zucchini Bread, 347
Zucchini Custard, 278